The Pearl
of Great Price

The Pearl
of Great Price:
A History
and Commentary

by H. Donl Peterson

Deseret Book Company
Salt Lake City, Utah

First Printing in hardbound edition, September 1987
First Printing in softbound edition, October 1992

Library of Congress Cataloging-in-Publication Data

Peterson, H. Donl
    The Pearl of Great Price.

    Bibliography: p.
    Includes index.
    1. Pearl of great price—Commentaries. I. Title.
BX8629.P53P48 1987   289.3′2   87-15672
ISBN 0-87579-096-8 (hardbound edition)
ISBN 0-87579-665-6 (softbound edition)

Printed in the United States of America

10   9   8   7   6   5   4

To my wife, Mary Lou,
and my children,
Terry, Diane, Jacque, Scott,
James, and Michael

Contents

Illustrations

Preface

The Pearl of Great Price, one of only four books upon which the Lord has placed his seal of approval, is holy scripture. The most compact of the standard works, it contains only sixty-one pages. Profound doctrine is pronounced in the first few verses, and that pattern continues throughout the entire text.

The original preface of the Pearl of Great Price states that it was "not adapted, nor designed, as a pioneer of the faith among unbelievers." It was compiled to strengthen the missionaries and the Saints in Great Britain, to "increase their abilty to maintain and to defend the holy faith by becoming possessors of it."

This *History and Commentary* has been written to fill the need of the Latter-day Saints for an up-to-date, comprehensive history and commentary on the Pearl of Great Price. The popular and respected histories and commentaries of the past are either out of print or were printed before 1981 when the new edition of the Pearl of Great Price was published. Considerable research in recent years has provided exciting new insights that update the historical material relied upon by previous publications. But perhaps the most significant contribution of this work is its unique collection of primary sources for doctrinal commentary on the Pearl of Great Price: statements of members of the First Presidency and the Quorum of the Twelve Apostles.

This book is divided into two major sections: the history and the commentary. The history section explains the origin and development of the Pearl of Great Price; the origins of the Joseph Smith Translation of the Bible, from which the book of Moses and Joseph Smith—Matthew

were extracted; the coming forth of the book of Abraham from its entomb-
ment in Egypt until it was safely in the hands of the Prophet Joseph
Smith; the origin and development of the history of the Church written
by the Prophet, a segment of which is found in the Pearl of Great Price
as Joseph Smith—History; and the origin of the Articles of Faith. The
commentary is the larger portion of this work. It contains three categories of quotations. The first category is statements selected from the
First Presidency and the Quorum of the Twelve Apostles, who are the
Lord's authorized teachers of the scriptures. The second category is scripture references selected from the standard works to support the topic
under which they are listed. They are not the only scripture references
that pertain to a particular topic but are some of the more closely related
ones. The third category is commentary from General Authorities other
than members of the First Presidency and the Quorum of the Twelve
Apostles and from historians and others who are knowledgeable on a
given topic. Naturally, a work such as this one cannot contain all the
relevant quotations that are available. In all three categories, choices
had to be made about what to include. I alone am responsible for the
final choices.

This is not an official Church publication, but it is my intention to
be orthodox in my representation of the views of the General Authorities of the Church. When an apostle of the Lord interviewed me on
three different occasions while I was a seminary teacher, he asked the
same searching question, "Do you delight in being orthodox?" That
was nearly thirty years ago. If I'm privileged to see him again, I hope
to answer in the affirmative a fourth time.

The Pearl of Great Price, a course in advanced theology, is an inspired
work. It is truly a "pearl of great price." (Matthew 13:46.) It is my hope
that this *History and Commentary* will help serious students of the
scriptures better understand its great truths.

Acknowledgments

Many friends have contributed in making this work possible. If I have left some unmentioned, it was not intentional.

My family, my colleagues, and my students over the years have helped me refine my thoughts about the holy scriptures and deepen my understanding of them.

Robert J. Matthews, dean of Religious Education at Brigham Young University, made it possible for me to serve as director of Pearl of Great Price research in the Religious Studies Center at Brigham Young University these past five years. He has encouraged me throughout this project.

Dr. James R. Harris, my friend and colleague and professor of Ancient Scripture at Brigham Young University, was kind enough to write, at my request, the chapter entitled "The Facsimiles of the Book of Abraham."

David G. Day, my research assistant, was tireless in collecting, sorting, and arranging the many quotations.

Carol Lee Pedersen faithfully typed and retyped the lengthy manuscript and was long-suffering through all the revisions and frustrations.

A host of proofreaders, especially Rebecca Brady, Alison Koritz, and Linda Adams's students from her editing class at Brigham Young University, patiently checked and rechecked the sources and the quotations.

Eleanor Knowles, executive editor at Deseret Book Company, recognized potential in this work.

Suzanne Brady, associate editor at Deseret Book Company, directed the manuscript through the various stages of turning it into a book.

Kent Ware, design director at Deseret Book Company, helped this work realize its visual potential.

PART I

HISTORY

Introduction

The history of the Pearl of Great Price is fascinating. Its complex background involves ancient Egypt and eighteenth- and nineteenth-century Egypt; the Napoleonic era in both Europe and Africa; the British invasion of Egypt; Italian studies and personalities in Venice, Trieste, Turin, and Castellamonte, Italy, and in Philadelphia, Pennsylvania; and research in Dublin and its environs and among Irish immigrants in the United States in the late 1820s and early 1830s. It also involves tracing the mummies around a circuit in New York, Pennsylvania, Maryland, and Ohio; learning about Joseph Smith and his associates in New York, Ohio, Missouri, and Illinois; becoming aware of the publication problems of the mid–nineteenth century in both Utah Territory and England; appreciating the intent and the contribution of the Joseph Smith Translation of the Bible; and recognizing the Wentworth Letter as a primary source of historical information.

Some names identified with the Pearl of Great Price history, some familiar, some not so familiar, include Joseph Smith, Bernardino Drovetti, Antonio Lebolo, Michael H. Chandler, Albano Oblasser, Oliver Cowdery, Mehemet Ali, Warren Parrish, John Taylor, Wilford Woodruff, Franklin D. Richards, Orson Pratt, James E. Talmage, Jean Francois Champollion, and more.

The Pearl of Great Price is a collection of extracts carefully hand-picked from various Church publications. The common thread is that Franklin D. Richards selected them from materials that had originally come about through the inspiration or by the authority of the Prophet Joseph Smith.

3

The Pearl of Great Price: Extracts from Divine Sources

This chapter details the origin of the Pearl of Great Price in Britain and explains its development. The Pearl of Great Price was canonized in 1880 as the fourth of the standard works.

The Book of Moses and Joseph Smith—Matthew: Extracts from the Joseph Smith Translation of the Bible

Joseph Smith spent three years laboring on his translation of the Bible. More than half the contents of the Pearl of Great Price are extracts from this revision of the Bible. Two of these, the book of Moses and Joseph Smith—Matthew, help to demonstrate the value of the Joseph Smith Translation.

The Book of Abraham: Extracts from the Larger Text Also Called the Book of Abraham

New information has been found in the last twenty years about how the writings of Abraham got from Egypt to Kirtland, Ohio.

The Facsimiles of the Book of Abraham

The facsimiles of the book of Abraham have been criticized by many who contend that they are unrelated to the accompanying text. In the chapter he wrote specifically for this volume, James R. Harris, who is trained in Egyptian hieroglyphics, presents some excellent arguments to support Joseph Smith's interpretations. Dr. Harris is a professor of Ancient Scripture at Brigham Young University, Provo, Utah.

Joseph Smith—History: Extracts from the History of Joseph Smith, the Prophet

Joseph Smith began dictating his history in 1838. It was finished in 1858, fourteen years after his death, by George A. Smith and Wilford Woodruff, who said of it at its publication: "The *History of Joseph Smith* is true, and is one of the most authentic histories ever written." (Joseph Smith, *History of the Church,* 1:vi.). The Pearl of Great Price contains extracts from the first forty-four pages of that history.

The Articles of Faith: Extracts from the Wentworth Letter

The Articles of Faith come from a document known as the Wentworth Letter, which was written by the Prophet Joseph Smith to John Wentworth, the editor of the *Chicago Democrat.* The Articles of Faith

are the last thirteen paragraphs of this letter. Elder B. H. Roberts characterized these paragraphs as "the epitome of the doctrines of the Church,
since called 'The Articles of Faith,' and published by millions. . . . These
Articles of Faith were not produced by the labored efforts and harmo-
nized contentions of scholastics, but were struck off by one inspired
mind at a single effort to make a declaration of that which is most
assuredly believed by the Church, for one making earnest inquiry about
the truth. The combined directness, perspicuity, simplicity and comprehensiveness of this statement of the principles of our religion may be
relied upon as strong evidence of a divine inspiration resting upon the
Prophet, Joseph Smith." (Smith, *History of the Church,* 4:535n.)

The Pearl of Great Price:
Extracts from Divine Sources

The Church of Jesus Christ of Latter-day Saints proclaims four books as holy scripture binding upon the conscience of the members: the Bible, the Book of Mormon, the Doctrine and Covenants, and the Pearl of Great Price. The small number of Christians who, on 6 April 1830, came together to organize the restored church of Jesus Christ had already accepted the Bible as the word of God. Furthermore, each of them had a testimony that the Book of Mormon, which had been published only about ten days before, was also a divinely inspired record. The newly organized church grew rapidly, and the Lord gave many revelations to the Prophet Joseph Smith, instructing him in his multifaceted role as leader of the Church. In 1835 a selection of these revelations was compiled and published as a handbook of instructions for the members of the Church. This publication, called the Doctrine and Covenants, was accepted by the Church as scripture in 1835. The Pearl of Great Price was not accepted as scripture until 1880, although all of its contents were brought to light through the instrumentality of the Prophet Joseph Smith, who had been murdered thirty-six years before. This is the fascinating story of the Pearl of Great Price.

The Church in 1837

The restored church endured some of its darkest days in the year 1837. The Prophet Joseph Smith wrote:

6

Franklin D. Richards
compiled the first Pearl of
Great Price in 1851

"At this time the spirit of speculation in lands and property of all kinds, which was so prevalent throughout the whole nation, was taking deep root in the Church. As the fruits of this spirit, evil surmisings, fault-finding, disunion, dissension, and apostasy followed in quick succession, and it seemed as though all the powers of earth and hell were combining their influence in an especial manner to overthrow the Church at once, and make a final end. . . . The enemy abroad, and apostates in our midst, united in their schemes. . . .

"No quorum in the Church was entirely exempt from the influence of those false spirits who are striving against me for the mastery; even some of the Twelve were so far lost to their high and responsible calling, as to begin to take sides, secretly, with the enemy.

"In this state of things, . . . God revealed to me that something new must be done for the salvation of His Church. And on or about the first of June, 1837, Heber C. Kimball, one of the Twelve, was set apart by the spirit of prophecy and revelation, prayer and laying on of hands, of the First Presidency, to preside over a mission to England, to be the first foreign mission of the Church of Christ in the last days." (*History of the Church*, 2: 487–89.)

Under Elder Kimball's leadership, the success of the mission was phenomenal. By 1842 there were more than seven thousand members of the Church in the British Isles. By 1850 the members in Great Britain numbered more than thirty thousand.

England in the Mid-1800s

England, with a high birthrate and in the midst of the industrial revolution, was not without its problems during the period from 1837 to 1850. A letter sent from Manchester to the Prophet Joseph Smith on 5 September 1840 by Elder Brigham Young and Elder Willard Richards aids us in understanding some of the deep-rooted concerns facing the British nation. These brethren spoke of "the great changes which have taken place in the nation, within a few years, with regard to money matters, which has caused a mighty revolution, in the affairs of the common people.

"A few years since, and almost every family had their garden, their cow on the common and their pig in the stye, which added greatly to the comforts of the household; but now we seldom find either garden, cow or pig." (As quoted in Ronald W. Walker, in *BYU Studies*, Spring 1978, p. 469.)

The commoners complained that the landlords had united the farms and forced the poor to go into the factory " 'to get a morsel of bread'; or [said another], 'I have taken to handloom weaving, to keep my wife & little one from starvation.'

" . . . There are taxes for living & taxes for dying, insomuch that it is very difficult for the poor to get buried any how, & a man may emigrate to America & find a grave, for less money, than he can get a decent burial for, in Old England." Consequently, the brethren explained, England was "filled with beggars. . . . Hunger & Rags are no curiosity here, & while things remain as they are what can we expect but theft, robbery, murder which now fill the land.

" . . . the people have enough to do, to keep from dying with hunger without taking much thought for the improvement of the mind. Many of the people cannot read, a great many cannot write, children are admitted into the factories at 8 years old, working a part of the day & attending school a part till they are 14 years old & then work continually. . . .

" . . . the masters . . . have reduced the workmens wages to almost, the lowest extremity, & if their hands should turn out for more wages, they have nothing before them but destruction for there [are] thousands & tens of thousands who cannot get one days work in a month, or six months, so they continue to labor 12 hours in a day for almost nothing rather than starve at once." (*Studies*, pp. 470–71.)

In this bleak setting the missionary work caught fire. Elder Young and Elder Richards further stated:

"We find the people of this land much more ready to receive the gospel, than those of America. . . . Consequently we have not & labor with a people month after month to break down their old notions, for their priests have taught them but little, & much of that is so foolish as to be detected at a glance. Viewing the subject in this light we find ignorance a blessing, for the more ignorant of false notions the more readily they sense truth." (*Studies*, p. 472.)

The two mission leaders informed Joseph Smith and the other brethren that a company of poverty-stricken Saints would soon sail from Liverpool to America to join the Saints in Nauvoo. This trek to Zion was the beginning of a mighty migration of over fifty thousand faithful European Saints that would continue for the next half century, proving to be indeed the salvation of the Church. The British converts hoped for temporal blessings as well as spiritual blessings through their Church membership.

Some Midcentury Concerns Facing the Church

The Church, led by Brigham Young after the death of the Prophet Joseph Smith, left the United States and moved west to what was then Mexican territory. The first company of pioneers arrived in the Salt Lake Valley on 24 July 1847.

As the Saints arrived, Brigham Young directed them to settle throughout the territory. By 1850 more than six thousand Saints lived in the Salt Lake Valley, and an additional five thousand lived in many small settlements scattered throughout the Great Basin.

Worldwide, Church membership in 1850 totaled more than fifty-seven thousand. Nearly thirty-one thousand were members living in Great Britain; only eleven thousand lived in Utah Territory; and fifteen thousand remained in the East or were making their way west across the plains to join the Saints in the Salt Lake Valley.

With more than half the entire membership of the Church living in Great Britain, communication and administrative problems were accentuated. Conditions in Utah contributed to the difficulties. For example, when the Saints were able to turn their attention to such matters, they found they lacked sufficient trees to produce paper in quantity. What little paper could be produced was used for the urgent printing needs of the Church in Utah and of the territorial government, newly established in 1850. It was not feasible for the scriptures and other Church literature to be printed in Utah Territory.

The administrative problems were more easily remedied. President Young sent effective leaders to administer Church affairs in England. Orson Pratt, a member of the first Quorum of the Twelve Apostles, was sent to preside over the British Mission from 14 August 1848 to 1 January 1851. Elder Pratt was succeeded as mission president by Elder Franklin D. Richards, then the newest member of the Quorum of the Twelve, who presided in Britain until 8 May 1852.

Shortage of Church Literature in Great Britain

Since the Prophet Joseph Smith's death in 1844, the Church had not printed the scriptures nor enough tracts to meet the needs of the rapidly expanding membership in Great Britain. Furthermore, the economic crisis that had troubled Great Britain in 1840 was still a major problem in 1850. As a result, most British Saints in 1850 did not own a copy of the Book of Mormon or of the Doctrine and Covenants or possess the popular Church pamphlets that once had been common among them. In 1850 Elder Richards encouraged the Saints "to read Elder Pratt's pamphlets, and lend them to others, so that people might know that Mormonism included all that is good." (British Mission Manuscript History, CR Mh 1140 #9, 2 June 1850, LDS Church Historical Department, Salt Lake City, Utah.)

Elder Pratt, on 14 July 1850, wrote to Elder John Davis about publishing and distributing Church literature: "I wish you to take every method of increasing the circulation of the publications of the church by offering inducements to agents and by lessening the price in proportion to the increase of circulation." On 3 December 1850 Elder Pratt and Elder Richards wrote to Elder Davis and a Brother Phillips:

"We are very thankful to learn that the circulation of the *Tracts* is producing so great and good results in the principality, and we pray that the printed word both of the English and Welsh Languages may run far and wide, have free course and be glorified in turning many from the error of their ways unto the living and true God.

"Concerning the 'Book of Mormon' and 'Doctrine & Covenants' we think they should both of them be entered duly at Stationers Hall in the name of Brigham Young, unless his absence from the Country or some other reason should prevent; if so, let them be entered in the name of Franklin D. Richards.

"This done they will be secure against trespassers upon the right to publish. . . .

"We are pleased to learn that these works are so nearly ready for the public eye in the Welsh tongue, and believe that when they come into general circulation you will realize great and glorious results, among both Saints and Sinners, as we your humble fellow Servants will ever pray." (LDS Church Historical Department, Salt Lake City, Utah.)

Elder Eli B. Kelsey from London wrote to Church headquarters at Liverpool on 7 January 1851 to propose a "more extensive circulation of the printed word":

"We should establish a central depot for the sale of our publications, wholesale and retail, to be called 'The Latter-day Saints' Book and Millennial Star Depot for the London Conference. . . . '

"During the time of my former visit to London, I called the attention of the Saints, both officers and members, to the importance of a more extensive circulation of the printed word. . . . The different branches are at present engaged in raising subscriptions, with the view of forming a Circulating Tract Society Fund in each branch. . . . I am satisfied that the aggregate of the number of tracts that will be called for by the whole of the branches forming this conference will not fall short of TWENTY-FIVE THOUSAND." (In *Millennial Star*, 13 [1 Feb. 1851]: 34.) Elder Kelsey then listed the books and tracts that would be needed for a lending library to serve fifty-six branches in the British Mission.

A New Pamphlet Is Proposed

On 1 February 1851, the day that Elder Orson Pratt set sail for America on the *Ellen Maria* from Liverpool, President Franklin D. Richards wrote a letter to his uncle Levi Richards, then serving a mission in Swansea, England, south of Liverpool. This is the first known mention of the new tract, yet untitled, that President Richards contemplated compiling from books, tracts, newspapers, and other publications of the Church in order to supply the British Saints with Church literature:

"You will perhaps recollect my naming to you that I thought of issueing a collection of revelations, prophecies &c., in a tract form of a character not designed to pioneer our doctrines to the world, so much as for the use of the Elders and Saints to arm and better qualify them for their service in our great *war*. The order of the work which I had thought to adopt so far as I have considered is about as follows:

"First the revelation to Moses then the translation of the first chap of Genesis. Then perhaps the revelation to Enoch after which or perhaps before it, items of revelation informing of Gods second law to Adam, viz faith repentance &c. as given to him by ministration of an Angel. The particular place could perhaps be better determined after close examination. Then perhaps, Mr. Chandler's letter about the mummies containing an account of the sale of them to the Church &c. &c. followed with a fac simile of the plates and the translation of the Book of Abraham. I have not particularly determined in my own mind as to the consecutive order of the other items such as translation of 24th Matthew. The destiny of the American Union &c., any further that I had thought it might perhaps be as well to close up with the Key to Revelation. Giving the whole a general feature of chronological order except it be Joseph's prophecy of the Union.

"Will you please to give me your views upon the matter in full with any suggestions which may occur to your mind relative to the subject at your earliest convenience. I desire that the whole thing may bear the dignity and weight of character which justly belongs to the revelations of God." (Used by permission from Mrs. Riley Richards, whose husband was a descendant of Levi Richards.)

The earliest documentation that this new publication was to be called the Pearl of Great Price is a notation made by Levi Richards on 8 May 1851: "With Franklin at 15 Wilton, Liverpool, reading proof sheets of Pearl of Great Price." (CHO 1 Box 1 MS/f 438 fd 1 fd 10 #1, LDS Church Historical Department, Salt Lake City, Utah.)

The Pearl of Great Price Is Published

On Sunday, 15 June 1851, the *Millennial Star* printed the prepublication notice of the Pearl of Great Price: "PEARL OF GREAT PRICE, is the title of a new work which will soon be ready for sale, containing 64 pages on beautiful paper of superior quality, and on new type of a larger size than any heretofore issued from this office. It contains

"Extracts from the prophecy of Enoch, including a revelation of the Gospel to our first parents after their expulsion from the Garden of Eden.

"The Words of God, which he spake unto Moses at the time when Moses was caught up into an exceedingly high mountain, and saw God face to face, and talked with him, and the Glory of God was upon Moses, so that he could endure the presence of the Lord. Including also the history of the creation of this heaven and this earth, together with the inhabitants thereof, and many historical items until the time of the flood, being items from the new translation of the scriptures by the Prophet Joseph.

"The Book of Abraham—a translation of some ancient records that fell into the hands of the Church a few years since from the catacombs of Egypt, purporting to be the writings of Abraham while he was in Egypt, called the Book of Abraham, written by his own hand upon Papyrus; translated from the Papyrus by Joseph Smith. Connected with this translation are three facsimiles from the Papyrus.

"An extract from a translation of the Bible—being the Twenty-fourth chapter of Matthew, commencing with the last verse of the Twenty-third chapter, by the Prophet, Seer, and Revelator, Joseph Smith.

"A Key to the Revelations of St. John, in a series of questions and answers. By the same.

"A Revelation given December, 1832, which has never before appeared in print.

"Extracts from the History of Joseph Smith, containing an account of the First Visions and Revelations which he received, also of his discovery and obtaining the Plates of Gold which contain the Record of Mormon; its translation, his baptism, and ordination by an Angel; items of doctrine from the revelations and commandments to the Church, &c.

"This little work though not particularly adapted nor designed as a pioneer of our faith to unbelievers of present revelation, will be a source of much instruction and edification to many thousands of the Saints, who will by an acquaintance with its precious contents, be more abundantly qualified to set forth and defend the principles of our Holy Faith before all men. The PEARL OF GREAT PRICE will recommend itself to all who appreciate the revelations of truth as hidden treasures of Everlasting Life. Prices printed on the covers." (In *Millennial Star*, 13 [15 July 1851]: 216–17.)

The Pearl of Great Price was published on 11 July 1851 at 15 Wilton Street, Liverpool, England. Following is the preface President Franklin D. Richards wrote for the first edition:

PREFACE

"The following compilation has been induced by the repeated solicitations of several friends of the publisher, who are desirous to be put in possession of the very important articles contained therein. Most of the Revelations composing this work were published at early periods of the Church, when the circulation of its journals was so very limited as to render them comparatively unknown at present, except to a few who have treasured up the productions of the Church with great care from the beginning. A smaller portion of this work has never before appeared in print; and altogether it is presumed, that true believers in the Divine mission of the Prophet JOSEPH SMITH, will appreciate this little collection of precious truths as a *Pearl of Great Price* that will increase their ability to maintain and to defend the holy faith by becoming possessors of it.

"Although not adapted, not designed, as a pioneer of the faith among unbelievers, still it will commend itself to all careful students of the scriptures, as detailing many important facts which are therein only alluded to, or entirely unmentioned, but consonant with the whole tenor of the revealed will of God; and, to the beginner in the Gospel, will add confirmatory evidence of the rectitude of his faith, by showing him that the doctrines and ordinances thereof are the same as were revealed to Adam for his salvation after his expulsion from the garden, and the same that he handed down and caused to be taught to his generations after him, as the only means appointed of God by which the generations of men may regain His presence.

"Nor do we conceive it possible for any unprejudiced person to arise from a careful perusal of this work, without being deeply impressed with a sense of the Divine calling, and holy ordination, of the man by whom these revelations, translations, and narrations have been communicated to us. As impervious as the minds of men may be at present to these convictions, the day is not far distant when sinners, as well as Saints, will know that JOSEPH SMITH was one of the greatest men that ever lived upon the earth, and that under God he was the Prophet and founder of the dispensation of the fulness of times, in which will be gathered together into one all things which are in Christ, both which are in heaven and which are on earth."

Following is the table of contents from the 1851 edition. The current location of each item is given in brackets at the end of each entry. The letter *a* after a verse number refers to the first half of that verse.

CONTENTS

Page

An Examination of the 1851 Preface and Contents

Paragraph one of the preface briefly explains the purpose and origin of the 1851 Pearl of Great Price. Much of the material in the Pearl of Great Price was first published in Ohio, Missouri, and Illinois and later in the British Mission publication *Millennial Star*. Even then, however, the material was scarce. More than twenty-six thousand converts had joined the Church in England since the Church had been compelled to stop printing the Book of Mormon and the Doctrine and Covenants. Because the revelations recorded in the Doctrine and Covenants were not otherwise available to the Saints, President Richards printed a number of them in the new mission tract.

President Richards also excerpted material from a variety of other Church publications to compose the first edition of the Pearl of Great Price. He made selections from the *Evening and Morning Star*, the *Times and Seasons*, the *Millennial Star, Lectures on Faith*, the Doctrine and Covenants, and a broadside published in Kirtland in 1836 or 1837. A few verses in Moses 4 were probably published for the first time in the 1851 Pearl of Great Price.

Most of the book of Moses came from the *Evening and Morning Star*, the *Millennial Star*, and the *Times and Seasons*. The book of Abraham had previously appeared in issues of the *Times and Seasons*, and Joseph Smith—Matthew had been published in a broadside on its own. Joseph Smith—History was drawn from the *Times and Seasons*. The Articles of Faith also were first published in the *Times and Seasons*.

Other material that appeared in the first edition of the Pearl of Great Price is no longer included in that volume of scripture. The selections from the Doctrine and Covenants appear only in the Doctrine and Covenants, and the poem "Truth" is set to music in the Latter-day Saint hymnal as "Oh Say, What Is Truth?" (*Hymns,* 1985, no. 272.)

A smaller part of the Pearl of Great Price was published for the first time in 1851. Such was the case of Joseph Smith's prophecy on the Civil War: "A Revelation given December, 1832, which has never before appeared in print." (In *Millennial Star*, 13 [15 July 1851]: 217.) A copy of this prophecy was given to Franklin D. Richards by Orson Pratt while they were serving together at Liverpool. (See Journal History, 10 Apr. 1896, LDS Church Historical Department, Salt Lake City, Utah.) Two other passages, Moses 4:14–19 and Moses 4:22–25, seem to have been printed for the first time in the 1851 Pearl of Great Price. Although there does not appear to be a statement such as the one about the prophecy of the Civil War to declare that these two passages had "never before appeared in print," neither have they been found in earlier printed sources.

EARLIEST PRINTED SOURCES
OF THE PEARL OF GREAT PRICE

1851 Edition Chapter Headings	1981 Edition Scripture References	Original Printed Source
"Extracts from the Prophecy of Enoch . . . "	Moses 6:43–68	*Evening and Morning Star* (Mar. 1833)
	Moses 7:1–69	*Evening and Morning Star* (Aug. 1832)
"The words of God, which he spake unto Moses at the time when Moses was caught up into an exceeding high mountain . . . "	Moses 1:1–42*a**	*Times and Seasons,* 4 [16 Jan. 1843]: 71–73
	Moses 2:1–4:13*a*	*Millennial Star,* 13 [15 Mar. 1851]: 90–93
	Moses 4:14–19	Probably Pearl of Great Price (1851 ed.)
	Moses 4:22–25	Probably Pearl of Great Price (1851 ed.)
	Moses 5:1–16*a*	*Evening and Morning Star* (Apr. 1833)
	Moses 5:19–23, 32–40	*Lectures on Faith,* 2:26; Doctrine and Covenants (1835 ed.)
	Moses 8:13–30	*Evening and Morning Star* [Apr. 1833]
"The Book of Abraham—A Translation of some Ancient Records, that have fallen into our hands from the Catacombs of Egypt . . . "	Abraham 1:1–2:18	*Times and Seasons,* 3 [1 Mar. 1842]: 704–6
	Abraham 2:19–5:21	*Times and Seasons,* 3 [15 Mar. 1842]: 719–22; [16 May 1842]: 783–84

*The first half of the verse.

1851 Edition Chapter Headings	1981 Edition Scripture References	Original Printed Source
"An Extract from a Translation of the Bible . . . "	Matthew 23:39–24:55	Printed as a broadside in Kirtland, Ohio, in 1836 or 1837
"A Key to the Revelations of St. John . . . "	Doctrine and Covenants 77	*Times and Seasons*, 5 [1 Aug. 1844]: 595–96
"A Revelation and Prophecy by the Prophet, Seer, and Revelator, Joseph Smith. Given December 25th, 1832 . . . "	Doctrine and Covenants 87	Pearl of Great Price (1851 ed.)
"Extracts from the History of Joseph Smith . . . "	Joseph Smith—History 1:1–14	*Times and Seasons*, 3 [15 Mar. 1842]: 726–28
	Joseph Smith—History 1:15–29	*Times and Seasons*, 3 [1 Apr. 1842]: 748–49
	Joseph Smith—History 1:30–49	*Times and Seasons*, 3 [15 Apr. 1842]: 753–54
	Joseph Smith—History 1:50–65	*Times and Seasons*, 3 [2 May 1842]: 771–73
	Joseph Smith—History 1:66–67	*Times and Seasons*, 3 [1 July 1842]: 832
	Joseph Smith—History 1:68–75	*Times and Seasons*, 3 [1 Aug. 1842]: 865–66
"Commandment to the Church concerning Baptism"	Doctrine and Covenants 20:71, 37, 72–74	*Evening and Morning Star* (June 1832)

1851 Edition Chapter Headings	1981 Edition Scripture References	Original Printed Source
"The Duties of the Members after they are received by Baptism"	Doctrine and Covenants 20:68–69	*Evening and Morning Star* (June 1832)
"Method of administering the Sacrament of the Lord's Supper"	Doctrine and Covenants 20:75–79	*Evening and Morning Star* (June 1832)
"The Duties of the Elders, Priests, Teachers, Deacons, and Members of the Church of Christ"	Doctrine and Covenants 20:38–44	*Evening and Morning Star* (June 1832)
	Doctrine and Covenants 107:11	Doctrine and Covenants (1835 ed.) 3:6
	Doctrine and Covenants 20:45–59, 70, 80	*Evening and Morning Star* (June 1832)
"On Priesthood"	Doctrine and Covenants 107:1–10, 12–20	Doctrine and Covenants (1835 ed.) 3:1–5, 7–10
"The Calling and Duties of the Twelve Apostles"	Doctrine and Covenants 107:23, 33	Doctrine and Covenants (1835 ed.) 3:11*a*, 12
"The Calling and Duties of the Seventy"	Doctrine and Covenants 107:34–35, 93–100	Doctrine and Covenants (1835 ed.) 3:13, 43–44
"Extract from a Revelation given July, 1830"	Doctrine and Covenants 27:5–18	Doctrine and Covenants (1835 ed.) 50:2–3
"Rise of the Church of Jesus Christ of Latter-day Saints"	Doctrine and Covenants 20:1–36	*Evening and Morning Star* (June 1832)

1851 Edition Chapter Headings	1981 Edition Scripture References	Original Printed Source
"Articles of Faith"	Pearl of Great Price, pages 60–61	*Times and Seasons,* 3 [1 Mar. 1842]: 709–10
"Truth"	*Hymns,* no. 272	*Millennial Star,* 12 [1 Aug. 1850]: 240
Fac-Simile No. 1 from the Book of Abraham	A Facsimile from the Book of Abraham, No. 1	*Times and Seasons,* 3 [1 Mar. 1842]: 703
Fac-Simile No. 2 from the Book of Abraham	A Facsimile from the Book of Abraham, No. 2	*Times and Seasons,* 3 [15 Mar. 1842]: 720 A
Fac-Simile No. 3 from the Book of Abraham	A Facsimile from the Book of Abraham, No. 3	*Times and Seasons,* 3 [16 May 1842]: 783–84

Paragraph two of the preface states that the Pearl of Great Price is not "adapted, nor designed, as a pioneer of the faith among unbelievers." It is important to understand that the tract was a mission publication whose purpose was to teach Church members; it was not intended as a missionary publication to be used in proselyting. The Book of Mormon, on the other hand, was specifically written "to the convincing of the Jew and Gentile that Jesus is the Christ, the Eternal God, manifesting himself unto all nations." (Title page of the Book of Mormon.)

The Pearl of Great Price speaks of eight dispensations of the gospel—dispensations to Adam, Enoch, Noah, Abraham, Moses, the apostles, Lehi, and Joseph Smith. President Richards emphasized that the doctrines and ordinances revealed to Adam and to the other prophets since his day are "the only means appointed of God by which the generations of men may regain His presence." In the words of Paul, there is "one Lord, one faith, one baptism." (Ephesians 4:5.)

The last paragraph of the preface is President Richards's testimony of the "Divine calling, and holy ordination" of the Prophet Joseph Smith. He prophesied that the "day is not far distant when sinners, as well as Saints, will know that Joseph Smith was one of the greatest men that ever lived upon the earth." The events that have transpired since Joseph Smith laid the foundation of this glorious dispensation attest to the truth of President Richards's prophecy.

The contents of the first edition of the Pearl of Great Price show that President Richards selected materials to strengthen the missionaries and the Saints. The tract described the duties of Church members; the method of administering the sacrament; the duties of the elders, priests, teachers, and deacons; the calling of the Twelve and the Seventy; and so on. It ended with a poem entitled "Truth," which had been written by a recent British convert to the Church, John Jaques. This poem was set to the music of Ellen Knowles Melling and has become one of the better known hymns of the Latter-day Saints. (See *Hymns*, 1985, no. 272.)

Not many of the Saints were immediately able to purchase the new mission publication because of the continuing financial crisis in Great Britain. In October 1852, a little over a year after the publication of the Pearl of Great Price, Elder Edward Frost wrote to Elder Levi Richards that Dorset, England, "is one of the poorest places that I was ever in but for all there poverty the Saints rejoice in the work of the Lord they are full of hope that a better day is at hand the Saints earnings do not average more than 6 pence per week from which there is not much to be got . . . the most that greeves me in this Conference is the poverty of the people from which my family suffers much for since I have been in this Conference the means that have been brought in my house have not been over 7 pence per week for sister Frost 2 children and myself still I am determined to hold on and go ahead in the work of God believing that after the bitter cometh the blessing." (MS/f 438-#2 Box 1 fd 11 Box 2 fd 15, LDS Church Historical Department, Salt Lake City, Utah.)

Elder Joseph F. Smith wrote to President Franklin D. Richards from Bedford a month later, on 30 November 1852, "of the extreme poverty of the Saints. I will do my best, but, my heart bleeds to see many of their circumstances." (MS/f 438-#2 Box 1 fd 11 box 2 fd 15, LDS Church Historical Department, Salt Lake City, Utah.)

The First American Edition, 1878

The Pearl of Great Price was soon popular with the Saints throughout the Church. The American Saints had access to it through returning missionaries and immigrating British Church members. John Taylor, acting president of the Church, called upon the Church historian, Elder Orson Pratt, to prepare an American edition of the British tract. Several changes were made for that edition, which was published in 1878. The preface was deleted because it was no longer pertinent, and it was not replaced by a new one. The first two entries in the table of contents were combined and placed in chronological order, and several passages not included in the 1851 edition were added. The source of most of these additions was the Inspired Version of the Bible (the Joseph Smith Translation), which had been published by the Reorganized Church of

Jesus Christ of Latter Day Saints in 1867. Several of the brethren, including Orson Pratt, had assisted Joseph Smith in preparing the Inspired Version, and they were persuaded that the Reorganized Church had been honest in preserving the original text. Another addition was the revelation on eternal marriage (now D&C 132). This revelation was also added to the new Doctrine and Covenants that was being prepared for publication. It seems that the brethren wanted it to be widely circulated because the Church at the time was under heavy attack from federal officials who opposed the practice of polygamy.

The Pearl of Great Price Is Canonized

Sunday, 10 October 1880, was a special day in Church history. President Wilford Woodruff said of the day, "This is a great day to Israel." (Wilford Woodruff Journal, LDS Church Historical Department, Salt Lake City, Utah.) The Church leaders and members met at 2:00 P.M. for the second Sunday session of the 50th Semiannual General Conference of the Church. Elder Orson Pratt presented the authorities for the sustaining vote of the conference. The voting was by priesthood quorums. John Taylor was sustained as the prophet, seer, and revelator and as president of the Church with George Q. Cannon and Joseph F. Smith as his counselors. President Taylor had been acting president of the Church since the death of Brigham Young three years before because he was president of the Quorum of the Twelve Apostles.

Orson Pratt prepared the first American edition of the Pearl of Great Price in 1878

The Pearl of Great Price was then canonized by the vote of the entire conference, becoming the fourth standard work of the Church:

"President George Q. Cannon said: I hold in my hand the Book of Doctrine and Covenants and also the book The Pearl of Great Price, which books contain revelations of God. In Kirtland, the Doctrine and Covenants in its original form, as first printed, was submitted to the officers of the Church and the members of the church to vote upon. As there have been additions made to it by the publishing of revelations which were not contained in the original edition, it has been deemed wise to submit these books and their contents as from God, and binding upon us as a people and as a Church.

"President Joseph F. Smith said, I move that we receive and accept the revelations contained in these books as revelations from God to the Church of Jesus Christ of Latter-day Saints, and to all the world. The motion was seconded and sustained by unanimous vote of the whole conference." (Journal History, 10 Oct. 1880, LDS Church Historical Department, Salt Lake City, Utah.)

Changes in the Pearl of Great Price, 1890–1981

In the October 1890 conference Elder Franklin D. Richards of the Quorum of the Twelve read the Articles of Faith to the congregation. They were confirmed as scripture by the vote of the conference. There must have been some confusion about their status because they had been canonized as part of the Pearl of Great Price ten years before.

In 1900 Dr. James E. Talmage, of the University of Utah, was called by the First Presidency to make some changes in the Pearl of Great Price. He divided it into chapters and verses and added numerous cross-references. He deleted the extracts from the Doctrine and Covenants because they were available in that book of scripture, and he deleted the poem "Truth" as well. These changes were approved by a Church reading committee consisting of General Authorities. The new format was accepted by the 1902 October general conference.

Dr. Talmage left the academic world in 1911 when he was sustained as a member of the Quorum of the Twelve Apostles. In 1920 he was called to chair a committee to make revisions in the latter-day scriptures. In 1920 he divided the Book of Mormon into double-column pages, added chapter headings, chronological data, a pronouncing vocabulary, and an index, and revised the footnote references. After completing the changes in the Doctrine and Covenants in 1921, Elder Talmage turned to the Pearl of Great Price. He organized this work also into double-column pages and added an index.

In the April general conference of 1976 two new revelations, Joseph Smith's vision of the celestial kingdom and Joseph F. Smith's vision of

James E. Talmage refined the format of the Pearl of Great Price in 1902 and 1921

the redemption of the dead, were sustained as scripture to be added to the Pearl of Great Price. The affirmative vote was unanimous. In June 1979 these two scriptures were moved from the Pearl of Great Price to become sections 137 and 138 of the Doctrine and Covenants.

The Church has made some changes in all the standard works in recent years. In August 1979 the Church published a new edition of the King James Version of the Bible. Hundreds of pages of footnotes, cross-references, chapter headings, a topical guide, and a Bible dictionary were included. Two years later, in August 1981, the Church published new editions of the three other standard works. The 1981 Pearl of Great Price had a preface, something it had been lacking since the 1851 edition. The titles of three of the four books in the Pearl of Great Price were changed. The book of Moses became Selections from the Book of Moses. Writings of Joseph Smith 1 was renamed Joseph Smith—Matthew, and Joseph Smith 2 was renamed Joseph Smith—History. Each chapter was given a new heading. Inaccurate dates in the headnotes of the Doctrine and Covenants were corrected, and minor textual corrections were made "to bring the text into conformity with earlier documents." (Introductory Note to the Pearl of Great Price.) All of the revisions were approved by the members of the Quorum of the Twelve Apostles who served as the Scripture Publications Committee of the Church.

Because the quality of the reproductions of the three Egyptian facsimiles in the book of Abraham had deteriorated in recent editions of the Pearl of Great Price, the 1981 edition used photoprints of the facsimiles as they appeared in the *Times and Seasons* in 1842 when Joseph Smith was the editor.

The Book of Moses and Joseph Smith–Matthew: Extracts from the Joseph Smith Translation of the Bible

Relationship of the Pearl of Great Price to the Bible

Moses and Joseph Smith—Matthew are extracts from the Joseph Smith Translation of the Bible that were revealed to the Prophet during the period from June 1830 through February 1831. (See headnotes to the Pearl of Great Price, Moses, and Joseph Smith—Matthew.) The new translation was necessary because "many plain and precious things" had been taken away from the Bible through the centuries. (1 Nephi 13:28.)

As Latter-day Saints we accept the Holy Bible as scripture and recognize it as the great worldwide witness of Jesus Christ. We also accept as scripture the Book of Mormon, which is subtitled Another Testament of Jesus Christ. The prophet Mormon explained, "This [the Book of Mormon] is written for the intent that ye may believe that [the Bible]; and if ye believe that ye will believe this also." (Mormon 7:9.) When the Bible was originally written, it "contained the fulness of the gospel of the Lord." (1 Nephi 13:24.) An angel explained to Nephi that "these things go forth from the Jews in purity unto the Gentiles, according to the truth which is in God." (1 Nephi 13:25.) But after the Bible was taken to the Gentiles, there was some deliberate tampering with the text by "that great and abominable church." (1 Nephi 13:26.) The angel further explained that "they have taken away from the gospel of the Lamb many parts which are plain and most precious; and also many covenants of the Lord have they taken away." (1 Nephi 13:26.)

Thus the Latter-day Saints recognize that the Bible has some deficiencies "because of the many plain and precious things which have been taken out of the book, which were plain unto the understanding of the children of men." (1 Nephi 13:29.) As Joseph Smith wrote in the Wentworth Letter, "We believe the Bible to be the word of God as far as it is translated correctly." (Articles of Faith 1:8.)

The angel who told Nephi how the Bible would be altered also told him how the Lord would provide his children with the missing teachings and covenants. The angel showed Nephi in vision "other books," which would come forth "by the power of the Lamb, from the Gentiles unto them, unto the convincing of the Gentiles and the remnant of the seed of my brethren, and also the Jews who were scattered upon all the face of the earth, that the records of the prophets and of the twelve apostles of the Lamb are true." (1 Nephi 13:39.)

Certainly the "other books" Nephi saw in vision include the Book of Mormon, the Doctrine and Covenants, the Pearl of Great Price, the Joseph Smith Translation of the Bible, and other sacred records such as the sealed portion of the plates and the lost books of the Bible.

Amid Persecution the Lord Provided "a Precious Morsel"

The restored church was only a few weeks old when considerable opposition arose. Newel Knight, who had shown interest in the new church, went to a wooded area to ask God about its truthfulness. He returned to his home feeling ill in body and mind. Shortly thereafter his body was twisted and distorted and finally he was caught up in the air and violently tossed about the room. Joseph Smith went to the home, and Newel Knight asked Joseph to cast out the devil that had possessed him. The Prophet replied, "If you know that I can, it shall be done." The devil was rebuked in the name of the Lord, and Brother Knight testified that he saw the devil leave him. Brother Knight, though very weakened, returned to normal. (Joseph Smith, *History of the Church*, 1:83.)

This episode, the first miracle of the Restoration, was witnessed by several adults. The experience helped convince them of the divinity of the work, and most of them were baptized. They were attended by the Holy Ghost, which was poured out upon the converts "in a miraculous manner," causing many to prophesy and others to see marvelous scenes as "the heavens were opened to their view." (Smith, *History of the Church*, 1:85.) Other converts applied for baptism because of their testimonies of the Book of Mormon and the accompanying witness of the Spirit.

Satan continued to incite his adherents to fight the restored Church of Jesus Christ. At one time a mob of about fifty men assembled, intending to harm the Prophet. On another occasion, Joseph was arrested on a charge of being a disorderly person. He was taken to a tavern where he was abused and ridiculed by men who spat upon him saying, "Prophesy, prophesy," ignorantly imitating those who had crucified the Savior of the world. (See Luke 22:64.) Twice he was subjected to court trials in front of a multitude of spectators who were convinced of his guilt and anxious for maximum punishment to be meted out. After two acquittals, he was released, but the hateful mobs continued to hinder the work. The Prophet recorded, "Amid all the trials and tribulations we had to wade through, the Lord, who well knew our infantile and delicate situation, vouchsafed for us a supply of strength, and granted us 'line upon line of knowledge—here a little and there a little,' of which the following was a precious morsel. [Moses 1]." (*History of the Church*, 1:98.)

Moses 1: The Prelude to the Bible

Moses 1 is indeed a "precious morsel," for it tells in plainness and simplicity of the nature of God, the nature of man, and the nature of the adversary. This revelation, given to Joseph Smith in June 1830, contained visions that had been given to Moses more than three thousand years before. The Savior had shown Moses the earth and the ends thereof and its innumerable inhabitants, and, in a succeeding vision, had allowed Moses to discern both the particles of the earth and its seemingly numberless inhabitants. Jehovah further opened the heavens to Moses to show him many worlds. Between the two visions, the adversary appeared to Moses and attempted to thwart the work of the Lord through impersonation and intimidation.

Both heavenly visions and the Satanic encounter were recorded by Moses. They preceded the more detailed vision of the creation of the earth that we have as Genesis 1 in the Bible. The Lord explained to Moses that "in a day when the children of men shall esteem my words as naught and take many of them from the book which thou shalt write, behold, I will raise up another like unto thee; and they shall be had again among the children of men—among as many as shall believe." (Moses 1:41.) The prophet "like unto" Moses, the great Lawgiver, was the Prophet Joseph Smith.

*Joseph Smith was the revelator,
translator, and narrator
of the contents of the
Pearl of Great Price*

The Joseph Smith Translation of the Bible

The exact date is not known, but it appears that soon after Joseph Smith received the great visions that had once been given to Moses (see Moses 1), the Lord gave the young prophet another important calling. He was to correct the King James Version of the Bible where meaning had been altered and restore the text where deletions had deprived it of purity and completeness.

This great undertaking occupied a good portion of Joseph's time between June 1830 and July 1833. Robert J. Matthews, a prominent Latter-day Saint authority on the Joseph Smith Translation of the Bible, wrote that procedurally "the Prophet and a scribe would sit at a table, with the Prophet having the King James Version of the Bible open before him. Probably he would read from the King James Version and dictate the revisions, while the scribe recorded what he said. . . .

"The translation was not a simple, mechanical recording of divine dictum, but rather a study-and-thought process accompanied and prompted by revelation from the Lord. That it was a revelatory process is evident from statements by the Prophet and others who were personally acquainted with the work." (*"A Plainer Translation": Joseph Smith's Translation of the Bible, a History and Commentary*, p. 39).

Many truths previously unknown to the young prophet came as a result of this extensive work. Several revelations now contained in the Doctrine and Covenants were given to him as he labored on the revision of the Bible (sections 76, 77, 84, 86, 88, 93, 102, 104, 107, 113, and

132). And most of what we now have as Moses and Joseph Smith—
Matthew was revealed to the Prophet in connection with his work on
the Bible. (See Introductory Note to the Pearl of Great Price; headnotes
to Moses and Joseph Smith—Matthew.)

Many Latter-day Saints are not fully aware of just how closely the
Joseph Smith Translation is related to the Pearl of Great Price and indeed
to the work of the Restoration. Robert J. Matthews answered many of
the questions Latter-day Saints ask about this translation of the Bible:

"*Q.* How did Joseph Smith make the translation of the Bible?

"*A.* The Prophet had a large, family-size edition of the King James
Version of the Bible. He read from this, marked certain passages, and
dictated the revisions, corrections, and additions to a scribe, who wrote
them on paper. Sometimes the entire verse was recorded, sometimes
only the part to be revised. The translation was done by divine revelation to the mind of the Prophet. . . .

"*Q.* How long did the Prophet Joseph work on his Bible translation?

"*A.* Some pages of the manuscript are dated. From this source and
from his own journal we know that he worked on the translation somewhat regularly from June 1830 until July 1833. Although there were
many interruptions, most of the work was accomplished during these
three years. However, he continued to make revisions and to prepare
the manuscript for printing until the time of his death in 1844. . . .

"*Q.* Did Joseph Smith finish the translation of the Bible? If not, how
much did he do?

"*A.* Although the Prophet stated in a letter of 2 July 1833 that he
had that day 'finished' the translation of the Bible, it is evident that he
did more to it later and did not consider the manuscript ready for publication at that time. The manuscript documents show that the Prophet
gave attention to every book in the Old and New Testaments. Although
in some of the books he made no changes, and in some of them he did
not make all the changes that could have been made, he did go all the
way through the Bible, giving consideration to every book from Genesis
to Revelation. . . .

"*Q.* What is the correct name for Joseph Smith's translation of the
Bible?

"*A.* The work has been known by several names. Joseph frequently
referred to it as the 'New Translation,' and as such it was known in the
early literature of the Church. The Reorganized Church (RLDS) published it in 1867 under the title *Holy Scriptures*. The 1936 edition was
the first to carry the title *Inspired Version*. In 1944 the book was again
published by the RLDS under the title *Holy Scriptures: Inspired Version*. It has been variously known as the Inspired Version, the Inspired
Revision, the Inspired Translation, and the New Translation. . . . [Since

Dr. Matthews wrote his book, The Church of Jesus Christ of Latter-day Saints approved the title Joseph Smith Translation of the Bible (JST).]

"*Q*. Is the Inspired Version of the Bible, as distributed by the Reorganized Church, published accurately?

"*A*. Comparison of the printed Inspired Version with the original manuscripts of the translation shows that the printed editions are accurate and faithful to the manuscript in almost every particular. Recent editions are more accurate than the first edition of 1867. . . .

"*Q*. Why does The Church of Jesus Christ of Latter-day Saints (LDS) not accept Joseph Smith's translation of the Bible?

"*A*. The Church does accept the 'work' of Joseph Smith as being divinely inspired, as evidenced by the book of Moses and by the twenty-fourth chapter of Matthew [Joseph Smith—Matthew] in the Pearl of Great Price, which are excerpts from the translation. The Church, however, does not accept the publication of the work by the RLDS as authoritative. This is based on a number of factors, including an awareness that the translation was not finished and the manuscript was not completely prepared by Joseph Smith for the press. Also, until recently the LDS Church has not had access to the original manuscripts of the translation. . . .

"*Q*. Why has no other prophet in the LDS Church completed the translation of the Bible?

"*A*. Such an undertaking would have to be by the command and direction of the Lord, and not by the volition and instigation of man. Apparently the Lord, in his timetable, has not desired that it be done. In its fullest sense, 'the restoration of all things' will surely include a restoration of ancient scriptures, which may someday call for the completion of the Bible translation. . . .

"*Q*. Does the LDS Church have a copy of the manuscript of Joseph Smith's Bible translation?

"*A*. A partial copy (less than half) of the original manuscripts was made privately by Dr. John M. Bernhisel in Nauvoo in the spring of 1845. His manuscript is valuable chiefly because of its early date, but it unfortunately consists only of *excerpts* from the Old and New Testaments. It was brought to the Salt Lake Valley in 1848 and is now in the archives of the Church Historical Department in Salt Lake City. . . .

"*Q*. Did Joseph Smith use the Urim and Thummim in the translation of the Bible?

"*A*. There is no evidence that he used the Urim and Thummim or a seer stone of any type during the actual translation. Elder Orson Pratt made a statement to the effect that it was not used. However, there is a report that prior to the translation the Prophet used the Urim and Thummim to 'look at' the Bible. . . .

"*Q*. Did Joseph Smith use Greek and/or Hebrew manuscripts or a knowledge of these languages in making the Bible translation?

"*A*. So far as we have any evidence, Joseph Smith did not use Biblical languages and manuscripts in the translation. His learning of Biblical languages came after his initial translation (ending in July 1833) and may have been employed by him in making some of the revisions and corrections in the manuscripts between 1835 and 1844.

"*Q*. If Joseph Smith dealt basically only with an English text and language, why is his work with the Bible called a 'translation'?

"*A*. Joseph himself called his work a 'translation.' This is apparently the sense in which he understood the work he was doing with the Bible. Since in part he was effecting a restoration of lost meaning and material, and since the Bible did not originate in English, his work to some degree would amount to an inspired, or revelatory, 'translation' into English of that which the ancient prophets and apostles had written in Hebrew, Aramaic, and/or Greek. . . .

"*Q*. Is there evidence that Joseph Smith intended to publish his Bible translation? If so, why did he not do it?

"*A*. Yes, there is a great amount of evidence that the Prophet and those who were associated with him intended to publish his translation of the Bible. Members and nonmembers of the Church were aware of plans for publication. Lack of financial resources appears to be a significant factor which prevented the Prophet's finishing the translation before his death and thus, of course, his publishing it. Parts of the translation were published in the Prophet's day in Church newspapers; also, portions of the translation were privately copied in longhand by interested persons. . . .

"*Q*. Does Joseph Smith's translation of the Bible contain any doctrines or principles not already found in the standard works of the Church?

"*A*. The New Translation has extensive doctrinal contributions that originally were available from no other source. However, since excerpts from the translation of Genesis and of Matthew (the book of Moses and the twenty-fourth chapter of Matthew) are now published in the Pearl of Great Price, some of the most important and unique doctrinal contributions are currently available from that source. There still remain several doctrinally important items that are available only from the New Translation itself. Some of these are hinted at in the other books of scripture but are enlarged upon and clarified in the New Translation. . . .

"*Q*. What is the proper place of Joseph Smith's translation of the Bible in the larger background of Church history?

"*A*. Familiarity with the facts and the history of Joseph Smith's translation of the Bible shows that it was the means by which many important doctrines of the gospel were revealed to the Prophet. He was translating the Bible, not because he already knew the answers and doctrines, but because by the process and experience of the translation he would learn things important for him to know. Thus the translation is inseparable from the history of the Church and the building up of the kingdom in the last days.

"*Q.* What differences exist between the first printed edition of the Inspired Version (1867 to 1936 printings) and the 'New Corrected Edition' (1944 and after)?

"*A.* Differences occur in about 352 verses in these two printings. Most of the differences are slight and do not affect doctrine, but some are quite significant doctrinally. Later printings (1944 and after) are more accurate than the 1867 edition. . . .

"*Q.* How does present-day non-LDS Biblical scholarship relate to the translation by Joseph Smith? Do recent translations of the Bible support Joseph Smith's translation?

"*A.* In most instances recent non-LDS translations of the Bible do not parallel the translation by Joseph Smith. Some passages, however, show similarities. Some apocryphal writings also show a similarity in content to some of the passages of Joseph Smith's translation. But in the overwhelming majority of passages there are no parallels to the work of Joseph Smith in supplying new material and information to the Bible.

"*Q.* How could I use Joseph Smith's Inspired Version of the Bible in teaching the gospel?

"*A.* Perhaps the best use of the Inspired Version is as a commentary or reference work. It is often an extremely rewarding experience to compare an unclear passage in the King James Version with the Inspired Version. It is an excellent study aid and supplement." ("*A Plainer Translation,*" pp. xxvii-xxxii.)

Mistranslations Clarified or Corrected

Part of Joseph Smith's work on the new translation of the Bible was correcting passages that had not been translated correctly. The following are a few of the hundreds of such textual corrections the Prophet Joseph was inspired to make.

King James Version	Joseph Smith Translation
"And the Lord repented of the evil which he thought to do unto his people." (Exodus 32:14.)	"And the Lord said unto Moses, if they will repent of the evil which they have done, I will spare them, and turn away my fierce wrath." (Exodus 32:14.)

"And the Lord said unto Moses, Go in unto Pharaoh: for I have hardened his heart, and the heart of his servants." (Exodus 10:1.)

"And the Lord said unto Moses, Go in unto Pharaoh: for he hath hardened his heart, and the hearts of his servants." (Exodus 10:1.)

"And it repented the Lord that he had made man on the earth, and it grieved him at his heart." (Genesis 6:6.)

"And it repented Noah, and his heart was pained that the Lord had made man on the earth, and it grieved him at the heart." (Moses 8:25)

"And I will establish my covenant between me and thee and thy seed after thee in their generations for an everlasting covenant, to be a God unto thee, and to thy seed after thee." (Genesis 17:7.)

"And I will establish a covenant of circumcision with thee, and it shall be my covenant between me and thee, and thy seed after thee, in their generations; that thou mayest know for ever that children are not accountable before me until they are eight years old." (Genesis 17:11.)

"And I appeared unto Abraham, unto Isaac, and unto Jacob, by the name of God Almighty, but by my name Jehovah was I not known to them." (Exodus 6:3.)

"And I appeared unto Abraham, unto Isaac, and unto Jacob. I am the Lord God Almighty; the Lord Jehovah. And was not my name known unto them?" (Exodus 6:3.)

"It is a shame for women to speak in the church." (1 Corinthians 14:35.)

"It is a shame for women to rule in the church." (1 Corinthians 14:35.)

"An evil spirit from the Lord troubled him." (1 Samuel 16:14.)

"And an evil spirit which was not of the Lord troubled him." (1 Samuel 16:14.)

"And Solomon did evil in the sight of the Lord, and went not fully after the Lord, as did David his father." (1 Kings 11:6.)

"And Solomon did evil in the sight of the Lord, as David his father, and went not fully after the Lord." (1 Kings 11:6.)

"Then was Jesus led up of the Spirit into the wilderness to be tempted of the devil." (Matthew 4:1.)	"Then was Jesus led up of the Spirit into the wilderness to be with God." (Matthew 4:1.)
"No man hath seen God at any time." (1 John 4:12.)	"No man hath seen God at any time, except them who believe." (1 John 4:12.)

Plain and Precious Truths Restored

Another part of Joseph Smith's work on the Bible was to restore many "plain and precious things" that were missing from the text. (1 Nephi 13:28.) Most of the book of Moses, for example, restores truths missing from the first chapters of the book of Genesis, which covers many hundreds of years in four pages. Following are some of the significant additions made to the book of Moses by the Prophet. (Compare Genesis 1:1–6:13.)

1. Several scriptures on the spiritual creation that preceded the physical creation were revealed. (See Moses 3:5, 7, 9.)

2. There were three actors in the great drama in the Garden of Eden: Adam, Eve, and Satan. Several verses in the King James Version refer to Adam and Eve, but little is said of Satan. An account that explains Satan's role was added. (See Moses 4:1–6.)

3. The more complete account in the book of Moses speaks of the sons and daughters of Adam and of their grandchildren, including the wife of Cain. The biblical account mentions only three sons of Adam and Eve: Cain, Abel, and Seth. (See Moses 5:2–3, 28.)

4. When Adam and Eve were cast out of the Garden of Eden, "after many days" they were taught the gospel of Jesus Christ. Our first parents were not left without hope or direction. The silence of the Bible has caused many to wonder about God's love and concern for the primal parents of the world and the first generations of the human family. (See Moses 5:6–12.)

5. Animal sacrifice, a solemn reminder of the infinite sacrifice of Jesus Christ, was first revealed to Adam. The particulars of animal sacrifice and its importance are not clear in the Bible text. (See Moses 5:4–8.)

6. The account of the first murder is given in outline in the Bible. Details of Cain's premeditated act, his reason for it, and the consequences of it were revealed to Joseph Smith. (See Moses 5:4–27.)

7. Satan's oath-bound wicked combinations that began with Cain and his followers are discussed in Moses. (See Moses 5:49–56.)

8. Adam and Eve and their extended family were intelligent beings who read and wrote and who frequently communed with Deity. They were record keepers, "having a language that was pure and undefiled." (Moses 6:6.)

9. One of the greatest visions ever given to man on the earth was given to the prophet Enoch. From it we learn of many great prophecies up to the end of the earth. Little is told about Enoch in the Bible account. (See Moses 6:26–7:69.)

The Book of Abraham: Extracts from the Larger Text Also Called the Book of Abraham

The book of Abraham in the Pearl of Great Price is an extract from a larger document also known as the book of Abraham. The record of Abraham was found buried with some Egyptian mummies exhumed from the west bank of the Nile across from the ancient city of Thebes about 1820. This record was "beautifully written on papyrus, with black, and a small part red, ink or paint, in perfect preservation." (Joseph Smith, *History of the Church*, 2:348.)

How Could Abraham's Writings Be in Egypt?

It is generally understood that Abraham was born and raised in the land of the Chaldeans in Mesopotamia. When he fell into disfavor with his family and the political leaders, and was consequently sentenced to death, the Lord rescued him and directed him to go to the land of Canaan, which was given to him and his posterity as a land of their inheritance. (See Abraham 1:1, 5–7, 12–16, 18–19.)

A famine that became "very grievous" caused Abraham to leave the land of Canaan and move to the richly endowed land of Egypt until the famine abated. (Abraham 2:21.) Abraham lived in Egypt where he mingled with royalty, instructed Pharaoh's court on the subject of astronomy,

The West Bank of the Nile near Thebes is where the papyri and the mummies were found

and no doubt taught the truths of the everlasting gospel whenever the occasion arose. When he left Egypt to return to his land of promise, he was "very rich in cattle, in silver, and in gold." (Genesis 13:2.)

The posterity of Abraham lived in Canaan from that time on. On several occasions, however, famines caused them to flee to Egypt with the magnificent Nile River and its fertile delta. Abraham's grandson Jacob and his family went to Egypt to seek food during a famine. Joseph, Jacob's son, was governor of the land, second only to Pharaoh, when Jacob's family arrived.

So there are many possibilities that could account for the writings of Abraham being in Egypt. First, Abraham may have kept records and left them in Egypt when he returned to Canaan. Second, the posterity of Abraham, perhaps Jacob himself, preserved his sacred writings and carried them to Egypt when they relocated there. Third, later Israelites who treasured the writings of their illustrious and honored ancestor could easily have taken his writings, or copies of them, to Egypt.

Events Leading to the Discovery of the Abraham Papyri

Europeans had paid little attention to their Egyptian neighbors to the south for several hundred years, until the Napoleonic Wars. Veterans of battles in Egypt took back to Europe stories and sketches that created a great sensation among all classes. After Napoleon and his forces were defeated at Waterloo in 1815, many restless Europeans looking for

new adventures moved to Egypt to engage in the profitable business of
stripping Egypt of her precious historical monuments. The land of Egypt
was robbed of much of its magnificent splendor during the first thirty
years of the nineteenth century.

Mehemet Ali, viceroy of Egypt, ruled with an iron hand. He was
anxious to increase Egypt's technology, which was far behind that of
European nations. So, in exchange for industrial assistance, Mehemet
Ali allowed the European visitors to rob graves and plunder the relics of
Egypt's illustrious past.

Antonio Lebolo

One of the prominent men working in the digs in Upper Egypt was
Antonio Lebolo. Lebolo, who was born in 1781 in the Piedmont of present
day Italy, close to the French and Swiss borders, served as a gendarme
under Napoleon. After Napoleon's defeat, Lebolo and many of his
comrades-in-arms were forced to leave their homes or face certain impris-
onment. By 1817, the exiled soldier was residing in Egypt, employed by
Bernardino Drovetti, the former French consul general, to supervise the
work of several hundred laborers in his excavations in Upper Egypt.
Lebolo became well known and was highly regarded by many important
people. One of them, Count Carlo Vidua, wrote of a visit to Thebes and
said of Lebolo:

"But, among so many marvelous things, that are possible to be
admired at Thebes, the most curious one of all is the valley where the
kings' sepulchers lay. It is rather a lonely valley, arid, horrible, in which
some holes like caverns are seen. Entering these caverns, long galleries,
halls, chambers, and cabinets are found, in short, they are underground
palaces, all covered with painted bas-relieves; and it is very marvelous. It
is wonderful the preservation of the colors, the amount of works, the
scrupulous attention used to make them. Lately, a new one was discovered which surpasses all the others in beauty, in the perfection of the
work, and in execution [Tomb of Seti I]. I visited it two times. The second time I spent the whole day there, examining everything; it was
already late evening, and I couldn't move myself away from there.

"I dined inside there in a beautiful hall, much more elegant than
our ballrooms. Also, I believe that, considering all, this sepulcher of the
king of Thebes is a much more sumptuous dwelling than the dwellings
of our living European kings. Who, do you think, gave me the honor of
those sepulchers, and who reigns in Thebes in exchange of the dead
king? A Piedmontese. Mr. Lebolo from Canavese, formerly a police officer
in the service of France. He came to Egypt and was employed by Mr.
Drovetti in the excavations, which he does continuously in Thebes. Our

Piedmonteses really have a ready spirit, and are capable of succeeding in everything; from police officer to antiques is a big jump. Well, Mr. Lebolo works successfully in his new career; he found beautiful pieces for the Drovetti museum; and since he was allowed by him to do some excavations of his own, he gathered for himself a small collection, which will bring him a moderate fortune. In those ten days that I lived in Thebes, Mr. Lebolo accompanied me, took me everywhere, had me come to dinner at his house, which is among monuments and half embedded in tombs, all filled with mummies, papyruses, and little statues. An Egyptian bas-relief was the top of the door; we made fire with pieces of mummies' coffins." (Balbo, *Letters of Count Carlo Vidua*, 2:177.)

Lebolo and his crews excavated various sites near Thebes, Karnak, and the west bank in Upper Egypt. In one of these sites, they discovered a catacomb containing several hundred mummies. They removed eleven mummies of the first order of burial, the only ones of the entire collection that were well enough preserved to be transported. (See Smith, *History of the Church*, 2:348–49.) The exact site of the tomb from which the eleven mummies were exhumed is unknown because Lebolo worked on several sites over the period from 1817 to 1821, and no record to identify the site has been found.

Lebolo left Egypt and returned to Castellamonte about 1826 where he died at his home on 19 February 1830 at the age of forty-nine. (Legal papers in the possession of H. Donl Peterson.) On 30 July 1831, Lebolo's twenty-one-year-old son, Pietro, was authorized by the family to go to Trieste to see why a shipping company owner, Albano Oblasser, had not paid the Lebolo family for the eleven mummies that he had been commissioned to sell.

On 5 October 1833 Pietro Lebolo went before a notary in Torino to give Francesco Bertola, who was then living in Philadelphia, "the authority to claim the eleven mummies and other antique objects located in various boxes belonging to the deceased Antonio Lebolo who sent them to Albano Oblasser of Trieste. Albano Oblasser sent them to New York to the custom house of Mr. Led and Quellerspie of Meetland and Kennedy." According to this notarized statement, the eleven mummies had been sent to New York City to the house of Mr. Led and Mr. Quellerspie "to be sold to anybody that would have paid the sum that they (Mr. Led and Quellerspie) would have thought appropriate and then sent quittance in any possible way." Mr. Bertola was given authority to sell the mummies, "and he will take care of all of the problems that might come up in order to obtain a quick liquidation of such objects." (The original documents are located in the State Archives in Turin, Italy. Photocopies and translations are in the possession of H. Donl Peterson.)

Michael H. Chandler

The *History of the Church* contains an intriguing story that raises several questions that have yet to be answered. "On his [Lebolo's] way from Alexandria to Paris, he put in at Trieste, and, after ten days' illness, expired. This was in the year 1832. Previous to his decease, he made a will of the whole, to Mr. Michael H. Chandler, (then in Philadelphia, Pa.,) his nephew, whom he supposed to be in Ireland. Accordingly, the whole were sent to Dublin, and Mr. Chandler's friends ordered them to New York, where they were received at the Custom House, in the winter or spring of 1833." (Smith, *History of the Church*, 2:349.)

There is evidence that Lebolo was in Alexandria and Trieste in the early 1820s. In Alexandria, Lebolo was engaged in selling Egyptian artifacts. In Trieste, where he visited several times between 1822 and 1824, he was listed as a merchant. No known documents substantiate Lebolo's illness in Trieste.

The year of Lebolo's death is recorded in Trieste as taking place in that city in 1832. Neither of those assertions is accurate. In fact, Lebolo died in his hometown of Castellamonte during the night of 18–19 February 1830. This fact is documented in church records of Castellamonte and is corroborated by several notarial documents relative to the Lebolo family that are maintained in the State Archives in Turin, Italy.

The archives in Trieste contain several oversized books in which are recorded the wills of those who filed them there. No will bearing Lebolo's name has been found in Trieste; however, Lebolo did prepare his last will and testament on 17 November 1829 in Castellamonte. (A copy of the will is in the possession of H. Donl Peterson.) Neither does Lebolo's genealogy mention a Michael H. Chandler, an Irishman, in any of the records. No documents have been found that in any way tie Lebolo and Chandler as relatives.

Research in Dublin has failed to document that any mummies moved through the Port of Dublin or were advertised in the maritime news sections of the newspapers of the day. The documents located in the State Archives of Turin mention only the shipment of the mummies from Trieste to New York City to be sold on the market to the highest bidder.

This segment of the story is still baffling. The route the mummies took to get to New York and the reasons for Michael Chandler's involvement with their handling have not yet been clearly established.

Despite the minor discrepancies between recent research findings and Oliver Cowdery's report in the *History of the Church* (see 2:348–51), the main facts in Oliver's account are borne out by recent research:

The mummies were found near Thebes. They were discovered by Antonio Lebolo, a celebrated French traveler. Lebolo was employed by

Drovetti, who was granted permission to excavate by Mehemet Ali. Lebolo did superintend several hundred men in the digs. Lebolo did own eleven mummies. Lebolo did have business connections in Trieste. The mummies were freighted to New York City. They did arrive in the winter or early spring of 1833. Seven mummies were sold to gentlemen in the east before Chandler took the remaining four to Kirtland.

In fact, the only discrepancies are that the early dates in Oliver Cowdery's account are not accurate and Lebolo did not die in Trieste. Documentation is lacking to establish or discredit the assertion of a blood relationship between Chandler and Lebolo and the route of the mummies to the United States. And it should be kept in mind that the information contained in the *History of the Church* was probably given to Oliver Cowdery by Michael Chandler, whose documentation relative to the origin of the mummies, if any, was probably written by the Lebolos or Mr. Oblasser in a foreign language.

The Mummies in America

Chandler, a resident of Philadelphia, had possession of the eleven mummies in the later part of March 1833. How he knew of their arrival in New York City is not known. Because no notice of the mummies' arrival appears to have been published in New York City newspapers, it seems Chandler must have had inside information about their arrival, location, and availability. Perhaps he had some connection with the customs house owners, fellow Irishmen McLoud, Gillespie, Maitland, and Kennedy. In any case, the following advertisement appeared in the *U.S. Gazette*, a Philadelphia newspaper, on 3 April 1833:

"The largest collection of Egyptian mummies ever exhibited in this city, is now seen at the Masonic Hall . . .

"They were found in the vicinity of Thebes, by the celebrated traveler Antonio Lebolo and Chevalier Drovetti, General Consul of France in Egypt.

"Some writings on papirus found with the mummies, can also be seen, and will afford, no doubt, much satisfaction to amateurs of antiquities.

"Admittance 25 cents, children half price."

Michael Chandler sold seven of the eleven mummies during the next few months. By 9 September 1833 he had sold five of them. When he exhibited the mummies in Harrisburg, Pennsylvania, the newspaper announcement read: "Six mummies now exhibiting in the Masonic Hall, Harrisburg." By 27 March 1835, he had sold two more of them. On that date a Painesville, Ohio, *Telegraph* article mentioned "the four mummies, now exhibiting in this place." These are the four mummies, along with the sacred writings, that were purchased by the Saints in Kirtland in July 1835.

Joseph Smith Acquired the Papyrus and the Four Remaining Mummies

"On the 3rd of July, Michael H. Chandler came to Kirtland to exhibit some Egyptian mummies. There were four human figures, together with some two or more rolls of papyrus covered with hieroglyphic figures and devices. As Mr. Chandler had been told I could translate them, he brought me some of the characters, and I gave him the interpretation, and like a gentleman, he gave me the following certificate:

"Kirtland, July 6, 1835.

"This is to make known to all who may be desirous, concerning the knowledge of Mr. Joseph Smith, Jun., in deciphering the ancient Egyptian hieroglyphic characters in my possession, which I have, in many eminent cities, showed to the most learned; and, from the information that I could ever learn, or meet with, I find that of Mr. Joseph Smith, Jun., to correspond in the most minute matters.

"Michael H. Chandler,
"Traveling with, and proprietor of, Egyptian mummies."
(Smith, *History of the Church*, 2:235.)

The Prophet Joseph Smith felt impressed to purchase the papyri. Orson Pratt recorded that Joseph did not want to purchase the mummies, but Chandler would not sell the documents independent of them.

The Papyrus Is Translated

Joseph Smith was anxious to begin translating the newly acquired papyrus to discover why he had been impressed to purchase them at the high price of $2,400. With W. W. Phelps and Oliver Cowdery acting as scribes, Joseph commenced translating the ancient scrolls and recorded, "Much to our joy found that one of the rolls contained the writings of Abraham, another the writings of Joseph of Egypt, etc." (*History of the Church*, 2:236.)

The Prophet spoke with great respect of the Egyptian documents. His journal entry for 1 October 1835 reads, "This afternoon I labored on the Egyptian alphabet, in company with Brothers Oliver Cowdery and W. W. Phelps, and during the research, the principles of astronomy as understood by Father Abraham and the ancients unfolded to our understanding." (*History of the Church*, 2:286.)

On 14 November 1835 Warren Parrish was selected as the scribe to assist the Prophet in translating the Egyptian records. In a revelation given to Joseph Smith for Warren Parrish, the Lord stated, "Behold, it shall come to pass in his day, that he shall see great things show forth

The four mummies were kept in the Kirtland Temple (far left, upper room), where Joseph Smith began translating the ancient Egyptian papyri

themselves unto my people; he shall see much of my ancient records, and shall know of hidden things, and shall be endowed with a knowledge of hidden languages; and if he desire and shall seek it at my hands, he shall be privileged with writing much of my word, as a scribe unto me for the benefit of my people." (Smith, *History of the Church*, 2:311.)

William E. M'Lellin, Brigham Young, and Jared Carter visited Joseph Smith on 16 December 1835, and Joseph reported, "I exhibited and explained the Egyptian records to them, and explained many things concerning the dealing of God with the ancients, and the formation of the planetary system." (*History of the Church,* 2:334.)

On 6 May 1838 the Prophet recorded: "I also gave some instructions in the mysteries of the kingdom of God; such as the history of the planets, Abraham's writings upon the planetary systems, etc." (*History of the Church*, 3:27.)

On 18 June 1840 Joseph wrote to the high council that "the time has now come, when he [Joseph] should devote himself exclusively to those things which relate to the spiritualities of the Church, and commence the work of translating the Egyptian records, the Bible, and wait upon the Lord for such revelations as may be suited to the conditions and circumstances of the Church." (*History of the Church*, 4:137.)

The following announcement was made by the Quorum of the Twelve on 21 February 1842: "Let all the different branches of the Church of Jesus Christ of Latter-day Saints in all the world, call meetings in their respective places and tithe themselves and send up to this place to the Trustee in Trust, so that his hands may be loosed, and the Temple go on, and other works be done, such as the new translation of the Bible, and the record of Father Abraham published to the world." (Smith, *History of the Church*, 4:517.)

The Book of Abraham Is Published

Joseph Smith was the editor of the Church newspaper, *Times and Seasons*, when the first two installments of the book of Abraham were printed. The following notice appeared on 1 March 1842 when the first installment was printed:

"This paper commences my editorial career, I alone stand responsible for it, and shall do all papers having my signature hence forward.

"Joseph Smith"

(*Times and Seasons*, 3 [1 Mar. 1842]: 710.)

What we currently have as the book of Abraham was printed in three installments. Abraham 1:1–2:18 was published in the 1 March 1842 edition of the *Times and Seasons*, Abraham 2:19–5:21 was published in the 16 March 1842 edition, and Facsimile 3 was published in the 16 May 1842 edition. Elder John Taylor, who succeeded Joseph Smith as the editor of the *Times and Seasons*, published the following notice in the 1 February 1843 paper (p. 95):

The papyri were stored and later translated in the red brick store in Nauvoo

"We would respectfully announce to those of our subscribers (and there are a good many of them) who commenced their subscriptions for the Times and Seasons at the time when brother Joseph took the editorial department, that the term for which they subscribed for is nearly at a close: most of those commenced at the seventh and eighth numbers; at the time when the translations from the Book of Abraham commenced. This is the sixth number, which only leaves four weeks until the time that they subscribed for, will be fulfilled.

"We have given this timely notice that our friends may prepare themselves. We would further state that we had the promise of Br. Joseph, to furnish us with further extracts from the Book of Abraham. These with other articles that we expect from his pen, the continuation of his history, and the resources that we have of obtaining interesting matter; together with our humble endeavors, we trust will make the paper sufficiently interesting."

The book of Abraham was a lengthy record. When the ancient writings first came to the Church, Oliver Cowdery wrote:

"When the translation of these valuable documents will be completed, I am unable to say; neither can I give you a probable idea how large volumes they will make; but judging from their size, and the comprehensiveness of the language, one might reasonably expect to see a sufficient to develop much upon the mighty acts of the ancient men of God, and of his dealing with the children of men when they saw him face to face. Be there little or much, it must be an inestimable acquisition to our present scriptures, fulfilling, in a small degree, the word of the prophet: For the earth shall be full of the knowledge of the Lord as the waters cover the sea." (In *Messenger and Advocate*, 2 [Dec. 1835]: 236.)

Unfortunately the Prophet Joseph Smith was unable to publish to the world additional passages from the writings of Abraham. The last months of his life were filled with heavy duties that did not allow him time to return to this great work.

The Contributions of the Book of Abraham

Even though we do not have the entire book of Abraham, nor the book of Joseph, what we do have is very significant. The book of Abraham contributes to the scriptures more information about—

1. The ten generations between Noah and Abraham, which are only briefly mentioned in the Bible.

2. The importance of the patriarchal order of the holy priesthood in Abraham's day.

3. The clash between the idolatrous world and the Lord's faithful.

4. The Abrahamic covenant.

5. The planetary system, as understood by the ancients. The planetary system and the organization of the spirits are paralleled in Abraham 3.

6. The premortal life. Perhaps the best statement in the standard works on this subject is recorded in Abraham 3.

7. Why Abraham had Sarai declare to the Egyptians that she was his sister.

8. Sacred truths pertaining to the temple ordinances.

The Facsimiles of the Book of Abraham

Introduction to the Facsimiles

The facsimiles of the book of Abraham, a trio of illustrations that complement the text of the book, have always been a curiosity, a conversation piece. They are incidental to the main business and real message of the book, which can be completely comprehended from the text. With the exception of a casual reference to the facsimiles, most teachers of the Pearl of Great Price successfully ignore them and focus nearly all of their attention on the text. It is hoped, however, that the information in this chapter will enable teachers and students alike to more fully appreciate the facsimiles and thereby deepen their faith.

The inspiration that guided Joseph Smith in the restoration and interpretation of the facsimiles was directed at illuminating and illustrating the text of the book of Abraham. Individual figures in the pictoral composition are authentic Egyptian ideograms that faithfully complement the text of Abraham and appropriately relate to each other. For the unlearned Joseph Smith to supply such accurate signs in meaningful relationships demanded that he must have had help from the world's most advanced Egyptologist or the God of heaven. Joseph was on speaking terms with the latter but not with the former.

Note: This chapter was written for inclusion in this volume by James R. Harris, professor of Ancient Scripture at Brigham Young University, Provo, Utah.

Facsimile 1

Facsimile 1 has been variously described as an embalming scene, a lion couch scene, a resurrection scene, and an altar of sacrifice scene. Egyptian scribes used the same basic backdrop and persons to illustrate a variety of mythological themes by manipulating secondary props. Osiris and his "couch" were basic, but all else could be relocated or substituted by other players or props. Some of over thirty variations of this scene include Osiris being renewed, Osiris being prepared for burial, Osiris ruling from the Netherworld, Osiris being resurrected, and Osiris triumphant.[1]

Because Abraham and Osiris are both types of the promised Messiah, some notable events in their lives will overlap or run parallel. It is not secret that the Osirian family so faithfully parallels the life of our Savior that Egypt was the most Christian nation of the first century of the common era.

Using Joseph Smith's figure numbers, we can examine each sign within Facsimile 1. Figure 1 is not a ba-bird (as it might have been in the original vignette); it is a hawk, the sign of a powerful celestial being. It was Horus (the hawk) who delivered his father Osiris from death just as a personage represented by a hawk delivered Abraham from death.[2]

Appropriately compatible with the text of Abraham 1:15, figure 2 is a determinative ideogram for the act of supplication or offering a prayer. Since generic determinatives cannot of themselves express specific meaning—in this case, praise, adore, supplicate, or greet are possible meanings—the specific meaning must be derived from the context of the vignette and the text it illustrates.

Figure 3, the priest of Elkenah, god of Canaan, does not represent Anubus, (the Greek equivalent for the Egyptian Anpu). Anubus was the embalmer of the dead Osiris; however, the person on this table is not dead but alive and pleading for life as his arm and leg positions indicate. The priest stands in back of Abraham, who is lying on the altar. If the lower body of the priest were not visible behind the altar, we could not see clearly his animal skin robe and apron, symbols of his priestly office. These symbols in turn help to explain his function in this scene.

Critics of Joseph Smith's interpretation of Facsimile 1 have for the most part been unwilling to consider figure 4 as anything but an embalming table. Lion couches and embalming tables of this design have been recovered and were authentic funerary furniture and palace furniture. It is also true that stone altars of this design have been recovered at Memphis (see research of Mustafer El Amir) and at Thebes.[3] The Prophet correctly identified this figure as "an altar for sacrifice."

The four canopic jars represented by figures 5 through 8 were accurately identified by Joseph Smith as gods, collectively known as the four

Sons of Horus. The individual identification of these four gods with the four lands adjacent to Egypt and the four cardinal points that supported the four pillars of heaven is quite remarkable. The four Sons of Horus were considered guardians of the four pillars of heaven based in the "four Pure Lands."[4] On the east is Egypt, represented by Elkenah, land of the god of Canaan, a hawk; on the west, Libnah, or Libya the white land, home of the jackal; on the north, Makmackrah (ancient Anatolia or Turkey, land of the ancient Hittites); and on the south, Korash, or Cush.[5]

Sebek the crocodile is figure 9, and the Prophet described him as "the idolatrous god of Pharaoh." Did this crocodile god have a special relationship with Pharaoh that would justify Joseph Smith's description? The answer is yes. Sebek was the champion of Osiris and the one who overpowered his enemies. When the young king Horus was in the process of claiming his seat on the throne, Sebek carried him on his back and devoured all that stood in his way. Pharaoh would not be Pharaoh without Sebek.

The lotus plant on an offering table with vials of perfume or ointment constitutes figure 10. It was appropriately identified as a sign of "Abraham in Egypt"—more specifically, as Abraham in the part of Egypt that produced the Joseph Smith Egyptian collection: Thebes. The papyrus plant is the symbol of Lower Egypt, and the lotus is a symbol of Upper Egypt, including Thebes.

Figure 11 is a mastaba-like facade "designed to represent the pillars of heaven," according to the explanation in the book of Abraham. Because pillars of heaven must hold up heaven, they are represented under figure 12, the heavens.

The heavens were seas above and beneath the earth. Sebek swam in both seas, and the sun god sailed through them in his solar bark.

Joseph Smith's explanations of figures 1 through 12 are within the range of probable Egyptian meaning for each specific sign. In restoration of damaged signs and interpretation of all twelve signs, the Prophet's accuracy demands respect and serious consideration of his claims to divine guidance.

Facsimile 3

Facsimile 3 is next in sequence and the final vignette of the original Egyptian document that contained the illustrations from which Facsimiles 1 and 3 were constructed. (Facsimile 2 was reconstructed from another funerary document of another time and substance.)

A general description of this scene is that it is the triumphant entry of the deceased owner of the papyrus into the presence of the gods.

Similar scenes are portrayed on the Papyrus Hu Nefer and on the Papyrus Ker Asher (B.M. 9995).

There cannot be the slightest doubt that the original vignette portrayed the figures of Hathor/Isis, a composite goddess combining the features of Hathor and Isis, Osiris, the goddess Maat, the deceased Osiris Hor, and Anubus (from left to right). It is also obvious that Facsimile 3 portrays a modification of that scene compatible with the life and times of Abraham. To understand other appropriately Egyptian interpretations of this scene, the concept of acquisition by impersonation must come into play. In his book on Egyptian funerary practices, Spencer explained that "the practice of acquiring the characteristics and attributes of the gods by impersonating them" was exploited by private individuals: it was not the exclusive right of royalty.[6] When the vignette is severed from the original text as it is in its facsimile variation, it can and does take on other possible meanings.

When an Egyptian king received an endowment, he was ceremonially clothed in the robes of the holy priesthood. The clothing and paraphernalia thus received represented powers, characteristics, and attributes of the divine ones. By this means he impersonated the gods and in the process became a partaker of the divine nature. An ordinary person, so it seems, would acquire the same divinity, not by going through the temple, which was closed to him, but by acquiring a papyrus which portrayed him becoming one with the gods, a sort of vicarious work for the living.

Figure 2 is a representation of Pharaoh dressed in ceremonial robes. The ancient Heb Sed festival alluded to here was a ceremonial drama intended to renew the king's vital power and divinity. In the course of the drama the king was dressed in the robes of Hathor/Isis. She is the house of Horus, indeed, she is Horus, who came forth from her and obtained his divinity from her. The king must renew his divinity by becoming one with her again. He acquires her attributes by impersonation. In this context the female figure is indeed Pharaoh, king of Egypt, impersonating Hathor/Isis.

While the king was engaged in the personification of Hathor/Isis, someone else had to impersonate the king, as represented by figure 1. Joseph Smith named this impersonator as Abraham, who then joined a long list of prominent persons who did the same thing. They played the role of rp't, meaning a substitute for the king. Among these illustrious persons were Joseph ben Jacob of Genesis 41, and Amenophis, son of Hapu, who played rp't during a Heb Sed festival.[7] The Pharaoh was both king and priest, and his two-plumed Atef crown was a symbol of power, priesthood, light, and holiness.[8] In his hands, as the Prophet Joseph's explanation indicates, are scepters of justice and judgment. He is the god of justice and mercy. He carries the shepherd's crook, for he is the good shepherd that lays down his life for his sheep. (See John 10:14–15.) His commitment to justice is such that he also carries the whip to mete out punishment and prod his sheep to do good.

Figure 3 is another offering table upon which is the lotus symbol of Upper Egypt (see figure 10 of Facsimile 1). The Prophet's explanation of figure 3 correctly states that this sign "signifies Abraham in Egypt."

Figure 4 is another male impersonating a female. He is identified as the "Prince of Pharaoh, King of Egypt," and the heir to the throne. When the time came for the prince to become king, one of his major responsibilities was to maintain Maat, that is, truth (moral and physical law) as it existed in the beginning. Maat personified eternal verities, that which always was and ever will be. She was the straight way. When endowed with her symbols and dress, the prince became a partaker of her essential nature—another case of acquisition by impersonation.

Figure 5 is "Shulem, one of the king's principal waiters." In the original vignette he was Osiris Hor, the deceased owner of the papyrus. In the ceremonial drama Heb Sed, he represented another level of the renewed king's constituents and is also an official witness of his renewal.

Figure 6 is "Olimlah [not Anubus], a slave belonging to the prince" and representing the lowest human level of the king's constituents. Egypt and everything in it belonged to the king, who was perceived as the living god of Egypt. Although the original meaning of the vignette in the context of the funerary document had no real value for Joseph Smith or for the Saints or for God's purpose in the Restoration, this very scene, when separated from the text, became a springboard to revelation about the life and divine mission of Abraham.

Facsimile 2

Facsimile 2 is a funerary document that originated about three hundred years earlier than the two vignettes that were modified into Facsimiles 1 and 3. This document is called a hypocephalus, meaning "under the head," a name given to it by Champollion, who had recognized the practice of placing the disk under the head of the deceased owner. Chapter 162 of the Book of the Dead contains the formula for its construction and the expectations that should arise from its proper use. Although the Book of the Dead requires the formula to be written on a piece of new papyrus, the surviving examples were made like a brass bowl or kepa hat that fit on the back of the head or of linen stiffened with plaster. Since white ants love to feast upon the grain that was used to make the plaster, many of these documents have damaged and missing portions. The Joseph Smith hypocephalus is no exception. Damaged parts were restored by Joseph Smith or under his direction. Some of the restored portions were interpreted by the Prophet, and some were not. When he was inspired to know the meaning of figures in various hemispheres of the hypocephalus, he gave an interpretation. Such interpretations are profound evidence that he received divine guidance and information from the Lord of heaven. Those figures or signs that he did not interpret were sometimes inappropriate to script or sequence or were placed upside down in the text. The Prophet's successes demanded divine assistance because he had no natural ability in this subject. When he was inspired, his interpretations are profound; when he was not inspired, his arrangements show glaring mistakes. Joseph was not an Egyptologist, but he was a prophet.

More Evidence of Divine Guidance in the Interpretations of Joseph Smith

Figure 1 represents "Kolob, signifying the first creation, nearest to the celestial, or the residence of God. First in government, the last pertaining to the measurement of time." (Explanation, Facsimile 2.) The Egyptian perception of this figure is that he is the two-bodied, four-faced Khnum-Ra combining the features of the Sun-god Ra with the great creator of all things, Khnum. Often featured with a ram's head he is seated at a potter's wheel shaping the bodies of mankind. His name Khnum, or Khnimu, means Molder. His major seat of popularity was the region of Elephantine. He personifies the earthly and heavenly Nile, the rivers of life. His mythical cavern on the Isle of Elephantine was the first place (the First Creation) from which all life flowed. The restoration by Joseph Smith replaced hieratic signs to the left of the head of Khnum. This composition of ideograms represents the primeval cavern, the first creation. From the top of the inscription the three horizontal lines are the hieratic form for Nun, or Nu. Nu was the deep, boundless, watery mass identified with the ocean and the Nile from which all life emerged. The half heaven sign is the determinative for the cavern on the island of Elephantine, and the line emerging from the cavern sign is the Nile. This combination of signs next to the head of a figure identified as Kolob, the First Creation, is remarkable and demands serious consideration of Joseph's claims to divine guidance.

Figure 2 "stands next to Kolob, called by the Egyptians Oliblish, which is the next grand governing creation near to the celestial or the place where God resides; holding the key of power also, pertaining to other planets." (Explanation, Facsimile 2.)[9] The Egyptian perception of figure 2 is Amen-Ra. Amen, the great ancient god of Thebes, is combined with Ra, the sun-god of Heliopolis. He is Amen the hidden one and Ra the manifest one (the Father and the Son). In his hand and on his shoulders are symbols of Anubus for he is Almighty. Even death, symbolized by Anubus, is subject to him. The inscription on the left says "the name of god." But his name itself is never given, for it is a key to power over the universe. He is indeed an awesome governor, holding keys to power over death and the universe.

Figure 3 "is made to represent God, sitting upon his throne, clothed with power and authority; with a crown of eternal light upon his head; representing also the grand Key-words of the Holy Priesthood." (Explanation, Facsimile 2.) This composition represents the bark (ship) of the great god, the bark of Ra, or "the Bark of Osiris defunct," as it was called by de Horrock.[10] He is the great God, the real God, however perceived. Over his head is the sun-disk symbol of eternal light, and in his hand is the W's scepter featuring the Wd't Eye. The W's scepter is a sign of dominion and power all by itself, but when combined with the Wd't Eye it becomes a key to completeness, resurrection, and eternal life. The secret of the eye is the key to life because each part of the eye represents a fraction of the whole.[11]

A point of great interest is the inscription to the left of the "bark of the great god." It is not found with the boat on any other hypocephalus. The marvelous thing about this inscription is its appropriate position and compatible message. It reads, "the sacred boat" and implies, "of the great god."[12] This brief but significant inscription was restored to the hypocephalus by Joseph Smith. He claimed divine assistance, and, as previously stated, his access to God was more ready than his access to Egyptologists.

Figure 4 represents "Raukeeyang, signifying expanse, or the firmament of the heavens; also a numerical figure, in Egyptian signifying one thousand." (Explanation, Facsimile 2.) The Sokar boat was indeed the ship of a thousand. It symbolized the cycles of the heavens and the universe. The mummified hawk with wings expanded is the ancient Memphite representation of the expanse of heaven.[13] This falcon spanned the expanse of heaven to push back the darkness and fill the expanse with light.[14] Joseph's explanation is again on target.

Figure 5 is "said by the Egyptians to be the Sun." The feminine figure holding a lotus scepter is obviously a goddess. Her proximity to the cow identifies her most benevolent aspects. She is the great Mother Hathor; she is the sky, the house of the stars, and the house of Horus (the literal meaning of her name, Hat = house, Hor = Horus the hawk). As goddess of the Tuat, all things passed through her to be renewed. Even the sun is in her, of her, and by her. It comes as no shock then that in her humanoid female form she is the sun. One large right eye fills her head. The right eye of the sun god is the sun. The figure is either Hathor as the sun goddess or the sun goddess just reborn of Hathor. Figure 5 is the sun.[15]

Figure 6 "represent[s] this earth in its four quarters." (See Facsimile 1, figures 5–8.) They are the guardians of the four pillars of heaven, which embraced the four pure lands.[16]

Figure 7 represents "God sitting upon his throne, revealing through the heavens the grand Key-words of the Priesthood; as, also, the sign of the Holy Ghost unto Abraham, in the form of a dove." (Explanation, Facsimile 2.) This scene is another example of acquisition by impersonation. The person on the throne is the deceased Osiris Sheshank, who in his hopes to acquire immortality and godhood is imitating and becoming one with the gods Horus and Min. He is seated on a throne, for he is to rule in heaven. He raises his arm to the square under a compass sign because he is also a priest. A dove, symbol of the Holy Spirit, feeds him the Wd't Eye, which symbolizes all good gifts, the food of the gods, and completeness (perfection). The same eye is encountered in discussion of figure 3.[17]

As Min, his eternal virility is insured: he will have eternal increase. As indicated above, the Wd't Eye contained the mystery of perfection. Each part was a fraction of the whole that could be verbalized, except for the last fraction. The sixth and last fraction, 1/64, was the secret key word that could be verbalized by those already acquainted with the mystery spoken only in the secret place.[18]

Figure 8 "contains writings that cannot be revealed unto the world; but is to be had in the Holy Temple of God." (Explanation, Facsimile 20.) That such a statement is made for this line is unlikely to have been a coincidence because the line contains the personal name of the deceased, which was to be remembered and preserved. Without this name, Osiris Sheshank, the deceased would cease to exist, as his name contains his essence.[19] Also the name was a key word that would allow him to enter the company of God.[20]

The facsimiles leave us with examples indicating that Joseph Smith made mistakes that no Egyptologist would have made. But he was not an Egyptologist. The facsimiles also leave us with an abundance of examples that Joseph Smith had to have had help from a Power above his own to make such accurate restorations of missing signs and such sound and appropriate interpretations. He was a prophet, seer, and revelator.

Notes
[1]E. A. Wallis Budge, *Osiris, Volume II* (New Hyde Park, New York: University Books, 1961), pp. 16–35.

[2]R. T. Rundle Clark, *Myth and Symbol in Ancient Egypt* (London: Thames and Hudson Ltd., 1978), pp. 130, 160–61.

[3]Catalogue, *The Luxor Museum of Ancient Egyptian Art* (Cairo: American Research Center in Egypt, 1979), pp. 40–41.

[4]*Introductory Guide to the Egyptian Collections* (British Museum Publication, 1964), p. 147.

[5]E. A. Wallis Budge, *The Gods of the Egyptians, Volume I* (New York: Dover Publications, 1969), pp. 157, 210).

[6]A. J. Spencer, *Death in Ancient Egypt* (Middlesex, England: Penguin Books, 1982), p. 141.

[7]H. E. Helck, "Rp-t auf dem Throne des Geb," *Orentalia* 19 (1950): 434.

[8]S. Morenz, *Religions en Egypte Hellenistique et Romaine,* Colloque de Strebourg, 16–18 May 1967 (Paris: University Press, 1969), p. 81.

[9]E. A. Wallis Budge, *The Gods of the Egyptians, Volume II* (New York: Dover Publications, 1969), pp. 52, 283–84, 774b.

[10]Peter J. de Horrack, *Proceedings of the Society of Biblical Archaeology* (London: British Museum, 1884), p. 128.

[11]Clark, pp. 179, 180, 219. Alan Gardiner, *Egyptian Grammar* (London: Oxford University Press, 1957), p. 179.

[12]A few years ago Edward Ashment wrote an article for a periodical in which he insisted that the line of signs next to the deity's head in figure 3 had come from a rubric near the aforementioned vignette of Papyrus Joseph Smith IV. A comparison of the two phrases proves that Ashment's assumption is inappropriate. PJS IV rubric: *dd md.w bft in,* "to recite a formula in front of," Fac. No. 2, fig. 3: *wi3,* "sacred bark." The Rubric phrase identified by Ashment is entirely inappropriate in the quarter of the disk in which it was supposedly placed. The phrase that is clearly represented in that quarter by Joseph Smith is entirely appropriate.

[13]Michael Dennis Rhodes, "A Translation and Commentary of the Joseph Smith Hypocephalus," *Brigham Young University Studies,* Spring 1977, p. 270.

[14]Clark, p. 213.

[15]Anthony S. Mercatante, *Who's Who in Egyptian Mythology* (New York: Clarkson N. Potter, 1978), p. 54; Clark, p. 185.

[16]Budge, *Osiris, Volume II.*

[17]Clark, pp. 218–30.

[18]Budge, *The Gods of the Egyptians, Volume II,* p. 164.

[19]Spencer, p. 71.

[20]Albert Champdor, *Das Agyptisch Totenbuch* (Zurich, 1979), p. 89.

Joseph Smith–History:
Extracts from the
History of Joseph Smith,
the Prophet

Joseph Smith—History is drawn from the first forty-four pages of volume 1 of *History of the Church*. It covers such important events as the First Vision, the first nine appearances of Moroni to Joseph Smith, the restoration of the Aaronic Priesthood through John the Baptist, the fulfillment of Isaiah's prophecy of the "book that is sealed" (Isaiah 29:11), and the beginning of the translation of the Book of Mormon.

Importance of Record Keeping

From the beginning of time the Lord has commanded his people to keep records. Adam kept a "book of remembrance" that was also kept by his faithful progeny, who wrote "by the spirit of inspiration." (Moses 6:5.) Along with records of religious matters, the early fathers kept "a genealogy . . . of the children of God." (Moses 5:8.)

Abraham, nearly two thousand years later, received the sacred records that contained the chronology of his predecessors. These sacred writings also clarified the "right of Priesthood" and "a knowledge of the beginning of the creation, and also of the planets, and of the stars, as they were made known unto the fathers." (Abraham 1:31.)

The Lord said to Moses, several hundred years later, "I will speak unto thee concerning this earth upon which thou standest; and thou shalt write the things which I shall speak." (Moses 1:40.)

Without the plates of brass, the sacred writings of the house of Joseph, the Lord explained, the Nephite nation "should dwindle and perish in unbelief." (1 Nephi 4:13.) He commanded the Nephites to "write the words which I speak unto them; for out of the books which shall be written I will judge the world, every man according to their works, according to that which is written.

"For behold, I shall speak unto the Jews and they shall write it; and I shall also speak unto the Nephites and they shall write it; and I shall also speak unto the other tribes of the house of Israel, which I have led away, and they shall write it; and I shall also speak unto all nations of the earth and they shall write it.

"And it shall come to pass that the Jews shall have the words of the Nephites, and the Nephites shall have the words of the Jews; and the Nephites and the Jews shall have the words of the lost tribes of Israel; and the lost tribes of Israel shall have the words of the Nephites and the Jews.

"And it shall come to pass that my people, which are of the house of Israel, shall be gathered home unto the lands of their possessions; and my word also shall be gathered in one. And I will show unto them that fight against my word and against my people, who are of the house of Israel, that I am God, and that I covenanted with Abraham that I would remember his seed forever." (2 Nephi 29:11-14.)

Record Keeping in the Last Dispensation

This last dispensation is under the same commandment to keep records as were previous dispensations. On the day that the church of Jesus Christ was restored, the Lord commanded, "Behold, there shall be a record kept among you. . . .

"Wherefore, meaning the church, thou shalt give heed unto all his [Joseph Smith's] words and commandments which he shall give unto you as he receiveth them, walking in all holiness before me;

"For his word ye shall receive, as if from mine own mouth, in all patience and faith." (D&C 21:1-5.)

The Prophet Joseph Smith did not have the opportunity for much formal education. Orson Pratt explained that Joseph was a slow and awkward writer. Along with that limitation Joseph Smith had the heavy burden of presiding over all of the multifaceted concerns of the restored kingdom of God on the earth. Nevertheless, said Franklin D. Richards, with the strict command of the 6 April 1830 revelation recorded in Doctrine and Covenants 21, accurate record keeping became a "duty imperative" with the Latter-day Saints. (Dean C. Jessee, in *BYU Studies*, Summer 1971, p. 439.)

Joseph Smith called many record keepers to record the historical data of the Church. Elder B. H. Roberts wrote:

"One difficulty the Prophet experienced in writing the annals of the Church, which he usually called his history, was the unfaithfulness of some whom he employed in this service, and the frequent change of historians, owing to the ever shifting conditions surrounding the Church in the early years of its existence. It would be marvelous indeed if under all these circumstances there had been no mistakes made in our annals, no conflict of dates, no errors in the relation of events. But whether these conditions are taken into account or not, the manuscript annals of the Church are astonishingly free from errors of dates, relation of facts, or anachronisms of every description." (Joseph Smith, *History of the Church*, 1:v.)

Joseph Smith "quite thoroughly supervised the writing of his history, with the result that more complete historical data have been written and preserved respecting the coming forth of the work of God in these last days than any other great movement whatsoever." (Smith, *History of the Church*, 1:iv–v.) An entry was made in the Prophet's history on 5 July 1839 as follows: "I was dictating history, I say dictating, for I seldom use the pen myself. I always dictate all my communications, but employ a scribe to write them." (*History of the Church*, 4:1.)

Attempts to Write a History

Joseph Smith explained some of the difficulties he faced in his attempt to write and preserve a history:

"Since I have been engaged in laying the foundation of the Church of Jesus Christ of Latter-day Saints, I have been prevented in various ways from continuing my journal and history in a manner satisfactory to myself or in justice to the cause. Long imprisonments, vexatious and long-continued law-suits, the treachery of some of my clerks, the death of others, and the poverty of myself and brethren from continued plunder and driving, have prevented my handing down to posterity a connected memorandum of events desirable to all lovers of truth; yet I have continued to keep up a journal in the best manner my circumstances would allow, and dictate for my history from time to time, as I have had opportunity so that the labors and suffering of the first Elders and Saints of this last kingdom might not wholly be lost to the world." (*History of the Church*, 4:470.)

Dean Jessee compiled a list of thirty men who wrote for Joseph Smith during his lifetime or did clerical work for the Church before 1846. Of these, "nine apostatized from the Church, two died at critical points in writing the History, and one retained Church records entrusted to him." (*Studies,* p. 461, n. 75.)

Seven attempts were made before 1839 to write the history of the Church:

"1. The history written by Oliver Cowdery covering the period 'from the time of the finding of the plates up to June 1831.'

"2. The John Whitmer history covering the post-1831 years after Oliver Cowdery's history left off. This record was retained by Whitmer after he left the Church.

"3. An unfinished 1832 history in the handwriting of Frederick G. Williams and Joseph Smith.

"4. An 1834 fragment of history in the handwriting of Oliver Cowdery.

"5. The 1834–35 history published in the *Messenger and Advocate.*

"6. An 1835–36 history in the handwriting of Frederick G. Williams, Warren Parrish, and Warren A. Cowdery.

"7. The 1838 history that was started by Joseph Smith, Sidney Rigdon, and George A. Robinson on April 27 of that year." (Jessee, in *Studies,* pp. 461–62.)

The final attempt to write the history of the Church was begun in 1839 and was completed in Salt Lake City in 1858. Joseph Smith began dictating the history of the Church in its present form to his clerk James Mulholland on 11 June 1839, using the 1838 history as a basis. James Mulholland completed the first fifty-nine pages of the Church's history in 1839. (See Jessee, in *Studies,* p. 464.) The Pearl of Great Price contains excerpts from the first forty-four pages of this history.

It should not be concluded that before that time (1820–1839) there were no letters, journals, newspaper clippings, and so on being kept by clerks and other Church members. Elder George A. Smith explained that the Prophet Joseph Smith himself established the format and style for the history:

" 'The plan of compiling the history of Joseph Smith from the Journals kept by his clerks, Willard Richards, William Clayton, Wilford Woodruff, and Thomas Bullock, was commenced by himself, extracting items of necessary information in regard to general and particular movements from the Times and Seasons, Millennial Star, Wasp, Neighbor, and other publications, extracts from City Councils, Municipal Courts, and Mayors Dockets, and Legion Records, which were all kept under his direction; also the movements of the Church as found in Conference minutes, High Council records, and the records of the several quorums, together with letters and copies preserved on file; also noted remarkable occurrences throughout the world, and compiled them under date of transaction, according to the above plan.' (Letter of George A. Smith to Wilford Woodruff, April 21, 1856 CHO.)" (As quoted in Jessee, in *Studies,* p. 464.)

When Joseph Smith's history was published in 1858, the two members of the Quorum of the Twelve who completed it, George A. Smith and Wilford Woodruff, wrote:

"The History of Joseph Smith is now before the world, and we are satisfied that a history more correct in its details than this was never published. To have it strictly correct, the greatest possible pains have been taken by the historians and clerks engaged in the work. They were eye and ear witnesses of nearly all the transactions recorded in this history, most of which were reported as they transpired, and, where they were not personally present, they have had access to those who were.

"Moreover, since the death of the Prophet Joseph, the history has been carefully revised under the strict inspection of President Brigham Young, and approved of by him.

"We, therefore, hereby bear our testimony to all the world, unto whom these words shall come, that the History of Joseph Smith is true, and it is one of the most authentic histories ever written." (As quoted in Jessee, in *Studies,* pp. 472–73.)

Elder B. H. Roberts edited the manuscript of Joseph Smith's history of the Church that was begun on 11 June 1839, and it was published in 1902 with the full title *History of the Church of Jesus Christ of Latter-day Saints.*

The Articles of Faith: Extracts from the Wentworth Letter

The Articles of Faith are thirteen statements of belief that are recorded in the last thirteen paragraphs of a letter Joseph Smith wrote to John Wentworth, which was published in the *Times and Seasons* 1 March 1842.

John Wentworth of Chicago

John Wentworth was born in New Hampshire on 5 March 1815. He was educated in the East and moved to Chicago where he was engaged in, among other things, the publishing business. He was a very tall man, about 6' 6", who was referred to by some as "Long John." Wentworth was soon involved in the political arena. He was elected mayor of Chicago on two different occasions and held other city offices as well. He eventually served seven terms in the United States Congress as a representative from Illinois.

The Wentworth Letter

About a year after Wentworth returned to Chicago from the East, he wrote to the Prophet Joseph Smith in Nauvoo, seeking information about the Latter-day Saints. Joseph Smith recorded: "At the request of Mr. John Wentworth, Editor and Proprietor of the *Chicago Democrat,* I have written the following sketch of the rise, progress, persecution, and faith

of the Latter-day Saints, of which I have the honor, under God, of being
the founder. Mr. Wentworth says that he wishes to furnish Mr. Bastow,
a friend of his, who is writing the history of New Hampshire, with this
document." Joseph seemed pleased that Mr. Bastow had taken "proper
steps to obtain correct information," and the Prophet requested only
"that he publish the account entire, ungarnished, and without
misrepresentation." (*History of the Church,* 4:535–36.) It must have been
refreshing to have an influential man seek correct information about
the Church. Too often Joseph had been maliciously treated by unscru-
pulous men who had used the power of the press to defame him and
the Church.

It is not known whether the letter was ever published by either
Wentworth or Bastow. Most of the Chicago newspapers were destroyed
in the great fire of 1871. Wentworth's friend, Mr. Bastow, has not been
located. A George Barstow did write a history of New Hampshire, but no
mention is made of Joseph Smith or the Church in his work. It does
seem that John Wentworth received Joseph Smith's letter. The 15 April
1842 *Times and Seasons* quoted the following article from the *Chicago
Democrat:*

"Gen. Joseph Smith, the President and founder of the sect called
"the Latter Day Saints of the Church of Jesus Christ" was born in Sharon,
Windsor co. Vt. in 1805, 23d of December. Old Windsor county is now
boasting of as many distinguished men in different spheres as any in
the Union. This poor farmer's son has built up a denomination of nearly
100,000 people in Europe, Asia, Africa, and nearly all the islands of the
great oceans. Besides, Gen. Smith did not invent his creed himself; but
an angel of the Lord delivered it to him on Mount Moriah, N.Y. on the
22nd September, 1827." (In *Times and Seasons,* 3 [15 Apr. 1842]: 759.)

That quotation was followed by a very complimentary editorial
response from the *Times and Seasons* editor, the Prophet Joseph Smith
himself, about John Wentworth:

"The above is from the able pen of that fearless champion of the
rights of man, Col. John Wentworth, Editor of the Chicago Democrat.
The west can boast of no more able editor, nor can any of her growing
cities produce a better conducted paper. As to Col. Wentworth's religious views we know nothing—we presume he has no particular pre-
dilections for us; but that he entertains the same noble and generous
feelings towards all professing christians, and all good men. He certainly is one of the most brilliant stars in the constellation of Illinois—
and as a political leader he has no superior." (In *Times and Seasons,* 3
[15 Apr. 1842]: 759.)

The Wentworth Letter provides answers to several questions a pol-
itician would have. Was Wentworth, with his political ambitions, sizing

up the Mormons for his political interest? The Latter-day Saints were potentially impressive politically, if they chose to be. Nauvoo was the largest city in Illinois. Joseph Smith was politically active, serving on the city council at the time of his writing to Wentworth. Many European emigrants were constantly increasing Nauvoo's population. The Prophet was soon to be elected mayor of Nauvoo, on 6 February 1843. If the Latter-day Saints voted as a bloc, they could have great influence on Illinois politics.

Highlights of the Wentworth Letter

The Wentworth Letter contains an informative summary of Joseph Smith's work and the Restoration. The following are only representative:

1. The Father and Son were described as "two glorious personages, who exactly resembled each other in features and likeness." (Smith, *History of the Church*, 4:536.)

2. The "angel of God," Moroni, explained that "the preparatory work for the second coming of the Messiah was speedily to commence; that the time was at hand for the Gospel in all its fullness to be preached in power, unto all nations that a people might be prepared for the Millennial reign." (Smith, *History of the Church*, 4:537.)

3. Before receiving the plates in 1827, Joseph Smith had had "many visits from the angels of God, unfolding the majesty and glory of the events that should transpire in the last days."

4. The plates "had the appearance of gold," and each was "six inches wide and eight inches long, and not quite so thick as common tin. . . . The volume was something near six inches in thickness." Joseph never did specifically state what portion of the volume of plates was sealed; he only stated, "a part of which was sealed." (Smith, *History of the Church*, 4:537.)

5. Jesus appeared on this continent after his resurrection and taught the gospel here in its fulness. The Nephites had apostles and prophets and all the powers and blessings that were had among the Jews.

6. The Church of Jesus Christ was organized 6 April 1830. The gifts of the Spirit were manifest, and "the work rolled forth with astonishing rapidity." (Smith, *History of the Church*, 4:538.) Branches of the Church were established in several states.

7. Amid the rapid growth, opposition mounted. About one-fourth of the letter deals with the terrible wrongs and atrocities that Church members suffered in Missouri.

8. Some of the accomplishments the Church had made since settling Nauvoo included building a city whose population numbered between six and eight thousand, "besides vast members in the country around";

receiving a city charter and a charter for the Nauvoo Legion, which numbered fifteen hundred soldiers; chartering a university and an "Agricultural and Manufacturing Society"; having their "own laws and administrators, and possess[ing] all the privileges that other free and enlightened citizens enjoy." (Smith, *History of the Church,* 4:540.)

9. The "Standard of Truth has been erected." Joseph listed nine foreign nations where that standard had been planted. He declared that the work of God, in spite of great opposition, "will go forth boldly, nobly, and independent, till it has penetrated every continent, visited every clime, swept every country, and sounded in every ear, till the purposes of God shall be accomplished, and the Great Jehovah shall say the work is done." (Smith, *History of the Church,* 4:540.)

10. The thirteen declarations of belief that we now call the Articles of Faith conclude this great letter.

Because the thirteen declarations did not include all the tenets of Latter-day Saint theology, other Church leaders have on occasion added articles to emphasize other Church teachings. Orson Pratt added an article on the resurrection in an 1849 publication. (See Edward K. Brandt, "The Origin and Importance of the Articles of Faith," in Robert L. Millet and Kent P. Jackson, eds., *The Pearl of Great Price,* Studies in Scripture, vol. 2 [Salt Lake City: Randall Book Co., 1985], p. 415.) The Reorganized Church of Jesus Christ of Latter Day Saints added a phrase about the Lord's Supper to article 4.

The thirteen articles of faith written by Joseph Smith in 1842 and canonized by the Church in 1880 are published today with only minor clarifications.

1 March 1842 *Times and Seasons*	1981 Pearl of Great Price
We believe in the literal gathering of Israel and in the restoration of the Ten Tribes. That Zion will be built upon *this continent.* That Christ will reign personally upon the earth, and that the earth will be renewed and receive its paradasaic glory.	We believe in the literal gathering of Israel and in the restoration of the Ten Tribes; that Zion *(the New Jerusalem)* will be built upon *the American continent*; that Christ will reign personally upon the earth; and, that the earth will be renewed and receive its paradisiacal glory.

The Articles of Faith, by James E. Talmage, and *A New Witness for the Articles of Faith,* by Bruce R. McConkie are two excellent resources for further study.

B. H. Roberts, who edited Joseph Smith's *History of the Church,* said of the Wentworth Letter and the thirteen popular extracts from it:

"The 'Wentworth Letter' is one of the choicest documents in our Church literature; as also it is the earliest published document by the Prophet making any pretension to consecutive narrative of those events in which the great latter-day work had its origin. . . .

"I may say that for combining conciseness of statement with comprehensiveness of treatment of the subject with which it deals, it has few equals among historical documents, and certainly none that excel it in our Church literature. In it one has in a few pages (less than six of these pages) a remarkably full history of the leading events in the Church, and an epitome of her doctrines, from the beginning (the birth of the Prophet, 1805) up to the date of publication, March, 1842, a period of thirty-six years." *(History of the Church,* 4:535n.)

PART II

COMMENTARY

Introduction

Each topic in the commentary is divided into three sections when relevant material is available: Selected Statements of the First Presidency and the Twelve Apostles, Selected Scripture References, and Other Commentary.

Selected Statements of the First Presidency and the Twelve Apostles

In the first section are included only statements from the First Presidency and members of the Quorum of the Twelve Apostles. The First Presidency is the source of official interpretation of the doctrine of the Church and the fountainhead for new truths that the Lord may choose to reveal. The members of the Quorum of Twelve, who are also sustained as prophets, seers, and revelators by the Church, are specially endowed to preach the doctrines of the Church throughout the world.

Because the First Presidency and the Quorum of the Twelve Apostles are sustained by the Church as prophets, seers, and revelators, their callings are unique among those of the General Authorities. President J. Reuben Clark, Jr., wrote: "Some of the General Authorities have assigned to them a special calling; they possess a special gift; they are sustained as prophets, seers, and revelators, which gives them a special spiritual endowment in connection with their teaching of the people. They have the right, the power, and authority to declare the mind and will of God to his people, subject to the over-all power and authority of the President of the Church. Others of the General Authorities are not given this special spiritual endowment and authority covering their teaching; they have a resulting limitation, and the resulting limitation upon their power and authority in teaching applies to every other officer and member of the Church, for none of them is spiritually endowed as a prophet, seer, and revelator. Furthermore . . . the President of the Church has a further and special spiritual endowment in this respect, for he is the Prophet, Seer, and Revelator for the whole Church." ("When Are Church Leader's Words Entitled to Claim of Scripture?" *Church News*, 31 July 1954, pp. 9–10.)

President Ezra Taft Benson explained that "doctrinal interpretation is the province of the First Presidency. The Lord has given that stewardship to them by revelation." ("The Gospel Teacher and His Message," in *Charge to Religious Educators*, 2d ed., pp. 51–52.)

President Marion G. Romney also stated: "Today the Lord is revealing his will to all the inhabitants of the earth, and to members of the Church in particular, on the issues of this our day through the living prophets, with the First Presidency at the head. What they say as a presidency is what the Lord would say if he were here in person. This is the rock foundation of Mormonism." (In Conference Report, Apr. 1945, p. 90.)

President Joseph Fielding Smith explained: "The First Presidency are the living oracles of God and the supreme adjudicators and interpreters of the law of the Church. They supervise the work of the entire Church in all matters of policy, organization, and administration. No part of the work of the church is beyond their authority." (In *Improvement Era*, Nov. 1966, p. 978.)

President Joseph Fielding Smith further explained that the "Apostles are traveling councilors or special witnesses who go into all the world to preach. By this is meant that the Twelve should *not* go forth without the counsel and direction of the First Presidency." (In *Improvement Era*, Nov. 1966, p. 979.)

Selected Scripture References

The second section contains references from the standard works, the four books of canonized scripture that are the only records on the face of the earth that have God's stamp of approval on them. Several prophets thus far in this dispensation have been directed to present revelations and declarations to the Church for acceptance and inclusion within the sacred texts. The Church members do not vote whether or not the revelations being presented are truly from God; they only signify their acceptance, or rejection, of revelations that the prophet declares as divine. The Lord has said of the standard works:

"For I command all men, both in the east and in the west, and in the north, and in the south, and in the islands of the sea, that they shall write the words which I speak unto them; for out of the books which shall be written I will judge the world, every man according to their works, according to that which is written." (2 Nephi 29:11.)

Elder Orson Pratt testified how the living oracles and the canonized scriptures work hand in glove: "The very moment that we set aside the living oracles we set aside the revelations of God. Why? Because the revelations of God command us plainly that we shall hearken to the living oracles. Hence, if we undertake to follow the written word, and at the same time do not give heed to the living oracles of God, the written word will condemn us: it shows that we do not follow it according to our profession." (In *Journal of Discourses,* 7:373.)

Other Commentary

The third section contains several kinds of commentary: statements selected from the General Authorities of the Church other than the First Presidency and the Quorum of the Twelve Apostles; quotations from respected scholars, both Latter-day Saints and others; and some editorial comments by the author. Entries in this section answer questions that are frequently asked about history, geography, archaeology, chronology, and so on.

Moses 1

Moses 1:1
"Moses was caught up into an exceedingly high mountain"

Selected Statements of the First Presidency and the Twelve Apostles

"In all the days of his goodness, mountain heights have been the places chosen by the Lord to commune with his people. The experiences of Enoch, and of Moriancumer, and of Moses show how the Lord deigned to deal with his servants when they lifted themselves temporally and spiritually toward heaven's heights.

" 'Turn ye, and get ye upon the mount Simeon,' was the divine command to Enoch. . . . 'and as I stood upon the mount, I beheld the heavens open, and I was clothed upon with glory; And I saw the Lord. . . .'

"Jared's brother, Moriancumer, scarcely a whit behind Enoch in faith and righteousness, took sixteen small stones 'upon the top of the mount.' . . .

"Moses, in like manner, 'was caught up into an exceedingly high mountain, And he saw God face to face, and he talked with him, and the glory of God was upon Moses,' and he saw the wonders of eternity and received the account of the creation and redemption of our planet and of worlds without number." (Bruce R. McConkie, *Millennial Messiah*, p. 274. See also Bruce R. McConkie, *Doctrinal New Testament Commentary*, 3:586.)

Selected Scripture References

"The hand of the Lord" set Ezekiel "upon a very high mountain" in Israel. (Ezekiel 40:1-2.)

"Jesus was in the Spirit, and it taketh him up into an exceeding high mountain." (JST Matthew 4:8.)

John the Beloved was carried away "to a great and high mountain." (Revelation 21:10.)

Nephi was caught away "into an exceedingly high mountain." (1 Nephi 11:1. See also 2 Nephi 4:25.)

The name of the mountain where Moses' theophany took place is not revealed. (See Moses 1:42.)

Other Commentary

The mountains of Israel and the Sinai are some of the highest in that region of the world. The Lord set Ezekiel upon a "very high mountain" in the land of Israel. (Ezekiel 40:2.) Israel's highest mountain, Mount Hermon, is approximately 9,200 feet high. Several mountains in the Sinaitic range are of comparable elevation, Saint Catherine's being the highest at about 8,600 feet. The Lord would not have had to carry Moses to a distant location to instruct him on "an exceedingly high mountain." (1 Nephi 11:1.)

Moses 1:2
"And he [Moses] saw God face to face, and he talked with him"

Selected Statements of the First Presidency and the Twelve Apostles

"It should be remembered that it was Christ before he was in the flesh who gave the law and the commandments to Moses, and who spoke for the Father, as He explained to the Nephites when he appeared to them after his resurrection. (3 Nephi 15:5.) He 'was in the beginning with God and was God' according to John 1:1. The Father was represented by Him and He acted and spoke for the Father, in the creation and from that time forward in all the divine dispensations." (The First Presidency: Joseph F. Smith, Anthon H. Lund, and Charles W. Penrose, in James R. Clark, comp., *Messages of the First Presidency*, 4:271.)

"All revelation since the fall has come through Jesus Christ, who is the Jehovah of the Old Testament. In all of the scriptures, where God is mentioned and where he has appeared, it was Jehovah who talked with Abraham, with Noah, Enoch, Moses and all the prophets. He is the God of Israel, the Holy One of Israel; the one who led that nation out of Egyptian bondage, and who gave and fulfilled the Law of Moses. The

Father has never dealt with man directly and personally since the fall, and he has never appeared except to introduce and bear record of the Son." (Joseph Fielding Smith, *Doctrines of Salvation*, 1:27.)

Other Commentary

The General Authorities authorized the Instructional Development Department of the Church to send out the following addendum to the first Relief Society Spiritual Living lesson for 1975–76.

"The following concepts should be emphasized in this lesson:

"1. *Jesus Christ is the God of Israel.*

"He is the Holy One of Israel, and the God of Abraham, Isaac, and Jacob. The Book of Mormon teaches that 'all the holy prophets . . . believed in Christ and worshiped the Father in his name.' (Jacob 4:4–5).

"When he appeared to the Nephites, he said: 'Behold, I am Jesus Christ, whom the prophets testified shall come into the world. . . . Arise and come forth unto me, that ye may thrust your hands into my side, and also that ye may feel the prints of the nails in my hands and in my feet, that ye may know that I am the God of Israel, and the God of the whole earth, and have been slain for the sins of the world.' (3 Nephi 11:10, 14).

"2. *Jesus Christ is the God of the Old Testament.*

"He is the great Jehovah and the one who has appeared to righteous and holy men from the beginning. To Abraham he said: "My name is Jehovah." (Abraham 2:8.) When he appeared to Joseph Smith and Oliver Cowdery in the Kirtland Temple, they also identified him as Jehovah. (D&C 110:1–4).

"3. *The Father appears only to bear record of the Son.*

"The Father appeared to Adam in the Garden of Eden, but since the day of the Fall, Christ has served as the Mediator and Intercessor between man and the Father. All appearances of God from that time on have been appearances of the Son, except in special cases when the Father has appeared to introduce and bear record of the Son. The appearance of the Father and the Son to Joseph Smith is the perfect illustration of this. The scripture says: 'No man hath seen God at any time, except he hath borne record of the Son; for except it is through him no man can be saved.' (Inspired Version, John 1:19).

"4. *Jesus Christ speaks in the Father's name as though he were the Father.*

"As set forth in a special pronouncement entitled "The Father and the Son: A Doctrinal Exposition by the First Presidency and the Twelve," the Father has placed his name upon the Son so that the Son can and does speak in the first person as though he were the Father. (See *Articles of Faith,* by Elder James E. Talmage, pages 465–473).

"5. Thus the God who appeared to Moses as recorded in the first chapter of Moses in the Pearl of Great Price was Jesus Christ though the language he used was spoken as though it came from the Father. The scriptures have a great many illustrations of this. For instance, section 29 in the Doctrine and Covenants begins 'Listen to the voice of Jesus Christ, your Redeemer, the Great I AM (meaning the Great Jehovah),' but soon says, 'I the Lord God,' sent 'forth angels to declare unto them repentance and redemption, through faith on the name of mine Only Begotten Son.' (D&C 29:1, 42.) That is to say—Jesus Christ is speaking but he speaks as though he were the Father."

Selected Scripture References

The "spiritual Rock" that followed Israel while they were in the Sinaitic wilderness was Jesus. (1 Corinthians 10:4; see also vv. 1–3.)

Jesus gave the law of Moses and covenanted with Israel. (See 3 Nephi 15:4–5.)

Jesus talked to the brother of Jared face to face. (See Ether 3:13–17.)

Moses 1:2

"The glory of God was upon Moses; therefore Moses could endure his presence"

Selected Statements of the First Presidency and the Twelve Apostles

"Moses declares he '. . . saw God face to face, and he talked with him. . . .' (Moses 1:2.) This experience of Moses is in harmony with the scripture, which says:

" '*For no man has seen God at any time in the flesh, except quickened by the Spirit of God. Neither can any natural man abide the presence of God, neither after the carnal mind.*' (D&C 67:11–12. Italics added.)

"It must be obvious then that to endure the glory of the Father or of the glorified Christ, a mortal being must be translated or otherwise fortified. Moses, a prophet of God, held the protecting Holy Priesthood: '. . . and the glory of God was upon Moses; therefore Moses could endure his presence.' (Moses 1:2.)

". . . There is a protective force which God brings into play when he exposes his human servants to the glories of his person and his works." (Spencer W. Kimball, in Conference Report, Apr. 1964, pp. 94–95.)

"God Almighty Himself dwells in eternal fire; flesh and blood cannot go there, for all corruption is devoured by the fire. 'Our God is a consuming fire.' . . .

" . . . Immortality dwells in everlasting burnings." (Joseph Smith, *Teachings of the Prophet Joseph Smith*, p. 367. See also Joseph Fielding Smith, *Seek Ye Earnestly . . .*, p. 275; Orson Pratt, in *Journal of Discourses*, 18:288–89.)

Selected Scripture References

The righteous "shall dwell with everlasting burnings." (Isaiah 33:14. See also v. 15.)

"No man has seen God at any time in the flesh, except quickened by the Spirit of God." (D&C 67:11.)

"Without this no man can see the face of God, even the Father, and live." (D&C 84:22.)

Moses 1:3
"I am the Lord God Almighty, and Endless is my name"

Selected Statements of the First Presidency and the Twelve Apostles

"*Endless*, used as a noun and not as an adjective, is one of the names of God and signifies his unending, eternal continuance as the supreme, exalted ruler of the universe. 'Behold, I am the Lord God Almighty, and *Endless* is my name,' he said, 'for I am without beginning of days or end of years; and is not this endless?' (Moses 1:3; 7:35.) '*Endless is my name*' he said to the Prophet. (D&C 19:10.) By using his name Endless and by combining it with other terms, the Lord has revealed some very significant truths in the scriptures. For instance: Endless life means God's life; 'Endless punishment is God's punishment.' (D&C 19:12.)" (Bruce R. McConkie, *Mormon Doctrine*, p. 226.)

" 'For, behold, I am endless, and the punishment which is given from my hand is endless punishment, for Endless is my name. Wherefore—

" 'Eternal punishment is God's punishment.'

" 'Endless punishment is God's punishment.'

"That is why it is called *endless*. Therefore, I say to you, eternal life is God's life; it is the life which he has, that which he possesses. Therefore, if he gives unto you that life which he has, you have eternal life, and you will not get it if you do not prove yourself worthy to enter into his presence. Now, that is the gospel of Jesus Christ, that is the great plan of salvation." (Joseph Fielding Smith, *Doctrines of Salvation*, 2:8.)

Selected Scripture References

"Endless" is defined. (D&C 19:10–12.)

"Then shall they be gods, because they have no end." (D&C 132:20.)
"Endless and Eternal is my name." (Moses 7:35.)

Moses 1:4

"Thou art my son" (literal)

Selected Statements of the First Presidency and the Twelve Apostles

"Man is the child of God, formed in the divine image and endowed with divine attributes, and even as the infant son of an earthly father and mother is capable in due time of becoming a man, so the undeveloped offspring of celestial parentage is capable, by experience through ages and aeons, of evolving into a God." (The First Presidency: Joseph F. Smith, John R. Winder, and Anthon H. Lund, in James R. Clark, comp., *Messages of the First Presidency*, 4:206.)

"I want to tell you, each and every one of you, that you are well acquainted with God our heavenly Father, or the great Eloheim. You are all well acquainted with Him, for there is not a soul of you but what has lived in His house and dwelt with Him year after year; and yet you are seeking to become acquainted with Him, when the fact is, you have merely forgotten what you did know. . . .

"There is not a person here to-day but what is a son or daughter of that Being. In the spirit world their spirits were first begotten and brought forth, and they lived there with their parents for ages before they came here. This, perhaps, is hard for many to believe, but it is the greatest nonsense in the world not to believe it. If you do not believe it, cease to call Him Father; and when you pray, pray to some other character." (Brigham Young, in *Journal of Discourses*, 4:216.)

"We are the offspring of God, born with the same faculties and powers as He possesses, capable of enlargement through experience that we are now passing through in our second estate." (Lorenzo Snow, in *Millennial Star* 56 [3 Dec. 1894]: 772.)

Selected Scripture References

"The Spirit shall return unto God who gave it." (Ecclesiastes 12:7.)
God is the "Father of spirits." (Hebrews 12:9.)
The Lord calls Moses "my son" four times in Moses 1. (Moses 1:4, 6, 7, 40.)

Moses 1:4

"Thou art my son" (through the gospel)

Selected Statements of the First Presidency and the Twelve Apostles

"Salvation is attainable only through compliance with the laws and ordinances of the Gospel; and all who are thus saved become sons and daughters unto God in a distinctive sense. In a revelation given through Joseph the Prophet to Emma Smith the Lord Jesus addressed the woman as 'My daughter,' and said: 'for verily I say unto you, all those who receive my gospel are sons and daughters in my kingdom' (D&C 25:1). In many instances the Lord has addressed men as His sons (e.g. D&C 9:1; 34:3; 121:7).

"That by obedience to the Gospel men may become sons of God, both as sons of Jesus Christ, and, through Him, as sons of His Father, is set forth in many revelations given in the current dispensation. . . .

"If it be proper to speak of those who accept and abide in the Gospel as Christ's sons and daughters—and upon this matter the scriptures are explicit and cannot be gainsaid nor denied—it is consistently proper to speak of Jesus Christ as the Father of the righteous, they having become His children and He having been made their Father through the second birth—the baptismal regeneration." ("The Father and The Son: A Doctrinal Exposition by The First Presidency and The Twelve," in James E. Talmage, *Articles of Faith*, pp. 468, 470.)

"The Gospel has been preached to us, and we have essayed to obey it, that we might become the sons and daughters of God—heirs of God and joint-heirs with his Son. We can never attain to the blessings of the Gospel by merely becoming acquainted with it and then sitting down and doing nothing ourselves to stem the current of evil that is preying upon us and upon the world." (Joseph F. Smith, in Conference Report, Apr. 1900, p. 40.)

Selected Scripture References

"Ye shall be called the children of Christ, his sons, and his daughters." (Mosiah 5:7.)

All mankind must be born of God into a "state of righteousness, being redeemed of God, becoming his sons and daughters." (Mosiah 27:25.)

"As many as would believe might become the sons of God." (D&C 34:3.)

Moses 1:4

"I will show thee the workmanship of mine hands; but not all"

Selected Statements of the First Presidency and the Twelve Apostles

"Is it hard to project ourselves from the elemental world of puny man to the world of Omnipotent God, who with great purpose has developed precision instruments operated through his omnipotent knowledge? Is it difficult to believe that the Urim and Thummim, carried down through the ages by the prophets, even in the hands of our own modern-day prophet, could be that precision instrument which would transmit messages from God himself to his supreme creation—man? Can God have limitations? Can atmosphere or distance or space hold back his pictures? Would it be so difficult for Moses or Enoch or Abraham or Joseph to see a colorful, accurate, moving picture of all things past and present, and even future? Could one doubt that the holy man, Moses, could stand on the mountain peak and see? Moses' Creator said 'look, and I will show thee the workmanship of mine hands; but not all, for my works are without end, . . .' [Moses 1:4] 'Wherefore, no man can behold all my works, except he behold all my glory; and no man can behold all my glory, and afterwards remain in the flesh on the earth.' (*Ibid.*, 1:5)." (Spencer W. Kimball, in Conference Report, Apr. 1962, p. 62.)

"Moses . . . at a certain time, was clothed upon with the glory of God; and while he was thus clothed upon, he was enabled to behold many things; and seeing some things that looked very glorious, he wanted to see more; . . . the sight would be so overwhelming that the mortal tabernacle would melt away. Should a mortal man be permitted to gaze upon all the works of God, which include all His glory, mortality could not endure it." (Orson Pratt, in *Journal of Discourses*, 2:245.)

Moses 1:6

"Moses, my son . . . thou art in the similitude of mine Only Begotten"

Selected Statements of the First Presidency and the Twelve Apostles

"In prophetic power, spiritual insight, and leadership qualifications, Moses ranks with the mightiest men who have ever lived. All succeeding generations have classed him as the great law-giver of Israel. The miracles and majesty attending his ministry can scarcely be duplicated. Indeed, his life and ministry stand as a prototype of the mortal life and ministry of our Lord himself. So great was Moses that even Christ is described as a Prophet like unto this ancient leader of Israel's host. (Deut. 18:15–19; Acts 3:22–23; 3 Ne. 20:23.)" (Bruce R. McConkie, *Mormon Doctrine*, p. 515.)

"To set forth in full how our Lord's life and ministry was patterned after and like unto that of Moses is beyond the scope of this work. . . .

"1. Both were among the noble and great in the premortal life. . . .

"2. Both were foreordained to perform the mortal labors chosen for them, and both were called by name, generations before their mortal births, with their specified labors being set forth in advance by the spirit of prophecy. . . .

"3. Moses delivered Israel from Egypt. . . . Christ, the Great Deliverer, offers freedom to all who are under the bondage of sin. . . .

"4. Moses was the lawgiver of Israel. . . . Christ was the great Lawgiver who set forth for all peoples of all ages the system of heavenly rule by which they can qualify for a celestial inheritance.

"5. As we have seen, Moses was the mediator of the old covenant, Christ of the new. . . .

"6. Jesus and Moses were both born in perilous times. . . .

"7. Moses performed many signs and wonders and miracles before Pharaoh and his court and in the presence of all Israel. Our Lord acted in like manner throughout his whole ministry. . . .

"8. Both Moses and Jesus had control over mighty waters. The one stretched forth his hand over the Red Sea, the waters divided, and Israel went through on dry ground. . . . The Other walked on the waters of the Galilean Sea and also commanded the wind and the waves to cease their tempestuous raging. . . .

"9. Under Moses' ministry manna fell from heaven, that Israel, for forty years, perished not for want of food. Jesus came to bring that bread from heaven which if men eat they shall never hunger more.

"10. Moses sat on the judgment seat, from morning to night, hearing the causes of the people and dispensing judgment, even as the great Judge shall dispense justice and judgment forever.

"11. 'Now the man Moses was very meek, above all the men which were upon the face of the earth.' (Num. 12:3.) Jesus said: 'I am meek and lowly in heart.' (Matt. 11:29.) The meek are the godfearing and the righteous.

"12. Moses and Christ were prophets, mighty prophets, the one foreshadowing the Other, but both acclaiming the divine Sonship of Him of whom all the prophets testify. . . .

"13. Those who defied Moses and rebelled against his law were destroyed. . . . At our Lord's Second Coming all those who are in rebellion against Christ and his laws shall be cut off from among the people. . . .

"14. . . . 'For had ye believed Moses, ye would have believed me: for he wrote of me. But if ye believe not his writings, how shall ye believe my words?' (John 5:45–47.) Christ and Moses go together. If one was a prophet, sent of God, so was the other. If the words of one are true, so are those of the other." (Bruce R. McConkie, *Promised Messiah*, pp. 445–48. See also Bruce R. McConkie, *Mortal Messiah*, 2:170.)

Selected Scripture References

Moses declared, "The Lord thy God will raise up unto thee a Prophet . . . like unto me." (Deuteronomy 18:15. See also Acts 3:19–26.)

The prophet of whom Moses spoke was the Holy One of Israel. (See 1 Nephi 22:20–21.)

Moroni stated that the prophet like unto Moses was Christ. (See Joseph Smith—History 1:40.)

Moses 1:6

"Mine Only Begotten is and shall be the Savior"

Selected Statements of the First Presidency and the Twelve Apostles

"The atonement is eternal—as eternal as the gospel, as eternal as the plan of salvation—because its saving and redeeming powers have always been manifest. It is the means by which Adam and all the ancient saints were saved. Through it they had the fulness of the everlasting gospel with all its gifts and glories. Baptism and celestial marriage had eternal efficacy and everlasting virtue for four thousand years before the Lord Jesus was even born in the flesh. The plan of salvation is always the same, and souls in those days were just as precious in the sight of the Lord as are souls today. All that was ever done by the ancient saints looked forward to and was built upon the foundation of the atonement that was to be. All was done in anticipation of an act that is eternal in nature. And the blessings of the atonement will continue to be manifest as long as there are men on earth—and, for that matter, everlastingly thereafter. It is truly an eternal, an everlasting, a perpetual thing that, like God, is to us without beginning and without end." (Bruce R. McConkie, *New Witness for the Articles of Faith*, p. 130.)

Selected Scripture References

"The Son of the Eternal Father, and the Savior of the world." (1 Nephi 13:40.)

The Old Testament prophets, speaking of the Messiah, taught the people to believe in Jesus as though he had already come. (See Jarom 1:11.)

The Nephites were taught to believe in Jesus "even as though he had already come among them." (Mosiah 3:13.)

"If Christ had not come . . . , speaking of things to come as though they had already come, there could have been no redemption." (Mosiah 16:6.)

"The Son of God hath atoned for original guilt." (Moses 6:54.)

Other Commentary

Sometimes prophets of God who lived before Christ was born deliberately spoke of the atonement of Jesus Christ in the past tense. It seems that they felt that by so doing some believers would better understand that the Atonement was retroactive and already in force. Except for resurrection, all of the benefits of the Atonement were available to the righteous from the days of Adam.

Moses 1:6

"There is no God beside me"

Selected Statements of the First Presidency and the Twelve Apostles

"A question has been discussed in some of the auxiliary societies, and finally has been submitted to us, in reference to a saying to be found in the Pearl of Great Price, as follows:

" 'And I have a work for thee, Moses, my son; and thou art in the similitude of my Only Begotten; and mine Only Begotten is and shall be the Savior, for He is full of Grace and truth; but there is no God beside me, and all things are present with me, for I know them all.' (Moses 1:6).

"The words particularly debated are, 'but there is no God beside me.' They appear to be in conflict with many other statements in scripture, both ancient and modern, but are not out of harmony with them when properly understood.

"Moses was reared in an atmosphere of idolatry. There were numerous deities among the Egyptians. In commencing the work which the Lord said he had for Moses to do, it was necessary to center his mind and faith upon God the Eternal Father as the only Being to worship. Therefore, the words now under consideration, or rather those that were actually spoken to Moses of which these are a translation, were made emphatic, not only as to the false gods of the times but delusive spirits, of whom Satan was the chief and who tried to pass himself off to Moses as a divine object of worship, as narrated in the same chapter. (Verses 12-15).

"This was repeated in substance, and for the same reasons, in the first of the Ten Commandments: 'Thou shalt have no other gods before me,'—that is, beside me, above me, or equal to me, or to be an object of worship, (Exodus 20:2-5). Or, as Paul put it: 'For though there be [many] that are called gods whether in heaven or in earth, (as there are gods many and lords many) yet to us there is but one God, the Father, of whom are all things, and one Lord, Jesus Christ, by whom are all things and we by Him.' (1 Cor. 8:5-6).

" . . . The sole object of worship, God the Eternal Father, stands supreme and alone, and it is in the name of the Only Begotten that we thus approach Him, as Christ taught always. 'God standeth in the congregation of the mighty; he judgeth among the gods.' (Psalm 82:1.) Jesus quoted this and did not dispute it (John 10:34-6). All the perfected beings who are rightly called gods, being, like the Savior, possessed of 'the fullness of the Godhead bodily,' are ONE, just as the Father and the Son and the Holy Ghost are one." (The First Presidency: Joseph F. Smith, Anthon H. Lund, and Charles W. Penrose, in James R. Clark, comp., *Messages of the First Presidency,* 4:270-71.)

"The Father *is* the one true God. *This* thing is certain: no one will ever ascend above Him; no one will ever replace Him. Nor will anything ever change the relationship that we, His literal offspring, have with Him. He is Elohim, the Father. He is God. Of Him there *is* only one. We revere our Father and our God; we *worship* Him." (Boyd K. Packer, in Conference Report, Oct. 1984, p. 85.)

Selected Scripture References

"Thou shalt have no other gods before me." (Exodus 20:3.)
"The Lord is God, and . . . there is none else." (1 Kings 8:60.)

Moses 1:6
"All things are present with me, for I know them all"

Selected Statements of the First Presidency and the Twelve Apostles

"Without the knowledge of all things, God would not be able to save any portion of his creatures; for it is by reason of the knowledge which he has of all things, from the beginning to the end, that enables him to give that understanding to his creatures by which they are made partakers of eternal life; and if it were not for the idea existing in the minds of men that God has all knowledge it would be impossible for them to exercise faith in him." (Joseph Smith, *Lectures on Faith*, 4:43. See also Bruce R. McConkie, *New Witness for the Articles of Faith*, pp. 52–53; Joseph Fielding Smith, *Doctrines of Salvation*, 1:10.)

"God does not deal in theories." (Richard L. Evans.)

"God is Omniscient—By Him matter has been organized and energy directed. He is therefore the Creator of all things that are created; and 'Known unto God are all his works from the beginning of the world.' His power and His wisdom are alike incomprehensible to man, for they are infinite. Being Himself eternal and perfect, His knowledge cannot be otherwise than infinite. To comprehend Himself, an infinite Being, He must possess an infinite mind. Through the agency of angels and ministering servants He is in continuous communication with all parts of creation, and may personally visit as He may determine." (James E. Talmage, *Articles of Faith*, pp. 43–44.)

Selected Scripture References

"I know their works and their thoughts." (Isaiah 66:18.)
"He knoweth all things, and there is not anything save he knows it." (2 Nephi 9:20.)
God has foreknowledge of all things. (See Alma 13:7.)
"All things are present before mine eyes." (D&C 38:2.)
"He comprehendeth all things." (D&C 88:41.)

Moses 1:7–8
"Moses beheld the world and the ends thereof"

Selected Statements of the First Presidency and the Twelve Apostles

> *I, Joseph, the prophet, in spirit beheld,*
>   *And the eyes of the inner man truly did see*
> *Eternity sketch'd in a vision from God.*
>   *Of what was, and now is, and yet is to be.*

(Joseph Smith, poetic explanation of the vision [D&C 76], stanza 11, in *Times and Seasons*, 4 [1 Feb. 1843]: 82.)

"When God manifests to his servants those things that are to come, or those which have been, he does it by unfolding them by the power of that Spirit which comprehends all things, always; and so much may be shown and made perfectly plain to the understanding in a short time, that to the world, who are occupied all their life to learn a little, look at the relation of it, and are disposed to call it false. . . . It is said, and I believe the account, that the Lord showed the brother of Jared (Moriancumer) all things which were to transpire from that day to the end of the earth, as well as those which had taken place. I believe that Moses was permitted to see the same, as the Lord caused them to pass, in vision before him as he stood upon the mount." (Oliver Cowdery, in *Messenger and Advocate*, 1 [Apr. 1835]: 112.)

Selected Scripture References

"And also others who have been, to them hath he shown all things." (1 Nephi 14:26.)

Adam "predicted whatsoever should befall his posterity unto the latest generation." (D&C 107:56.)

Enoch was shown all things, even until the end of the world. (See Moses 7:4-67.)

Other Commentary

"The ancient prophets have known a great deal about our age of miracles for many centuries.

"Moses was permitted to see the history of our earth from its beginning to its end." (Sterling W. Sill, in Conference Report, Apr. 1966, p. 19.)

Moses 1:10

"Man is nothing"

Selected Statements of the First Presidency and the Twelve Apostles

"There is but a small degree—a very small degree, indeed, of the purposes of God unfolded to the mind of man. The amount of knowledge, which we in our present state are in possession of, is extremely limited, so that when compared with that vast amount of knowledge that fills eternity, we might say that man, in his highest attainments here in this life, is, as it were, nothing. However far he may expand his intellectual powers, and faculties by studying, by meditation, by seeking unto the Lord diligently for the inspiration of the Spirit, yet all that he can possibly receive and attain to here is, comparatively speaking, nothing. Moses was a man possessed of like passions with other men; he was a man similar to ourselves, but he had by his perseverance, diligence, and faithfulness obtained great favor and power with God; so that by this favor and through this power, he was enabled to obtain greater information and knowledge than the rest of the human family that were on the earth at that period; and far greater in some things than what we have attained to in this generation; at the same time, when the grand and wonderful intelligence of heaven was portrayed before the mind of Moses, and knowledge was poured out from the heavens upon him, he exclaimed before the Lord, *'Now I know for this once that man is nothing.'*

"If there were a being then upon the face of the earth, that had a reason to suppose that man was something, it was Moses; but yet in the midst of the visions of the Almighty, and the vast field of knowledge that was opened to his mind—while he was yet gazing upon the workmanship of the hands of God, and looking into the intricacies of the construction of this world—in the midst of all this, he considered himself nothing. That is just the way I feel; and I presume it is the way that almost every one feels who contemplates the greatness of God, and the immensity of knowledge that there is far beyond our reach in this present state of existence." (Orson Pratt, in *Journal of Discourses*, 3:97.)

" 'For as the heavens are higher than the earth, so are my ways higher than your ways, and my thoughts than your thoughts.' (Isa. 55:8-9.)

"Perhaps this statement will cause us to remember how small we are in comparison to our God, who is all-knowing and all-powerful. The Lord taught Moses a great lesson in this regard. After he had shown Moses by vision the workmanship of his hands, he withdrew from Moses, and his glory was not upon him. Moses was left unto himself, and he fell unto the earth exhausted. It was many hours before he again received his natural strength, and when he did, he humbly said: 'Now for this cause I know that man is nothing, which thing I never had supposed.' (Moses 1:10.) This counsel should remind all of us to be meek and contrite of spirit." (Delbert L. Stapley, in Conference Report, Apr. 1967, p. 34.)

"The great law-giver, Moses, has given us the key to the beginning of heavenly wisdom. After he had sought God on Mt. Sinai, a soul-stirring vision was given him in which he was permitted to enter into the presence of the Lord. When the vision was ended and he was left unto himself, he made this profound statement: 'Now, for this cause I know that man is nothing, which thing I had never supposed.' (Moses 1:10.)

"That was the beginning of his wisdom unto the obtaining of the spiritual power necessary for him to perform his great mission. He had found himself by losing himself in the great work to which God had now called him." (Harold B. Lee, in Conference Report, Oct. 1966, p. 116.)

Selected Scripture References

A knowledge of God's goodness awakens men to a sense of their own nothingness. (See Mosiah 4:5-7, 11.)

"Yea, I know that I am nothing." (Alma 26:12.)

See Selected Statements and Scripture References under Moses 1:39.

Moses 1:11

"Mine own eyes have beheld God; but not my natural, but my spiritual eyes"

Selected Statements of the First Presidency and the Twelve Apostles

"All things whatsoever God in his infinite wisdom has seen fit and proper to reveal to us, while we are dwelling in mortality, in regard to our mortal bodies, are revealed to us in the abstract, and independent of affinity of this mortal tabernacle, but are revealed to our spirits precisely as though we had no bodies at all; and those revelations which will save our spirits will save our bodies. God reveals them to us in view of no eternal dissolution of the body, or tabernacle." (Joseph Smith, *Teachings of the Prophet Joseph Smith*, p. 355.)

"But still, we have the faculties within us; we have the power; there is merely an obstacle, or obstruction, in the way; and when this obstruction is removed it shows the godlike powers that are planted within the tabernacles of men, by which they can behold and pierce those portions of creations that are not discernable by the natural man." (Orson Pratt, in *Journal of Discourses*, 21:260. See also 16:336-37.)

"It is not given to every man to look upon the face of God as did Moses [Moses 1:11], as did Joseph Smith. One must be specially prepared before he can see what Joseph saw. . . . I do not expect the Lord to manifest Himself to me in the same way that he did to Joseph the Prophet. I expect Him to communicate with me through the gifts He has endowed me with, not through those with which He has endowed my brother or sister, unless they have the right to receive for me a message from Him. When the Lord speaks to me or to you, it will be in a method or manner justified by our preparation, our gifts, our powers; for we have all been endowed in some degree." (Orson F. Whitney, in Conference Report, Apr. 1910, p. 60. See also Bruce R. McConkie, *Mormon Doctrine*, p. 803.)

Selected Scripture References

Paul was "caught up to the third heaven," that is, the celestial kingdom. (2 Corinthians 12:2; see also vv. 1, 3–4.)

The Three Nephites were translated. (See 3 Nephi 28:13–17.)

"You shall see me . . . not with the carnal . . . but with the spiritual." (D&C 67:10.)

Joseph Smith and Sidney Rigdon were transfigured during this vision. (See D&C 76.)

Joseph Smith saw in vision the celestial kingdom. (See D&C 137.)

Enoch "beheld also things which were not visible to the natural eye." (Moses 6:36.)

Moses 1:11

"His glory was upon me; and I beheld his face, for I was transfigured before him"

See Selected Statements, Scripture References, and Other Commentary under Moses 1:2.

Moses 1:12

"Satan came tempting him, saying: Moses, son of man, worship me"

Selected Statements of the First Presidency and the Twelve Apostles

"Satan came up before Moses, not in all his ugliness and maliciousness, but assuming the form of an angel of light. Satan said, 'Moses, son of man, worship me!' Moses looked upon Satan and said, 'Who art thou, that I should worship thee? For I could not look upon God except his glory should come upon me, but I can look upon thee as a natural man.' Here was the difference. He could look upon this individual who came to him pretending to be an angel of goodness and light, and have none of the glorious feelings that he had before. Hence said Moses, 'I can discern the difference between God and thee. Get thee hence, Satan!' Satan did not feel disposed to give up the attack, and he commanded him again to worship him, and he exerted a great power and the earth shook and trembled, and Moses was filled with fear and trembling, but he nevertheless called upon God for he was convinced in his own mind that his visitor was one from the infernal regions, a personage of darkness, and he felt to rebuke him." (Orson Pratt, in *Journal of Discourses*, 15:235.)

"It is not every revelation that is of God, for Satan has the power to transform himself into an angel of light; he can give visions and revelations as well as spiritual manifestations and table-rappings." (John Taylor, in *Millennial Star* 19 [28 Mar. 1857]: 197. See also Joseph Smith, *Teachings of the Prophet Joseph Smith*, pp. 214-15; Bruce R. McConkie, *Mormon Doctrine*, p. 195.)

"People are liable in many ways to be led astray by the power of the adversary, for they do not fully understand that it is a hard matter for them to always distinguish the things of God from the things of the devil. There is but one way by which they can know the difference, and that is by the light of the spirit of revelation, even the spirit of our Lord Jesus Christ." (Brigham Young, in *Journal of Discourses*, 3:43. See also John A. Widtsoe, *Evidences and Reconciliations*, 1:92-93.)

"This arch enemy of God and man, called the devil, the 'Son of the Morning,' who dwells here on the earth, is a personage of great power; he has great influence and knowledge. He understands that if this kingdom, which he rebelled against in heaven, prevails on the earth, there will be no dominion here for him. He has great influence over the children of men; he labors continually to destroy them. He labored to destroy them in heaven; he labored to destroy the works of God in heaven, and he had to be cast out. He is here, mighty among the children of men. There is a vast number of fallen spirits, cast out with him, here on the earth. They do not die and disappear; they have not bodies only as they enter the tabernacles of men. They have not organized bodies, and are not to be seen with the sight of the eye. But there are many evil spirits amongst us, and they labor to overthrow the Church and kingdom of God. There never was a prophet in any age of the world but what the devil was continually at his elbow." (Wilford Woodruff, in *Journal of Discourses*, 13:163.)

Selected Scripture References

Satan "transformeth himself nigh unto an angel of light, and stirreth up the children of men unto secret combinations." (2 Nephi 9:9.)

"What do we hear? . . . The voice of Michael on the banks of the Susquehanna, detecting the devil when he appeared as an angel of light!" (D&C 128:20.)

"If it be the devil as an angel of light, when you ask him to shake hands he will offer you his hand, and you will not feel anything; you may therefore detect him." (D&C 129:8; see also vv. 4-7.)

Other Commentary

The phrase "son of man" appears to have three different uses in the scriptures:

1. A title emphasizing the divine sonship of Jesus Christ. "In the language of Adam, Man of Holiness is his name [God the Father], and the name of his Only Begotten is the Son of Man." (Moses 6:57.)

2. A greeting between friends. The Lord uses the phrase more than ninety times in the book of Ezekiel in speaking to his prophet. (See Bible Dictionary, s.v. "Son of Man.")

3. Satan's patronizing of Moses. Satan emphasized Moses' mortality in contrast to his own nonmortality, which gives him the ability to appear as an angel of light. (See Moses 1:12–13.) In other words, Satan called Moses a mere man.

The physical appearance of Satan must have been impressive. Moses explains, however, that the "glory" of Satan is darkness in comparison to God's glory. In verse 15 Moses states that God's Spirit had not altogether withdrawn from him; therefore, Moses could detect Satan's spirit as darkness.

Moses 1:14

"I can look upon thee in the natural man"

Selected Statements of the First Presidency and the Twelve Apostles

"Moses the priesthood bearer must be protected to see Jehovah but could face this imposter with his natural eyes and without discomfort." (Spencer W. Kimball, in Conference Report, Apr. 1964, pp. 95–96.)

"The good spirits, in the superlative sense of the word, are they who, in this life, partook of the Holy Priesthood and of the fulness of the gospel. This class of spirits minister to the heirs of salvation, both in this world and in the world of spirits. They can appear unto men when permitted; but not having a fleshly tabernacle, they cannot hide their glory. Hence, an unembodied spirit, if it be a holy personage, will be surrounded with a halo of resplendent glory, or brightness, above the brightness of the sun; whereas spirits not worthy to be glorified will appear without this brilliant halo, and, although they often attempt to pass as angels of light, there is more or less darkness about them. So it is with Satan and his hosts who have not been embodied." (Parley P. Pratt, *Key to the Science of Theology*, p. 72.)

Selected Scripture References

The devil is "that being who beguiled our first parents, who transformeth himself nigh unto an angel of light." (2 Nephi 9:9.)

"Satan himself is transformed into an angel of light. Therefore it is no great thing if his ministers also be transformed as the ministers of righteousness." (2 Corinthians 11:14-15; see also vv. 12-13.)

Moses 1:15

"I can judge between thee and God"

Selected Statements of the First Presidency and the Twelve Apostles

"Who can describe an angel of light? If Satan should appear as one in glory, who can tell his color, his signs, his appearance, his glory, or what is the manner of his manifestation? . . . Who can drag into daylight and develop the hidden mysteries of the false spirits that so frequently are made manifest among the Latter-day Saints? We answer that no man can do this without the Priesthood, and having a knowledge of the laws by which spirits are governed; for as no man knows the things of God, but by the Spirit of God, so no man knows the spirit of the devil, and his power and influence, but by possessing intelligence which is more than human, and having unfolded through the medium of the Priesthood the mysterious operations of his devices; without knowing the angelic form, the sanctified look and gesture, and the zeal that is frequently manifested by him for the glory of God, together with the prophetic spirit, the gracious influence, the godly appearance, and the holy garb, which are so characteristic of his proceedings and his mysterious windings.

"A man must have the discerning of spirits before he can drag into daylight this hellish influence and unfold it unto the world in all its soul-destroying, diabolical, and horrid colors." (Joseph Smith, *Teachings of the Prophet Joseph Smith*, pp. 204-5.)

"The only sure way to know the truth and have the gift of discernment and be able to distinguish between truth and error is by following the admonition of our Lord Jesus Christ, and then we will know the truth which will make us free from error. Members of the Church have been baptized and confirmed and they have the right to the companionship of the Holy Ghost. This gift is bestowed upon them, but only those who are contrite in spirit, obedient in the keeping of divine commandments, who are faithful and true, will have this great gift of discernment. If they comply with the laws of the kingdom of God and earnestly, faithfully, seek to know the truth, they shall find it and will not be deceived. The great trouble with so many members of the Church is that they do not live in strict accordance with divine law, therefore they have not freed themselves from darkness, and they are unable to distinguish the truths from heaven from the theories and doctrines of men. The word of the Lord will never fail the honest humble person who will do the will of the Father, he will be given an abiding knowledge that no theory or false doctrine can destroy. This is the promise of our Lord whose promises do not fail." (Joseph Fielding Smith, *Man: His Origin and Destiny*, pp. 7–8.)

Selected Scripture References

"And whatsoever thing persuadeth men to do good is of me; for good cometh of none save it be of me." (Ether 4:12.)

"That ye may not be deceived seek ye earnestly the best gifts." (D&C 46:8.)

Bishops and other Church leaders shall discern all gifts of the Spirit to detect those that are not of God. (See D&C 46:27.)

"He that asketh in Spirit shall receive in Spirit." (D&C 46:28.)

Moses 1:16

"Thou art after the similitude of mine Only Begotten"

See Selected Statements, Scripture References, and Other Commentary under Moses 1:6.

Moses 1:17

"Call upon God in the name of mine Only Begotten, and worship me"

Selected Scripture References

"Call upon God in the name of the Son forevermore." (Moses 5:8.)

Moses 1:19

"Satan . . . commanded, saying: I am the Only Begotten, worship me"

Selected Statements of the First Presidency and the Twelve Apostles

"Satan is irrevocably committed to countering and overcoming the influence of the Spirit of Christ upon men. He is the representative, promoter, and advocate of that 'opposition in all things' referred to by Lehi in his instructions to his son Jacob. (See 2 Nephi 2:11, 14–18.)

"Satan's methods are various, devious, and countless.

" . . . by every possible means he seeks to darken the minds of men and then offers them falsehood and deception in the guise of truth. . . .' (Joseph F. Smith [as quoted in] Daniel H. Ludlow, *Latter-day Prophets Speak* [Bookcraft, 1948], pp. 20–21.)" (Marion G. Romney, in Conference Report, Apr. 1971, p. 24.)

"The nearer a person approaches the Lord, a greater power will be manifested by the adversary to prevent the accomplishment of His purposes." (Joseph Smith, as quoted in Orson F. Whitney, *Life of Heber C. Kimball*, p. 32.)

Selected Scripture References

Satan is "that old serpent, who is the devil, who is the father of all lies." (2 Nephi 2:18; see also v. 17.)

Satan is "the devil, the father of all lies." (Moses 4:4.)

Moses 1:20

"Calling upon God, he received strength"

Selected Statements of the First Presidency and the Twelve Apostles

"Your greatest weakness will be the point at which Satan will try to tempt you, will try to win you; and if you have made yourself weak, he will add to that weakness. Resist him, and you will gain in strength. If he tempts you in another way, resist him again and he will become weaker. In turn, you become stronger, until you can say, no matter what your surroundings may be, 'Get thee behind me, Satan: for it is written, Thou shalt worship the Lord thy God, and him only shalt thou serve.' (Luke 4:8). . . .

"Remember, you cannot tamper with the evil one. Resist temptation, resist Satan, and he will flee from you." (David O. McKay, in *Improvement Era*, July 1968, p. 3.)

Moses 1:21–22

Moses commanded Satan, "saying: In the name of the Only Begotten, depart hence, Satan. . . . and he departed hence"

Selected Statements of the First Presidency and the Twelve Apostles

"It would seem also, that wicked spirits have their bounds, limits, and laws by which they are governed or controlled, and know their future destiny; . . . When Satan presented himself before the Lord, among the sons of God, he said that he came 'from going to and fro in the earth, and from wandering up and down in it;' and he is emphatically called the prince of the power of the air; and, it is very evident that they possess a power that none but those who have the Priesthood can control." (Joseph Smith, *Teachings of the Prophet Joseph Smith*, p. 208.)

"God, men, and angels will not condemn those that resist everything that is evil, and devils cannot; as well might the devil seek to dethrone Jehovah, as overthrow an innocent soul that resists everything which is evil." (Joseph Smith, *Teachings of the Prophet Joseph Smith*, p. 226.)

"Any person that he can find that will yield to him, he will bind him, and take possession of the body and reign there, glorying in it mightily, not caring that he had got merely a stolen body; and by and by some one having authority will come along and cast him out and restore the tabernacle to its rightful owner. The devil steals a tabernacle because he has not one of his own: but if he steals one, he is always liable to be turned out of doors." (Joseph Smith, *Teachings of the Prophet Joseph Smith*, p. 298.)

"Not even Lucifer, the Star of the Morning, the arch-enemy of mankind can withstand the power of the priesthood of God." (Spencer W. Kimball, in Conference Report, Apr. 1964, p. 96.)

"Satan can be resisted. You know the evil one has opposed us all the way from before the beginning. He has promised himself that he is going to disturb every person in this earth and try to get him to do evil. But remember that the evil one is a spirit only. He has no body. Therefore, every one of you is stronger than Satan. If you will exercise your brain, your morals, your teachings, you can be superior to him." (Spencer W. Kimball, *Teachings of Spencer W. Kimball*, p. 33.)

Selected Scripture References

"Whoso shall ask it in my name in faith, they shall cast out devils." (D&C 35:9.)

"It shall be given unto you, power over that spirit." (D&C 50:32; see also v. 33.)

Moses 1:23

Moses recorded his encounter with Satan, "but because of

wickedness it is not had among the children of men"

Selected Statements of the First Presidency and the Twelve Apostles

"In these days of sophistication and error men depersonalize not only God but the devil. Under this concept Satan is a myth, useful for keeping people straight in less enlightened days but outmoded in our educated age. Nothing is further from reality. Satan is very much a personal, individual spirit being, but without a mortal body. His desires to seal each of us his are no less ardent in wickedness than our Father's are in righteousness to attract us to his own eternal kingdom." (Spencer W. Kimball, *Teachings of Spencer W. Kimball*, p. 35.)

Selected Scripture References

The devil teaches that there is no hell and no devil. (See 2 Nephi 28:22.)

Other Commentary

The Old Testament and Satan. Latter-day Saints may look upon the few references to Satan, or the devil, in the Old Testament as a deliberate attempt to nullify the concept of Satan as a spirit being opposed to God. Nephi was informed through revelation that because many plain and precious things would be taken from the Bible, many people would stumble in unbelief. In fact, the angel told him, because of these deletions from the Bible "Satan hath great power over them." (1 Nephi 13:29; see also vv. 24–28.)

The first time Satan is mentioned in the Bible is in the book of Chronicles (see 1 Chronicles 21:1), and his name appears in only thirteen verses in the Old Testament, ten of which are in the book of Job. The devil or devils are mentioned only four times in the Old Testament. (See Leviticus 17:7; Deuteronomy 32:17; 2 Chronicles 11:15; Psalm 106:37.) There are, however, numerous references to the devil or devils in the New Testament.

The book of Genesis records that it was the serpent who tempted Adam and Eve. (See Genesis 3:1–2.) But the account in Genesis does not identify the serpent as Satan. Some critics of the Bible have concluded from this and from the few references to Satan in the Old Testament that the Jewish people acquired the idea of Satan at a late date, probably during the Babylonian exile (609–539 B.C.). This view of the Bible indicates a belief in the evolution of religious ideas rather than in direct revelation from God.

The Book of Moses and Satan. "In the eight chapters of the Book of Moses, the name Satan appears twenty-eight times. Satan is also referred to as the devil. (Moses 4:4.) It is evident that in the beginning a knowledge of the devil as an individual was known, according to the revelations. (2 Nephi 2:17; D&C 29:36–37; 76:25–29.)

"Examples of scriptures in the Book of Moses which refer to Satan, but are lost from the Bible are:

"1. The temptation of Moses (Moses 1:12–22).

"2. The temptation of Adam and Eve (Moses 3:25; 4:5–8; compare Genesis 2:25; 3:1–6).

"3. The origin of Satan (Moses 4:1–4).

"4. The tempter of the sons and daughters of Adam and Eve (Moses 5:12–13).

"5. Cain and Satan (Moses 5:17–23; compare Genesis 4:2–7).

"6. Other references to Satan's power, but which are not found in the Bible (Moses 5:28–31, 38, 49, 52, 55; 6:15, 29, 49; 7:24, 26, 38, 57)." (Roy W. Doxey, *Pearl of Great Price: Education Weeks Lectures 1970*, p. 64.)

Moses 1:24
"The Holy Ghost . . . beareth record of the Father and the Son"

Selected Statements of the First Presidency and the Twelve Apostles

"I have always declared God to be a distinct personage, Jesus Christ a separate and distinct personage from God the Father, and that the Holy Ghost was a distinct personage and a Spirit: and these three constitute three distinct personages and three Gods." (Joseph Smith, *Teachings of the Prophet Joseph Smith*, 6:474.)

"The Holy Ghost 'witnesses of the Father and the Son' (2 Nephi 2:18); he 'beareth record of the Father and the Son' (Moses 1:24); he, and he only, makes known those holy beings whom it is life eternal to know. Jesus said: 'He shall testify of me' (John 15:26); and, he 'beareth record of the Father and me' (3 Nephi 11:32). And Paul said: 'no man can say [meaning know] that Jesus is the Lord, but by the Holy Ghost.' (1 Corinthians 12:3.) Thus the Holy Ghost is the source of saving knowledge; his mission, assigned by the Father, is to bear witness to the truth of those things which enable men to gain eternal life. His witness is sure; it cannot be controverted; it will stand forever." (Bruce R. McConkie, *New Witness for the Articles of Faith*, p. 267. See also Bruce R. McConkie, *Mormon Doctrine*, p. 785.)

"The Holy Ghost is the third member of the Godhead. He is a Spirit, in the form of a man. The Father and the Son are personages of tabernacle; they have bodies of flesh and bones. The Holy Ghost is a personage of Spirit, and has a spirit body only. His mission is to bear witness of the Father and the Son and of all truth." (Joseph Fielding Smith, *Doctrines of Salvation*, 1:38.)

Selected Scripture References

"The Holy Ghost beareth record of the Father and me." (3 Nephi 28:11.)

"The Holy Ghost . . . beareth record of the Father and of the Son." (D&C 20:27.)

"The Comforter . . . beareth record of the Father and of the Son." (D&C 42:17.)

Moses 1:25

"Blessed art thou Moses, for I, the Almighty, have chosen thee"

See Selected Statements and Scripture References under Abraham 3:22–23.

Moses 1:25

Many waters "shall obey thy command as if thou wert God"

Selected Statements of the First Presidency and the Twelve Apostles

"Water is subject not alone to the natural laws that man must learn and to which he must conform, but it is subject also to the eternal law of faith, a law that in the eternal sense is also a natural law. And further, water is used by the Lord to further his own purposes—to give life to men; to cleanse them from their sins; to drown them in death when his judgments are poured out. . . .

"But our concern, with reference to the miracle we are about to witness, is to know that Jehovah rules the waters, and that what he does to and with them—whether it be by his own voice or by the voice of his servants, it is the same. . . .

"We see Moses, the man of God—by his own voice, which was the voice of Jehovah . . . stretch forth his hand over the Red Sea and divide it so that all Israel, numbering in the millions, 'went into the midst of the sea upon the dry ground: and the waters were a wall unto them on the right hand, and on their left.' We learn that 'the floods stood upright as an heap, and the depths were congealed in the heart of the sea.' (Ex. 14:19–31; 15:8.) And we see the pursuing armies of Pharaoh drowned in the depths of the sea as the congealing power is withdrawn and the floods surge forth in all their unchecked fury." (Bruce R. McConkie, *Mortal Messiah*, 2:354–56.)

Selected Scripture References

The Israelites passed through the Red Sea on dry ground. (See Exodus 14:13–31.)

Moses "spake unto the waters of the Red Sea and they divided." (1 Nephi 4:2; see also 17:26.)

Moses smote the waters of the Red Sea, and they parted. (See Helaman 8:11.)

Other Commentary

Moses 1:25, together with verse 17, allows us to approximate the time of Moses' vision of the world in the lifetime of Moses. Moses lived about forty years as a prince in Egypt, the next forty years as a shepherd in the Sinai, and the last forty years as a prophet of God leading the children of Israel in the Sinai. Since the call from the burning bush had happened (see Moses 1:17) and the parting of the Red Sea had not yet happened (see Moses 1:25), we can estimate that Moses was about eighty years of age when he received the vision recorded in Moses 1.

See Selected Statements and Scripture References under Moses 7:13.

Moses 1:26

"I am with thee, even unto the end of thy days; for thou shalt deliver my people from bondage, even Israel my chosen"

Selected Statements of the First Presidency and the Twelve Apostles

"A dispensation of the gospel is defined as the granting to divinely chosen officers, by a commission from God, of power and authority to dispense the word of God, and to administer in all the ordinances thereof. However, a dispensation has frequently embraced additional power and included a special commission or warning to the people, the making of a special and definite covenant with man, and the conferring of special powers upon chosen prophets beyond what other prophets may have received.

" . . . Moses was given a dispensation of gathering and led Israel from Egypt to their promised land." (Joseph Fielding Smith, *Doctrines of Salvation*, 1:160–61.)

"Moses had two missions. One was to rescue Israel from Egyptian bondage, restoring the nation to the Land of Promise. The other was to convert the tribes to the worship of the true God. In both of these missions he was constantly taught and directed by the Almighty himself; he had such a close relationship with the Lord that it even approached

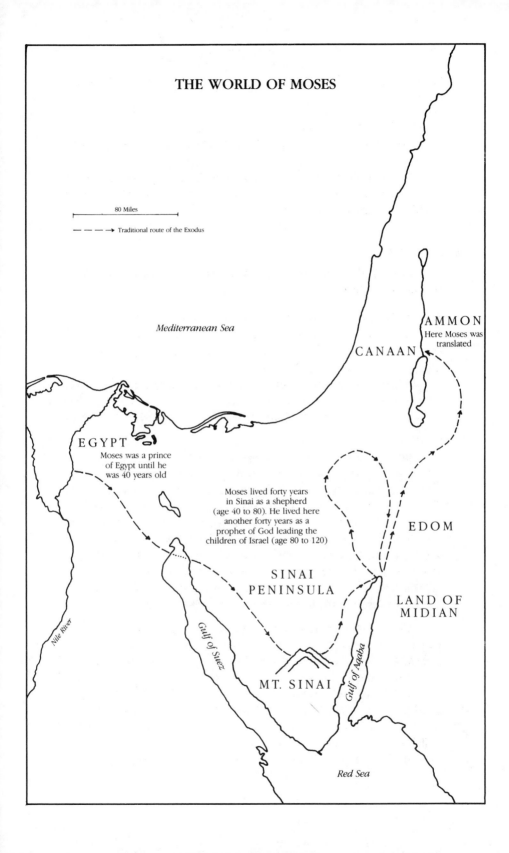

THE WORLD OF MOSES

80 Miles

— — — → Traditional route of the Exodus

Mediterranean Sea

AMMON
Here Moses was
translated

CANAAN

EGYPT
Moses was a prince
of Egypt until he
was 40 years old

Moses lived forty years
in Sinai as a shepherd
(age 40 to 80). He lived here
another forty years as a
prophet of God leading the
children of Israel (age 80 to 120)

EDOM

SINAI
PENINSULA

LAND OF
MIDIAN

Nile River

Gulf of Suez

Gulf of Aqaba

MT. SINAI

Red Sea

being a companionship." (Mark E. Petersen, *Moses, Man of Miracles*, p. 154.)

Selected Scripture References

"Bring forth my people the children of Israel out of Egypt." (Exodus 3:10.)

The children of Israel "should be brought out of bondage. Now ye know that Moses was commanded of the Lord to do that great work." (1 Nephi 17:25–26; see also v. 24.)

Moses 1:27

"Moses cast his eyes and beheld the earth . . . , discerning it by the spirit of God"

Selected Statements of the First Presidency and the Twelve Apostles

"How comforting it is to know that on judgment day we shall be treated fairly and justly and in the light of the total, true picture and the discernment of the Judge!

"A similar power of discernment and perception comes to men as they become perfect and the impediments which obstruct spiritual vision are dissolved." (Spencer W. Kimball, *Teachings of Spencer W. Kimball*, p. 156.)

"Before the Lord revealed to him the history of its creation Moses beheld every particle of the earth, and the account says there was not a particle that he did not behold, discerning it by the Spirit of God. One of the revelations says, that whatsoever is light is spirit, and there are degrees of this spiritual influence that will affect the natural or mortal eye; then there are other degrees more refined, perhaps, which do not affect the mortal eye, but will affect the immortal eye, yet the Lord would be able to touch the eyes of a man like unto Moses or any other man of God, so as to show him every particle of the earth, inside and outside." (Orson Pratt, in *Journal of Discourses*, 16:337.)

"You . . . who are acquainted with . . . 'The Pearl of Great Price'—a very precious book, because it contains many important ideas given by revelation—will recollect the revelation given to Moses. He inquired of God concerning the creation of this heaven and this earth, and obtained the information now contained in the Book of Genesis respecting the creation of the world. But before this he had a great vision in relation to the earth. . . . Now, this was a very extended vision. He saw something which you and I have never seen, unless we have had a similar vision. Only think of a man, here in a state of mortality, being permitted to look down into the earth, which is about eight thousand miles in diameter, and seeing not only large portions of its interior, but discerning every particle of it. There was not a particle of it that he did not behold, discerning it by the Spirit of God." (Orson Pratt, in *Journal of Discourses,* 16:362.)

Selected Scripture References

"By the power of the Spirit our eyes were opened and our understandings were enlightened, so as to see and understand the things of God." (D&C 76:12.)

"All spirit is matter, but it . . . can only be discerned by purer eyes." (D&C 131:7, see also v. 8.)

Moses 1:28

Moses beheld the inhabitants of the earth, and "he discerned them by the Spirit of God"

Other Commentary

Moses not only beheld the earth, discerning every particle of it, but also beheld all the inhabitants of the earth and even, it appears, discerned them as individuals. That is, he was able to perceive, as God does, the unique individuality of each of God's multitudinous children, comprehending their eternal souls.

Moses 1:29

Moses "beheld many lands; and each land was called earth, and there were inhabitants on the face thereof"

Selected Scripture References

There are many kingdoms throughout the universe. The Savior will visit the inhabitants in each kingdom at a designated time. (See D&C 88:45–61.)

The Lord has created "millions of earths," and he has "taken Zion" (or the righteous people) to his "own bosom, from all [his] creations." (Moses 7: 30–31.)

Other Commentary

Moses was given a panoramic view of the universe. Not only did he see many worlds, but he also saw and recorded that they were inhabited. The headnote to Moses 1, approved by the three members of the Quorum of the Twelve Apostles who were the Scriptures Publication

Committee, says, "Many inhabited worlds seen." The interpretation of Moses 1:29 in context with the next few verses (vv. 30–38) seems clear.

Moses 1:30

"Tell me . . . why these things are so, and by what thou madest them"

Other Commentary

Moses, after seeing the vastness of creation and the innumerable inhabitants of the various worlds, "called upon God, saying: Tell me, I pray thee, why these things are so, and by what thou madest them?" (Moses 1:30.) In other words, Moses was asking, "Why all of this? How was it done?" The Lord did not want to discourage his prophet from inquiring, since inquiry is the wellspring of learning, but to properly channel his inquiry, the Lord very briefly answered both questions: "For mine own purpose have I made these things. Here is wisdom and it remaineth in me. . . . For behold, this is my work and my glory—to bring to pass the immortality and eternal life of man." (Moses 1:33, 39.) The Lord wanted Moses to be aware of the eternal nature of the Creation, but he also wanted him to concentrate his time and talents on his own calling—that of being the prophet of God to the children of Israel.

Moses 1:31

"The glory of the Lord was upon Moses, so that Moses stood in the presence of God"

See Selected Statements and Scripture References under Moses 1:2.

Moses 1:32–33

Jesus Christ is the Creator and Redeemer of many worlds

Selected Statements of the First Presidency and the Twelve Apostles

"The Father operated in the work of creation through the Son, who thus became the executive through whom the will, commandment, or word of the Father was put into effect. It is with incisive appropriateness therefore, that the Son, Jesus Christ, is designated by the apostle John as the Word; or as declared by the Father 'the word of my power.' The part taken by Jesus Christ in the creation, a part so prominent as to justify our calling Him the Creator, is set forth in many scriptures. The author of the Epistle to the Hebrews refers in this wise distinctively to the Father and the Son as separate though associated Beings: 'God, who at sundry times and in diverse manners spake in time past unto the fathers by the prophets, hath in these last days spoken unto us by his Son, whom he hath appointed heir of all things, by whom also he made the worlds.' Paul is even more explicit in his letter to the Colossians, wherein, speaking of Jesus the Son, he says: 'For by him were all things created, that are in heaven, and that are in earth, visible and invisible, whether they be thrones, or dominions, or principalities, or powers: all things were created by him, and for him: and he is before all things, and by him all things consist.' And here let be repeated the testimony of John, that by the Word, who was with God, and who was God even in the beginning, all things were made; 'and without him was not any-thing made that was made.' (James E. Talmage, *Jesus the Christ*, pp. 33–34.)

"From this [Moses 1:30–33, 35, 38–39] and other scriptures we learn that, representing the Father and serving his purpose 'to bring to pass the immortality and eternal life of man,' Jesus Christ, in the sense of being its Creator and Redeemer, is the Lord of the whole universe. Except for his mortal ministry accomplished on this earth, his service and relationship to other worlds and their inhabitants are the same as his service and relationship to this earth and its inhabitants. . . .

". . . In short, Jesus Christ, through whom God created the universe, was chosen to put into operation throughout the universe Elohim's great plan, 'to bring to pass the immortality and eternal life of man'— the gospel of Jesus Christ—the only way whereby man can obtain eternal life." (Marion G. Romney, in *Improvement Era*, Nov. 1968, pp. 46, 48.)

> *And I heard a great voice, bearing record from heav'n,*
> *He's the Savior, and only begotten of God—*
> *By him, of him, and through him, the worlds were all made,*
> *Even all that career in the heavens so broad,*
>
> *Whose inhabitants, too, from the first to the last,*
> *Are sav'd by the very same Saviour of ours;*
> *And, of course, are begotten God's daughters and sons,*
> *By the very same truths, and the very same pow'rs.*

(Joseph Smith, poetic explanation of the vision [D&C 76], stanzas 19–20, in *Times and Seasons,* 4 [1 Feb. 1843]: 82–83.

"He [Jesus] has other worlds or creations and other sons and daughters, perhaps just as good as those dwelling on this planet, and they, as well as we, will be visited, and they will be made glad with the counte-

nance of their Lord." (Orson Pratt, in *Journal of Discourses*, 17:332.)
See also Joseph Fielding Smith, *Answers to Gospel Questions*, 3:211–12;
Spencer W. Kimball, in Conference Report, Apr. 1962, p. 61; Bruce R.
McConkie, *Promised Messiah*, p. 55.)

Selected Scripture References

"God . . . hath in these last days spoken unto us by his Son, . . . by
whom also he made the worlds." (Hebrews 1:1–2.)

"For by him [Jesus] were all things created, that are in heaven, and
that are in earth, visible and invisible, . . . and by him all things consist."
(Colossians 1:16–17.)

"He [Jesus] was in the world, and the world was made by him."
(John 1:10. See also vv. 1, 3, 14.)

"By him [Jesus], and through him, and of him, the worlds are and
were created, and the inhabitants thereof are begotten sons and daughters unto God." (D&C 76:24; see also vv. 22–23.)

Moses 1:33
"Worlds without number have I created"

Selected Scripture References

"There are many worlds that have passed away by the word of my
power. . . . and there is no end to my works, neither to my words."
(Moses 1:35, 38.)

Moses 1:34
"The first man of all men have I called Adam"

Selected Statements of the First Presidency and the Twelve Apostles

"I might enlarge the subject by connecting the family of Adam with
other branches of Christ's kingdom, and of the celestial family in other
planets and worlds, many of which are older and much larger than our
earth, but peopled by branches of the celestial family, who are of the
same kindred and race that we are: viz., the sons and daughters of God.

"I might also tell you of the continued exertions of creative power
by which millions of new worlds will yet be formed and peopled by
king Adam and his descendants, in the name, and by the authority of
Jesus Christ." (Parley P. Pratt, in *Millennial Star*, 5 [May 1845]: 191.)

" 'And the first man of all men have I called Adam,' the Lord says,
'which is many.' (Moses 1:34; 3:7; 6:45; Abra. 1:3; 1 Ne. 5:11; D&C

84:16.) That is, Adam was placed on earth as the first of the human family and given a name which signifies many as pertaining to the greatness of the posterity which should flow from him." (Bruce R. McConkie, *Mormon Doctrine*, p. 17. See also Joseph Smith, *Teachings of the Prophet Joseph Smith*, p. 167.)

" 'Adam fell that man might be.' (2 Nephi 2:25.) There were no pre-Adamic men in the line of Adam. The Lord said that Adam was the first man. (Moses 1:34, 3:7; D&C 84:16.) It is hard for me to get the idea of a man ahead of Adam, before the first man. The Lord also said that Adam was the first flesh (Moses 3:7) which, as I understand it, means the first mortal on the earth. I understand from a statement in the book of Moses, which was made by Enoch, that there was no death in the world before Adam. (Moses 6:48; see also 2 Nephi 2:22.) . . .

"I am not a scientist. I do not profess to know anything but Jesus Christ, and him crucified, and the principles of his gospel. If, however, there are some things in the strata of the earth indicating there were men before Adam, they were not the ancestors of Adam." (Marion G. Romney, in Conference Report, Apr. 1953, p. 123. See also "The Origin of Man," in James R. Clark, comp., *Messages of the First Presidency*, 4:200–206.)

Selected Scripture References

"The first man Adam was made a living soul." (1 Corinthians 15:45.)

The brass plates of Laban contained an account of "Adam and Eve, who were our first parents." (1 Nephi 5:11.)

"Adam, who was the first man," received the priesthood of God. (D&C 84:16.)

"Abraham received the same priesthood held by the first man, who is Adam, or first father." (Abraham 1:3.)

Moses 1:35

"There are many worlds that have passed away. . . . And there are many that now stand"

Selected Statements of the First Presidency and the Twelve Apostles

"To Moses, to Joseph Smith, and to others of the great prophets, came visions and revelations unbelievable, so clear, so distinct, so complete that it will yet be long, if ever, when, through observation and exploration only, men will gain the knowledge, for the prophets saw unbelievable things in kaleidoscopic vision. 'But only an account of this earth, and the inhabitants thereof, give I unto you,' said the Lord to

Moses. 'For behold, there are many worlds that have passed away by the word of my power and there are many that now stand, and innumerable are they unto man; but all things are numbered unto me, for they are mine and I know them.' (Moses 1:35.)" (Spencer W. Kimball, in Conference Report, Apr. 1962, pp. 61–62.)

"Our heavens are filled with eternal worlds that have attained their exaltation. They are not dying. They have passed through the stage of death and have become eternal, glorious bodies, the habitations of sons and daughters of God who likewise have attained to glory." (Joseph Fielding Smith, *Man: His Origin and Destiny*, pp. 28–29.)

"This passing away does not mean that earths grow old and die, becoming cold, lifeless bodies, wandering through space, perhaps to disintegrate, be broken up and in some unknown manner be recreated, by some natural force working on the energy in the universe. We have every reason to believe that the passing away of an earth simply means that it will undergo, or has undergone, the same definite course which is destined for our earth, and the Lord has made that perfectly clear. This earth is a living body. It is true to the law given it. It was created to become a celestial body and the abode for celestial beings." (Joseph Fielding Smith, *Doctrines of Salvation*, 1:72. See also Joseph Fielding Smith, *Man: His Origin and Destiny*, p. 391; Orson Pratt, *Masterful Discourses and Writings of Orson Pratt*, p. 71.)

Selected Scripture References

"As one earth shall pass away, and the heavens thereof even so shall another come." (Moses 1:38.)

Moses 1:37

"The heavens . . . cannot be numbered unto man; but they are numbered unto me"

Selected Statements of the First Presidency and the Twelve Apostles

"The scriptures postulate that worlds have gone out of existence through self-destruction, but other worlds have gone on unto perfection, and communication between the higher and the lower is not only possible but is an actuality. At the controlling center of the universe in such a perfected world is God. He knows all things that could possibly affect us, and because of his experience in his creation of us in his image, he is eager that we become like him—perfect. Accordingly, he has continued communication with us through the millennia. Without plane or rocket, messengers have come." (Spencer W. Kimball, *Faith Precedes the Miracle*, p. 54.)

Selected Scripture References

"No man can behold all my works." (Moses 1:5.)
"Worlds without number have I created." (Moses 1:33.)

Other Commentary

"It is natural for me to worship the Supreme Intelligence of the universe. This Supreme Intelligence necessarily exists since the world is full of unequally intelligent beings. Harlow Shapley estimates there are some 10^{20} suns having companion satellites analogous to our earth. Most of these satellites are at such distances from their suns that they are either too hot or too cold to support life as we know it. Still others lack life-giving water, while others lack the necessary oxygen. However, after guessing that at least one in every 10^{12} of these planets should be uninhabitable, Professor Shapley is left with at least 10^{8}, or 100,000,000 planets on which it is reasonable to suppose that life could and does exist. (Harlow Shapley, *Of Stars and Men*; Beacon Press, Beacon Hill, Boston, 1958; page 74 and following.)

"It is accordingly natural to conclude that the universe is flooded with intelligent beings and, presumably, always has been. Any unfolding of intelligences that may eventuate on this earth only repeats what has happened previously elsewhere. The biblical account of an all-wise Providence shaping human destiny is a natural expectation for me, and this belief is shared by a large fraction of mankind." (Henry Eyring, *Faith of a Scientist*, p. 97.)

Moses 1:39

"For behold, this is my work and my glory—to bring to pass the immortality and eternal life of man"

Selected Statements of the First Presidency and the Twelve Apostles

"The whole object of the creation of this world is to exalt the intelligences that are placed upon it, that they may live, endure, and increase for ever and ever. We are not here to quarrel and contend about the things of this world, but we are here to subdue and beautify it. Let every man and woman worship their God with all their heart." (Brigham Young, *Discourses of Brigham Young*, pp. 87–88.)

"Mortal life is a probationary state where we are to be tried, proved, as gold is tried in the crucible, to see if we will keep all of the commandments of God. If we pass through this probation successfully we will be entitled to eternal life, if we fail we will be given immortality. Eternal life is to have the same kind of life, with its glory, that God possesses; immortality is to have the blessing of living forever, after the resurrection of the dead, but not with the same glory and blessings which are held in store for those who are just and true. We learn from these teachings given to Moses that Man is the greatest of all the creations— for he is the offspring of God." (Joseph Fielding Smith, *Man: His Origin and Destiny*, p. 272.)

"The Lord Almighty never created a world like this and peopled it for 6,000 years, as he has done, without having some motive in view. That motive was, that we might come here and exercise our agency. The probation we are called upon to pass through, is intended to elevate us so that we can dwell in the presence of God our Father." (Wilford Woodruff, in *Journal of Discourses*, 25:9.)

"God's plan, God's purpose, is the perfection of humanity." (David O. McKay, in Conference Report, Apr. 1968, p. 92. See also Marion G. Romney, in Conference Report, Apr. 1975, p. 125.)

"What would a loving Father want for his children? What would any father want for his children? Peace and health and happiness; learning and progress and improvement; and everlasting life, and everlasting assocation with those we love. What less could heaven be? What less would a Father plan or propose, for those he loves, for those whom he made 'in his own image'? (Genesis 1:27.) He has declared his work and his glory 'to bring to pass the immortality and eternal life of man.' (Pearl of Great Price, Moses 1:39.) This is the ultimate objective. This is the whole purpose of the Gospel he has given." (Richard L. Evans, in Conference Report, Oct. 1959, p. 127.)

"Here, then, is eternal life—to know the only wise and true God; and you have got to learn how to be Gods yourselves, and to be kings and priests to God, the same as all Gods have done before you, namely, by going from one small degree to another, and from a small capacity to a great one; from grace to grace, from exaltation to exaltation, until you attain to the resurrection of the dead, and are able to dwell in everlasting burnings, and to sit in glory, as do those who sit enthroned in everlasting power." (Joseph Smith, *Teachings of the Prophet Joseph Smith*, pp. 346–47. See also Gordon B. Hinckley, in *Ensign*, Nov. 1986, pp. 49–50; LeGrand Richards, in *Ensign*, Nov. 1981, p. 27.)

Selected Scripture References

"God bringeth about his great and eternal purposes, which were prepared from the foundation of the world." (Alma 42:26.)

"By his natural death he might be raised in immortality unto eternal life." (D&C 29:43.)

Moses 1:41
"I will raise up another like unto thee"

Selected Statements of the First Presidency and the Twelve Apostles

"In modern revelation the President of the Church is frequently compared to Moses. Soon after the organization of the Church, the Lord said, 'No one shall be appointed to receive commandments and revelations in this church excepting my servant Joseph Smith, Jun., for he receiveth them even as Moses' (D&C 28:2). In one of the great revelations upon Priesthood, this is more specifically expressed: 'the duty of the President of the office of the High Priesthood is to preside over the whole church, and to be like unto Moses' (D&C 107:91).

"The discussion of this question among the Saints, led to the following statement in the *Times and Seasons* (6:922) by John Taylor, then the editor: 'The President [of the Church] stands in the Church as Moses did to the children of Israel, according to the revelations.'

"The man like unto Moses in the Church is the President of the Church." (John A. Widtsoe, *Evidences and Reconciliations*, 1:197. See also Joseph Fielding Smith, *Doctrines of Salvation*, 3:187.)

Selected Scripture References

"These last records . . . shall establish the truth of the first [Bible], . . . and shall make known the plain and precious things which have been taken away from them." (1 Nephi 13:40.)

"Other records have I, that I will give unto you." (D&C 9:2.)

Joseph Smith received "commandments and revelations . . . even as Moses." (D&C 28:2.)

"I will raise up unto my people a man, who shall lead them like as Moses." (D&C 103:16.)

"The duty of the President . . . is to preside over the whole church, and to be like unto Moses." (D&C 107:91.)

Other Commentary

"I bear my testimony that the Prophet Joseph Smith is one of the greatest (if not the greatest) of the prophets, seers, and revelators that the world has known. A study and evaluation of the prophecies he made, the visions and revelations he had, the scriptures he produced, and his numerous mighty works and marvelous accomplishments force this conclusion upon the honest investigator. Joseph Smith shall stand always as superior among God's elect—the noble and great ones whom he selected to be his rulers. Joseph was indeed a prophet, seer, and revelator 'great like unto Moses.' " (Milton R. Hunter, in Conference Report, Oct. 1968, p. 37.)

Moses 1:41

"The children of men shall esteem my [God's] words as naught and take many of them from the book which thou [Moses] shalt write"

Selected Statements of the First Presidency and the Twelve Apostles

"God alone can add to or diminish from holy writ. What he has spoken, he has spoken, and none but he can alter. When a prophet speaks by the power of the Holy Ghost, it is the voice of God; and none can change it without suffering the penalty prescribed for perverting the pronouncements of Deity." (Bruce R. McConkie, *Doctrinal New Testament Commentary*, 3:593.)

Selected Scripture References

"Ye shall not add unto the work which I command you, neither shall ye diminish ought from it." (Deuteronomy 4:2.)

"If any man shall add unto these things, God shall add unto him the plagues . . . and if any man shall take away from the words of the book of this prophecy, God shall take away his part out of the book of life." (Revelation 22:18–19.)

"They have taken away from the gospel of the Lamb many parts which are plain and most precious." (1 Nephi 13:26.)

"These last records . . . shall establish the truth of the first, which are of the twelve apostles of the Lamb, and shall make known the plain and precious things which have been taken away from them." (1 Nephi 13:4.)

Moses 2

Moses 2:1

"By mine Only Begotten . . . I created the heaven, and the earth"

Selected Statements of the First Presidency and the Twelve Apostles

"You ask the learned doctors why they say the world was made out of nothing; and they will answer, 'Doesn't the Bible say He created the world?' And they infer, from the word create, that it must have been made out of nothing. Now, the word create came from the word *baurau*, which does not mean to create out of nothing; it means to organize; the same as a man would organize materials and build a ship. Hence, we infer that God had materials to organize the world out of chaos—chaotic matter, which is element, and in which dwells all the glory." (Joseph Smith, *Teachings of the Prophet Joseph Smith*, pp. 350-51. See also Joseph F. Smith, in James R. Clark, comp., *Messages of the First Presidency*, 4:329.)

"It must be very difficult to reach out into the great universe and bring to one's self the priesthood, which is the power to create, and . . . to make something out of nothing. Of course, we do not do that. We take one element, and we transform it and organize it into another. . . . You look out there in the starry night and you see the sky is filled with stars. There are in the universe numerous bits or quantities of materials—gases and other elements—which brought together in the proper way can create an earth and can eventually produce fruit trees, and grain fields, and forests." (Spencer W. Kimball, *Teachings of Spencer W. Kimball*, p. 53.)

"Latter-day Saints believe that the Lord formed or organized the earth from existing universal materials. That it is impossible to create something from nothing is a spiritual as well as a scientific axiom. It is an established doctrine of the Church that the ultimate elements which constitute the universe are eternal, indestructible, everlasting. Whether these ultimate realities be, in the language of present-day science, molecules, atoms, electrons, or pure energy is of little concern. Whatever is the ultimate reality is eternal. Matter as we know it, and which forms the earth, is made from eternal elements. In that sense the formation of the earth was an organization rather than a creation." (John A. Widtsoe, *Evidences and Reconciliations*, 1:140. See also Charles W. Penrose, *"Mormon" Doctrine, Plain and Simple*, pp. 10, 12.)

"Our knowledge about the Creation is limited. We do not know the how and why and when of all things. Our finite limitations are such that we could not comprehend them if they were revealed to us in all their glory, fulness, and perfection. What has been revealed is that portion of the Lord's eternal word which we must believe and understand if we are to envision the truth about the Fall and the Atonement and thus become heirs of salvation. This is all we are obligated to know in our day.

"In a future day the Lord will expect more of his Saints in this regard than he does of us. 'When the Lord shall come, he shall reveal all things,' our latter-day revelations tell us—'Things which have passed, and hidden things which no man knew, things of the earth, by which it was made, and the purpose and the end thereof.' (D&C 101:32-33.) Pending that Millennial day it is our responsibility to believe and accept that portion of the truth about the Creation that has been dispensed to us in our dispensation." (Bruce R. McConkie, in *Ensign*, June 1982, p. 10. See also Parley P. Pratt, *Key to the Science of Theology*, p. 29; Brigham Young, in *Journal of Discourses*, 7:2-3.)

"Man is . . . the offspring of God, and he will, if he is obedient to eternal divine law, become a son of God and possess the powers by which earths are created." (Joseph Fielding Smith, *Man: His Origin and Destiny*, p. 28.)

Selected Scripture References

"By him, and through him, and of him, the worlds are and were created." (D&C 76:24.)

"The elements are eternal." (D&C 93:33.)

"All spirit is matter." (D&C 131:8.)

"Worlds without number have I created; ... by the Son I created them." (Moses 1:33.)

Moses 2:1

"In the beginning" (time)

Selected Statements of the First Presidency and the Twelve Apostles

"Any question as to when that beginning was is largely futile because unanswerable. In the first place we have no time unit by which to measure back through the ages to the time when at which, so far as the earth began, time began." (James E. Talmage, *Earth and Man*, p. 1.)

"The information given in the scriptures on the time involved in the first great acts of creation, refers only to the spiritual creation. President Joseph Fielding Smith tells us: 'Life did not commence upon this earth, life existed long before our solar system was called into being.' (Vol. 1.) Dr. John A. Widtsoe made this statement: 'It seems reasonable to suppose that the great acts of creation could well have continued through eons of time.' In fact, it is doubtful if man can measure, according to man's methods of measurements, the time involved, and Dr. Talmage said that the earth passed through ages of preparation, unmeasured and immeasurable." (Hugh B. Brown, *What Is Man and What He May Become*, Brigham Young University Speeches of the Year [Provo, 25 Mar. 1958], pp. 5–6.)

"In these two creations that took place in the beginning, represented as the beginning of this creation—not absolutely the beginning of all the creations of God; for his works are without beginning, and without end, they never cease, nor does his word cease; he speaks to us, so far as this creation is concerned, according to our natural ideas and understanding." (Orson Pratt, *Masterful Discourses of Orson Pratt*, p. 70.)

"How old is the earth?

"This is an ancient question which has occasioned much controversy. There are at least three prevailing answers among faithful Bible-believing Latter-day Saints. The fact appears to be that no man knows the age of the earth.

"The first group believe that the earth was created in six days of twenty-four hours each. That is, the earth was six days old at the coming of Adam. This view is based upon the literal acceptance of the story of the creation as given in King James' translation of Genesis (Genesis, chapter 1; Exodus 20:11). . . .

"The second group hold that each day of creation was really one thousand years, and that the earth therefore was six thousand years old at the coming of Adam. Those who uphold this view quote as their support the statement of the Apostle Peter, 'one day is with the Lord as a thousand years, and a thousand years as one day' (2 Peter, 3:8). . . .

"The third group believe that the creation of the earth extended over immensely long periods of time, not yet correctly known by revelation or by man's scientific advance, and that the earth therefore is very old. . . .

"Every person must decide for himself, on the basis of the evidence produced, which of these three opinions as to the age of the earth, before Adam, seems most reasonable to him, whether (1) six days, or (2) six thousand years, or (3) many millions of years. Clearly it does not matter to one's daily welfare or ultimate salvation which view he adopts, except that every Latter-day Saint must seek and cherish truth above all else." (John A. Widtsoe, *Evidences and Reconciliations*, pp. 134–35, 138.)

"The adaptation of a thousand years to one day of celestial time is inapplicable to the years of all other planetary bodies of our system. Among the great variety of celestial kingdoms or glorified worlds, there may be many methods of measuring celestial time. There can be no doubt that each planet has its set time of creation, its set time of temporal continuance, and its set time of the period of rest." (Orson Pratt, *Masterful Discourses of Orson Pratt*, p. 81.)

Selected Scripture References

"All is as one day with God, and time only is measured unto men." (Alma 40:8.)

"All these are one year with God, but not with man." (D&C 88:44.)

Other Commentary

Genesis 1:1 in the King James Bible reads, "In the beginning God created the heaven and the earth." Because the book of Moses records the revelation that gives a context to the story of the Creation, the information in Genesis 1 corresponds to the information in Moses 2 in the Pearl of Great Price.

Moses 2:2

"The earth was without form, and void"

Selected Statements of the First Presidency and the Twelve Apostles

"In the translation 'without form and void' it should be read, empty and desolate. The word created should be formed, or organized." (Joseph Smith, *Teachings of the Prophet Joseph Smith*, p. 181.)

Selected Scripture References

"They, that is the Gods, organized and formed the heavens and the earth. And the earth, after it was formed, was empty and desolate." (Abraham 4:1–2.)

Moses 2:2

"I caused darkness to come up upon the face of the deep"

Selected Statements of the First Presidency and the Twelve Apostles

"It would seem, that light had been shining previous to this time. The universe, probably was lighted up, so far as it existed, and that light shone forth over the face of this embryo creation. Where that light came from or how it was produced is not mentioned; but the Lord was obliged to create darkness in order to envelop the earth therein. There are many ways in which this might have been accomplished. The sun was not permitted to shine forth on the first, second, or third day of creation, but on the fourth day it was permitted to give its light to the earth. Whether the sun shone upon the face of this creation, before the Lord created darkness, is not for me to say. If it did, it would be an easy matter for him to withhold the rays of that bright luminary in such a manner as seemed good in his sight, the same as he did among the ancient Nephites who dwelt on this continent at the time of the crucifixion. . . . The Lord had some method by which he created or produced that darkness by shading the earth from the rays of the sun; but by and by he said, 'Let there be light,' and light was again restored." (Orson Pratt, in *Journal of Discourses*, 16:314–15.)

Moses 2:2

"My Spirit moved upon the face of the water"

See Selected Statements under Abraham 4:2.

Moses 2:3

"And I, God, said: Let there be light"

Selected Statements of the First Presidency and the Twelve Apostles

"The Lord of earth, air, and sea spoke and was obeyed. He it was who, amidst the black chaos of creation's earliest stages, had commanded with immediate effect—Let there be light . . . and, as He had decreed, so it was. . . . His word of command is but a sound-wave in air, except as it is followed by labor. Through the Spirit that emanates from the very Person of Deity, and which pervades all space, the command of God is immediately operative." (James E. Talmage, *Jesus the Christ*, p. 309.)

"When he says—'I created darkness and I created light,' what does he do? Does he absolutely form light out of nothing? No, he causes the light that existed from all eternity to shine where darkness existed, and it is light creating light, the same as you, when you attend meeting, lock up your house and blow out the lights. When you return, supposing you say in your own heart, or to your wife, daughter, or son, 'Let there be light.' Do you create it out of nothing? No, you look for a match, or for some means by which you can start the light and cause it to be exhibited, where darkness was before. So when God creates light he calls forth and makes to shine that light which has existed from all eternity." (Orson Pratt, in *Journal of Discourses*, 16: 315–16.)

"They next caused light to shine upon it before the sun appeared in the firmament; for God is light, and in him there is no darkness. He is the light of the sun and the power thereof by which it was made; he is also the light of the moon and the power by which it was made; he is the light of the stars and the power by which they were made. He says it is the same light that enlightens the understanding of men. What, have we a mental light and a visual light, all proceeding from the same source? Yes, so says the scripture, and so says science when rightly comprehended." (John Taylor, in *Journal of Discourses*, 18:327.)

"The First Day—Elohim, Jehovah, Michael, a host of noble and great ones—all these played their parts. 'The Gods' created the atmospheric heavens and the temporal earth. It was 'without form, and void'; as yet it could serve no useful purpose with respect to the salvation of man. It was 'empty and desolate'; life could not yet exist on its surface; it was not yet a fit abiding place for those sons of God who shouted for joy at the prospect of a mortal probation. The 'waters' of the great 'deep' were present, and 'darkness reigned' until the divine decree: 'Let there be light.' The light and the darkness were then 'divided,' the one being called 'Day' and the other 'Night.' Clearly our planet was thus formed as a revolving orb and placed in its relationship to our sun. (See Moses 2:1-5; Abr. 4:1-5.)" (Bruce R. McConkie, in *Ensign,* June 1982, p. 11.)

Selected Scripture References

The light of Christ is the light of the sun, the moon, the stars, and the earth also, and is the power thereof by which they were made. (See D&C 88:7-10.)

"The light which shineth, which giveth you light, is through him who enlighteneth your eyes." (D&C 88:11.)

Moses 2:5
"The evening and the morning were the first day"

Selected Statements of the First Presidency and the Twelve Apostles

"Now these two states of being in which our earth existed are called first, the evening, and second, the morning—and the evening and the morning were the first day. Whether the day here mentioned was a period such as the one to which we now apply that term, we are not informed in the Bible, but from what has been revealed to the Latter-day Saints we have great reason to believe that it was a very long period of time, and that this darkness existed over the face of the great deep for a long time. It might have been for many centuries, we have no definite information on this point." (Orson Pratt, in *Journal of Discourses,* 16:315.)

Moses 2:6
"Let there be a firmament"

Selected Statements of the First Presidency and the Twelve Apostles

"The waters above the firmament is a reference to the clouds and the waters which exist in the atmosphere above the earth.

"The meaning of the 'firmament' as we find it in Genesis, chapter two, verse eight as given in the *Standard Dictionary*, is 'The expanse of heaven; the sky.' The word 'firmament' according to its original meaning connotes something compact, solid, or firm. . . .

"Dr. D. E. E. Hart-Davies, in an article published in the *Journal of Transactions* (Victoria Institute) in discussing this question has this to say:

" ' . . . The R. V. rendering is "expanse" which is correct. The Hebrew is a strictly accurate term. The word, "firmament" is a mistranslation due to the false astronomy of Alexandria in the third century B.C.' " (Joseph Fielding Smith, *Answers to Gospel Questions*, 4:116–17.)

"The Second Day—On this day 'the waters' were 'divided' between the surface of the earth and the atmospheric heavens that surround it. A 'firmament' or an 'expanse' called 'Heaven' was created to divide 'the waters which were under the expanse from the waters which were above the expanse.' Thus, as the creative events unfold, provision seems to be made for clouds and rain and storms to give life to that which will yet grow and dwell upon the earth. (See Moses 2:6–8; Abraham 4: 6–8.)" (Bruce R. McConkie, in *Ensign*, June 1982, p. 11.)

Moses 2:9

"Let the waters under the heaven be gathered together unto one place; . . . Let there be dry land"

Selected Statements of the First Presidency and the Twelve Apostles

"All the water was brought together in one place. That means the land was in one place, does it not, and you did not have a variety of islands and continents." (Joseph Fielding Smith, *Signs of the Times,* p. 23.)

"In the morning of our creation the gathering together of the particles was accomplished under such regular, harmonious and systematic laws, that there were no elevations of the land above the water. All the successive strata seemed to have arranged themselves in a perfect spheroidal form, conforming to the laws of gravity and rotation, as if they had been a fluid substance. . . .

"But soon the commandment came for the waters to be gathered together into one place, and for the dry or solid land to appear. . . .

"From the revelations which God has given, there is no doubt but there has been a most wonderful change. By them we learn that the Eastern and Western Continents were one; whilst the waters occupied the polar regions of our globe." (Orson Pratt, in *Seer*, Apr. 1854, pp. 249–50. See also Bruce R. McConkie, *Millennial Messiah*, pp. 622–23.)

"The Third Day—This is the day when life began. In it 'the waters under the heaven' were 'gathered together unto one place,' and the 'dry land' appeared. The dry land was called 'Earth,' and the assembled waters became 'the Sea.' " (Bruce R. McConkie, in *Ensign*, June 1982, pp. 11–12.)

Moses 2:11

"The herb yielding seed, the fruit tree yielding fruit, after his kind"

Selected Statements of the First Presidency and the Twelve Apostles

"Having in mind the coming fall and consequent entrance of death and mortality into the world, the Lord in that first primeval day commanded that all forms of life, after mortality entered the picture, should bring forth posterity, each after his own kind. (Moses 2:3.) These principles accord with the one announced by Paul that 'All flesh is not the same flesh: but there is one kind of flesh of men, another of beasts, another of fishes, and another of birds.' (1 Cor. 15:39.)" (Bruce R. McConkie, *Mormon Doctrine*, pp. 252–53.)

"He commanded them to reproduce themselves. They too would bring forth only 'after their kind.' It could be in no other way. Each form of life was destined to bring forth after its own kind so that it would be perpetuated in the earth and avoid confusion.

"Man was always man, and always will be, for we are the offspring of God. The fact that we know of our own form and image and the further fact that we are God's offspring give us positive knowledge of the form and image of God, after whom we are made and of whom we are born as his children." (Mark E. Petersen, *Moses, Man of Miracles*, pp. 162–63.)

Moses 2:14

"Let there be lights in the firmament of the heaven"

Selected Statements of the First Presidency and the Twelve Apostles

"The Fourth Day—After seeds in all their varieties had been planted on the earth; after these had sprouted and grown; after each variety was prepared to bring forth fruit and seed after its own kind—the Creators organized all things in such a way as to make their earthly garden a productive and beautiful place. They then 'organized the lights in the expanse of the heaven' so there would be 'seasons' and a way of measuring 'days' and 'years.' We have no way of knowing what changes then took place in either the atmospheric or the sidereal heavens, but during this period the sun, moon, and stars assumed the relationship to the earth that now is theirs. At least the light of each of them began to shine through the lifting hazes that enshrouded the newly created earth so they could play their parts with reference to life in all its forms as it soon would be upon the new orb. (See Moses 2:14–19; Abraham 4:14–19.)" (Bruce R. McConkie, in *Ensign,* June 1982, p. 12.)

Selected Scripture References

"He appointed the moon for seasons: the sun knoweth his going down." (Psalm 104:19.)

The light of Christ is the light of the sun, the moon, the stars, and the earth also, and is the power thereof by which they were made. (See D&C 88:7–10.)

Moses 2:20–23

The creatures of the water and the fowls of the air were brought forth

Selected Statements of the First Presidency and the Twelve Apostles

"The Fifth Day—Next came fish and fowl and 'every living creature' whose abode is 'the waters.' Their Creators placed them on the newly organized earth, and they were given the command: 'Be fruitful, and multiply, and fill the waters in the sea; and let fowl multiply in the earth.' This command—as with a similar decree given to man and applicable to all animal life—they could not then keep, but they soon would be able to do so. Appended to this command to multiply was the heaven-sent restriction that the creatures in the waters could only bring forth 'after their kind,' and that 'every winged fowl' could only bring forth 'after his kind.' There was no provision for evolvement or change from one species to another. (See Moses 2:20–23; Abraham 4:20–23.)" (Bruce R. McConkie, in *Ensign*, June 1982, p. 12.)

Moses 2:24–25

The animals that live on land were placed upon the earth

Selected Statements of the First Presidency and the Twelve Apostles

"By His almighty power He organized the earth, and all that it contains, from spirit and element, which exist co-eternally with Himself. He formed every plant that grows, and every animal that breathes, each after its own kind, spiritually and temporally—'that which is spiritual being in the likeness of that which is temporal, and that which is temporal in the likeness of that which is spiritual.' [D&C 77:2.] He made the tadpole and the ape, the lion and the elephant but He did not make them in His own image, nor endow them with Godlike reason and intelligence. Nevertheless, the whole animal creation will be perfected and perpetuated in the Hereafter, each class in its 'distinct order or sphere,' and will enjoy 'eternal felicity.' That fact has been made plain in this dispensation. (Doctrine & Covenants 77:3)." (The First Presidency: Joseph F. Smith, John R. Winder, and Anthon H. Lund, in James R. Clark, comp., *Messages of the First Presidency*, 4:206.)

"The Sixth Day—The crowning day of creation is at hand. In its early hours, the great Creators 'made the beasts of the earth after their kind, and cattle after their kind, and everything which creepeth upon the earth after his kind.' And the same procreative restrictions applied to them that apply to all forms of life; they too are to reproduce only after their kind." (Bruce R. McConkie, in *Ensign*, June 1982, p. 12.)

Moses 2:26

"And I, God, said unto mine Only Begotten . . . : Let us make man in our image"

Selected Statements of the First Presidency and the Twelve Apostles

"The Father of Jesus is our Father also. Jesus Himself taught this truth, when He instructed His disciples how to pray: 'Our Father which art in heaven,' etc. Jesus, however, is the firstborn among all the sons of God—the first begotten in the spirit, and the only begotten in the flesh. He is our elder brother, and we, like Him, are in the image of God. All men and women are in the similitude of the universal Father and Mother, and are literally the sons and daughters of Deity." (The First Presidency: Joseph F. Smith, John R. Winder, and Anthon H. Lund, in James R. Clark, comp., *Messages of the First Presidency*, 4:203.)

"The Church of Jesus Christ of Latter-day Saints, basing its belief on divine revelation, ancient and modern, proclaims man to be the direct and lineal offspring of Deity. . . .

"Man is the child of God, formed in the divine image and endowed with divine attributes, and even as the infant son of an earthly father and mother is capable in due time of becoming a man, so that undeveloped offspring of celestial parentage is capable, by experience through ages and aeons, of evolving into a God." (The First Presidency: Heber J. Grant, Anthony W. Ivins, and Charles W. Nibley, in James R. Clark, comp., *Messages of the First Presidency*, 5:243–44.)

"If God made man in the likeness of God then he is like God and God is like man." (Joseph F. Smith, in James R. Clark, comp., *Messages of the First Presidency*, 4:328. See also Wilford Woodruff, in *Journal of Discourses*, 18:32; John Taylor, *Mediation and Atonement*, p. 160;

Brigham Young, in *Journal of Discourses*, 13:146; Charles W. Penrose, *"Mormon Doctrine," Plain and Simple*, pp. 11–12; James E. Talmage, *Articles of Faith*, p. 528.)

"God made man in his own image and certainly he made woman in the image of his wife-partner." (Spencer W. Kimball, *Teachings of Spencer W. Kimball*, p. 25.)

" 'And I, God said unto mine Only Begotten, which was with me from the beginning: Let us make man [not a separate man, but a complete man, which is husband and wife] in our image, after our likeness; and it was so.' (Moses 2:26.) What a beautiful partnership! Adam and Eve were married for eternity by the Lord. Such a marriage extends beyond the grave." (Spencer W. Kimball, in *Ensign*, Mar. 1976, p. 71.)

"In the account of the creation of the earth, 'God said, Let us make man in our image, after our likeness' (Genesis 1:26).

"Could any language be more explicit? Does it demean God, as some would have us believe, that man was created in His express image? Rather, it should stir within the heart of every man and woman a greater appreciation for himself or herself as a son or daughter of God." (Gordon B. Hinckley, in Conference Report, Oct. 1986, p. 65. See also Bruce R. McConkie, *New Witness for the Articles of Faith*, p. 63.)

"One of the most vital facts in the entire creation story is the account of the formation of man. When God spoke of making man in his image he spoke of *mankind*—male and female, not just of an isolated person or even a single couple as Adam and Eve. He thereby provided mortal life for us all." (Mark E. Petersen, *Moses, Man of Miracles*, p. 162.)

Moses 2:26
"Let them have dominion over . . . all the earth"

Selected Statements of the First Presidency and the Twelve Apostles

"All the creations are his work, and they are for his glory and for the benefit of the children of men; and all things are put into the possession of man for his comfort, improvement and consolation, and for his health, wealth, beauty and excellency." (Brigham Young, *Discourses of Brigham Young*, p. 27.)

"Now, this mortal life is the time to prepare to meet God, which is our first responsibility. Having already obtained our bodies, which become the permanent tabernacle for our spirits through the eternities, now we are to train our bodies, our minds, and our spirits. Preeminent, then, is our using this life to perfect ourselves, to subjugate the flesh, subject the body to the spirit, to overcome all weaknesses, to govern self so that one may give leadership to others, and to perform all necessary ordinances. Secondly comes the preparation for the subduing of the earth and the elements. . . .

"To subdue self is not only the more important but the more difficult. Many men have power over certain natural forces who cannot control their own desires, urges, passions." (Spencer W. Kimball, *Teachings of Spencer W. Kimball*, pp. 31–32.)

"The dominion of the Creator over the created is real and absolute. A small part of that dominion has been committed to man [Genesis 1:28; Moses 2:26; 5:1] as the offspring of God, tabernacled in the very image of his divine Father. But man exercises that delegated control through secondary agencies, and by means of complicated mechanism. Man's power over the objects of his own devising is limited. . . .

" . . . But the earth shall yet be 'renewed and receive its paradisiacal glory'; then soil, water, air, and the forces acting upon them, shall directly respond to the command of glorified man, as now they obey the word of the Creator." (James E. Talmage, *Jesus the Christ*, pp. 309–10.)

Selected Scripture References

"All things which come of the earth . . . are made for the benefit and the use of man . . . for food and for raiment, for taste and for smell, to strengthen the body and to enliven the soul." (D&C 59:18–19.)

Moses 2:28
"Be fruitful, and multiply, and replenish the earth"

Selected Statements of the First Presidency and the Twelve Apostles

"The Lord has told us that it is the duty of every husband and wife to obey the command given to Adam to multiply and replenish the earth, so that the legions of choice spirits waiting for their tabernacles of flesh may come here and move forward under God's great design to become perfect souls, for without these fleshly tabernacles they cannot progress to their God-planned destiny. Thus, every husband and wife should become a father and a mother in Israel to children born under the holy, eternal covenant." (The First Presidency: Heber J. Grant, J. Reuben Clark, Jr., and David O. McKay, in James R. Clark, comp., *Messages of the First Presidency*, 6:177.)

"It is true that the original meaning of the word *replenish* connotes something is being filled again that was once filled before: *Re*-again, *plenus*-full. Why the translators of the King James Version of the Bible used the word *replenish* may not be clearly known, but it is not the word used in other translations and is not the correct meaning of the Hebrew word from which the translation was originally taken. It is true that the Prophet Joseph Smith followed the King James Version in the use of this word, perhaps because it had obtained common usage among the English-speaking peoples. *Replenish*, however, is incorrectly used in the King James translation. The Hebrew verb is Mole . . . meaning fill, to fill, or make full." (Joseph Fielding Smith, *Answers to Gospel Questions*, 1:208. See also Bruce R. McConkie, *Promised Messiah*, pp. 220–21.)

Selected Scripture References

"God himself that formed the earth and made it; . . . he formed it to be inhabited." (Isaiah 45:18.)

"The Lord hath created the earth that it should be inhabited." (1 Nephi 17:36.)

Moses 2:29
"To you it [the herb and the fruit] shall be for meat"

Selected Statements of the First Presidency and the Twelve Apostles

"There is no statement in the scriptures indicating that the flesh of animals and birds and other living creatures was used as food before the days of Noah. It was after the landing of the ark that the Lord gave his commandment concerning the eating of flesh." (Joseph Fielding Smith, *Answers to Gospel Questions*, 4:42.)

"Instead of our first parents eating animal food, they subsisted upon herbs and the fruits of the earth, which were originally designed for the food of man." (Orson Pratt, in *Times and Seasons*, 6 [1 June 1845]: 918.)

Moses 2:31
"All things which I had made were very good"

Selected Statements of the First Presidency and the Twelve Apostles

"In the morning of creation all things were pronounced good by the Creator, as they rolled into organized existence unsullied and without a curse." (Orson Pratt, in *Times and Seasons*, 6 [1 June 1845]: 918.)

"When the earth was created, the Lord pronounced it good. Everything on its face was created without the seeds of death and could have endured forever. This is taught, among other places, in 2 Nephi 2:22. Death had not entered the world, and Adam was immortal in the sense that he was not subject to death. However, he had not passed through the resurrection, and, therefore, he was in a condition by which he could fall so that his body would become subject to death or mortality. This happened and this condition then passed upon the earth and all creatures living upon it." (Joseph Fielding Smith, *Doctrines of Salvation*, 1:82.)

"In that Edenic day, the earth and all life were pronounced very good by the Creator. There was no disease or evil or death. Life was destined to go on forever. The lion ate straw like the ox, and the wolf and the lamb were friends. Light and life and peace and immortality reigned in every department of creation. Such was life on the Edenic earth, on the temporal earth that had been created in a paradisiacal state. The earth was in a terrestrial state; it was temporal and earthy, and neither a spiritual nor celestial." (Bruce R. McConkie, *New Witness for the Articles of Faith*, p. 648. See also Joseph F. Smith, *Gospel Doctrine*, p. 21.)

" 'Tell the brethren if they will follow the Spirit of the Lord, they will go right. Be sure to tell the brethren to keep the Spirit of the Lord; and if they will, they will find themselves just as they were organized by our Father in Heaven before they came into the world. Our Father in Heaven organized the human family, but they are all disorganized and in great confusion.' " (Joseph Smith, as quoted by Marion G. Romney, in Conference Report, Apr. 1944, p. 141.)

Selected Scripture References

"All things which are good cometh of God; and that which is evil cometh of the devil." (Moroni 7:12.)

Other Commentary

There is no consensus among writers on the Creation. The subject becomes even more confusing when we realize that a spirit creation preceded the gross matter creation. Elder Bruce R. McConkie explained:

"Mankind's knowledge of the creation of the heavens and the earth, and of life in all its forms and varieties, comes by revelation from the Creator himself. The Lord has revealed only that portion of eternal truth relative to the creation of all things that finite minds are capable of understanding. He has given man only what he needs to know to comprehend the true doctrine of the fall, and thus to gain that salvation which comes because of the fall." (*New Witness for the Articles of Faith,* p. 82.)

There are many more questions than answers about the Creation. For example, Was man placed on the earth on the sixth or the seventh day? (See Moses 2:27; Abraham 5:7.) Was Eve placed on the earth before or after the animals? (See Moses 3:19–23; Abraham 5:14–21.) How long did the creation of the earth take? If Adam and Eve are the primal parents of the human race, how do we explain the evidences of so-called prehistoric man? If there was no death before the Fall, how do we explain the ancient fossilized animals that have been discovered?

The Doctrine and Covenants gives us this answer:

"Yea, verily I say unto you, in that day when the Lord shall come, he shall reveal all things—things which have passed, and hidden things which no man knew, things of the earth, by which it was made, and the purpose and the end thereof—things most precious, things that are above, and things that are beneath, things that are in the earth, and upon the earth, and in heaven." (D&C 101:32–34.)

We conclude from this passage of scripture that there will be confusion on the subject of the Creation until Christ returns and reveals all things. Understanding this topic is not necessary for us to gain salvation; otherwise it would be very clear in the scriptures. As Jacob explained, "No man knoweth of his ways save it be revealed unto him." (Jacob 4:8.)

Moses 3

Moses 3:1

"The heaven and the earth were finished, and all the host of them"

Selected Statements of the First Presidency and the Twelve Apostles

"The creation was accomplished; it was done. This earth, and man, and life in all its forms and varieties existed in physical form. But none of these had the same nature they now possess. The great Creator had created a paradisiacal earth, an edenic earth, an earth of the kind and nature that will exist during the Millennium, when it will be renewed and receive again its paradisiacal glory. There was as yet neither procreation nor death. These would enter the scheme of things only after the fall. The earth, man, and all created things were in a deathless state of immortality, but they were so organized that they could become mortal through the fall." (Bruce R. McConkie, *New Witness for the Articles of Faith*, p. 84.)

" 'Thus the heaven and the earth were finished, and all of the host of them.' That is, the physical creation was completed. Then the account explains, by way of interpolation, that nevertheless all things had been created spiritually before this physical creation. But hosts of the earth were not on the earth, although they had been created preparatory to

127

coming to the earth." (Joseph Fielding Smith, *Man: His Origin and Destiny*, p. 284.)

Moses 3:2-3

"On the seventh day I, God, ended my work, and all things which I had made. . . . And I, God, blessed the seventh day, and sanctified it"

Selected Statements of the First Presidency and the Twelve Apostles

"Latter-day Saints should not permit these commandments regarding the Sabbath to slip from their minds. All during this, the Last Dispensation, the Prophets of the Lord have urged Sabbath-observance upon the people. Different concepts of Sabbath-observance have been urged upon us by unbelievers, partial-believers, and by the thoughtless, concerned primarily with the pleasures of the world, sometimes under the guise of recreation, sometimes by activities the Lord has told us were sinful.

"The Sabbath is not just another day on which we merely rest from work, free to spend it as our lightmindedness may suggest. It is a holy day, the Lord's Day, to be spent as a day of worship and reverence. All matters extraneous thereto should be shunned.

"We must bear in mind all these principles. We must remember particularly actual Sabbath-breaking labor which might be required from a great number of Lesser Priesthood members in any Sabbath-breaking activities, including interference with their duties and attendance at quorum meetings. For all these and for many other reasons affecting injuriously the religious duties and activities of the whole Church membership, Latter-day Saints, with a testimony of the Gospel and a knowledge of the spiritual blessings that come from keeping the Sabbath, will never permit themselves to make it a shopping day, an activity that has no place in a proper observance of the Holy Day of the Lord, on which we are commanded to pour out our souls in gratitude for the many blessings of health, strength, physical comfort, and spiritual joy which come from the Lord's bounteous hand." (The First Presidency: David O. McKay, J. Reuben Clark, Jr., and Henry D. Moyle, in *Deseret News*, 20 June 1959.)

Selected Scripture References

"Six days shalt thou labour and do all thy work." (Exodus 20:9.)

"This is a day appointed unto you to rest from your labors, and to pay thy devotions unto the Most High." (D&C 59:10.)

Moses 3:4–5

"I, the Lord God, made the heaven and the earth, and every plant of the field"

Selected Statements of the First Presidency and the Twelve Apostles

" 'God is not the Father of the earth as one of the worlds in space, nor of the heavenly bodies in whole or in part, nor of the inanimate objects and the plants and the animals upon the earth, in the literal sense in which He is the Father of the spirits of mankind. Therefore, scriptures that refer to God in any way as the Father of the heavens and the earth are to be understood as signifying that God is the Maker, the Organizer, the Creator of the heavens and the earth.' " (The First Presidency and the Council of the Twelve Apostles, in Joseph Fielding Smith, *Church History and Modern Revelation*, 2:161.)

Selected Scripture References

"All things were made by him; and without him was not any thing made that was made." (John 1:3.)

"God . . . hath in these last days spoken unto us by his Son, . . . by whom also he made the worlds." (Hebrews 1:1–2.)

Moses 3:5

"I, the Lord God, created all things, of which I have spoken, spiritually, before they were naturally upon the face of the earth"

Selected Statements of the First Presidency and the Twelve Apostles

"The creation was two fold—firstly spiritual, secondly temporal. This truth, also, Moses plainly taught—much more plainly than it has come down to us in the imperfect translations of the Bible that are now in use. Therein the fact of a spiritual creation, antedating the temporal creation, is strongly implied, but the proof of it is not so clear and conclusive as in other records held by the Latter-day Saints to be of equal authority with the Jewish scriptures. The partial obscurity of the latter upon the point in question is owing, no doubt, to the loss of those 'plain and precious' parts of sacred writ, which, as the Book of Mormon informs us, have been taken away from the Bible during its passage down the centuries (1 Nephi 13:24–29). Some of these missing parts the Prophet Joseph Smith undertook to restore when he revised those scriptures by the spirit of revelation, the result being that more complete account of the creation which is found in the book of Moses, previously cited. Note the following passages: [Moses 3:4–7]." (The First

Presidency: Joseph F. Smith, John R. Winder, and Anthon H. Lund, in James R. Clark, comp., *Messages of the First Presidency*, 4:201–2. See also Bruce R. McConkie, *Mormon Doctrine*, p. 251; Joseph Fielding Smith, *Doctrines of Salvation*, 1:63–64.)

"Man, as a spirit, was begotten and born of heavenly parents and reared to maturity in the eternal mansions of the Father, prior to the coming upon the earth in a temporal body to undergo an experience in mortality." (The First Presidency: Heber J. Grant, Anthony W. Ivins, and Charles W. Nibley, in James R. Clark, comp., *Messages of the First Presidency*, 5:244. See also Joseph Fielding Smith, *Man: His Origin and Destiny*, p. 285; Bruce R. McConkie, *Millennial Messiah*, p. 643.)

Selected Scripture References

"The spirits of all men . . . are taken home to that God who gave them life." (Alma 40:11.)

"By the power of my Spirit created I them; yea, all things both spiritual and temporal." (D&C 29:31.)

"That which is spiritual [is] in the likeness of that which is temporal." (D&C 77:2.)

"Man was also in the beginning with God." (D&C 93:29.)

"I made the world, and men before they were in the flesh." (Moses 6:51.)

Moses 3:7, 22
"I, the Lord God, formed man from the dust of the ground"

Selected Statements of the First Presidency and the Twelve Apostles

" 'Our father Adam—that is our earthly father—the progenitor of the human race of man, stands at the head being 'Michael the Archangel, the Ancient of Days,' and that he was not fashioned from earth life and adobe but begotten by his Father in Heaven.' " (The First Presidency: Joseph F. Smith, Anthon H. Lund, and Charles W. Penrose, as quoted in Melvin A. Cook and M. Garfield Cook, *Science and Mormonism*, p. 156.)

"At length a Moses came, who knew his God, and would fain have led mankind to know him too, and see him face to face. But they could not receive his heavenly laws or abide his presence. Thus the holy man was forced again to veil the past in mystery, and in the beginning of his history assign to man an earthly origin.

"Man, moulded from the earth, as a brick!

"Woman, manufactured from a rib!

"Thus, parents still would fain conceal from budding manhood the mysteries of procreation, or the sources of life's ever-flowing river, by relating some childish tale of new-born life." (Parley P. Pratt, *Key to the Science of Theology*, p. 30.)

"Here let me state to all the philosophers of every class upon the earth, When you tell me that father Adam was made as we make adobies from the earth, you tell me what I deem an idle tale. When you tell me that the beasts of the field were produced in that manner, you are speaking idle words devoid of meaning. There is no such thing in all the eternities where the Gods dwell." (Brigham Young, in *Journal of Discourses*, 7:285. See also Brigham Young, in *Journal of Discourses*, 11:122; 3:319.)

"If the body of man be analyzed, the elements from which it is made are found to be those which exist in the air and in the soil, that is, the earth's crust....

OUT OF THE GROUND

Approximate Elementary Composition of the Adult Human Body		Approximate Elementary Composition of the Earth's Crust with Its Oceans and Atmosphere (Clarke)	
Chemical Element	Percent	Chemical Element	Percent
Oxygen	65.0	Oxygen	50.02
Carbon	18.0	Carbon	0.18
Hydrogen	10.0	Hydrogen	0.95
Nitrogen	3.0	Nitrogen	0.03
Calcium	1.5	Calcium	3.22
Phosphorus	1.0	Phosphorus	0.11
Potassium	0.35	Potassium	2.88
Sulphur	0.25	Sulphur	0.11
Sodium	0.15	Sodium	2.36
Chlorine	0.15	Chlorine	0.20
Magnesium	0.05	Magnesium	2.08
Iron	0.004	Iron	4.18
Manganese	0.0003	Manganese	0.08
Iodine	0.00004	Silicon	25.80
Copper, zinc, fluorine, silicon (aluminum?)	Very minute amounts	Aluminum	7.30
		Titanium	0.43
		Fluorine	0.10
		Barium	0.08
		Others in lesser amounts.	

"The inorganic elements of air and soil are built by plants into forms suitable and necessary for the use of man. Thus, all life depends upon Mother Earth. In very deed man is made of the 'dust of the earth.' " (John A. Widtsoe, *Word of Wisdom*, pp. 102–3.)

Selected Scripture References

"Who shall say that it was not a miracle that . . . by the power of his word man was created of the dust of the earth." (Mormon 9:17.)

"On the seventh day he finished his work, and sanctified it, and also formed man out of the dust of the earth." (D&C 77:12.)

"For man is spirit. The elements are eternal. . . . the elements are the tabernacle of God." (D&C 93:33, 35.)

Moses 3:7

"I, the Lord God, . . . breathed into his nostrils the breath of life; and man became a living soul, the first flesh upon the earth, the first man also"

Selected Statements of the First Presidency and the Twelve Apostles

"Adam, our progenitor, 'the first man,' was, like Christ, a pre-existent spirit, and like Christ he took upon him an appropriate body, the body of a man, and so became a 'living soul.' The doctrine of the pre-existence, revealed so plainly, particularly in latter days, pours a wonderful flood of light upon the otherwise mysterious problem of man's origin. It shows that man, as a spirit, was begotten and born of heavenly parents, and reared to maturity in the eternal mansions of the Father, prior to coming upon the earth in a temporal body to undergo an experience of mortality. It teaches that all men existed in the spirit before any man existed in the flesh, and that all who have inhabited the earth since Adam have taken bodies and become souls in like manner." (The First Presidency: Joseph F. Smith, John R. Winder, and Anthon H. Lund, in James R. Clark, comp., *Messages of the First Presidency*, 4:205.)

"Man became a living soul—mankind, male and female. The Creators breathed into their nostrils the breath of life and man and woman became living souls. We don't know exactly how their coming into this world happened, and when we're able to understand it the Lord will tell us." (Spencer W. Kimball, in *Ensign*, Mar. 1976, p. 72.)

"The thought that man was the first living thing upon the earth and that he was placed here in a state of desolation, before there was any vegetation or animal life on the land, in the air, or in the sea, does violence to the entire account of creation as well as to reason. . . . The expression, 'the first flesh upon the earth' is simply a statement of the fact that Adam—the first man on earth—was, by reason of his transgression the first to partake of mortality. That is to say, the fall brought the mortal as well as the spiritual death. 'Mortality' and 'flesh' are often used as synonymous terms." (Joseph Fielding Smith, *Man: His Origin and Destiny*, p. 328. See also Bruce R. McConkie, in *Ensign*, June 1982, p. 14.)

Selected Scripture References

"Adam was first formed, then Eve." (1 Timothy 2:13.)

The priesthood is "the right of the firstborn, or the first man, who is Adam, or first father." (Abraham 1:3.)

Moses 3:8
"I, the Lord God, planted a garden eastward in Eden, and there I put the man whom I had formed"

Selected Statements of the First Presidency and the Twelve Apostles

"Man, the last and noblest of God's creation was placed in the garden of Eden, being governed by laws and restricted by commandments, not being subject to sickness, disease, or death. Adam was placed upon the earth an immortal being. He was placed in the garden to dress, beautify and adorn it, and to hold the supremacy of power over all the things of God's creation." (Orson Pratt, in *Times and Seasons*, 6 [1 June 1845]: 918.)

"Does it not appear to you that it is a foolish and ridiculous notion that when God created this earth he had to begin with a speck of protoplasm, and take millions of years, if not billions, to bring conditions to pass by which his sons and daughters might obtain bodies made in his image? Why not the shorter route and transplant them from another earth as we are taught in the scriptures." (Joseph Fielding Smith, *Man: His Origin and Destiny*, pp. 276-77.)

"Since Adam called together seven generations of his descendants at Adam-ondi-Ahman, it can well be believed that there was his old homestead. If so, the Garden of Eden was probably not far distant, for it was the entrance at the east of the Garden which was closed against them at the time of the 'fall.' " (John A. Widtsoe, *Gospel Interpretations*, p. 253.)

"The spot chosen for the garden of Eden was Jackson County, in the State of Missouri, where Independence now stands; it was occupied in the morn of creation by Adam." (Heber C. Kimball, in *Journal of Discourses*, 10:235.)

"In the beginning, after this earth was prepared for man, the Lord commenced his work upon what is now called the American continent, where the Garden of Eden was made. In the days of Noah, in the days of the floating of the ark, he took the people to another part of the earth." (Brigham Young, *Discourses of Brigham Young*, p. 157. See also Joseph Fielding Smith, *Doctrines of Salvation*, 1:139–40.)

Moses 3:9

"And it [every tree] became also a living soul. For it was spiritual in the day that I created it"

Selected Statements of the First Presidency and the Twelve Apostles

"The idea prevails in general, I believe, in the religious world where the gospel truth is misunderstood, that man is the only being on the earth that has what is called a soul or a spirit. We know this is not the case, for the Lord has said that not only has man a spirit, and is thereby a living soul, but likewise the beasts of the field, the fowl of the air, and the fish of the sea have spirits, and hence are living souls. But this does not make them kinsmen to the sons and daughters of God. They are our Father's creations, not his offspring, and that is the great difference between man and beast." (Joseph Fielding Smith, *Doctrines of Salvation*, 1:63.)

Moses 3:10–14

The four rivers

Other Commentary

"A careful reading of the account in Genesis and also of the one in the Book of Moses makes it clear that one 'river went out of Eden' and it had 'four heads.' In other words, four rivers flowed together, making one. It is very evident that since the river that ran through Ethiopia (Nile) and the Euphrates River are hundreds of miles apart, they could never have been joined together. Therefore, the geography of the western part of Persia or the Mesopotamia Valley fails to fit the description given in the scriptures.

"Where then in the world are there four rivers that flow together, making one? The Mississippi River and its tributaries fit well with the description given in Genesis and in the Book of Moses. Among the principal rivers that flow together in the upper Mississippi Valley are the Mississippi, Missouri, Ohio, and Illinois." (Milton R. Hunter, *Pearl of Great Price Commentary*, p. 108.)

Moses 3:17

"Thou shalt not eat of it [the tree of the knowledge of good and evil], nevertheless, thou mayest choose for thyself"

Selected Statements of the First Presidency and the Twelve Apostles

"God himself grants this right to every human being upon the earth irrespective of race or color; it is part of the divine economy not to force any man to heaven, not to coerce the mind but to leave it free to act for itself. He lays before His creature man the everlasting Gospel, the principles of life and salvation, and then leaves him to choose for himself or to reject for himself, with the understanding that he becomes responsible to Him for the results of his acts." (Wilford Woodruff, in *Journal of Discourses*, 23:77.)

"Just why the Lord would say to Adam that he forbade him to partake of the fruit of that tree is not made clear in the Bible account, but in the original as it comes to us in the Book of Moses it is made definitely clear. It is that the Lord said to Adam that if he wished to remain as he was in the garden, then he was not to eat the fruit, but if he desired to eat it and partake of death he was at liberty to do so. So really it was not in the true sense a transgression of a divine commandment. Adam made the wise decision, in fact the only decision he could make." (Joseph Fielding Smith, *Answers to Gospel Questions*, 4:81. See also 1:180–81; John A. Widtsoe, *Gospel Interpretations*, pp. 77–78; Bruce R. McConkie, *New Witness for the Articles of Faith*, p. 91.)

"What is meant by partaking of the fruit of the tree of the knowledge of good and evil is that our first parents complied with whatever laws were involved so that their bodies would change from their state of paradisiacal immortality to a state of natural mortality." (Bruce R. McConkie, in *Ensign*, June 1982, p. 15.)

Moses 3:17

If Adam and Eve ate of the forbidden fruit, they would surely die

Selected Statements of the First Presidency and the Twelve Apostles

"Adam could have remained in the Garden of Eden indefinitely if he had not transgressed the law which brought to pass mortality. Since Adam had not passed through the resurrection his spirit and body were not inseparably connected, hence it was possible for him to become mortal by partaking of the fruit of the tree of knowledge of good and evil. By so doing he received the seeds of death and brought to pass mortality in himself and caused all of his posterity to partake of like conditions and be subject to death." (Heber J. Grant, in James R. Clark, comp., *Messages of the First Presidency*, 5:290.)

"After the fall, which came by a transgression of the law under which Adam was living, the forbidden fruit had the power to create blood and change his nature and mortality took the place of immortality, and all things, partaking of the change, became mortal." (Joseph Fielding Smith, *Doctrines of Salvation*, 1:77.)

"When Adam and Eve were in the garden of Eden, before this transgression took place, they were not subject to death; they were not subject to any kind of pain, or disease, or sickness, or any of the afflictions of mortality. Now, perhaps those who are not in the habit of reflecting upon this matter, may suppose that when Adam was placed on the earth, and Eve, his wife, they were mortal, like unto us; but that was not so. God did not make a mortal being. It would be contrary to his great goodness to make a man mortal, subject to pain, subject to sickness, subject to death. When he made this creation, and when he made these two intelligent beings and placed them upon this creation he made them after his own likeness and his own image. He did not make them mortal, he made them immortal, like unto himself. If he had made them mortal, and subject to pain, there would have been some cause, among intelligent beings, to say that the Lord subjected man, without a cause, to afflictions, sorrows, death and mortality. But he could not do this; it was contrary to the nature of his attributes, contrary to the nature of that infinite goodness which dwells in the bosom of the Father and the Son, to make a being subject to any kind of pain." (Orson Pratt, in *Journal of Discourses*, 21:289.)

Selected Scripture References

"If Adam had not transgressed he would not have fallen, but he would have remained in the garden of Eden." (2 Nephi 2:22.)

"Adam should fall because of his partaking of the forbidden fruit." (Mosiah 3:26.)

"We see that Adam did fall by the partaking of the forbidden fruit." (Alma 12:22.)

Moses 3:18

"It was not good that the man should be alone"

Selected Statements of the First Presidency and the Twelve Apostles

"The Lord has revealed to us by His special revelations, as clearly and positively as He ever did to any of the ancient Prophets, certain principles associated with the eternity of the marriage covenant, has given definite commands pertaining thereto, and made them obligatory upon us to carry out. He has made manifest to us those great and eternal principles which bind woman to man and man to woman, children to parents and parents to children, and has called upon us in the most emphatic and pointed manner to obey them. These glorious principles involve our dearest interests and associations in time and throughout the eternities that are to come. We are told that this is His everlasting covenant, and that it has existed from eternity." (The First Presidency: John Taylor and George Q. Cannon, in James R. Clark, comp., *Messages of the First Presidency*, 3:9–10.)

"As an indication of the importance the gods gave to women the Lord said,

" 'Therefore shall a man leave his father and his mother, and shall cleave unto his wife: and they shall be one flesh.' (Genesis 2:24.)

"Do you note that? She, the woman, occupies the first place. She is preeminent, even above the parents who are so dear to all of us. Even the children must take their proper but significant place." (Spencer W. Kimball, in *Ensign*, Mar. 1976, p. 72.)

Selected Scripture References

"Marriage is honourable in all." (Hebrews 13:4.)

"Marriage is ordained of God unto man." (D&C 49:15.)

"In order to obtain the highest [degree of glory], a man must enter into this order of the priesthood [meaning the new and everlasting covenant of marriage]." (D&C 131:1–2.)

Other Commentary

"In the beginning, after the earth was prepared, God brought man and woman together in the Garden, and the first wedding occurred. They were not yet subject to mortal death, and no time limitations were placed upon their marriage." (Marion D. Hanks, in *Ensign*, Nov. 1984, p. 36.)

Moses 3:22

"The rib which I, the Lord God, had taken from man, made I a woman"

Selected Statements of the First Presidency and the Twelve Apostles

" 'And I, God, created man in mine own image, in the image of mine Only Begotten created I him; male and female created I them. [The story of the rib, of course, is figurative.]' " (Spencer W. Kimball, in *Ensign*, Mar. 1976, p. 71.)

Moses 3:24

"Therefore shall a man leave his father and his mother, and shall cleave unto his wife; and they shall be one flesh"

Selected Statements of the First Presidency and the Twelve Apostles

"The first marriage recorded in scripture was the union of immortals. The curse of death had not been pronounced when the ceremony was solemnized. There was no sin then, and therefore there was no death. The man and woman became one as eternal beings, and dominion was given to them over all earthly things together. . . .

"Here is a sample marriage. It was not for time alone, but for eternity. Death intervened, but only as an incident. The bond that bound them in matrimony was not sundered. The seal set upon them was of heavenly stamp. Its virtue reached within the vail. Its force extended into the world to come. There was no end to it. God had a hand in it and it was His seal and sanction that made it valid and everlasting." (Charles W. Penrose, *"Mormon" Doctrine, Plain and Simple,* p. 49.)

Selected Scripture References

"Whoso findeth a good wife hath obtained favor of the Lord." (JST Proverbs 18:22.)

"Husbands, love your wives, even as Christ also loved the church, and gave himself for it." (Ephesians 5:25.)

"So ought men to love their wives as their own bodies. He that loveth his wife loveth himself." (Ephesians 5:28.)

"Thou shalt love thy wife with all thy heart, and shalt cleave unto her and none else." (D&C 42:22.)

Moses 4

Moses 4:1

"Behold, here am I [Satan], send me, . . . and I will redeem all mankind . . . ; wherefore give me thine honor"

Selected Statements of the First Presidency and the Twelve Apostles

"Just what authority Lucifer held before his rebellion we do not know, but he was an angel of light, his name Lucifer, meaning torchbearer. Agency was given unto the spirits of men, and they had their talents and individual traits of character there as they do here. It was due to this fact that Lucifer, who was proud and ambitious, rebelled against the Father when his plan for the salvation of fallen man was rejected." (Joseph Fielding Smith, *Church History and Modern Revelation*, 2:51–52.)

"This angel was a mighty personage, without doubt. The record that is given to us concerning him clearly shows that he occupied a very high position; that he was thought a great deal of, and that he was mighty in his sphere, so much so that when the matter was debated concerning the earth and the plan of salvation, he was of sufficient importance to have a plan, which he proposed as the plan by which this earth should be peopled and the inhabitants thereof redeemed. His plan, however, was not accepted; but it was so plausible and so attractive that out of the whole hosts of heaven one-third accepted his plan and were willing to cast their lot with him." (George Q. Cannon, in *Millennial Star,* 57 [5 Sept. 1895]: 563–64.)

Selected Scripture References

"O Lucifer, son of the morning!" (Isaiah 14:12.)

"I will ascend above the heights of the clouds; I will be like the most High." (Isaiah 14:14.)

"An angel of God who was in authority in the presence of God . . . rebelled." (D&C 76:25.)

"And the Lord said: Whom shall I send? . . . And another answered and said: Here am I, send me." (Abraham 3:27.)

Moses 4:2

Jesus said, "Father, thy will be done, and the glory be thine forever"

Selected Statements of the First Presidency and the Twelve Apostles

"We read also in the scriptures that Jesus was the 'Lamb slain from the foundation of the world,' meaning that our Savior was chosen before the foundations of the world to come and be the sacrifice for the redemption of man and all the creatures who partook of death through Adam's fall." (Joseph Fielding Smith, *Answers to Gospel Questions*, 4:81.)

"Although we sometimes hear it said that there were two plans—Christ's plan of freedom and agency, and Lucifer's of slavery and compulsion—such teaching does not conform to the revealed word. Christ did not present a plan of redemption and salvation nor did Lucifer. There were not two plans up for consideration; there was only one; and that was the plan of the Father: originated, developed, presented, and put in force by him. Christ, however, made the Father's plan his own by his willing obedience to its terms and provisions." (Bruce R. McConkie, in *Improvement Era*, May 1953, p. 322.)

Selected Scripture References

Christ "verily was foreordained before the foundation of the world." (1 Peter 1:20.)

"I am he who was prepared from the foundation of the world to redeem my people. Behold, I am Jesus Christ." (Ether 3:14.)

"The Lord said: Whom shall I send? . . . I will send the first." (Abraham 3:27.)

Moses 4:3

"Satan rebelled against me, and sought to destroy the agency of man; . . . [therefore] I caused that he should be cast down"

Selected Statements of the First Presidency and the Twelve Apostles

"The contention in heaven was—Jesus said there would be certain souls that would not be saved; and the devil said he could save them all, and laid his plans before the grand council, who gave their vote in favor of Jesus Christ. So the devil rose up in rebellion against God, and was cast down, with all who put up their heads for him." (Joseph Smith, *Teachings of the Prophet Joseph Smith*, p. 357.)

"Long before you were born a program was developed by your creators. There was rebellion in the ranks. The proposed program called for total controls by each individual of his personal life, including restraints, sacrifices, and self-mastery. The rebellion with its warring elements and conflicts was of such proportion that our civil war of rebellion, and even our World War II are insignificant as to number of people involved in the conflicting armies and the principles fought for. Had the rebels won that great war you and I would have been in a totally different position. Ours would have been a life under force. You could make no decisions. You would *have* to comply. Every determination would be made for you regardless of your will. Under compulsion you would do the bidding of your dictator leader in whose image the Khrushchevs, Hitlers, Napoleons, and Alexanders were but poor and ineffectual novices in comparison. Your life would be cut out for you and you *would* fit into the mold made for you.

"But thank God that there were enough sane and sagacious souls on the side of truth and wisdom and the rebellious souls were vanquished as to the eternal and ultimate program. The principal personalities in this great drama were a Father Elohim, perfect in wisdom, judgment, and person, and two sons, Lucifer and Jehovah." (Spencer W. Kimball, *Teachings of Spencer W. Kimball*, pp. 32–33. See also George Q. Cannon, *Gospel Truth*, 1:137–38; Harold B. Lee, as quoted by ElRay L. Christiansen, in *Ensign*, Nov. 1974, p. 23; Joseph Fielding Smith, *Answers to Gospel Questions*, 5:31.)

"There was war in heaven. That war was a war of words; it was a conflict of ideologies; it was a rebellion against God and his laws. Lucifer sought to dethrone God, to sit himself on the divine throne, and to save all men without reference to their works. He sought to deny men their agency so they could not sin. He offered a mortal life of carnality and sensuality, of evil and crime and murder, following which all men would be saved. His offer was a philosophical impossibility." (Bruce R. McConkie, *Millennial Messiah*, pp. 666–67.)

"If Lucifer had not known the effects of his rebellion, how would he ever have become perdition? If he were ignorant he could not have become perdition. He was not ignorant, and therefore, he became perdition. They who followed him were sons of perdition, because he and they sinned knowingly. They did what they did with their eyes open, and he was in rebellion against God." (Joseph Fielding Smith, *Answers to Gospel Questions*, 5:189.)

Selected Scripture References

"I beheld Satan as lightning fall from heaven." (Luke 10:18.)

"And they were thrust down, and thus came the devil and his angels." (D&C 29:37.)

Moses 4:4
"He became . . . the devil, the father of all lies, to deceive and to blind men"

Selected Statements of the First Presidency and the Twelve Apostles

"We do not consider that the rebellion which took place in heaven prior to this creation was the first rebellion that had ever existed. . . . But this seems to be the origin of evil so far as the inhabitants intended for this earth, and who were then living in heaven, were concerned. They had their agency; and when I speak of the inhabitants that dwell in heaven, pertaining to this creation, I mean the spirits of men and women." (Orson Pratt, in *Journal of Discourses*, 21:287.)

"The adversary presents his principles and arguments in the most approved style, and in the most winning tone, attended with the most graceful attitudes; and he is very careful to ingratiate himself into the favor of the powerful and influential of mankind, uniting himself with popular parties, floating into offices of trust and emolument by pandering to popular feeling, though it should seriously wrong and oppress the innocent." (Brigham Young, *Discourses of Brigham Young*, p. 106.)

"Every person who desires and strives to be a Saint is closely watched by fallen spirits that came here when Lucifer fell, and by the spirits of wicked persons who have been here in tabernacles and departed from them, but who are still under the control of the prince of the power of the air. Those spirits are never idle; they are watching every person who wishes to do right and are continually prompting them to do wrong."

(Brigham Young, in *Journal of Discourses*, 7:239. See also Brigham Young, in *Journal of Discourses*, 3:208; Wilford Woodruff, in *Journal of Discourses,* 13:163.)

"We are all familiar with the facts: how Lucifer—a personage of prominence—sought to amend the plan, while Jehovah sustained the plan. . . .

"The central issue in that council, then, was: Shall the children of God have untrammeled agency to choose the course they should follow, whether good or evil, or shall they be coerced and forced to be obedient? Christ and all who followed Him stood for the former proposition—freedom of choice; Satan stood for the latter—coercion and force. Because Satan and those who stood with him would not accept the vote of the council, but rose up in rebellion, they were cast down to the earth, where they have continued to foster the same plan. The war that began in heaven is not yet over. The conflict continues on the battlefield of mortality. And one of Lucifer's primary strategies has been to restrict our agency through the power of earthly governments. Proof of this is found in the long history of humanity." (Ezra Taft Benson, *The Constitution, a Heavenly Banner*, pp. 2–3.)

"From the above [Moses 4:1–4] we gather: First, that the proposition of Lucifer was an act of rebellion 'against me'—God.

"Second, that God had already decreed that man should have his free agency, and this agency had been given to him by the Lord, as it is said, 'which I, the Lord God, had given him.'

"Third, that Lucifer coveted and asked for a power which was the prerogative of the Almighty and alone belonged to God; and which He called 'mine own power.'

"Fourth, that for this rebellion Lucifer was cast out and became Satan.

"Fifth, that the power by which he was cast out, was by a certain power or Priesthood which had been conferred by God on His Only Begotten; for he said, 'By the power of mine Only Begotten I caused that he should be cast down.'

"Sixth, that being cast down and becoming Satan, 'even the devil, the father of lies,' his office was to deceive and to blind men; as it is stated, 'to deceive, and to blind men, and to lead them captive at his will, even as many as would not hearken unto my voice.' " (John Taylor, *Mediation and Atonement*, p. 98.)

"Let it not be forgotten that the evil one has great power in the earth, and that by every possible means he seeks to darken the minds of men and then offers them falsehood and deception in the guise of truth.

Satan is a skillful imitator, and as genuine gospel truth is given the world in ever-increasing abundance, so he spreads the counterfeit coin of false doctrine. Beware of his spurious currency, it will purchase for you nothing but disappointment, misery and spiritual death. The 'father of lies' he has been called, and such an adept has he become through the ages of practice in his nefarious work, that were it possible he would deceive the very elect." (Joseph F. Smith, in *Juvenile Instructor*, vol. 37, no. 18 [15 Sept. 1902], p. 562. See also Spencer W. Kimball, *Teachings of Spencer W. Kimball*, pp. 33–34.)

Selected Scripture References

"And there was war in heaven; Michael and his angels fought against the dragon. . . . Neither was there place found in heaven for the great dragon, who was cast out; that old serpent called the devil . . . ; he was cast out into the earth; and his angels were cast out with him." (JST Revelation 12:6, 8.)

"They were thrust down, and thus came the devil and his angels." (D&C 29:37.)

Satan "was thrust down from the presence of God and the Son, and was called Perdition." (D&C 76:25–26.)

Moses 4:6

"He [Satan] knew not the mind of God"

Selected Statements of the First Presidency and the Twelve Apostles

"There is a difference between knowledge and pure intelligence. Satan possesses knowledge, far more than we have, but he has not intelligence or he would render obedience to the principles of truth and right." (Joseph F. Smith, *Gospel Doctrine*, p. 58.)

"Eve was fulfilling the foreseen purposes of God by the part she took in the great drama of the fall; yet she did not partake of the forbidden fruit with that object in view, but with intent to act contrary to the divine command, being deceived by the sophistries of Satan, who also, for that matter, furthered the purposes of the Creator by tempting Eve; yet his design was to thwart the Lord's plan. We are definitely told that 'he knew not the mind of God, wherefore he sought to destroy the world.' [Moses 4:6]. Yet his diabolical effort, far from being the initiatory step toward destruction, contributed to the plan of man's eternal progression." (James E. Talmage, *Articles of Faith*, pp. 69–70.)

Selected Scripture References

"Satan stirreth them up, that he may lead their souls to destruction. And thus he has laid a cunning plan, thinking to destroy the work of God." (D&C 10:22–23.)

Moses 4:6

"And Satan put it into the heart of the serpent"

Selected Statements of the First Presidency and the Twelve Apostles

"It was in the Garden of Eden that the devil, or one of those foul spirits, entered into a certain animal or beast, called a serpent, and came before our first parents and beguiled them." (Orson Pratt, in *Journal of Discourses*, 13:63.)

"Satan presented himself before Eve in the garden, and, speaking by the mouth of the serpent, questioned her about the commandments that God had given respecting the tree of knowledge of good and evil." (James E. Talmage, *Articles of Faith*, p. 64.)

Selected Scripture References

"The great dragon was cast out, that old serpent, called the Devil, and Satan." (Revelation 12:9.)

The devil is "that old serpent that did beguile our first parents." (Mosiah 16:3.)

"We beheld Satan, that old serpent, even the devil." (D&C 76:28.)

Moses 4:6

"He sought also to beguile Eve"

Selected Statements of the First Presidency and the Twelve Apostles

"The devil can adapt himself to the belief of any person. . . . If he could get you to swallow down one or two great lies that would effect your destruction, and which you would preach and destroy many others, he would not mind how many truths you might believe. He would be willing that you should believe a great many things absolutely true if he could only deceive you and lead you astray and get you to reject some of the fundamental principles of your salvation, and the salvation of the people." (Orson Pratt, in *Journal of Discourses*, 13:73.)

"The powerful Lucifer has his day. He whispers into every man's ears. Some reject his enticing offers, others yield. Satan whispers, 'This is no sin. You are no transgressor. I am no devil. There is no evil one. There is no black. All is white.' " (Spencer W. Kimball, in Conference Report, Oct. 1967, p. 30.)

Selected Scripture References

"The serpent beguiled Eve through his subtilty." (2 Corinthians 11:3.)

"He [Satan] sought also the misery of all mankind. Wherefore, he said unto Eve. . . . " (2 Nephi 2:18.)

The father of lies is "that being who beguiled our first parents, who transformeth himself nigh unto an angel of light." (2 Nephi 9:9.)

Moses 4:10

"Ye shall not surely die"

Selected Statements of the First Presidency and the Twelve Apostles

"The devil in tempting Eve told a truth when he said unto her that when she should eat of the tree of knowledge of good and evil they should become as Gods. He told the truth in telling that, but he accompanied it with a lie as he always does. He never tells the complete truth. He said that they should not die. The Father had said that they should die. The devil had to tell a lie in order to accomplish his purposes; but there was some truth in his statement. Their eyes were opened. They had a knowledge of good and evil just as the Gods have. They became as Gods; for that is one of the features, one of the peculiar attributes of those who attain unto that glory—they understand the difference between good and evil." (George Q. Cannon, *Gospel Truth*, 1:16.)

Moses 4:12

"She took of the fruit thereof, and did eat, and also gave unto her husband with her, and he did eat"

Selected Statements of the First Presidency and the Twelve Apostles

"The Apostle Paul plainly declared that the man was not in the transgression, but the woman; hence we infer that Adam was acquainted of the penalty annexed to the law of God, and with his future destiny, before he partook of the fruit. It might be said that out of two evils the man upon reflection chose the least. The first was the seduction of the woman, by the tempter, which evil would terminate in the banishment of the woman from the garden of Paridise [sic], it being one of the penalties annexed to the law, for the offence already committed. Adam knowing this fact chose to suffer the penalty of the law with the woman, rather than to be deprived of her society; consequently he followed her into the transgression." (Orson Pratt, in *Times and Seasons*, 6 [1 Feb. 1845]: 798–99.)

"Adam had the privilege of making a choice, with the penalty of death awaiting him if he ate the fruit of the tree. We may assume that

Adam would not have eaten if Eve had not partaken. When she did, Adam realized that he had to partake or he and Eve would have been separated forever." (Joseph Fielding Smith, in *Improvement Era*, Apr. 1962, p. 230.)

"Don't go around whispering the fall consisted in the mother of the race losing her chastity and her virtue. It is not truth, the human race is not born of fornication. These bodies that are given unto us are given in the way that God has provided. Let it not be said that the patriarch of the race, who stood with the gods before he came here upon the earth, and his equally royal consort, were guilty of any such foul offense. The adoption of that belief has led many to excuse departures from the path of virtue, by saying that it is the sin of the race, it is as old as Adam. It was not introduced by Adam. It was not committed by Eve. It was the introduction of the devil and came in order that he might sow the seeds of early death in the bodies of men and women, that the race should degenerate as it has degenerated whenever the laws of virtue and of chastity have been transgressed." (James E. Talmage, in Conference Report, Oct. 1913, pp. 118–19.)

Selected Scripture References

"Adam was not deceived, but the woman being deceived was in the transgression." (1 Timothy 2:14.)

"The devil tempted Adam, and he partook of the forbidden fruit." (D&C 29:40.)

Moses 4:21

The seed of woman

Selected Statements of the First Presidency and the Twelve Apostles

"Adam, the patriarch of the race, rejoiced in the assurance of the Savior's appointed ministry, through the acceptance of which, he, the transgressor, might gain redemption. Brief mention of the plan of salvation, the author of which is Jesus Christ, appears in the promise given of God following the fall—that though the devil, represented by the serpent in Eden, should have power to bruise the heel of Adam's posterity, through the seed of the woman should come the power to bruise the adversary's head. It is significant that this assurance of eventual victory over sin and its inevitable effect, death, both of which were introduced to earth through Satan, the arch-enemy of mankind, was to be realized through the offspring of woman; the promise was not made specifically to the man, nor to the pair. The only instance of offspring from woman dissociated from mortal fatherhood is the birth of Jesus the Christ, who was the earthly Son of a mortal mother, begotten by an immortal Father. He is the Only Begotten of the Eternal Father in the flesh, and was born of woman." (James E. Talmage, *Jesus the Christ*, p. 43.)

Selected Scripture References

"God shall wound the head of his enemies." (Psalm 68:21.)

"The God of peace shall bruise Satan under your feet." (Romans 16:20.)

"Through death he [Christ] might destroy him that had the power of death, that is, the devil." (Hebrews 2:14.)

Moses 4:22

"Unto the woman, I, the Lord God, said: I will greatly multiply thy sorrow. . . . thy desire shall be to thy husband"

Selected Statements of the First Presidency and the Twelve Apostles

"The Lord said to the woman: ' . . . in sorrow thou shalt bring forth children.' I wonder if those who translated the Bible might have used the term distress instead of sorrow. It would mean much the same, except I think there is a great gladness in most Latter-day Saint homes when there is to be a child there. As He concludes this statement He says, 'and thy desire shall be to thy husband, and he shall rule over thee.' (Genesis 3:16.) I have a question about the word *rule*. It gives the wrong impression. I would prefer to use the word *preside* because that's what he does. A righteous husband presides over his wife and family." (Spencer W. Kimball, in *Ensign*, Mar. 1976, p. 72.)

Selected Scripture References

"Wives, submit yourselves unto your own husbands, as unto the Lord. . . . Husbands, love your wives, even as Christ also loved the church, and gave himself for it." (Ephesians 5:22, 25.)

"They shall be saved in childbearing, if they continue in faith and charity and holiness with sobriety." (JST 1 Timothy 2:15.)

Moses 4:23

"Cursed shall be the ground for thy sake; in sorrow shalt thou eat of it all the days of thy life"

Selected Statements of the First Presidency and the Twelve Apostles

"Then came the curse upon the fruit, upon the vegetables, and upon our mother earth; and it came upon the creeping things, upon the grain in the field, the fish in the sea, and upon all things pertaining to this earth, through man's transgression." (Brigham Young, in *Journal of Discourses*, 10:312.)

"Note that the curse was not placed upon Adam, but upon the ground for Adam's sake. Rather than a curse upon Adam, it was a blessing to him." (Marion G. Romney, in Conference Report, Oct. 1976, p. 168.)

Selected Scripture References

"I, the Lord, in the beginning cursed the land, even so in the last days have I blessed it, . . . for the use of my saints." (D&C 61:17.)

"The ground which the Lord has cursed." (Moses 8:9.)

Moses 4:25

"For thou shalt surely die"

Selected Statements of the First Presidency and the Twelve Apostles

"Adam and Eve transgressed a law and were responsible for a change that came to all their posterity, that of mortality. Could it have been the different food which made the change? Somehow blood, the life-giving element in our bodies, replaced the finer substance which coursed through their bodies before. They and we became mortal, subject to illness, pains, and even the physical dissolution called death. But the spirit, which is supreme in the dual man, transcends the body. It does not decompose but proceeds to the spirit world for further experience, with the assurance that after sufficient preparation there, a reunion will take place where the spirit will be housed eternally in a remodeled body of flesh and bones. This time the union will never be dissolved, since there will be no blood to disintegrate and cause trouble. A finer substance will give life to the body and will render it immortal." (Spencer W. Kimball, *Teachings of Spencer W. Kimball*, p. 44.)

Selected Scripture References

"As in Adam all die, even so in Christ shall all be made alive." (1 Corinthians 15:22.)

"By reason of transgression cometh the fall, which fall bringeth death." (Moses 6:59.)

Moses 4:26

"Eve, . . . the mother of all living"

Selected Statements of the First Presidency and the Twelve Apostles

"Martin Luther penned a meaningful statement regarding woman's place when he wrote, 'When Eve was brought unto Adam, he became filled with the Holy Spirit, and gave her the most sanctified, the most glorious of appellations. He called her Eve—that is to say, the Mother of All. He did not style her wife, but simply mother—mother of all living creatures. In this consists the glory and the most precious ornament of woman.'

"To be what God intended you to be as a woman depends on the way you think, believe, live, dress, and conduct yourselves as true examples of Latter-day Saint womanhood, examples of that for which you were created and made." (Harold B. Lee, *Ye Are the Light of the World*, p. 280.)

Selected Scripture References

"Adam and Eve . . . were our first parents." (1 Nephi 5:11.)

"And they [Adam and Eve] have brought forth children; yea, even the family of all the earth." (2 Nephi 2:20.)

Moses 4:28
"The tree of life"

Selected Statements of the First Presidency and the Twelve Apostles

"The tree of life will be on the earth in the midst of that city that will descend on the earth, and whoever eats of the fruit of that tree will live forever, just the same as the tree of life was placed upon the earth before Adam transgressed. Any one eating of the fruit of that tree could not die, for the decree of the Lord had gone forth, and his word must be fulfilled." (Orson Pratt, in *Journal of Discourses*, 21:328.)

"The result of their fall could have been of none but ill effect had they been immediately brought to a condition of immortality, without repentance, without atonement. In the despair following their realization of the great change that had come upon them, and in the light of the knowledge they had gained at such cost as to the virtues of the tree of life, it would have been natural for them to seek the seeming advantage of an immediate escape by partaking of the immortalizing food. In mercy they were prevented from so doing." (James E. Talmage, *Articles of Faith*, p. 66.)

Selected Scripture References

"If . . . our first parents could have gone forth and partaken of the tree of life . . . the plan of redemption would have been frustrated." (Alma 12:26.)

"If Adam had put forth his hand immediately, and partaken of the tree of life, he would have lived forever, . . . having no space for repentance." (Alma 42:5.)

Moses 4:31
"I placed at the east of the Garden of Eden, cherubim and a flaming sword"

Selected Statements of the First Presidency and the Twelve Apostles

"Apparently a cherub is an angel of some particular order or rank to whom specific duties and work are assigned. That portion of the Lord's word which is now available among men does not set forth clearly either the identity or work of these heavenly beings." (Bruce R. McConkie, *Mormon Doctrine*, p. 124.)

"Little is known about the beings known under the above names [Cherubim and Seraphim] beyond the fact that they are creatures in the service of the Lord. Genesis states that the Lord, after driving Adam and Eve out of the Garden of Eden, 'placed at the east of the garden of Eden cherubims, and a flaming sword.' . . .

"Undoubtedly, the golden cherubim of the mercy seat, and the seraphim seen in vision by Isaiah were, similarly, figurative of certain heavenly beings. Their wings were symbolical of their power to move and act as in the case of the four beasts of the book of Revelation. Such symbolical representations in scripture and painting, of human or divine qualities, have always been commonly used for the easier comprehension of the mind. The symbolic use of wings is however never used in the Church today." (John A. Widtsoe, *Evidences and Reconciliations*, 3:182–83.)

Moses 5

Moses 5:1
Adam and Eve were driven out of the Garden of Eden

Selected Statements of the First Presidency and the Twelve Apostles

"Satan and his cohorts, including evil and designing men, are determined to keep man wandering in the wilderness so that eventually he will be destroyed and the work of the Lord will be thwarted. Adam and Eve were the first wanderers of record when they listened to Satan rather than the Lord. They were cast out of the Garden of Eden and had a period of wandering until they committed themselves to keeping the commandments of God." (N. Eldon Tanner, in Conference Report, Oct. 1974, p. 121.)

Moses 5:1
Adam ate his bread "by the sweat of his brow"

Selected Statements of the First Presidency and the Twelve Apostles

"Not man alone, but also the earth and all the elemental forces pertaining thereto came under the Adamic curse; and as the soil no longer brought forth only good and useful fruits, but gave of its substance to nurture thorns and thistles, so the several forces of nature ceased to be obedient to man as agents subject to his direct control." (James E. Talmage, *Jesus the Christ*, p. 309.)

"Waste is unjustified, and especially the waste of time—limited as that commodity is in our days of probation. One must live, not only exist; he must do, not merely be; he must grow, not just vegetate.

" . . . One of the numerous rewards in girding ourselves to do hard things is in the creation of a capacity for doing of the still harder things." (Spencer W. Kimball, *Teachings of Spencer W. Kimball*, pp. 359-62.)

"I assert with confidence that the law of success, here and hereafter, is to have a humble and a prayerful heart, and to work, *work*, WORK.

" . . . I do not know of anything that destroys a person's health more quickly than not working. It seems to me that lazy people die young while those who are ready and willing to labor and who ask the Lord day by day to help them to do more in the future than they have ever done in the past, are the people whom the Lord loves, and who live to a good old age." (Heber J. Grant, *Gospel Standards*, pp. 182-83.)

"I am a firm believer that work does not kill anyone, but that laziness does kill a man at an early age.

"There should be in the heart of every man and woman, the cry, 'I am going to live. There is nothing given to me but time in which to live, and I am going to endeavor each day of my life to do some labor which will be acceptable in the sight of my Heavenly Father, and if it is possible, do a little better today than I did yesterday.' " (Heber J. Grant, *Gospel Standards*, p. 108.)

Selected Scripture References

"Go to the ant, thou sluggard; consider her ways, and be wise." (Proverbs 6:6.)

"Neither be idle but labor with your might." (D&C 75:3.)

Moses 5:1
"And Eve, also, his wife, did labor with him"

Selected Statements of the First Presidency and the Twelve Apostles

"They were partners, each given a part of the work of life to do. The fact that some women and men disregard their work and their opportunities does not change the program." (Spencer W. Kimball, in *Ensign,* Mar. 1976, p. 72.)

Moses 5:4

"They were shut out from his presence"

Selected Statements of the First Presidency and the Twelve Apostles

"After he was driven out of the Garden of Eden the scene changed. Adam was banished because of his transgression from the presence of the Father. The scriptures say he became spiritually dead—that is, he was shut out from the presence of God." (Joseph Fielding Smith, *Answers to Gospel Questions*, 1:16.)

"When Adam was driven out of the Garden of Eden, he was not left without direction, but the Lord sent messengers to him and even spoke to him by his own voice. Although Adam had been driven from his presence and he could not behold him, yet he received commandments and revelation for his guidance." (Joseph Fielding Smith, *Doctrines of Salvation*, 3:313-14.)

Selected Scripture References

"All mankind were in a lost and in a fallen state." (1 Nephi 10:6.)

"The fall had brought upon all mankind a spiritual death as well as a temporal, that is, they were cut off from the presence of the Lord." (Alma 42:9.)

"Neither can any natural man abide the presence of God." (D&C 67:12.)

Moses 5:5–7

God commanded Adam and Eve to offer sacrifice. It was in similitude of the atonement of Jesus Christ.

Selected Statements of the First Presidency and the Twelve Apostles

"Sacrifice is a similitude. It is performed to typify the coming sacrifice of the Son of God. For four thousand long years, from Adam to that bleak day when our Lord was lifted up by sinful men, all of his righteous followers sought remission of their sins through sacrifice. It was an ordinance of the Melchizedek Priesthood; it antedated the law of Moses by two and a half millenniums, although that lesser law did give rise to many sacrificial requirements not theretofore practiced." (Bruce R. McConkie, *Promised Messiah*, pp. 379-80.)

"It would seem that Adam, until instructed by the angel, did not know the reasons for the offering up of sacrifices, nor the object that the Lord had in view in requiring this offering at his hands; for, being asked by the angel why he performed this rite, he said, 'I know not, save the Lord commanded me;' and the object of the visit of this holy being to Adam evidently was to show him why he was called to offer a sacrifice to the Lord, as, on Adam expressing his ignorance of the intent of this offering, the angel stated very explicitly that this thing was 'a similitude of the sacrifice of the Only Begotten of the Father.' We have here given a reason why Adam offered up this sacrifice." (John Taylor, *Mediation and Atonement*, pp. 62–63. See also Wilford Woodruff, in *Journal of Discourses*, 23:127.)

Other Commentary

THE SIMILITUDE OF ANIMAL SACRIFICE AND THE ATONEMENT OF JESUS CHRIST

Symbol	Sacrifice	Atonement
A lamb	"Take to them . . . A lamb for an house." (Exodus 12:3.)	"Behold the Lamb of God." (John 1:29, 36)
Male	"Your lamb shall be . . . A male of the first year." (Exodus 12:5.)	"This is the Son of God." (John 1:34.)
Firstborn	"Offer the firstlings of their flock." (Moses 5:5.)	"Christ is the image of the invisible God, the firstborn of every creature." (Colossians 1:15.)
Perfect	"If there be any blemish therein, as if it be lame, or blind, or have any ill blemish, thou shalt not sacrifice it unto the Lord." (Deuteronomy 15:21.)	"Christ, . . . a lamb without blemish and without spot." (1 Peter 1:19.)
Shedding of blood	"They shall take of the blood." (Exodus 12:7.)	"Suffering caused Christ . . . to bleed at every pore." (D&C 19:18.)

Symbol	Sacrifice	Atonement
No broken bones	"Neither shall ye break a bone thereof." (Exodus 12:46.)	"A bone of him shall not be broken." (John 19:36.)
Proper authority	"The *priests* sprinkled the blood . . . , and the *Levites* flayed them." (2 Chronicles 35:11.)	Jesus was God incarnate. (See John 1:1–5, 14.)

Moses 5:9

"As thou hast fallen thou mayest be redeemed, and all mankind, even as many as will"

Selected Statements of the First Presidency and the Twelve Apostles

"Christ came, as we know, not subject to death, but always having the mastery over death, to atone for Adam's transgression. The Saviour said that he had life in himself as the Father had life in himself (John 5:26) and that he had power to lay down his life of himself and take it again, which commandment he had received from his Father. (John 10:15.)

"Adam, like all of his posterity, became a benefactor through the mission of Jesus Christ. Through the atonement made by our Lord, Adam was redeemed from his transgression and received the resurrection." (Heber J. Grant, in James R. Clark, comp., *Message of the First Presidency*, 5:290.)

"The difference between Jesus Christ and other men is this: Our fathers in the flesh are mortal men, who are subject unto death; but the Father of Jesus Christ in the flesh is the God of Heaven. Therefore Jesus, as he declared, received the power of life from his Father and was never subject unto death but had life in himself as his father had life in himself. Because of this power he overcame death and the grave and became master of the resurrection and the means of salvation to us all." (Joseph F. Smith, in James R. Clark, comp., *Messages of the First Presidency*, 4:329. See also Brigham Young, in *Journal of Discourses*, 13:328.)

"A man who says he does not believe in the atoning blood of Jesus Christ, who professes to be a member of the Church of Jesus Christ of Latter-day Saints, but who ignores and repudiates the doctrine of the atonement . . . —the man who denies that truth and who persists in his unbelief is not worthy of membership in the Church." (Joseph F.

Smith, in *Improvement Era*, Nov. 1917, p. 7. See also John Taylor, *Mediation and Atonement*, p. 179.)

"In a manner to us incomprehensible and inexplicable, he [Christ] bore the weight of the sins of the whole world; not only of Adam, but of his posterity; and in doing that, opened the kingdom of heaven, not only to all believers and all who obeyed the law of God, but to more than one-half of the human family who die before they come to years of maturity, as well as to the heathen, who, having died without law, will, through His mediation, be resurrected without law, and be judged without law, and thus participate, according to their capacity, works and worth, in the blessings of His atonement." (John Taylor, *Mediation and Atonement*, pp. 148–49. See also Heber J. Grant, in *Juvenile Instructor*, 64 [Dec. 1929]: 697; Wilford Woodruff, in *Millennial Star*, 51 [21 Oct. 1889]: 659.)

Other Commentary

"CONDITIONS BEFORE AND AFTER THE FALL

Before	After
"1. In the presence of God	1. Banished from God's presence (spiritual death)
"2. Not subject to physical death	2. Subject to physical death
"3. Not subject to pain or sorrow	3. Subject to pain and sorrow
"4. Only a partial knowledge of good and evil	4. Knowledge of good and evil
"5. A state of innocence	5. Possibility of joy in mortality
"6. No posterity	6. Possibility of bearing children

"The conditions 'after the fall' are headed by three conditions which would be undesirable if permanent. However, when Adam and Eve understood that Jesus Christ would (1) provide the means to overcome spiritual death, (2) overcome physical death, and (3) then give man commandments to minimize the third condition, it was discovered that mortality with a few limitations is a most desirable condition where man can receive a body and can prove himself in a probationary state."

(*Messages for Exaltation* [Sunday School Gospel Doctrine manual, 1967], p. 63.)

Moses 5:9
"I am the Only Begotten of the Father"

Selected Statements of the First Presidency and the Twelve Apostles

"We are told in scriptures that Jesus Christ is the only begotten Son of God in the flesh. Well, now for the benefit of the older ones, how are children begotten? I answer just as Jesus Christ was begotten of his father. The Christian denominations believe that Christ was begotten not of God but of the spirit that overshadowed his mother. This is nonsense. Why will not the world receive the truth? Why will they not believe the Father when he says that Jesus Christ is His only begotten Son? Why will they try to explain this truth away and make mystery of it?" (Joseph F. Smith, in James R. Clark, comp., *Messages of the First Presidency*, 4:329. See also Orson Pratt, in *Times and Seasons*, 6 [1 Feb. 1845]: 798.)

Selected Scripture References

"For God so loved the world, that he gave his only begotten Son." (John 3:16.)

"We heard the voice bearing record that he is the Only Begotten of the Father." (D&C 76:23.)

Moses 5:10–11
"Because of my transgression my eyes are opened"

Selected Statements of the First Presidency and the Twelve Apostles

"Adam and Eve both considered that they had gained, instead of suffered loss, through their disobedience to that law; for they made the statement, that if it had not been for their transgression they never would 'have known good and evil.' And again, they would have been incapable of increase; and without that increase the designs of God in relation to the formation of the earth and man could not have been accomplished." (John Taylor, *Mediation and Atonement*, p. 130. See also Brigham Young, in *Journal of Discourses*, 10:312.)

"What was that transgression? It was violating a single commandment of God, and disregarding the counsel of those immortal beings who stood above them in authority. The Creator placed in the garden a certain tree and warned Adam that in the day he eat the fruit thereof he should surely die. He commanded him not to eat the fruit. His was a simple commandment; but the violation of it subjected Adam to a fall from his exalted station in the favor of God. Consequently a curse was passed upon all created things, and in the posterity of Adam were sown the seeds of dissolution." (Orson Pratt, in *Times and Seasons*, 6 [1 June 1845]: 918.)

Moses 5:10–11
"We never should have had seed"

Selected Statements of the First Presidency and the Twelve Apostles

"If Adam and Eve had not partaken of the forbidden fruit, they would have had no children, and we would not have been. (2 Nephi 2:23–25; Moses 5:11.)

"I do not look upon Adam's action as a sin. I think it was a deliberate act of free agency. He chose to do that which had to be done to further the purposes of God. The consequences of his act made necessary the atonement of the Redeemer." (Marion G. Romney, in Conference Report, Apr. 1953, p. 124.)

"They would have been incapable of increase; and without that increase the designs of God in relation to the formation of the earth and man could not have been accomplished; for one great object of the creation of the world was the propagation of the human species, that bodies might be prepared for those spirits who already existed, and who, when they saw the earth formed, shouted for joy." (John Taylor, *Gospel Kingdom*, p. 96. See also James E. Talmage, *Articles of Faith*, p. 69.)

"If we then accept the truth of the existence of God and his parentage then there immediately devolves upon us a responsibility to him and his children, our fellowmen. If he organized and planned the world, is it not most likely that he has made a perfect plan by which we might become closer to him and by which we might progress?

"God has given us a plan. He has sent us all to earth to obtain bodies and to gain experience and growth. He anticipated the fall of Adam and Eve and the consequent change in their mortal condition and provided his Son Jesus Christ to redeem man from the effects of the fall and to show to man a perfect example of right living so that man, too, might improve and become more godly." (Spencer W. Kimball, *Teachings of Spencer W. Kimball*, p. 25.)

Selected Scripture References

"Adam fell that men might be." (2 Nephi 2:25.)
"Because that Adam fell, we are." (Moses 6:48.)

Other Commentary

CONSEQUENCES OF THE FALL
AFTER THE TEACHING OF THE GOSPEL

Eve	Adam
1. Have the possibility of joy in mortality	1. Have the possibility of joy in mortality
2. Be a homemaker	2. Preside over the family
3. Be a mother	3. Provide for the family
4. Have the promise of resurrection for all and eternal life for the righteous	4. Have the promise of resurrection for all and eternal life for the righteous

Moses 5:12

"They made all things known unto their sons and their daughters"

Selected Statements of the First Presidency and the Twelve Apostles

"By bringing these choice spirits to earth, each father and each mother assume towards the tabernacled spirit and towards the Lord Himself by having taken advantage of the opportunity He offered, an obligation of the most sacred kind, because the fate of that spirit in the eternities to come, the blessings or punishments which shall await it in the hereafter, depend, in great part, upon the care, the teachings, the training which the parents shall give to that spirit.

"No parent can escape that obligation and that responsibility, and for the proper meeting thereof, the Lord will hold us to a strict accountability. No loftier duty than this can be assumed by mortals." (The First Presidency: Heber J. Grant, J. Reuben Clark, Jr., and David O. McKay, in James R. Clark, comp., *Messages of the First Presidency*, 6:178.)

"Another great and important duty devolving upon this people is to teach their children, from their cradle until they become men and women, every principle of the gospel, and endeavor, as far as it lies in the power of the parents, to instill into their hearts a love for God, the truth, virtue, honesty, honor and integrity to everything that is good. That is important for all men and women who stand at the head of a family in the household of faith. Teach your children the love of God, teach them to love the principles of the gospel of Jesus Christ." (Joseph F. Smith, *Gospel Doctrine*, p. 292.)

"No wonder the Lord wants the plan taught plainly and repetitively.

"And why not? It is God's plan—not ours! And, given the unimpressive outcomes of man's plans to solve the world's problems, aren't we glad!" (Neal A. Maxwell, in Conference Report, Apr. 1984, p. 30. See also Bruce R. McConkie, *Mortal Messiah*, 1:229.)

"Because no one can be saved without a knowledge of the gospel, the Lord himself set the pattern as to how it should be taught in order that everyone can be taught. He himself came to his son Adam and taught him the gospel, and directed him to teach his children. The record says that 'Adam and Eve . . . made all things known unto their sons and their daughters . . . ' (Moses 5:12.)" (Marion G. Romney, in Conference Report, Apr. 1969, p. 107. See also John A. Widtsoe, *Evidences and Reconciliations*, 1:83.)

"Neither can there be a doubt existing on the mind of any person, that Adam was the first who did communicate the knowledge of the existence of a God to his posterity; and that the whole faith of the world, from that time down to the present, is in a certain degree dependent on the knowledge first communicated to them by their common progenitor; and it has been handed down to the day and generation in which we live, as we shall show from the face of the sacred records." (Joseph Smith, *Lectures on Faith*, 2:36. See also Bruce R. McConkie, *Mormon Doctrine*, p. 113.)

Selected Scripture References

"Train up a child in the way he should go." (Proverbs 22:6.)

"Inasmuch as parents have children . . . that teach them not to understand the doctrine . . . , the sin be upon the heads of the parents." (D&C 68:25.)

"I have commanded you to bring up your children in light and truth." (D&C 93:40.)

Moses 5:13

"And men began from that time forth to be carnal, sensual, and devilish"

Selected Statements of the First Presidency and the Twelve Apostles

"Thus apostasy began; men fell away from the truth even in the day of righteous Adam; men turned to carnal and ungodly practices even in the day when there were living witnesses to tell them of Eden's beauty, of the fall and promised redemption, and of angelic ministrations and heavenly revelations of the mind and will of Him whose they and we are." (Bruce R. McConkie, *Mortal Messiah*, 1:229–30.)

"In this mortal condition, which has continued since the days of Adam until now, wickedness has prevailed on the earth. Satan has had sway. He has usurped authority and found favor with men. Through his power, his cunning and craftiness, he has won mankind very largely over to his side." (Joseph Fielding Smith, *Doctrines of Salvation*, 1:83.)

Moses 5:13
"And they loved Satan more than God"

Selected Statements of the First Presidency and the Twelve Apostles

"In tragic contrast with the blessed state of those who become children of God through obedience to the Gospel of Jesus Christ is that of the unregenerate, who are specifically called the children of the devil. Note the words of Christ, while in the flesh, to certain wicked Jews who boasted of their Abrahamic lineage: 'If ye were Abraham's children, ye would do the works of Abraham. . . . Ye do the deeds of your father. . . . If God were your Father, ye would love me. . . . Ye are of your father the devil, and the lusts of your father ye will do' (John 8:39, 41, 42, 44). Thus Satan is designated as the father of the wicked, though we cannot assume any personal relationship of parent and children as existing between him and them. A combined illustration showing that the righteous are the children of God and the wicked the children of the devil appears in the parable of the Tares: 'The good seed are the children of the kingdom; but the tares are the children of the wicked one' (Matt. 13:38)." (The First Presidency: Joseph F. Smith, Anthon H. Lund, Charles W. Penrose, and The Council of the Twelve Apostles, in James R. Clark, comp., *Messages of the First Presidency*, 5:30.)

Selected Scripture References

"Satan had great power, unto the stirring up of the people to do all manner of iniquity." (3 Nephi 6:15.)

"In those days Satan had great dominion among men, and raged in their hearts." (Moses 6:15.)

Moses 5:14
"The Lord God called upon men by the Holy Ghost everywhere

and commanded them that they should repent"

Selected Statements of the First Presidency and the Twelve Apostles

"When the scripture says, 'The Lord called upon men by the Holy Ghost everywhere and commanded them that they should repent' (Moses 5:14), it means that the Lord called upon them by the mouths of his servants who were inspired and guided by the Holy Ghost, not that unclean persons received the promptings of that Holy Being." (Bruce R. McConkie, *Promised Messiah*, p. 76.)

Moses 5:17
"And Abel hearkened unto the voice of the Lord"

Selected Statements of the First Presidency and the Twelve Apostles

"In early ages of the world, also in the days of the Apostles, people came into possession of spiritual powers and various privileges by obtaining an understanding of, and faithfully attending to, certain rules which the Lord established; as, for instance, Abel, obtaining information that offering up sacrifices was an order instituted of God, through which men might receive blessings, he set himself to work, observed the order, and performed the sacrifice, whereby he obtained glorious manifestations of the Most High." (Lorenzo Snow, *Teachings of Lorenzo Snow*, p. 42. See also Joseph Smith, *Teachings of the Prophet Joseph Smith*, p. 59.)

Selected Scripture References

"By faith Abel offered unto God a more excellent sacrifice than Cain." (Hebrews 11:4.)

Moses 5:18
"And Satan commanded him [Cain], saying: Make an offering unto the Lord"

Selected Statements of the First Presidency and the Twelve Apostles

"Cain offered of the fruit of the ground, and was not accepted, because he could not do it in faith, he could have no faith, or could not exercise faith contrary to the plan of heaven. . . . Without the shedding of blood was no remission; and as the sacrifice was instituted for a type, by which man was to discern the great Sacrifice which God had prepared; to offer a sacrifice contrary to that, no faith could be exercised, . . .

consequently Cain could have no faith; and whatsoever is not of faith, is sin." (Joseph Smith, *Teachings of the Prophet Joseph Smith*, p. 58.)

"Every good and perfect gift comes from the Father of Light, who is no respecter of persons and in whom there is no variableness, nor shadow of turning. To please him we must not only worship him with thanksgiving and praise but render willing obedience to his commandments. By so doing he is bound to bestow his blessings; for it is upon this principle (obedience to law) that all blessings are predicated." (Joseph F. Smith, in *Improvement Era*, Dec. 1917, p. 104.)

"The power, glory and blessings of the Priesthood could not continue with those who received ordination only as their righteousness continued; for Cain also being authorized to offer sacrifice, but not offering it in righteousness, was cursed. It signifies, then, that the ordinances must be kept in the very way God has appointed; otherwise their Priesthood will prove a cursing instead of a blessing." (Joseph Smith, *Teachings of the Prophet Joseph Smith*, p. 169.)

Selected Scripture References

"If any man of you bring an offering unto the Lord, ye shall bring your offering of the cattle. . . . he shall offer it of his own voluntary will." (Leviticus 1:2-3.)

"Hath the Lord as great delight in burnt offerings and sacrifices, as in obeying the voice of the Lord?" (1 Samuel 15:22.)

Moses 5:20
"The Lord had respect unto Abel, and to his offering"

Selected Statements of the First Presidency and the Twelve Apostles

"By faith in this atonement or plan of redemption, Abel offered to God a sacrifice that was accepted, which was the firstlings of the flock. . . . Abel offered an acceptable sacrifice, by which he obtained witness that he was righteous, God Himself testifying of his gifts. . . .

"Then certainly God spoke to him: indeed, it is said that God talked with him; and if He did, would He not, seeing that Abel was righteous deliver to him the whole plan of the Gospel? And is not the Gospel the news of the redemption? How could Abel offer a sacrifice and look forward with faith on the Son of God for a remission of his sins, and not understand the Gospel? The mere shedding of the blood of beasts or offering anything else in sacrifice, could not procure a remission of sins, except it were performed in faith of something to come; if it could, Cain's offering must have been as good as Abel's. And if Abel was taught of the coming of the Son of God, was he not taught also of His ordinances? We all admit that the Gospel has ordinances, and if so, had it not always ordinances, and were not its ordinances always the same?" (Joseph Smith, *Teachings of the Prophet Joseph Smith*, pp. 58–59.)

Moses 5:22

"And the Lord said unto Cain: . . . Why is thy countenance fallen?"

Selected Statements of the First Presidency and the Twelve Apostles

"Cain conversed with his God every day, and knew all about the plan of creating this earth, for his father told him. But, for the want of humility, and through jealousy, and an anxiety to possess the kingdom, and to have the whole of it under his own control, and not allow anybody else the right to say one word, what did he do? He killed his brother." (Brigham Young, *Discourses of Brigham Young*, p. 160.)

Moses 5:23

"If thou doest well, thou shalt be accepted"

Selected Statements of the First Presidency and the Twelve Apostles

"Every soul coming into this world came here with the promise that through obedience he would receive the blessings of salvation. No person was foreordained or appointed to sin or to perform a mission of evil. No person is ever predestined to salvation or damnation. Every person has free agency. Cain was promised by the Lord that if he would do well, he would be accepted. . . . If men were appointed to sin and betray their brethren, then justice could not demand that they be punished for sin and betrayal when they are guilty." (Joseph Fielding Smith, *Doctrines of Salvation*, 1:61.)

"The gospel is so very simple when we understand it properly. It is always right, it is always good, it is always uplifting. Obedience to gospel principles brings forth joy and happiness. Disobedience has a day of reckoning and will only bring forth heartache, misery, strife, and unhappiness." (L. Tom Perry, in Conference Report, Oct. 1984, p. 21.)

"In reality, therefore, a man who has command of himself does not need to fear the evil one. He is not a force that can work harm, unless man places himself under the subjection of evil; but, if the devil be allowed a hearing, he may become the master of the man." (John A. Widtsoe, *Rational Theology*, p. 85.)

Moses 5:23

"And thou [Cain] shalt rule over him [Satan]"

Selected Statements of the First Presidency and the Twelve Apostles

"Now as to whether or not those who in mortal life rebel and become sons of perdition will be able to exercise greater dominion than those who followed Lucifer, who became the devil and arch-enemy of Jesus Christ, might be a moot question. However, the Lord has made it definitely clear that Cain will hold that ascendency in the realm of wickedness; [and] that Satan desired to have him. . . .

"As far as Cain is concerned, the information given is definite that he became Perdition, and that Lucifer who is Satan, became subject to him. It appears that the reason Satan desired to have him was due to the fact that Cain had obtained a body of flesh and bones and therefore had superior power, and Satan was willing to accept and be obedient to him because of that condition. The natural conclusion is, therefore, that a devil with a body of flesh and bones has some power greater than one who was denied the physical body." (Joseph Fielding Smith, *Answers to Gospel Questions*, 2:170–72.)

"The spirits in the eternal world are like the spirits in this world. When those have come into this world and received tabernacles, then died and again have risen and received glorified bodies, they will have an ascendency over the spirits who have received no bodies, or kept not their first estate, like the devil. The punishment of the devil was that he should not have a habitation like men. The devil's retaliation is, he comes into this world, binds up men's bodies, and occupies them himself. When the authorities come along, they eject him from a stolen habitation." (Joseph Smith, *Teachings of the Prophet Joseph Smith*, pp. 305–6.)

"Satan wanted him because Cain had a body. He wanted more power. A man with a body of course will have greater power than just a spirit without a body. Cain sinned with his eyes open, so he became Perdition, the father of lies." (Joseph Fielding Smith, *Doctrines of Salvation*, 2:279–80.)

Moses 5:24

"Thou shalt be called Perdition"

Selected Statements of the First Presidency and the Twelve Apostles

"Say to the brothers Hulet and to all others, that the Lord never authorized them to say that the devil, his angels or the sons of perdition, should ever be restored; for their state of destiny was not revealed to man, is not revealed, nor ever shall be revealed, save to those who are made partakers thereof: consequently those who teach this doctrine, have not received it of the Spirit of the Lord. Truly Brother Oliver declared it to be the doctrine of devils. We therefore command that this doctrine be taught no more in Zion." (Joseph Smith, *History of the Church*, 1:366. See also Bruce R. McConkie, *Mormon Doctrine*, p. 566.)

"Cain's great sin was not committed in ignorance. We have every reason to believe that he had the privilege of standing in the presence of messengers from heaven. In fact the scriptures infer that he was blessed by communication with the Father and was instructed by messengers from his presence. No doubt he held the Priesthood; otherwise his sin could not make of him Perdition. He sinned against the light. And this he did, so we are told, because he loved Satan more than he loved God." (Joseph Fielding Smith, *Way to Perfection*, p. 98.)

"Both Satan and Cain bear the title *father of lies*, both have been liars from the beginning. (2 Nephi 9:9; Moses 5:18–27.) The name signifies authorship and sponsorship of all that is dishonest and which leads away from the truth. In a similar sense Satan is the *master of sin* (Mosiah 4:14) and the father of secret combinations and every evil thing. (2 Nephi 26:22; Helaman 6:26; Moroni 7:12.)" (Bruce R. McConkie, *Mormon Doctrine*, p. 278.)

Selected Scripture References

Jesus is the Savior, "who glorifies the Father, and saves all the works of his hands, except those sons of perdition who deny the Son after the Father has revealed him." (D&C 76:43.)

Moses 5:26

"Cain was wroth, and listened not any more to the voice of the Lord, neither to Abel, his brother, who walked in holiness before the Lord"

Selected Statements of the First Presidency and the Twelve Apostles

"Adam received commandments and instructions from God: this was the order from the beginning.

"That he received revelations, commandments and ordinances at the beginning is beyond the power of controversy; else how did they begin to offer sacrifices to God in an acceptable manner? And if they offered sacrifices they must be authorized by ordination. We read in Genesis 4:4, that Abel brought of the firstlings of the flock and the fat thereof, and the Lord had respect to Abel and to his offering. And, again, 'By faith Abel offered unto God a more excellent sacrifice than Cain, by which he obtained witness that he was righteous, God testifying of his gifts; and by it he being dead, yet speaketh.' (Hebrews 11:4.) How doth he yet speak? Why he magnified the Priesthood which was conferred upon him, and died a righteous man, and therefore has become an angel of God by receiving his body from the dead, holding still the keys of his dispensation; and was sent down from heaven unto Paul to minister consoling words, and to commit unto him a knowledge of the mysteries of godliness.

"And if this was not the case, I would ask, how did Paul know so much about Abel, and why should he talk about his speaking after he was dead? Hence, that he spoke after he was dead must be by being sent down out of heaven to administer." (Joseph Smith, *Teachings of the Prophet Joseph Smith*, pp. 168–69.)

"And Cain listened to the advice of Satan, and as the devil was a murderer and a liar from the beginning, so he induced Cain to become the same, and he instigated him to kill his brother Abel. Here were the two powers represented in the two men, that of God in Abel, and that of Satan in Cain; and thus the warfare commenced, and the opposition was inaugurated, for we are told it was necessary there should be an opposition in all things." (John Taylor, in *Journal of Discourses*, 22:301.)

Selected Scripture References

"They have gone in the way of Cain, and ran greedily after the error of Balaam for reward." (Jude 1:11.)

Moses 5:29
Secret combinations

Selected Statements of the First Presidency and the Twelve Apostles

"I would further suggest the impropriety of the organization of bands or companies, by covenant or oaths, by penalties or secrecies; but let the time past of our experience and suffering by the wickedness of Doctor Avard suffice and let our covenant be that of the Everlasting Covenant, as is contained in the Holy Writ and the things that God hath revealed unto us. Pure friendship always becomes weakened the very moment you undertake to make it stronger by penal oaths and secrecy." (Joseph Smith, *Teachings of the Prophet Joseph Smith*, p. 146.)

"Latter-day Saints should have nothing to do with the secret combinations and groups antagonistic to the constitutional law of the land, which the Lord 'suffered to be established,' and which 'should be maintained for the rights and protection of all flesh according to just and holy principles.' " (David O. McKay, *Gospel Ideals*, p. 306.)

"From the day of Cain, who slew his brother Abel, to the present, there have always been secret combinations whose members have reveled in carnal deeds and sought power and dominion over others by evil means. Through the ages these have taken many forms and borne many names. There are powers and forces and combinations of nations and kingdoms where freedom is denied today. Some of these are as autocratic and deny freedom of worship as forcefully as any of the ancient empires. Some profess to be godless; others mandate the worship of a particular God. Some have political philosophies that run counter to gospel principles; others wage wars against neighboring nations to spread and impose their views upon the minds of men. There are those who would control, govern, and enslave the whole world if they could. . . . They are part of the church of the devil and will be overthrown when the Lord comes to take vengeance upon the ungodly." (Bruce R. McConkie, *New Witness for the Articles of Faith*, pp. 625–26. See also Bruce R. McConkie, *Mormon Doctrine*, p. 698.)

"Lucifer and his followers know the habits, weaknesses, and vulnerable spots of everyone and take advantage of them to lead us to spiritual destruction. With one person it may be thirst for liquor; another may have an insatiable hunger; another has permitted his sex urges to dominate; another loves money, and the luxuries and comforts it can buy; another craves power; and so on." (Spencer W. Kimball, *Miracle of Forgiveness*, pp. 218–19.)

Selected Scripture References

"There are also secret combinations, . . . according to the combinations of the devil, for he is the founder of all these things." (2 Nephi 26:22.)

"And they did enter into a covenant . . . , which covenant was given and administered by the devil." (3 Nephi 6:28.)

"And Akish did administer unto them the oaths . . . , which had been handed down even from Cain." (Ether 8:15.)

Moses 5:31

"Wherefore Cain was called Master Mahan, and he gloried in his wickedness"

Selected Statements of the First Presidency and the Twelve Apostles

"Is it not possible that he rejoiced in the knowledge that through his wickedness he should rule in the kingdom of wickedness? What glory and honor could Cain expect to obtain in becoming the "father of lies" and becoming Perdition? Such an attitude of mind is hard to understand. To think that Cain would glory in obtaining dominion in the empire of evil, and in becoming the author of falsehood and holding the scepter of power in the kingdom of darkness, is almost beyond belief. . . .

" . . . Here we have the first and most pronounced case in history of one glorying in wickedness. Cain chose knowingly but not intelligently. He killed his brother, not so much for his flocks as for the glory of being Master Mahan. Not so much with the expectancy of obtaining his brother's worldly possessions, but to cut off without posterity that righteous brother, and, because Satan had commanded him!" (Joseph Fielding Smith, *Way to Perfection*, pp. 100–101.)

"The difference between God and the devil is that God creates and organizes while the whole study of the devil is to destroy." (Brigham Young, in *Journal of Discourses*, 13:4.)

Moses 5:32
"Cain rose up against Abel, his brother, and slew him"

Selected Statements of the First Presidency and the Twelve Apostles

"This knowledge that God is near to us, and hears and answers our prayers, is an unceasing cause of thankfulness and praise. For a wise purpose in His providence He permits the wicked, in the exercise of their agency, from time to time to afflict His followers. Since the days of our father Adam this has always been the case, and it will continue to be, so long as Satan has any power over the hearts of the children of men." (The First Presidency: John Taylor and George Q. Cannon, in James R. Clark, comp., *Messages of the First Presidency*, 3:5.)

"The hatred of the wicked always has and always will follow the Priesthood and the Saints. The devil will not lose sight of the power of God vested in man—the Holy Priesthood. He fears it, he hates it, and will never cease to stir up the hearts of the debased and corrupt in anger and malice towards those who hold this power, and to persecute the Saints, until he is bound." (Joseph F. Smith, in *Journal of Discourses*, 19:24.)

Selected Scripture References

Cain slew his brother "because his own works were evil, and his brother's righteous." (1 John 3:12.)

Other Commentary

The Joseph Smith Translation of the Bible records that the Lord explained to Abraham, "My people have gone astray from my precepts . . . ; and have said that the blood of the righteous Abel was shed for sins; and have not known wherein they are accountable before me." (JST Genesis 17:4, 7.)

Moses 5:34
"And the Lord said unto Cain"

Selected Statements of the First Presidency and the Twelve Apostles

"It is interesting to note that God even appeared to the first murderer, Cain, and talked with him face to face after his crime. Not even Cain and his children—banished as they were into the land of Nod— would have any excuse for not serving God, for the Lord did appear to and talk with Cain." (Mark E. Petersen, *One Lord . . . One Faith!*, p. 184.)

Moses 5:34
"Am I my brother's keeper?"

Selected Statements of the First Presidency and the Twelve Apostles

"Are we our brothers' keepers? In other words, are we responsible to look after the well-being of our neighbors as we seek to earn our daily bread? The Savior's Golden Rule says we are. Satan says we are not.

"Tempted of Satan, some have followed the example of Cain. They covet property and then sin to obtain it. The sin may be murder, robbery, or theft. It may be fraud or deception. It may even be some clever but legal manipulation of facts or influence to take unfair advantage of another. Always the excuse is the same: 'Am I my brother's keeper?' " (Dallin H. Oaks, in *Ensign*, Nov. 1986, p. 20.)

Moses 5:36–40
"A fugitive and a vagabond shalt thou be in the earth"

Selected Statements of the First Presidency and the Twelve Apostles

"The taking of life was condemned when Cain slew Abel, and for his dreadful sin Cain was punished far worse than to have been put to death." (Joseph Fielding Smith, *Answers to Gospel Questions*, 4:132.)

Moses 5:38

"Satan tempted me [Cain] because of my brother's flocks. I was wroth also; for his offering thou didst accept and not mine"

Selected Statements of the First Presidency and the Twelve Apostles

"One of his [Satan's] most effective tools is the temptation to take unfair advantage in order to get gain. It has been so from the beginning.

"Cain set the pattern of the world. Cain coveted the flocks of his brother Abel, and Satan showed him how to obtain them (see JST Genesis 5:14, 23; Moses 5:29, 38). Satan taught Cain that a man could get worldly wealth by committing some evil against its owner (see JST Genesis 5:16; Moses 5:31)." (Dallin H. Oaks, in *Ensign*, Nov. 1986, p. 20.)

"First, we must eliminate the individual tendency to selfishness that snares the soul, shrinks the heart, and darkens the mind. President Romney recently referred to the tragic cycle of civilization, a cycle propelled by anyone who seeks for power and gain. Was it not this that led Cain to commit the first murder 'for the sake of getting gain'?" (Spencer W. Kimball, in Conference Report, Apr. 1978, p. 123.)

Other Commentary

Not only did Cain glory in that which he had done (see Moses 5:33), but he seems never to have felt remorse for his heinous sin. Sadly, he divorced himself from any responsibility when he blamed Satan for tempting him to covet Abel's flocks and blamed God for not accepting a satanically inspired, bloodless sacrifice. (See Moses 5:38.)

Moses 5:41–42

Cain built a city and named it after his son Enoch

Other Commentary

The city of Enoch named after Cain's son should not be confused with the city that was built several hundred years later by righteous Enoch, son of Jared, who was six generations from Adam. It was this later city of Enoch that was called Zion and was translated because of the righteousness of the people. (See Moses 7:19–21.)

Moses 5:43–46

The children and followers of Cain

Other Commentary

It appears that the followers of Cain were bright people of varied skills and trades. There were city builders and tent dwellers, cattlemen, musicians, and artisans. They, like the first Pharaoh, were blessed with "the blessings of the earth and . . . of wisdom, but cursed . . . as pertaining to the Priesthood." (Abraham 1:26.)

Moses 5:51

"From the days of Cain, there was a secret combination"

Selected Statements of the First Presidency and the Twelve Apostles

"[The war in heaven], so bitter, so intense, has gone on, and it has never ceased. It is the war between truth and error, between agency and compulsion, between the followers of Christ and those who have denied Him. His enemies have used every stratagem in that conflict. They've indulged in lying and deceit. They've employed money and wealth. They've tricked the minds of men. They've murdered and destroyed and engaged in every other unholy and impure practice to thwart the work of Christ.

"It began in the earth when Cain slew Abel. The Old Testament is replete with accounts of the same eternal struggle." (Gordon B. Hinckley, in *Ensign*, Nov. 1986, p. 42.)

Moses 5:55

"The works of darkness began to prevail among all the sons of men"

Selected Statements of the First Presidency and the Twelve Apostles

"When the devil got possession of the earth, his power extended to that which pertains to the earth. He obtained influence over the children of men in their present organization, because the spirits of men yielded to the temptations of the evil principle that the flesh or body is subjected to." (Brigham Young, in *Journal of Discourses*, 3:208.)

"Because of this agency, and the activity of Satan, wickedness has prevailed in the world from the beginning. Contrary to the commandments of the Lord that men should live in peace and righteousness and respect the rights of others, they have used this agency to rebel against God and commit all manner of sin. The mission of Lucifer, as we all should know, is to fight truth and destroy the works of the Lord and the salvation of mankind if he can." (Joseph Fielding Smith, *Answers to Gospel Questions*, 3:73.)

Moses 5:57

"His Only Begotten Son . . . [who] should come in the meridian of time"

Selected Statements of the First Presidency and the Twelve Apostles

"In this scripture appears the earliest mention of the expressive and profoundly significant designation of the period in which the Christ should appear—the meridian of time. If the expression be regarded as figurative, be it remembered the figure is the Lord's.

"The term 'meridian,' as commonly used, conveys the thought of a principal division of time or space. . . . So the years and the centuries of human history are divided by the great event of the birth of Jesus Christ." (James E. Talmage, *Jesus the Christ*, p. 57.)

Selected Scripture References

"He [Christ] came in the meridian of time, in the flesh." (D&C 20:26.)

"The same which came in the meridian of time." (D&C 39:3.)

"The name of his Only Begotten is the Son of Man, even Jesus Christ, a righteous Judge, who shall come in the meridian of time." (Moses 6:57.)

Moses 5:58–59

"The Gospel began to be preached, from the beginning"

Selected Statements of the First Presidency and the Twelve Apostles

"Now, any man acquainted with the Scriptures can clearly understand that there is but one true Gospel. There never was but one Gospel. Whenever that Gospel has been upon the earth it has been the same in every dispensation. The ordinances of the Gospel have never been changed from the days of Adam to the present time, and never will be to the end of time. While there were many sects and parties in existence in the early times, Jesus gave his disciples to understand that there was but one Gospel. He told them what it was. He declared unto them its ordinances. He commissioned them to preach the Gospel to every creature." (Wilford Woodruff, in *Journal of Discourses*, 24:239–40. See also N. Eldon Tanner, in Conference Report, Oct. 1964, p. 44; Joseph Smith, *History of the Church*, 2:16–17.)

"To help men to come back to him, our Heavenly Father has from the beginning shown the way leading back into his presence, by proclaiming the saving principles of the Gospel to his children [Moses 5:56–58], not always in their fullness, but sufficiently so to save men if they harken and obey. Remnants of the Gospel plan have clung in the minds of men from Adam down, part as corrupted memories, part as tradition; some few things God made instinctive in his children." (J. Reuben Clark, Jr., *On the Way to Immortality and Eternal Life,* pp. 32–33.)

"Although not adapted, nor designed, as a pioneer of faith among unbelievers, still it [the Pearl of Great Price] will commend itself to all careful students of the scriptures, as detailing many important facts which are therein only alluded to, or entirely unmentioned, but consonant with the whole tenor of the revealed will of God; and, to the beginner in the Gospel, will add confirmatory evidence of the rectitude of his faith, by showing him that the doctrines and ordinances thereof are the same as were revealed to Adam for his salvation after his expulsion from the garden, and the same that he handed down and caused to be taught to his generations after him, as the only means appointed of God by which the generations of men may regain His presence." (Franklin D. Richards, Preface to Pearl of Great Price, 1851 ed., pp. v–vi.)

Selected Scripture References

"Unto us was the gospel preached, as well as unto them." (Hebrews 4:2.)

"And they began from that time forth to call on his name; therefore God . . . made known unto them the plan of redemption." (Alma 12:30.)

Moses 6

Moses 6:2–3

"God hath appointed me another seed [Seth], instead of Abel, whom Cain slew"

Selected Statements of the First Presidency and the Twelve Apostles

"There is a principle developed here pertaining to the economy of God with the human family. Abel held a representative position, as also did Cain, and that position, it would seem, associated Abel with what may be denominated the chosen seed. Cain slew Abel; but that the purposes relating to the perpetuation of that seed might stand, and the plan of God not be frustrated by the adversary, He gave to Adam Seth, who inherited the priesthood and promises of his martyred brother." (John Taylor, *Mediation and Atonement*, p. 67. See also pp. 68–69.)

Selected Scripture References

"Seth . . . was ordained by Adam at the age of sixty-nine years, and was blessed by him three years previous to his [Adam's] death." (D&C 107:42.)

Seth was "a perfect man," expressly like Adam. (D&C 107:43.)

Seth was "one of the mighty ones, who was in the express image of his father, Adam." (D&C 138:40.)

Moses 6:5–6
"And a book of remembrance was kept"

Selected Statements of the First Presidency and the Twelve Apostles

"Adam kept a written account of his faithful descendants in which he recorded their faith and works, their righteousness and devotion, their revelations and visions, and their adherence to the revealed plan of salvation. To signify the importance of honoring our worthy ancestors and of hearkening to the great truths revealed to them, Adam called his record a *book of remembrance*." (Bruce R. McConkie, *Mormon Doctrine*, p. 100.)

"The Lord has always impressed upon his people the necessity of keeping records. In Adam's day, we are informed by Moses, the Lord commanded that records be kept. . . .

"And so they were commanded to keep records. They were not only commanded to keep a record of important *events*, but they were also to keep a record of their *families* and preserve it that it might be of benefit in time to come." (Joseph Fielding Smith, *Doctrines of Salvation*, 2:200–201. See also Bruce R. McConkie, *Mortal Messiah*, 1:269.)

"Please follow the counsel you have been given in the past and maintain your personal journals. Those who keep a book of remembrance are more likely to keep the Lord in remembrance in their daily lives. Journals are a way of counting our blessings and of leaving an inventory of these blessings for our posterity." (Spencer W. Kimball, in *Ensign*, May 1978, p. 77.)

Other Commentary

"When a person receives a patriarchal blessing, he is entitled to receive a pronouncement of the blessings of Israel, or a declaration of the tribe of Israel through which his blessings shall come. This is the right to the blessings of those recorded in the book of remembrance started in the days of Adam." (Eldred G. Smith, in Conference Report, Apr. 1971, p. 146.)

Moses 6:6
"And by them their children were taught to read and write"

Selected Statements of the First Presidency and the Twelve Apostles

"I understand from this that Enoch could read about Adam in a book which had been written under the tutelage of Almighty God. Thus there were no prehistoric men who could not write because men living in the days of Adam, who was the first man, wrote." (Marion G. Romney, in *Improvement Era*, June 1953, p. 442.)

Moses 6:8

"And a genealogy was kept of the children of God"

Selected Scripture References

"The plates of brass . . . contained the genealogy of my father [Lehi]." (1 Nephi 3:12.)

"My father, Lehi, also found upon the plates of brass a genealogy of his fathers." (1 Nephi 5:14.)

"These plates of brass . . . have the genealogy of our forefathers, even from the beginning." (Alma 37:3.)

"I [Abraham] shall endeavor . . . to delineate the chronology running back from myself to the beginning of the creation, for the records have come into my hands." (Abraham 1:28.)

Other Commentary

" 'Now this prophecy Adam spake, as he was moved upon by the Holy Ghost, and a genealogy was kept of the children of God. . . . ' (Moses 6:7–8.)

"This became the record of the royal seed, which is a record in part, at least, of the fulfillment of this promise. This we have today, at least in part, which is known as the Bible." (Eldred G. Smith, in Conference Report, Apr. 1971, p. 146.)

Moses 6:8

"And this was the book of the generations of Adam"

Selected Statements of the First Presidency and the Twelve Apostles

"This ancient book of remembrance and genealogical record of the children of God, which contained the generations of Adam, was intended to be preserved and handed down from generation to generation. These records were kept by the Church. Those whose names were found therein, were known as the 'children of God.' " (Joseph Fielding Smith, *Way to Perfection*, pp. 78–79.)

Moses 6:9

"In the image of his own body, male and female, created he them . . . and called their name Adam"

Selected Statements of the First Presidency and the Twelve Apostles

" 'Male and female created he them; and blessed them, and called their name Adam [Mr. and Mrs. Adam, I suppose, or Brother and Sister

Adam], in the day when they were created.' (Genesis 5:1-2)." (Spencer W. Kimball, in *Ensign*, Mar. 1976, p. 71.)

Moses 6:10-25

Longevity among the antediluvian prophets

Selected Statements of the First Presidency and the Twelve Apostles

"The age of man is very short indeed in this day to what it was in ancient days. Men anciently lived to a very great age. When four or five hundred years old they took wives, begat children, and raised up posterity. Today our age is limited to something like three score years and ten." (Wilford Woodruff, in James R. Clark, comp., *Messages of the First Presidency*, 3:253. See also Wilford Woodruff, in *Journal of Discourses*, 13:319.)

Selected Scripture References

The first generations of men were given much longer life spans "that they might repent while in the flesh." (2 Nephi 2:21.)

The Lord will lengthen the Lamanites' days because they have not sinned against greater knowledge. (See Helaman 7:24.)

Other Commentary

Two lists in the scriptures deal with the antediluvian prophets. One list gives the ages of the prophets when their successors in the patriarchal priesthood were born and also the ages when the prophets died. (See Moses 6:10-25; 8:1-2.) The second list gives the ages of the ten patriarchs when they were ordained to the holy priesthood and the names of those who ordained them. (See D&C 107:40-52.)

"Now when Noah had lived three hundred and fifty years after the Flood, and that all that time happily, he died, having lived the number of nine hundred and fifty years. But let no one, upon comparing the lives of the ancients with our lives, and with the few years which we now live, think that what we have said of them is false; or make the shortness of our lives at present an argument that neither did they attain to so long a duration of life, for those ancients were beloved of God, and [lately] made by God himself; and because their food was then fitter for the prolongation of life, might well live so great a number of years: and besides, God afforded them a longer time of life on account of their virtue, and the good use they made of it in astronomical and geometrical discoveries, which would not have afforded the time of foretelling [the periods of the stars] unless they had lived six hundred years; for the great year is completed in that interval. Now I have for witnesses to what I have said, all those that have written Antiquities, both among the Greeks and barbarians; for even Manetho, who wrote the Egyptian History, and Berosus, who collected the Chaldean Monuments, and Mochus, and Hestiaeus, and, besides these, Hieronymus the Egyptian, and those who composed the Phoenician History, agree to what I here say: Hesiod also, and Hecataeus, Hellanicus, and Acusilaus; and, besides these, Ephorus and Nicolaus relate that the ancients lived a thousand years. But as to these matters, let every one look upon them as he thinks fit." (Josephus *Antiquities of the Jews*, bk. 1, chap. 3, par. 9.)

LONGEVITY OF THE ANTEDILUVIAN PROPHETS

Name	Age at Death	Reference
Adam	930	Moses 6:12
Seth	912	Moses 6:16
Enos	905	Moses 6:18
Cainan	910	Moses 6:19
Mahalaleel	895	Moses 6:20
Jared	962	Moses 6:24
Enoch	430 (translated)	Moses 8:1
Methuselah	969	Moses 8:7
Lamech	777	Moses 8:11
Noah	950	Genesis 9:29

Moses 6:15

"And in those days Satan had great dominion among men, and raged in their hearts"

Selected Statements of the First Presidency and the Twelve Apostles

"There is this difference between God and Satan in the treatment of mankind. Satan is perfectly reckless as to what the consequences may be of anything he may give to the children of men. He will heap temptation upon temptation before them, give them honor, riches, and position, and, if necessary, he will give them revelation. What for? To damn them. He does not care anything as to what may become of them; but he offers them all he can control without judgment or discrimination. God does not do so." (George Q. Cannon, in *Journal of Discourses*, 11:174.)

Selected Scripture References

In the last days Satan shall "rage in the hearts of the children of men." (2 Nephi 28:20.)

"Satan had great power, unto the stirring up of the people to do all manner of iniquity." (3 Nephi 6:15.)

Moses 6:22

"And this is the genealogy of the sons of Adam, who was the son of God"

Selected Statements of the First Presidency and the Twelve Apostles

"We are not to understand that these ten men were the only ones who held the divine authority before the flood, but that they were called to positions of responsibility, or presiding authority, among their fellows. It is hardly reasonable to suppose that these ten men were left in their day and generation to perform all the labor required of men holding the Priesthood. They had a church organization." (Joseph Fielding Smith, *Way to Perfection*, p. 73.)

Other Commentary

In the book of remembrance kept in the days of Adam, "a genealogy was kept of the children of God." (Moses 6:8.) The record refers to God in a most familiar manner: "And this was the book of the generations of Adam, saying: In the day that God created man, in the likeness of God made he him; in the image of his own body, male and female, created he them, and blessed them, and called their name Adam." (Moses 6:8-9.) Similar phrasing was used to tell about Seth: "Adam . . . begat a son in his own likeness, after his own image, and called his name Seth." The book of remembrance once again listed God's name in the genealogy: "And this is the genealogy of the sons of Adam, who was the son of God, with whom God, himself, conversed." (Moses 6:22.)

Moses 6:28

"Ever since the day that I created them, have they gone astray"

Selected Statements of the First Presidency and the Twelve Apostles

"Satan succeeded in those early days to turn many from righteous lives. These people lived sinfully. Yet, as they departed from association with the people of the Lord, they carried with them the knowledge of the gospel. Such parts of it as seemed to fit their desires they retained, often warped beyond recognition. But, from the days of Adam, gospel truth was diffused among the peoples of the earth." (John A. Widtsoe, *Evidences and Reconciliations*, 1:83.)

Moses 6:31

"Why is it that I [Enoch] have found favor in thy [the Lord's] sight?"

Selected Statements of the First Presidency and the Twelve Apostles

"We read of Enoch who was called when but a lad. He describes himself as a lad whom the people despised and who was slow of speech; yet he did his duty in love and compassion with stunning success. (See Moses 6.) I marvel at the empathy of these men in all ages, because even prophets have no immunity from thorns in the flesh. They learn to cast all their cares upon the Lord." (Spencer W. Kimball, in Conference Report, Apr. 1978, p. 116.)

Other Commentary

"Do you think it is difficult to be a prophet? As you read the scriptures, you cannot help but be impressed with the fact that the calling of a prophet is a most difficult assignment. In fact, you will be astonished to find that when some of the prophets first received their callings they pleaded with the Lord not to send them forth. . . .

"These men felt incapable. They felt there were others who would be more readily accepted. But in spite of their own feelings to the contrary, they went forth and delivered their messages because God had called them." (Paul H. Dunn, in Conference Report, Oct. 1969, pp. 128–29.)

"A special dispensation of the Gospel seems to have been given to Enoch. He was called of God to preach the plan of redemption to the 'sons of men' (non-Church members). . . .

"Enoch accepted the call and became a powerful preacher of righteousness. . . . He understood thoroughly the doctrine of the fall, the atonement, and the accompanying principles and ordinances of the gospel." (Milton R. Hunter, *Gospel through the Ages*, p. 70.)

Doctrine and Covenants 107:48 tells us that Enoch was twenty-five years old when he was called to serve. Until Noah's day Enoch was the youngest man ever ordained. He was "but a lad" compared to his forefathers. (See D&C 107: 41–52.)

Moses 6:33
"Choose ye this day, to serve the Lord God"

Selected Statements of the First Presidency and the Twelve Apostles

"If our service is to be most efficacious, it must be accomplished for the love of God and the love of his children. . . .

"Service with all our heart and mind is a high challenge for all of us. Such service must be free of selfish ambition. It must be motivated only by the pure love of Christ." (Dallin H. Oaks, in Conference Report, Oct. 1984, p. 16.)

"We came to mortal life to encounter resistance. It was part of the plan for our eternal progress. Without temptation, sickness, pain, and sorrow, there could be no goodness, virtue, appreciation for well-being, or joy. The law of opposition makes freedom of choice possible; therefore, our Heavenly Father has commanded his children, 'Choose ye this day, to serve the Lord God who made you' (Moses 6:33). He has counseled us to yield to his spirit and resist temptation. Free agency, of course, permits us to oppose his directions; thus, we see many who resist the truth and yield to temptation." (Howard W. Hunter, in Conference Report, Apr. 1980, p. 34.)

Selected Scripture References

"Choose you this day whom ye will serve; . . . as for me and my house, we will serve the Lord." (Joshua 24:15.)

"Thus saith the scripture: Choose ye this day, whom ye will serve." (Alma 30:8.)

Other Commentary

Could Joshua's famous saying (see Joshua 24:15) possibly be based upon an earlier statement of the prophet Enoch?

Moses 6:34

"All thy words will I justify; and the mountains shall flee before you, and the rivers shall turn from their course"

Selected Statements of the First Presidency and the Twelve Apostles

"Deity intervenes in temporal things, even controlling and moderating the elements for the faithful. True, he makes the sun to shine and sends his rains upon the just and the unjust (Matthew 5:45), for all men have come to earth to receive the experiences and undergo the vicissitudes of mortality. But he maintains special watch care over those who by obedience and righteousness become his especial friends. For them storms are stilled, barren soil becomes productive (Isaiah 35), special needed rains fall and bounteous harvests mature (Leviticus 26:3–5; Deuteronomy 11:13–15; 28:11–12), vines do not cast off their ripened fruits untimely (Malachi 3:11), climatic conditions of whole regions are changed, mountains are moved, and rivers are turned out of their courses. (Moses 6:34; 7:13–14.)" (Bruce R. McConkie, *Doctrinal New Testament Commentary*, 1:307.)

Moses 6:36

"A seer hath the Lord raised up"

Selected Statements of the First Presidency and the Twelve Apostles

"A seer is one who sees with spiritual eyes. He perceives the meaning of that which seems obscure to others; therefore he is an interpreter and a clarifier of eternal truth. He foresees the future from the past and the present. This he does by the power of the Lord operating through him directly, or indirectly with the aid of divine instruments such as the Urim and Thummim. In short, he is one who sees, who walks in the Lord's light with open eyes." (John A. Widtsoe, *Evidences and Reconciliations*, 1:205–6.)

Selected Scripture References

"Whosoever is commanded to look in them [Urim and Thummim], the same is called seer." (Mosiah 8:13.)

"A seer is a revelator and a prophet also." (Mosiah 8:16.)

"A seer can know of things which are past, and also of things which are to come, and by them shall all things be revealed." (Mosiah 8:17.)

"Whosoever has these things [Urim and Thummim] is called seer." (Mosiah 28:16.)

Moses 6:43

"Why counsel ye yourselves, and deny the God of heaven?"

Selected Statements of the First Presidency and the Twelve Apostles

"Lucifer turned men from the truth to fables. He changed men from revelation to human logic and mental gymnastics and convinced them that man was on his own, to make all his own determinations without the aid of God and his prophets and apostles. . . .

"Many men with no pretense nor claim to revelation, speaking without divine authority or revelation, depending only upon their own brilliant minds, but representing as they claim the congregations of the Christians and in long conference and erudite councils, sought the creation process to make a God which all could accept.

"The brilliant minds with their philosophies, knowing much about the Christian traditions and the pagan philosophies, would combine all elements to please everybody." (Spencer W. Kimball, *Teachings of Spencer W. Kimball*, p. 425.)

Other Commentary

When men reject an omniscient supreme being, they often seek counsel from experts whom they regard as superior in understanding. The wisdom of men is so shallow and so tentative. How many textbooks used in the universities even ten years ago are still considered authoritative? The wisdom of finite man is foolishness before God. The self-appointed wise men of Enoch's day who counseled each other and denied God were as some still are in this day, only multiplying ignorance.

Moses 6:46

"A book of remembrance we have written"

See Statements and Scripture References under Moses 6:6.

Moses 6:48

"Because that Adam fell, we are; and by his fall came death"

See Statements and Scripture References under Moses 5:10–11.

Moses 6:49

"Satan hath come among the children of men, and tempteth them to worship him"

Selected Statements of the First Presidency and the Twelve Apostles

"First, he flatters. He tells men of their gifts and virtues as compared with those of others. He tempts them with praise and glory, and promises power, if they do as he suggests. In the distance he beckons with the rewards of gain, gold and silver. Fleshly satisfactions are his common baits." (John A. Widtsoe, *Man and the Dragon*, p. 159.)

Moses 6:51

"I made the world, and men before they were in the flesh"

See Statements and Scripture References under Moses 3:4-5; 3:5; 3:7, 22.

Moses 6:52

"Jesus Christ, the only name which shall be given under heaven, whereby salvation shall come unto the children of men"

Selected Statements of the First Presidency and the Twelve Apostles

"The Lord's revelation to Adam making known the ordained plan whereby the Son of God was to take upon Himself flesh in the meridian of time, and become the Redeemer of the world, was attested by Enoch, son of Jared and father of Methuselah. From the words of Enoch we learn that to him as to his great progenitor, Adam, the very name by which the Savior would be known among men was revealed." (James E. Talmage, *Jesus the Christ*, p. 44.)

Selected Scripture References

"Neither is there salvation in any other: for there is none other name under heaven given among men, whereby we must be saved." (Acts 4:12.)

"There is none other name given under heaven save it be this Jesus Christ, of which I have spoken, whereby man can be saved." (2 Nephi 25:20.)

"This is the means whereby salvation cometh." (Mosiah 4:8.)

Moses 6:52

"Ye shall receive the gift of the Holy Ghost"

Selected Statements of the First Presidency and the Twelve Apostles

"Through the Holy Ghost a knowledge of things past, present and to come is communicated and the mind and will of the Father made known. In this way the Almighty reveals His purposes to those who obey His commandments and whose lives are pure and acceptable before Him, so that they can be prepared for all the events and trials that may lie in their pathway." (Wilford Woodruff, in James R. Clark, comp., *Messages of the First Presidency*, 3:158.)

Selected Scripture References

"Repent, and be baptized every one of you in the name of Jesus Christ . . . , and ye shall receive the gift of the Holy Ghost." (Acts 2:38.)

"Then cometh the baptism of fire and of the Holy Ghost; and then can ye speak with the tongue of angels, and shout praises unto the Holy One of Israel." (2 Nephi 31:13.)

"They shall receive the Holy Ghost by the laying on of the hands." (D&C 35:6.)

Moses 6:53

"Why is it that men must repent and be baptized in water?"

Selected Statements of the First Presidency and the Twelve Apostles

"Adam and Eve, cut off from the presence of God, were given instruction concerning the necessity of repentance as a means to regain their place in God's presence, there to continue in the way of light and intelligence to the attainment of ultimate perfection. Adam, seeking earnestly to know the will of God, asked this question of the Lord: 'Why is it that men must repent and be baptized in water?' (Moses 6:53.)

"The Lord's answer was clear and distinct, for unto Adam and Eve, upon whom darkness had come, having fallen from God, came this vital instruction of the need of repentance: 'Wherefore teach it unto your children, that all men, everywhere, must repent, or they can in nowise inherit the kingdom of God. . . . ' (Moses 6:57.)" (Alvin R. Dyer, in Conference Report, Oct. 1969, p. 54.)

Selected Scripture References

"It becometh us to fulfil all righteousness." (Matthew 3:15.)

"Except a man be born of water and of the Spirit, he cannot enter into the kingdom of God." (John 3:5.)

"If the Lamb of God, he being holy, should have need to be baptized by water, . . . how much more need have we, being unholy, to be baptized, yea, even by water." (2 Nephi 31:5.)

Moses 6:54

"The Son of God hath atoned for original guilt . . . , for [children] are whole from the foundation of the world"

Selected Statements of the First Presidency and the Twelve Apostles

"There is no such thing as original sin as such is defined in the creeds of Christendom. Such a concept denies the efficacy of the atonement. Our revelation says: 'Every spirit of man was innocent in the beginning'—meaning that spirits started out in a state of purity and innocence in pre-existence—'and God having redeemed man from the fall, men became again, in their infant state, innocent before God' (D&C 93:38)—meaning that all children start out their mortal probation in purity and innocence because of the atonement. Our revelations also say, 'The Son of God hath atoned for original guilt, wherein the sins of the parents cannot be answered upon the heads of the children, for they are whole from the foundation of the world.' (Moses 6:54.)" (Bruce R. McConkie, in *Ensign*, Apr. 1977, p. 4. See also Joseph Fielding Smith, *Man: His Origin and Destiny*, pp. 51–52.)

"Through the atonement of Jesus Christ all little children are redeemed, for they cannot sin, and the power is not given to Satan to tempt them. The question naturally may arise as to the meaning of the words of the Lord (verse 46) that 'little children are redeemed from the foundation of the world, through the Only Begotten.' This does not mean that redemption was made for them before, or at, the foundation of the world, but at that time when the plan of salvation was received provision was made for the redemption of little children and also for those who are without the law, and this was consummated in the atonement made by Jesus Christ." (Joseph Fielding Smith, *Church History and Modern Revelation*, 1:133–34.)

"This being 'conceived in sin,' [Moses 6:55], as I understand it, is only that they are in the midst of sin. They come into the world where sin is prevalent, and it will enter into their hearts, but it will lead them 'to taste the bitter, that they may know to prize the good.' " (George Q. Morris, in Conference Report, Apr. 1958, p. 38. See also Anthony W. Ivins, in *Improvement Era*, Sept. 1923, p. 986.)

Selected Scripture References

"Wherefore, it must needs be an infinite atonement—save it should be an infinite atonement this corruption could not put on incorruption." (2 Nephi 9:7.)

"Even if it were possible that little children could sin they could not be saved; but I say unto you they are blessed; . . . as in Adam, or by nature, they fall, even so the blood of Christ atoneth for their sins. . . . The infant perisheth not that dieth in his infancy." (Mosiah 3:16, 18.)

"Little children are whole, for they are not capable of committing sin." (Moroni 8:8.)

"Little children are redeemed from the foundation of the world through mine Only Begotten." (D&C 29:46.)

"Little children are holy, being sanctified through the atonement of Jesus Christ." (D&C 74:7.)

Moses 6:56

"Wherefore they are agents unto themselves"

Selected Statements of the First Presidency and the Twelve Apostles

"Intelligent obedience on the part of His Saints is desired by our Father in heaven. He has given us our agency to think and act for ourselves, on our own volition, to obtain a testimony for ourselves from Him concerning the truth of the principles which He teaches, and then be firm and unshaken in the performance of all which is necessary for salvation." (Wilford Woodruff, in James R. Clark, comp., *Messages of the First Presidency*, 3:137.)

"He [Joseph Smith] then observed that Satan was generally blamed for the evils which we did, but if he was the cause of all our wickedness, men could not be condemned. The devil could not compel mankind to do evil; all was voluntary. Those who resisted the Spirit of God, would be liable to be led into temptation, and then the association of heaven would be withdrawn from those who refused to be made partakers of such great glory. God would not exert any compulsory means, and the devil could not; and such ideas as were entertained [on these subjects] by many were absurd." (Joseph Smith, *Teachings of the Prophet Joseph Smith*, p. 187.)

"Men may choose the right or they may choose the wrong; they may walk in darkness or they may walk in the light. The Lord has given them, in the various dispensations of the world, the light of the gospel, wherein they could walk and not stumble." (David O. McKay, in

Improvement Era, Feb. 1964, p. 84. See also John A. Widtsoe, *Evidences and Reconciliations*, 3:126.)

Selected Scripture References

"It must needs be, that there is an opposition in all things." (2 Nephi 2:11.)

"Men are free according to the flesh." (2 Nephi 2:27.)

"Behold, ye are free; ye are permitted to act for yourselves." (Helaman 14:30.)

"It must needs be that the devil should tempt the children of men, or they could not be agents unto themselves." (D&C 29:39.)

"All these things shall give thee experience, and shall be for thy good." (D&C 122:7.)

Other Commentary

"In denying our own responsibility, we frequently blame Satan for much of the misery that we are bringing upon ourselves. Satan has no power over us except as we give it to him. And temptations without imply desires within; and rather than say, 'How powerfully the devil tempts,' we might say, 'How strongly I am inclined.' God never forces us to do right, and Satan has no power to force us to do wrong. As someone has said, 'God always votes for us and Satan always votes against us, and then we are asked to vote to break the tie.' It is how we vote that gives our lives their significance." (Sterling W. Sill, in Conference Report, Apr. 1970, pp. 29–30.)

Moses 6:57

"All men, everywhere, must repent, . . . for no unclean thing can dwell . . . in his presence"

Selected Statements of the First Presidency and the Twelve Apostles

"The prophets and apostles from Adam and Enoch down, and all men, whether cleansed and sanctified from sin or not, are yet subject to and do in fact commit sin. This is the case even after men have seen the visions of eternity and been sealed by the Holy Spirit of Promise which makes their calling and election sure. Since these chosen ones have the sure promise of eternal life, and since 'no unclean thing can enter into' the Father's 'kingdom' (3 Nephi 27:19), 'or dwell in his presence' (Moses 6:57), what of sins committed after being sealed up into eternal life?

"Obviously the laws of repentance still apply, and the more enlightened a person is, the more he seeks the gift of repentance, and the harder he strives to free himself from sin as often as he falls short of the divine will and becomes subject in any degree to the Master of Sin who is Lucifer. It follows that the sins of the godfearing and the righteous are continually remitted because they repent and seek the Lord anew every day and every hour." (Bruce R. McConkie, *Doctrinal New Testament Commentary*, 3:342-43.)

Selected Scripture References

"Who shall ascend into the hill of the Lord? . . . He that hath clean hands, and a pure heart." (Psalm 24:3-4.)

"No unclean thing can dwell with God." (1 Nephi 10:21.)

"If they be filthy it must needs be that they cannot dwell in the kingdom of God." (1 Nephi 15:33.)

"Every man must repent or suffer." (D&C 19:4.)

"He that sinneth and repenteth not shall be cast out." (D&C 42:28.)

"They can in nowise inherit the kingdom of God, for no unclean thing can dwell there." (Moses 6:57.)

Moses 6:58
"Teach these things freely unto your children"

See Statements and Scripture References under Moses 5:12.

Moses 6:59
"By reason of transgression cometh the fall"

Selected Statements of the First Presidency and the Twelve Apostles

"It may seem very cruel to us without any understanding of all the circumstances, to know that the Fall brought upon us all such awful consequences, and made it possible for an infinite atonement to be offered to amend the broken law. Adam and Eve did not come here in a mortal state. They had to come in the manner in which they did and then transgress the law. The transgression of that law, contrary to the view of many, was not a sin. It was not a sin any more than the transgression in the laboratory by a chemist in combining two substances and creating another entirely different from the first. It was not a sin to bring to pass mortality, a condition which was essential to the eternal welfare of man. The Fall changed the nature of Adam and Eve to fit them for the condition in which we now are." (Joseph Fielding Smith, *Answers to Gospel Questions*, 2:214-15.)

Selected Scripture References

"If Adam had not transgressed he would not have fallen, but he would have remained in the garden of Eden." (2 Nephi 2:22.)

"The fall came by reason of transgression; and because man became fallen they were cut off from the presence of the Lord." (2 Nephi 9:6.)

Moses 6:59

"Inasmuch as ye were born into the world by water, and blood, and the spirit, . . . even so ye must be born again"

Selected Statements of the First Presidency and the Twelve Apostles

"Every child that comes into this world is carried in water, is born of water, and of blood, and of the spirit. So when we are born into the kingdom of God, we must be born in the same way. By baptism, we are born of the water. Through the shedding of the blood of Christ, we are cleansed and sanctified; and we are justified, through the Spirit of God, for baptism is not complete without the baptism of the Holy Ghost. You see the *parallel* between birth into the world and birth into the kingdom of God." (Joseph Fielding Smith, *Doctrines of Salvation*, 2:324-25.)

"Baptism in water for the remission of sins, and the laying on of hands for the gift of the Holy Ghost, constitute the birth of the water and of the Spirit. This is essential to salvation. It is more than a symbol; it is a reality, a birth in very deed." (Joseph Fielding Smith, *Way to Perfection*, p. 190.)

Moses 6:60

"By the Spirit ye are justified"

Selected Statements of the First Presidency and the Twelve Apostles

"To be justified is to be made righteous and therefore to be saved. Men are justified in what they do when their deeds conform to divine standards. Righteous acts are approved of the Lord; they are ratified by the Holy Ghost; they are sealed by the Holy Spirit of Promise; or, in other words, they are justified by the Spirit. Such divine approval must be given to 'all covenants, contracts, bonds, obligations, oaths, vows, performances, connections, associations, or expectations'—that is, to all things—if they are to have 'efficacy, virtue, or force in and after the resurrection from the dead.' (D&C 132:7.) Such a requirement is part of the terms and conditions of the gospel covenant." (Bruce R. McConkie, *Promised Messiah*, p. 344.)

Selected Scripture References

"By works a man is justified, and not by faith only." (James 2:24.)

"We know that justification through the grace of our Lord and Savior Jesus Christ is just and true." (D&C 20:30.)

Moses 6:60

"By the blood ye are sanctified"

Selected Statements of the First Presidency and the Twelve Apostles

"The atonement of Christ is the rock foundation upon which all things rest which pertain to salvation and eternal life. Hence the Lord said to Adam: 'By the blood ye are sanctified' (Moses 6:60), although the usual scriptural pronouncement is that men are 'sanctified by the reception of the Holy Ghost.' (3 Nephi 27:20.) The meaning is that although men are sanctified by the power of the Holy Ghost, such sanctifying process is effective and operative because of the shedding of the blood of Christ." (Bruce R. McConkie, *Doctrinal New Testament Commentary*, 3:188.)

Selected Scripture References

"Sanctification cometh because of their yielding their hearts unto God." (Helaman 3:35.)

"Sanctification through the grace of our Lord and Savior Jesus Christ is just and true." (D&C 20:31.)

Moses 6:61

"Therefore it [the Comforter] is given to abide in you"

Selected Statements of the First Presidency and the Twelve Apostles

"The Holy Ghost as a personage does not inhabit the bodies of mortal men, but that member of the Godhead dwells in a man in the sense that his promptings, the whisperings of the Spirit, find lodgment in the human soul. When the Holy Spirit speaks to the spirit in man, the Holy Ghost is thereby dwelling in man, for the truths that man then gives forth are those which have come from the Holy Ghost." (Bruce R. McConkie, *Doctrinal New Testament Commentary*, 1:738.)

Moses 6:63

"All things are created and made to bear record of me"

Selected Scripture References

"All things which have been given of God . . . are the typifying of him." (2 Nephi 11:4.)

"All things denote there is a God." (Alma 30:44.)

"Any man who hath seen [the planetary system] . . . hath seen God moving in his majesty and power." (D&C 88:47.)

Moses 6:64–68

Adam and Eve received the ordinances of the gospel

Selected Statements of the First Presidency and the Twelve Apostles

"Adam and Eve—our first parents, our common ancestors, the mother and father of all living—had the fulness of the everlasting gospel. They received the plan of salvation from God himself. . . . They saw God, knew his laws, entertained angels, received revelations, beheld visions, and were in tune with the Infinite. They exercised faith in the Lord Jesus Christ; repented of their sins; were baptized in similitude of the death, burial, and resurrection of the Promised Messiah; and received the gift of the Holy Ghost. They were endowed with power from on high, were sealed in the new and everlasting covenant of marriage, and received the fulness of the ordinances of the house of the Lord.

"After baptism, and after celestial marriage, they walked in paths of truth and righteousness, kept the commandments, and endured to the end. Having charted for themselves a course leading to eternal life, they pressed forward with a steadfastness in Christ—believing, obeying, conforming, consecrating, sacrificing—until their calling and election was made sure and they were sealed up unto eternal life." (Bruce R. McConkie, *Mortal Messiah*, 1:228–29.)

"Adam was taught the gospel, was baptized, received the gift of the Holy Ghost, and was ordained to the Priesthood. While details are not given, the inference seems justified that the father of the human race received a knowledge of the fulness of the gospel and all its gifts. We know that he was ordained a presiding high priest." (John A. Widtsoe, *Evidences and Reconciliations*, 1:82.)

Moses 6:67

"And thou art after the order of him who was without beginning of days or end of years"

Selected Statements of the First Presidency and the Twelve Apostles

"The Prophet Joseph taught us that father Adam was the first man on the earth to whom God gave the keys of the everlasting priesthood.

He held the keys of the presidency, and was the first man who did hold them." (Wilford Woodruff, *Discourses of Wilford Woodruff*, p. 66.)

Selected Scripture References

Alma "ordained priests and elders by laying on his hands according to the order of God." (Alma 6:1.)

Alma taught "according to the holy order of God, by which he had been called." (Alma 8:4.)

"The Lord God ordained priests, after his holy order, which was after the order of his Son." (Alma 13:1.)

Before Melchizedek, the priesthood "was called the Holy Priesthood, after the Order of the Son of God." (D&C 107:2.)

"This order was instituted in the days of Adam." (D&C 107:41.)

Moses 6:68

"Thou art one in me, a son of God; and thus may all become my sons"

Selected Statements of the First Presidency and the Twelve Apostles

"We have power to become the sons of God, to be adopted into the family of the Lord Jesus Christ, to have him as our Father, to be one with him as he is one with his Father." (Bruce R. McConkie, in Conference Report, Oct. 1977, p. 50.)

Selected Scripture References

"All those who receive my gospel are sons and daughters in my kingdom." (D&C 25:1.)

"Who so loved the world that he gave his own life, that as many as would believe might become the sons of God." (D&C 34:3.)

Moses 7

Moses 7:1

"Enoch continued his speech, saying: Behold, our father Adam taught these things"

Selected Statements of the First Presidency and the Twelve Apostles

"If you were to meet with Father Adam, with Seth, Moses, Aaron, Christ, or the Apostles, they would all teach the same principles that we have been taught; they would not vary one particle. This Gospel is everlasting in its nature and unchangeable in its character. It might be urged that the house of Israel had the law of carnal commandments; but that only acted as a schoolmaster to bring them to Christ, because they would not receive a celestial law. They had the Priesthood of Aaron for a series of years amongst them; but the old Apostles, Prophets, and Saints were saved by the Gospel, and not by the law of carnal commandments." (Wilford Woodruff, in *Journal of Discourses*, 8:265.)

Selected Scripture References

See Statements and Scripture References under Moses 5:12.

Moses 7:1

"Many have believed and become the sons of God"

See Statements and Scripture References under Moses 1:4.

Moses 7:2

"As I [Enoch] was journeying, and stood upon the place Mahujah, . . . there came a voice out of heaven, saying—Turn ye, and get ye upon the mount Simeon"

Other Commentary

Simeon is the English equivalent of the Hebrew *Shim'om*, which means "hearing." (See Moses 7:2 n. *a*.)

Moses 7:3

"I beheld the heavens open, and I was clothed upon with glory"

See Statements, Scripture References, and Other Commentary under Moses 1:11.

Moses 7:4

"And he [the Lord] talked with me, even as a man talketh one with another, face to face"

Selected Statements of the First Presidency and the Twelve Apostles

"In order for Adam and Eve and their children clearly to understand their relationship to the Almighty, it was necessary that God appear to them and talk with them face to face, so that they could see him, hear him, and know him.

"They were commanded to worship him, and to make their worship intelligent, they were permitted to see and talk with him." (Mark E. Petersen, *One Lord . . . One Faith!* p. 184.)

Moses 7:8

"There was a blackness came upon all the children of Canaan"

Selected Statements of the First Presidency and the Twelve Apostles

"The opinion is held by many members of the church that because the negro was a neutral in the great council, held in the heavens before the foundations of the earth were laid, he has been punished with a black skin. There is no evidence, as far as found, to justify this belief. On the other hand, there is ample evidence to support the Church doctrine that all who have been permitted to come upon this earth and take upon themselves bodies, accepted the plan of salvation." (John A. Widtsoe, *Gospel Interpretations*, 2:255.)

Moses 7:13

"So great was the faith of Enoch that he led the people of God, and their enemies came to battle against them"

Selected Statements of the First Presidency and the Twelve Apostles

"They [Zion's enemies] rejected their testimony, and not only that, but, like some of the very pious people in our day do towards us, they thought it would be doing God service to sweep these men off the face of the earth. And they thought so in earnest for they gathered together their armies for that purpose. The Saints were under the immediate direction and guidance of the Lord, and were, therefore, governed by revelation, and the power and Spirit of the Lord rested upon Enoch. And he rose up and prophesied and told the wicked of the fate that awaited them; and the power of God rested upon him in a marvelous manner, so much so, that the mountains trembled and the earth shook, and the people were afraid and fled away from his presence, because they could not endure it. Their armies were scattered, and they failed to accomplish that which they in their wickedness had designed to do." (John Taylor, in *Journal of Discourses*, 26:90.)

Moses 7:13

"The earth trembled, and the mountains fled"

Selected Statements of the First Presidency and the Twelve Apostles

"Faith is power; by faith the worlds were made; nothing is impossible to those who have faith. If the earth itself came rolling into existence by faith, surely a mere mountain can be removed by that same power. 'Let Mount Hermon be cast into the Great Sea.' Such would not be one whit different than the brother of Jared saying 'unto the mountain Zerin, Remove—and it was removed.' (Ether 12:30.)" (Bruce R. McConkie, *Mortal Messiah*, 3:73.)

Selected Scripture References

"If ye have faith as a grain of mustard seed, ye shall say unto this mountain, Remove hence to yonder place; and it shall remove." (Matthew 17:20.)

"Our faith becometh unshaken, insomuch that we truly can command in the name of Jesus and the very trees obey us, or the mountains, or the waves of the sea." (Jacob 4:6.)

Moses 7:13-21
Enoch and the perfecting of the Saints

Selected Statements of the First Presidency and the Twelve Apostles

"He stood at the head of the dispensation in which he lived. He, in the course of time, some 350 years, built and perfected the city called Zion. He, however, met with all kinds of opposition from the people among whom he labored; but the power of God was manifested to such an extent that his enemies stood and trembled through fear; and through that power he was enabled to perform the mighty work which he and his people did; it was not because the devil and his party were any more kindly disposed towards the Saints of God, but because they could not help themselves; and in the wisdom of God, Enoch and his people and their city were taken away from the earth." (Wilford Woodruff, in *Journal of Discourses,* 24:53.)

"Excluding, as we necessarily must, the events surrounding the creation and the fall, it is clear that the most transcendent happenings involved Enoch and his ministry. And it is interesting to note that what John saw was not the establishment of Zion and its removal to heavenly spheres, but the unparalleled wars in which Enoch, as a general over the armies of the saints, 'went forth conquering and to conquer.' ...

"Truly, never was there a ministry such as Enoch's, and never a conqueror and general who was his equal! How appropriate that he should ride the white horse of victory in John's apocalyptic vision!" (Bruce R. McConkie, *Doctrinal New Testament Commentary,* 3:477-78.)

Moses 7:15
"Giants of the land"

Selected Statements of the First Presidency and the Twelve Apostles

"A Bible dictionary says that the Nephilim referred to in this passage were giant demigods who lived in those days. (*New Analytical Bible and Dictionary of the Bible.*) Enoch spoke of them as a depraved lot who sought to murder him. But part divine and part human they were not, for God at no time consorted with the 'daughters of men.' It is sacrilege even to mention such a thing. ...

"The Nephilim were described as giants—how big we do not know. Were they like Goliath? In any case, the giants who lived in Enoch's day were a depraved lot who sought to murder him. But part divine and part human they were not, for neither God, angels, nor 'the sons of the gods' consorted with earthly women as implied." (Mark E. Petersen, *Noah and the Flood*, pp. 27–29.)

Selected Scripture References

"We saw the giants, the sons of Anak, . . . and we were in our own sight as grasshoppers." (Numbers 13:33.)
"Giants dwelt therein in old time." (Deuteronomy 2:20.)
"In those days there were giants on the earth." (Moses 8:18.)

Moses 7:17
"The Lord blessed the land"

Selected Statements of the First Presidency and the Twelve Apostles

"As the Lord has repeatedly warned that breaking His commandments would bring on calamity, so has He promised that observance of His commandments would avert calamity and bring blessings.

"As disobedience brought on the flood, so obedience sanctified Enoch's Zion.

" 'And the Lord blessed the land, and they . . . did flourish.' [Moses 7:17.]" (Marion G. Romney, in Conference Report, Apr. 1977, p. 76.)

Selected Scripture References

"And he leadeth away the righteous into precious lands." (1 Nephi 17:38.)
"If it so be that they shall keep his commandments they shall be blessed upon the face of this land." (2 Nephi 1:9.)
"I would that ye should keep the commandments of God, that ye may prosper in the land." (Mosiah 1:7.)

Moses 7:18
"The Lord called his people Zion, because they were of one heart and one mind"

Selected Statements of the First Presidency and the Twelve Apostles

"Always the aim has been unity, oneness, and equality among the members of the church of Christ. As an example, I call your attention to the record of Enoch, how he and his people reached a state of unity when the rest of the world was at war. [Moses 7:15–17.]

" 'And the Lord called his people Zion,' Why? 'Because they were of one heart and one mind, and dwelt in righteousness; and there was no poor among them.' " (Marion G. Romney, in *Ensign*, May 1983, p. 17.)

Selected Scripture References

"Seek to bring forth and establish the cause of Zion." (D&C 6:7.)

"Keep my commandments, and seek to bring forth and establish the cause of Zion." (D&C 11:6.)

"This is Zion—the pure in heart." (D&C 97:21.)

Moses 7:19

"He [Enoch] built a city that was called the City of Holiness, even Zion"

Selected Statements of the First Presidency and the Twelve Apostles

"Our first scriptural account relative to Zion concerns Enoch and his city. That prophet of transcendent faith and power lived while father Adam yet dwelt in mortality. It was a day of wickedness and evil, a day of darkness and rebellion, a day of war and desolation, a day leading up to the cleansing of the earth by water. Enoch, however, was faithful. He saw the Lord, and talked with him face to face as one man speaks with another. (Moses 7:4.) . . .

" . . . Enoch made converts and assembled a congregation of true believers, all of whom became so faithful 'that the Lord came and dwelt with his people, and they dwelt in righteousness,' and were blessed from on high." (Bruce R. McConkie, in *Ensign,* May 1977, p. 117.)

"*Zion* is a name given by the Lord to his covenant people, who are characterized by purity of heart and faithfulness in caring for the poor, the needy, and the distressed. (See D&C 97:21.) . . .

"This highest order of priesthood society is founded on the doctrines of love, service, work, self-reliance, and stewardship, all of which are circumscribed by the covenant of consecration." (Spencer W. Kimball, in *Ensign*, Nov. 1977, p. 78.)

Moses 7:21

"The Lord showed unto Enoch all the inhabitants of the earth"

See Statements, Scripture References, and Other Commentary under Moses 1: 7–8.

Moses 7:21, 69

"Zion, in process of time, was taken up into heaven"

Selected Statements of the First Presidency and the Twelve Apostles

"Enoch and his whole city were translated, taken up bodily into heaven without tasting death. There they served and labored with bodies of flesh and bones, bodies quickened by the power of the Spirit, until that blessed day when they were with Christ in his resurrection. Then, in the twinkling of an eye, they were changed and became immortal in the full sense of the word." (Bruce R. McConkie, *Mortal Messiah*, 3:52. See also Brigham Young, *Discourses of Brigham Young*, p. 179.)

"Now this Enoch God reserved unto Himself, that he should not die at that time, and appointed unto him a ministry unto terrestrial bodies, of whom there has been but little revealed. He is reserved also unto the presidency of a dispensation, and more shall be said of him and terrestrial bodies in another treatise. He is a ministering angel, to minister to those who shall be heirs of salvation. . . .

"Many have supposed that the doctrine of translation was a doctrine whereby men were taken immediately into the presence of God, and into an eternal fullness, but this is a mistaken idea. Their place of habitation is that of the terrestrial order, and a place prepared for such characters He held in reserve to be ministering angels unto many planets, and who as yet have not entered into so great a fullness as those who are resurrected from the dead. 'Others were tortured, not accepting deliverance, that they might obtain a better resurrection.' (See Hebrews 11:35.)" (Joseph Smith, *Teachings of the Prophet Joseph Smith*, p. 170. See also Bruce R. McConkie, *Doctrinal New Testament Commentary*, 3:199; Delbert L. Stapley, in Conference Report, Apr. 1969, p. 47.)

"According to the Pearl of Great Price, when Enoch was translated, the inhabitants of the city of Zion were also taken and were also translated. How many others have been given this great honor we do not know, but there may have been many of whom we have no record. . . . Moreover, the Lord, of necessity, has kept authorized servants on the earth bearing the priesthood from the days of Adam to the present time; in fact, there has never been a moment from the beginning that there were not men on the earth holding the Holy Priesthood. Even in the days of apostasy, and apostasy has occurred several times, the Lord never surrendered this earth and permitted Satan to have complete control." (Joseph Fielding Smith, *Answers to Gospel Questions*, 2:45. See also Wilford Woodruff, in *Journal of Discourses*, 22:232.)

"Translated beings are still mortal and will have to pass through the experience of death, or the separation of the spirit and the body, although this will be instantaneous, for the people of the City of Enoch, Elijah, and others who received this great blessing in ancient times, before the coming of our Lord, could not have received the resurrection, or the change from mortality to immortality, because our Lord had not paid the debt which frees us from mortality and grants to us the resurrection and immortal life." (Joseph Fielding Smith, *Answers to Gospel Questions*, 1:165.)

Selected Scripture References

"I am the same which have taken the Zion of Enoch into mine own bosom." (D&C 38:4.)

"Enoch, and his brethren, . . . were separated from the earth, and were received unto myself—a city reserved until a day of righteousness shall come." (D&C 45:11–12.)

"He [Enoch] walked with God three hundred and sixty-five years, . . . [then] he was translated." (D&C 107:49.)

Moses 7:22

"The seed of Cain were black, and had not place among them"

Selected Statements of the First Presidency and the Twelve Apostles

"When one considers marriage, it should be an unselfish thing, but there is not much selflessness when two people of different races plan marriage. They must be thinking selfishly of themselves. They certainly are not considering the problems that will beset each other and that will beset their children. . . .

"If your son thinks he loves this girl, he would not want to inflict upon her loneliness and unhappiness; and if he thinks that his affection for her will solve all her problems, he should do some more mature thinking.

"We are unanimous, all of the Brethren, in feeling and recommending that Indians marry Indians, and Mexicans marry Mexicans; the Chinese marry Chinese and the Japanese marry Japanese; that the Caucasians marry the Caucasians, and the Arabs marry Arabs." (Spencer W. Kimball, *Teachings of Spencer W. Kimball*, pp. 302–3.)

Selected Scripture References

"All worthy male members of the Church may be ordained to the priesthood without regard for race or color." (Official Declaration—2.)

Other Commentary

"For a number of years, President Spencer W. Kimball has counseled young members of the Church to not cross racial lines in dating and marrying.

"Following are some excerpts of his messages on the subject:

"In an address to seminary and institute teachers at Brigham Young University on June 27, 1958, President Kimball, then a member of the Council of the Twelve, said:

" ' . . . there is one thing that I must mention, and that is the inter-racial marriages. When I said you must teach your young people to overcome their prejudices and accept the Indians, I did not mean that you would encourage intermarriage.'

"Speaking to Indian students at Brigham Young University on January 5, 1965, President Kimball, as a member of the Council of the Twelve, said:

" 'Now, the brethren feel that it is not the wisest thing to cross racial lines in dating and marrying. There is no condemnation. We have had some of our fine young people who have crossed the lines. We hope they will be very happy, but experience of the brethren through a hundred years has proved to us that marriage is a very difficult thing under any circumstances and the difficulty increases in interrace marriages.'

"Addressing a Brigham Young University devotional on September 7, 1976, President Kimball counseled the students:

" 'We are grateful that this one survey reveals that about 90 percent of the temple marriages hold fast. Because of this, we recommend that people marry those who are of the same racial background generally, and of somewhat the same economic and social and educational background (some of those are not an absolute necessity, but preferred), and above all, the same religious background, without question.' " (*Church News*, 17 June 1978, p. 4.)

See Selected Statements under Moses 7:8.

Moses 7:24

"Enoch was high and lifted up, even in the bosom of the Father, and of the Son of Man"

Selected Statements of the First Presidency and the Twelve Apostles

"And yet there are those—a favored few—who break the time-bound bands, who see beyond the veil, who come to know the things of eternity. Portions of what they learn they are permitted to reveal to the rest of us." (Bruce R. McConkie, *Mortal Messiah*, 4:393.)

"Enoch 'was high and lifted up, even in the bosom of the Father, and of the Son of Man,' and he beheld marvelous visions beyond anything that the mind of man can conceive. He saw all the spirits that God had created, the nations of mortal men, the coming of Christ and his crucifixion, the Second Coming of the Son of Man, the millennial era, and many other things that are not recorded." (Bruce R. McConkie, *Mortal Messiah*, 1:409.)

"Understand eternity? There is not and never was a man in finite flesh who understands it. Enoch has been referred to in this matter. How many of the Gods and kingdoms he saw when the vision of his mind was opened, matters not. If he had seen more than he could have enumerated throughout his long life, and more than all the men on earth could multiply from the time his vision opened until now, he would not have attained to the comprehension of eternity. How much Enoch saw, how many worlds he saw, has nothing to do with the case. This is a matter that wise men know nothing about." (Brigham Young, *Discourses of Brigham Young*, p. 148.)

Moses 7:27

"The Holy Ghost fell on many, and they were caught up by the powers of heaven into Zion"

Selected Statements of the First Presidency and the Twelve Apostles

"In his day [the day of Enoch] the Lord gathered together all the righteous and they with Enoch were taken from the earth, and later before the flood if any repented and accepted the truth they too were caught up to the people of Enoch." (Joseph Fielding Smith, *Signs of the Times*, p. 10. See also Bruce R. McConkie, *Mormon Doctrine*, p. 804; John Taylor, in *Journal of Discourses*, 26:90.)

"We come down to the days of Noah. He was a righteous man, and called of God to preach the Gospel among the nations as it was revealed to his forefathers, and before the days of the flood, so great was the faith of many of the people, after the days that Enoch's city was caught up, that the Holy Ghost fell upon them, and they were caught up by the power of heaven into the midst of Zion—the Zion of Enoch." (Orson Pratt, *Masterful Discourses of Orson Pratt*, p. 435.)

"During the first 2200 or so years of the earth's history—that is, from the fall of Adam to the ministry of Melchizedek—it was a not uncommon occurrence for faithful members of the Church to be translated and taken into the heavenly realms without tasting death. Since that time there have been occasional special instances of translation, instances in which a special work of the ministry required it." (Bruce R. McConkie, *Mormon Doctrine*, p. 804.)

"After those in the City of Holiness were translated and taken up
into heaven without tasting death, so that Zion as a people and a congregation had fled from the battle-scarred surface of the earth, the Lord
sought others among men who would serve him. From the days of
Enoch to the flood, new converts and true believers, except those needed
to carry out the Lord's purposes among mortals, were translated. . . .
'And men having this faith'—the faith of Enoch and his people—'coming up unto this order of God'—the holy order of priesthood which we
call the Melchizedek Priesthood—'were translated and taken up into
heaven.' (JST, Genesis 14:32.)" (Bruce R. McConkie, *Millennial Messiah*, p. 284.)

Moses 7:28

"How is it that the heavens weep"

Selected Scripture References

"The whole heavens shall weep over them, even all the workmanship of mine hands; wherefore should not the heavens weep, seeing
these shall suffer?" (Moses 7:37.)

Moses 7:29

"And Enoch said unto the Lord: How is it that thou canst weep?"

Selected Statements of the First Presidency and the Twelve Apostles

"Do you not see, then, the increased powers and faculties which
the Almighty has? His creations are so numerous that the number of
particles composing this earth would not be a beginning to them, yet
the Lord's eye can pierce all these creations, and he can hold them, as it
were, in his hand. Not physically, not hold them in the hollow of his
hand as we can a ball or an orange; but by the power which he possesses he can hold them and his eye can pierce them." (Orson Pratt, in
Journal of Discourses, 16:363.)

Selected Scripture References

"The heavens wept over him—he was Lucifer, a son of the
morning." (D&C 76:26.)

"Until that day they shall be in torment; wherefore, for this shall
the heavens weep." (Moses 7:39-40.)

Other Commentary

"God, from whom all blessings come, asked of his children only that they should love each other and choose him, their Father.

"But as in our day, many neither sought the Lord nor had love for each other, and when God foresaw the suffering that would inevitably follow this self-willed, rebellious course of sin, *he wept*. That, he told Enoch, was what he had to cry about." (Marion D. Hanks, in Conference Report, Apr. 1980, pp. 40–41.)

Moses 7:30
"It would not be a beginning to the number of thy creations"

See Statements, Scripture References, and Other Commentary under Moses 1:33, 34, 35, 37.

Moses 7:32
"In the Garden of Eden, gave I unto man his agency"

Selected Statements of the First Presidency and the Twelve Apostles

"While perhaps it is seldom, if ever, contended that either political independence or economic freedom alone brings perfect liberty, it is not, however, uncommon for free agency to be considered as synonymous with freedom of the soul. And it is true that the God-given right to choose one's course of action is an indispensable prerequisite to such freedom. Without it we can scarcely enjoy any type of liberty—political, economic, or personal. It is one of our greatest heritages. For it we are deeply indebted to our Father in Heaven, to the Founding Fathers, and to the pioneers. God gave it to man in the Garden of Eden. (See Moses 7:32.) The Founding Fathers, under the Lord's inspiration, wrote a guarantee of it into the fundamental law of the land. And the pioneers, led by the inspiration of heaven, gave their all to perpetuate it. Surely we ought always to be alert in its defense and willing, if necessary, to give our lives for its preservation." (Marion G. Romney, in *Ensign*, Nov. 1981, p. 43.)

Selected Scripture References

"The Lord God gave unto man that he should act for himself." (2 Nephi 2:16.)

"It is given unto them to know good from evil; wherefore they are agents unto themselves." (Moses 6:56.)

Moses 7:34

"Will I send in the floods upon them"

Selected Statements of the First Presidency and the Twelve Apostles

"God's work has included mighty natural processes at various times in the history of the world. Noah's deluge was one of them. The flood had a far greater purpose than merely to wipe out Noah's neighbors. God baptized the earth! He would not baptize a portion of it any more than we would be satisfied with a partial immersion if we were baptizing some person. He baptized Adam by a miracle, when there was no one there to perform the ordinance. And now He baptized the earth by His own almighty power, for His own purposes, and the destruction of the wicked was only incidental thereto. And He will yet baptize it with fire, according to the baptismal pattern for us all. (Matthew 3:11; 3 Nephi 19:13.)" (Mark E. Petersen, *Noah and the Flood*, p. 61.)

Selected Scripture References

"By faith Noah, being warned of God of things not seen as yet, . . . prepared an ark to the saving of his house." (Hebrews 11:7.)

God "saved Noah . . . , a preacher of righteousness, bringing in the flood upon the world of the ungodly." (2 Peter 2:5.)

"If men do not repent, I will send in the floods upon them." (Moses 8:17.)

Moses 7:35

"Man of Holiness is my name"

See Statements and Scripture References under Moses 6:57.

Moses 7:35

"Endless and Eternal is my name"

See Statements and Scripture References under Moses 1:3.

Moses 7:38

"And behold, I will shut them up; a prison have I prepared for them"

Selected Statements of the First Presidency and the Twelve Apostles

"In the realm of departed spirits there are two divisions—paradise, where the spirits of the righteous go to await the day when they shall come forth in the resurrection of the just; and hell, where the spirits of the wicked go to be buffeted and tormented until that day when they shall come forth in the resurrection of the unjust. Our Lord did not go in person to the spirits in hell, which is the spirit prison as such. His ministry in the spirit world was among the righteous in paradise, but even these considered their disembodied state as one of bondage. Thus the designation *spirit prison* may be said to have two meanings—*hell*, which is the prison proper; and the *whole spirit world*, in the sense that all who are therein are restricted and cannot gain a fulness of joy until after their resurrection. (D&C 93:33-34.)" (Bruce R. McConkie, *Doctrinal New Testament Commentary*, 3:309.)

"All this was shown unto Enoch; and he was shown that those who had thus acted, or who should thus act, 'would be consigned to prison,' they would be consigned to a place of torment, and because of their sufferings, because of that which they should have to pass through, the heavens themselves wept over their fate. Enoch was told that they should remain there until the day of the Lord Jesus Christ." (George Q. Cannon, in *Journal of Discourses*, 26:81.)

"The people swept off by the flood of Noah were imprisoned in the world of spirits, in a kind of hell, without justification, without priesthood or gospel, without the true knowledge of God or a hope of resurrection, during those long ages which intervened between the flood and the death of Christ. It was only by the personal ministry of the Spirit of Jesus Christ, during his sojourn in the spirit world, that they were at length privileged to hear the gospel and to act upon their own agency the same as men in the flesh; whereas, if they had repented at the preaching of Noah, they might have been justified and filled with the hope and knowledge of the resurrection while in the flesh." (Parley P. Pratt, *Key to the Science of Theology*, p. 82.)

Selected Scripture References

Jesus "preached unto the spirits in prison." (1 Peter 3:19.)

"The gospel [was] preached also to them that are dead." (1 Peter 4:6.)

Doctrine and Covenants 138 contains an account of the Savior's visit to the spirits of the dead. (See D&C 138; headnote to D&C 138.)

"A hell I have prepared for them, if they repent not." (Moses 6:29.)

Moses 7:39
"And That which I have chosen hath pled before my face.

Wherefore, he suffereth for their sins"

Selected Statements of the First Presidency and the Twelve Apostles

"Men in Noah's day rebelled, rejected the Lord and his gospel, and were buried in a watery grave. Their spirits then found themselves in that prison prepared for those who walk in darkness when light is before them. Are they lost forever? Who will plead their cause?

"To Enoch, concerning them, came these words of the Father: 'And That which I have chosen hath pled before my face. Wherefore, he suffereth for their sins; inasmuch as they will repent in the day that my Chosen shall return unto me, and until that day they shall be in torment.' (Moses 7:39.)" (Bruce R. McConkie, *Promised Messiah*, pp. 330–31.)

Selected Scripture References

"He is the firstfruits unto God, inasmuch as he shall make intercession for all the children of men." (2 Nephi 2:9.)

"He advocateth the cause of the children of men; and he dwelleth eternally in the heavens." (Moroni 7:28.)

"Listen to him who is the advocate with the Father, who is pleading your cause before him." (D&C 45:3.)

Moses 7:41

"The Lord spake unto Enoch, and told Enoch all the doings of the children of men"

Selected Statements of the First Presidency and the Twelve Apostles

"A most important revelation, this, to Enoch, showing unto him the fate of the wicked after his city should be translated and taken to heaven. The inhabitants of the earth should grow worse and worse, more abandoned than ever in their wickedness, until the time should come for the Lord to send forth His floods and drown the inhabitants of the earth except Noah, and those who received His testimony." (George Q. Cannon, in *Journal of Discourses*, 26:80–81.)

Moses 7:43

"Enoch saw that Noah built an ark"

Selected Statements of the First Presidency and the Twelve Apostles

"Noah, after having preached the gospel and published glad tidings among the nations, was commanded to build an ark. He had a Urim and

Thummim by which he was enabled to discern all things pertaining to the ark and its pattern." (Orson Pratt, *Masterful Discourses of Orson Pratt*, p. 435.)

"It was not blind faith when the patriarch Noah built an ark some forty-two centuries ago or when the prophet Nephi built a boat about twenty-five centuries ago. . . . Each knew the goodness of God and that he had a purpose in his strange commands. And so each with his eyes wide open, with absolute freedom of choice, built by faith." (Spencer W. Kimball, in Conference Report, Oct. 1954, p. 52.)

Moses 7:43

"But upon the residue of the wicked the floods came and swallowed them up"

Selected Statements of the First Presidency and the Twelve Apostles

"Some doubt that there was a flood, but by modern revelation we know that it did take place. By modern revelation we know that for more than a century, Noah pleaded with the people to repent, but in their willful stubbornness they would not listen." (Mark E. Petersen, in *Ensign*, Nov. 1981, p. 65.)

"The whole family of man was destroyed, except Noah and those seven souls who received his testimony, a part of his family, and a part only, for there were children that Noah had who rejected his testimony, and who also shared in the destruction that came upon the inhabitants of the earth." (George Q. Cannon, in *Journal of Discourses*, 26:81.)

Other Commentary

"So wicked did mortals become, the sacred record declares, that God sent upon the earth a great flood or deluge which destroyed all of the human race but one family." (Milton R. Hunter, *Gospel through the Ages*, p. 253.)

Moses 7:45

"When shall the blood of the Righteous be shed?"

See Statements and Scripture References under Moses 5:57.

Moses 7:49

"Enoch heard the earth mourn"

Selected Statements of the First Presidency and the Twelve Apostles

"Those millions of spirits who had thus committed sin and iniquity until it could be borne no longer, until the earth groaned under their wickedness, and cried aloud as with a human voice against the wickedness upon its surface of which those inhabitants had been guilty." (George Q. Cannon, in *Journal of Discourses*, 26:81.)

"The Lord here informs us that the earth on which we dwell is a living thing, and that the time must come when it will be sanctified from all unrighteousness. In the Pearl of Great Price, when Enoch is conversing with the Lord, he hears the earth crying for deliverance from the iniquity upon her face. . . . It is not the fault of the earth that wickedness prevails upon her face, for she has been true to the law which she received and that law is the celestial law. Therefore the Lord says that the earth shall be sanctified from all unrighteousness." (Joseph Fielding Smith, *Church History and Modern Revelation*, 2:131.)

"The earth is a living thing. Is there not great significance in the scriptural references to the earth? While Enoch and the Lord discussed the wickedness of men, 'it came to pass that Enoch looked upon the earth; and he heard a voice from the bowels thereof, saying: Wo, wo is me, . . . When will my Creator sanctify me, that I may rest, and righteousness for a season abide upon my face? . . . '

"How are men cleansed of their sins? By baptism, and not only by water, but also by fire and the Holy Ghost. . . .

"Should not the earth—a living thing—be similarly sanctified? It was baptized with water in the flood. Eventually it will be baptized with fire, thus becoming cleansed and sanctified, to be made into a celestial sphere as the eternal home for the righteous." (Mark E. Petersen, *Noah and the Flood*, pp. 62-63. See also Wilford Woodruff, in *Journal of Discourses*, 13:163.)

"The earth, as a living body, will have to die and be resurrected, for it, too, has been redeemed by the blood of Jesus Christ." (Joseph Fielding Smith, *Doctrines of Salvation*, 1:74.)

"This earth, after wading through all the corruptions of men, being cursed for his sake, and not permitted to send forth its full lustre and glory, must yet take its proper place in God's creations; be purified from that corruption under which it has groaned for ages, and become a fit place for redeemed men, angels, and God to dwell upon." (John Taylor, *Government of God*, p. 82.)

Moses 7:50

Enoch pleaded with the Lord "that the earth might never more be covered by the floods"

Selected Statements of the First Presidency and the Twelve Apostles

"Among the things revealed to Enoch was the knowledge of the flood, which was to take place. And the Lord made a covenant with Enoch, that He would set his bow in the clouds—just as it afterwards was given to Noah—not as a mere token alone that the Lord would no more drown the world, but as a token of the new and everlasting covenant that the Lord made with Enoch." (Orson Pratt, in *Journal of Discourses*, 16:49.)

Selected Scripture References

"I will establish my covenant with you [Noah]; neither shall all flesh be cut off any more by the waters of a flood." (Genesis 9:11. See also v. 15.)

The Lord's covenant with Noah is recorded in Joseph Smith Translation, Genesis 9:17–25.

"I have sworn that the waters of Noah should no more go over the earth." (3 Nephi 22:9; Isaiah 54:9.)

Moses 7:56

"The saints arose, and were crowned at the right hand of the Son of Man, with crowns of glory"

Selected Statements of the First Presidency and the Twelve Apostles

"For those who lived prior to the time of the resurrection of Christ, the first resurrection, itself a resurrection of the just, was the one which accompanied the coming forth of the Son of God from the grave." (Bruce R. McConkie, *Doctrinal New Testament Commentary*, 1:847.)

"The doctrine of the Resurrection is the single most fundamental and crucial doctrine in the Christian religion. It cannot be overemphasized, nor can it be disregarded.

"Without the Resurrection, the gospel of Jesus Christ becomes a litany of wise sayings and seemingly unexplainable miracles—but sayings and miracles with no ultimate triumph. No, the ultimate triumph is in the ultimate miracle: for the first time in the history of mankind, one who was dead raised himself into living immortality. He *was* the Son of God, the Son of our immortal Father in Heaven, and his triumph over physical and spiritual death is the good news every Christian tongue should speak." (Howard W. Hunter, in Conference Report, Apr. 1986, p. 18.)

"Question.... How, and where did you obtain the book of Mormon?

"Answer. Moroni, the person who deposited the plates, from whence the book of Mormon was translated... being dead, and raised again therefrom, appeared unto me, and told me where they were; and gave me directions how to obtain them." (Joseph Smith, in *Elder's Journal*, July 1838, pp. 42–43.)

Selected Scripture References

"The graves were opened; and many bodies of the saints which slept arose." (Matthew 27:52.)

"The souls and the bodies are reunited, of the righteous, at the resurrection of Christ." (Alma 40:20.)

"There were many saints who should arise from the dead, and should appear unto many." (3 Nephi 23:9.)

Moses 7:61
"Great tribulations shall be among the children of men"

Selected Statements of the First Presidency and the Twelve Apostles

"When we become ripe in iniquity, then the Lord will come. I get annoyed sometimes at some of our elders who when speaking say the Lord will come when we all become righteous enough to receive him. The Lord is not going to wait for us to get righteous. When he gets ready to come, he is going to come—when the cup of iniquity is full—and if we are not righteous then, it will be just too bad for us, for we will be classed among the ungodly, and we will be as stubble to be swept off the face of the earth, for the Lord says wickedness shall not stand." (Joseph Fielding Smith, *Doctrines of Salvation*, 3:3.)

"What is the matter with the world today? What has created this change that we see coming over the world? Why these terrible earthquakes, tornadoes, and judgments? What is the meaning of all these mighty events that are taking place? The meaning is, these angels that have been held for many years in the temple of our God have got their liberty to go out and commence their mission and their work in the earth, and they are here today in the earth. I feel bold in saying this to the Latter-day Saints. There is a meaning in these judgments. The word of the Lord cannot fall unfulfilled." (Wilford Woodruff, *Discourses of Wilford Woodruff*, p. 251.)

"The Lord gave that good old prophet Enoch, president of the Zion of God, who stood in the midst of his people three hundred and sixty-five years, a view of the earth in its various dispensations, showing him that the time would come when it would groan under the wickedness, blasphemy, murders, whoredoms and abominations of its inhabitants." (Wilford Woodruff, *Discourses of Wilford Woodruff*, p. 109.)

"I will prophesy that the signs of the coming of the Son of Man are already commenced. One pestilence will desolate after another. We shall soon have war and bloodshed. The moon will be turned into blood. I testify of these things, and that the coming of the Son of Man is nigh, even at your doors." (Joseph Smith, *History of the Church*, 3:390.)

Selected Scripture References

"The wrath of God shall be poured out upon the wicked without measure." (D&C 1:9.)

"I will take vengeance upon the wicked, for they will not repent." (D&C 29:17.)

"The wrath of God [is] the desolation of abomination which awaits the wicked, both in this world and in the world to come." (D&C 88:85.)

Moses 7:61

"But my people will I preserve"

Selected Statements of the First Presidency and the Twelve Apostles

"The pathway of the people of God has been beset with difficulties. They have been environed with dangers. Dark clouds have almost enshrouded them. But amidst all these, the still, small voice of the Spirit of God has been heard. His Saints have had a testimony from Him that the course they have been led to take is the right one and that He will never fail to make known His mind and will to them so long as they live up to His requirements.

"It appears plain that it is God's purpose to suffer His Saints to be thoroughly tried and tested, so that they may prove their integrity and know the character of the foundation upon which they build." (Wilford Woodruff, in James R. Clark, comp., *Messages of the First Presidency*, 3:160.)

"The scriptures say that many will not listen. But they also say that true believers in the Lord will follow his servants and give ear to their warning voices. God will protect the faithful regardless of all the tribulations that will come upon the wicked." (Mark E. Petersen, in *Ensign*, Nov. 1981, p. 66.)

" 'Great tribulations shall be among the children of men, but my
people will I preserve.' (Moses 7:61.)

"The kingdom of God will not fail; it shall not be destroyed; it will
not be left to other people; it will stand forever until 'the kingdoms of
this world [will] become the kingdoms of our Lord, and of his Christ.'
(Revelation 11:15.)" (Ezra Taft Benson, in Conference Report, Apr. 1978,
p. 48. See also Ezra Taft Benson, in *Ensign,* Nov. 1986, p. 79.)

Selected Scripture References

"Wherefore, the righteous need not fear." (1 Nephi 22:17. See also
vv. 18–26.)

"The wicked will he destroy; and he will spare his people." (2 Nephi
30:10.)

Moses 7:62

"Righteousness will I send down out of heaven; and truth will I send forth out of the earth . . . to gather out mine elect"

Selected Statements of the First Presidency and the Twelve Apostles

"Enoch, whose mortal ministry preceded by five thousand years
the coming forth of the Book of Mormon, saw in vision both the Second Coming and the coming forth of the volume of holy scripture that
would prepare the way for that glorious day. To him the Lord said:
'And righteousness will I send down out of heaven'—that is, revelation
shall commence anew and the gospel shall be restored—'and truth will
I send forth out of the earth, to bear testimony of mine Only Begotten:
his resurrection from the dead; yea, and also the resurrection of all
men.' (Moses 7:62.) The Book of Mormon shall come forth from American soil, from plates buried in Cumorah, from the soil that supported
the people of whom it speaks. The Book of Mormon shall come forth
containing the *word* of the gospel which will unite with the *power* of
the gospel that comes down from heaven." (Bruce R. McConkie, *Millennial Messiah*, p. 150.)

"The Lord promised, therefore, that righteousness would come from
heaven and truth out of the earth. We have seen the marvelous fulfillment of that prophecy in our generation. The Book of Mormon has
come forth out of the earth, filled with truth, serving as the very 'key-
stone of our religion' (see Introduction to the Book of Mormon). God
has also sent down righteousness from heaven. The Father Himself
appeared with His Son to the Prophet Joseph Smith. The angel Moroni,
John the Baptist, Peter, James, and numerous other angels were directed

by heaven to restore the necessary powers to the kingdom. Further, the Prophet Joseph Smith received revelation after revelation from the heavens during those first critical years of the Church's growth. These revelations have been preserved for us in the Doctrine and Covenants." (Ezra Taft Benson, in *Ensign*, Nov. 1986, pp. 79–80.)

Other Commentary

The Lord's promise that he would send forth truth out of the earth may include, along with the Book of Mormon, the books of Abraham and Joseph, the sealed part of the Book of Mormon, and other sacred documents that have been promised to be revealed to the Lord's faithful in the latter days. Peter promised that in this dispensation there will be a "restitution of all things, which God hath spoken by the mouth of all his holy prophets since the world began." (Acts 3:21. See also vv. 19–20.)

Moses 7:62
"The resurrection of all men"

Selected Statements of the First Presidency and the Twelve Apostles

"This body will come forth in the resurrection. It will be free from all imperfections and scars and infirmities which came to it in mortality which were not self-inflicted. Would we have a right to expect a perfect body if we carelessly or intentionally damaged it?" (Spencer W. Kimball, *Teachings of Spencer W. Kimball*, p. 37.)

Selected Scripture References

"The day cometh that all shall rise from the dead and stand before God." (Alma 11:41.)

"The atonement bringeth to pass the resurrection of the dead." (Alma 42:23.)

"Then shall all the dead awake, for their graves shall be opened, and they shall come forth." (D&C 29:26.)

Moses 7:62
The Latter-day Saints shall build a holy city called Zion, a place of gathering

Selected Statements of the First Presidency and the Twelve Apostles

"Without Zion, and a place of deliverance, we must fall; because the time is near when the sun will be darkened, and the moon turn to blood, and the stars fall from heaven, and the earth reel to and fro.

Then, if this is the case, and if we are not sanctified and gathered to the places God has appointed, with all our former professions and our great love for the Bible, we must fall; we cannot stand; we cannot be saved; for God will gather out His Saints from the Gentiles, and then comes desolation and destruction, and none can escape except the pure in heart who are gathered." (Joseph Smith, *History of the Church*, 2:52.)

"The Latter-Day Zion will resemble, in most particulars, the Zion of Enoch: it will be established upon the same celestial laws—be built upon the same gospel, and be guided by continued revelation. Its inhabitants, like those of the antediluvian Zion, will be the righteous gathered out from all nations: the glory of God will be seen upon it; and His power will be manifested there, even as in the Zion of old. All the blessings and grand characteristics which were exhibited in ancient Zion will be shown forth in the Latter-Day Zion." (Orson Pratt, in *Seer*, May 1854, p. 265.)

Selected Scripture References

"The New Jerusalem shall be prepared, that ye may be gathered in one, that ye may be my people and I will be your God." (D&C 42:9.)

Zion in the last days will be "the only people that shall not be at war one with another." (D&C 45:69.)

"It shall be called the New Jerusalem, a land of peace, a city of refuge, a place of safety for the saints of the Most High God." (D&C 45:66.)

The new song of Zion is recorded in Doctrine and Covenants 84:99–102.

Moses 7:63

"Then shall thou and all thy city meet them there, and we will receive them into our bosom"

Selected Statements of the First Presidency and the Twelve Apostles

"And then when the time comes that these calamities we read of, shall overtake the earth, those that are prepared will have the power of translation, as they had in former times, and the city will be translated. And Zion that is on the earth will rise, and the Zion above will descend, as we are told, and we will meet and fall on each other's necks and embrace and kiss each other. And thus the purposes of God to a certain extent will then be fulfilled. But there are a great many things to be brought about before that time. And we are here in an organized capacity trying to prepare ourselves for all the providences of the Almighty." (John Taylor, in *Journal of Discourses*, 21:253. See also 10:147.)

"When we go back to Jackson County, we are to go back with power. Do you suppose that God will reveal his power among an unsanctified people, who have no regard nor respect for his laws and institutions, but who are filled with covetousness? No. When God shows forth his power among the Latter-day Saints, it will be because there is a union of feeling in regard to doctrine, and in regard to everything that God has placed in their hands; and not only a union, but a sanctification on their part, that there shall not be a spot or wrinkle as it were, but everything shall be as fair as the sun that shines in the heavens." (Orson Pratt, in *Journal of Discourses*, 15:361.)

"Yes, there will be wrenching polarization on this planet, but also the remarkable reunion with our colleagues in Christ from the City of Enoch. Yes, nation after nation will become a house divided, but more and more unifying Houses of the Lord will grace this planet. Yes, Armageddon lies ahead. But so does Adam-ondi-Ahman!" (Neal A. Maxwell, in *Ensign*, Nov. 1981, p. 10. See also Neal A. Maxwell, in *Ensign,* Nov. 1986, p. 59.)

Selected Scripture References

See Joseph Smith Translation, Genesis 9:17–25.

Moses 7:64

"For the space of a thousand years the earth shall rest"

Selected Statements of the First Presidency and the Twelve Apostles

"The Millennium is dawning upon the world, we are at the end of the six thousand years, and the great day of rest, the Millennium of which the Lord has spoken, will soon dawn, and the Savior will come in the clouds of heaven to reign over his people on the earth one thousand years." (Wilford Woodruff, *Discourses of Wilford Woodruff*, p. 252.)

"Christ and the resurrected Saints will reign over the earth during the thousand years. They will not probably dwell upon the earth, but will visit it when they please, or when it is necessary to govern it." (Joseph Smith, *History of the Church*, 5:212.)

"The government of individuals, communities, and nations throughout this Millennium is to be that of a perfect theocracy, with Jesus the Christ as Lord and King. The more wicked part of the race shall have been destroyed; and during the period Satan shall be bound. . . . The righteous dead shall have come forth from their graves. . . . Men yet in the flesh shall mingle with immortalized beings; children shall grow to maturity and then die in peace or be changed to immortality 'in the twinkling of an eye.' There shall be surcease of enmity between man and beast." (James E. Talmage, *Jesus the Christ*, p. 790.)

Moses 7:69

"And Enoch and all his people walked with God, and he dwelt in the midst of Zion"

Selected Statements of the First Presidency and the Twelve Apostles

"It may well be that more people saw the Lord in Enoch's day than at any other time in the entire history of the earth, or that more people saw him than at all other times combined." (Bruce R. McConkie, *Promised Messiah*, pp. 598–99.)

"When Enoch preached among the wicked, made converts, and built his City of Holiness, that original Zion operated so perfectly upon theocratic principles that the Lord of heaven himself came and dwelt with his people. So perfect was the system and so righteous were the people that they received instruction from the Lord in person as well as from his duly constituted servants on earth. What better system of government could there be?" (Bruce R. McConkie, *New Witness for the Articles of Faith*, p. 659.)

"Yet Enoch had to talk with and teach his people during a period of three hundred and sixty years, before he could get them prepared to enter into their rest, and then he obtained power to translate himself and his people, with the region they inhabited, their houses, gardens, fields, cattle, and all their possessions. He had learned enough from Adam and his associates to know how to handle the elements, and those who would not listen to his teachings were so wicked that they were fit to be destroyed, and he obtained power to take his portion of the earth and move out a little while, where he remains to this day." (Brigham Young, in *Journal of Discourses*, 3:320. See also John Taylor, in *Journal of Discourses*, 24:291.)

"3382 B.C. to 3017 B.C.—A duration of 365 years, a period of one year for each day of our years, during which the Lord Jesus Christ personally dwelt on earth and was seen by his people. We assume, of course, that he came and went during this period, as he will during that millennial age when he is destined, again, to dwell personally upon the earth." (Bruce R. McConkie, *Promised Messiah*, p. 607. See also Lorenzo Snow, in *Journal of Discourses*, 20:191.)

Moses 7:69

"It came to pass that Zion was not, for God received it up into his own bosom"

See Statements and Scripture References under Moses 7:21.

Moses 8

Moses 8:2

"Methuselah, the son of Enoch, was not taken"

Selected Statements of the First Presidency and the Twelve Apostles

"It is generally thought that the Lord called Noah, when he had determined to cleanse the earth with the flood, and sent him out alone to preach to the wicked inhabitants. It is sometimes said, without basis in fact, that Noah preached 120 years; and nothing is said of the preaching of other witnesses.

"Let me call your attention to the fact that Noah was not alone in bearing witness. [Moses 8:2-3.]

"Now Methuselah, grandfather of Noah, was a righteous man and a prophet. He knew by the spirit of revelation that the flood would come in the days of Noah. Moreover, he lived until the year of the flood when he died. Do you not think that this righteous man was also declaring repentance to the perverse world, and warning them of the flood which was to come? Again, Lamech, father of Noah, was also a righteous man and he lived until five years before the flood. It is reasonable to suppose that he, too, was preaching to the people, as well as his father and his son." (Joseph Fielding Smith, *Doctrines of Salvation*, 1:204.)

Moses 8:3

"Methuselah prophesied that from his loins should spring all the kingdoms of the earth"

Selected Statements of the First Presidency and the Twelve Apostles

"Now, with regard to Noah and his day. God made arrangements before hand, and told Methuselah that when the people should be destroyed, that a remnant of his seed should occupy the earth and stand foremost upon it. And Methuselah was so anxious to have it done that he ordained Noah to the Priesthood when he was ten years of age. Noah then stood in his day as the representative of God." (John Taylor, in *Journal of Discourses*, 22:304.)

Selected Scripture References

"A remnant of his seed should always be found among all nations, while the earth should stand." (Moses 7:52.)

Moses 8:7

"All the days of Methuselah were nine hundred and sixty-nine years"

Selected Statements of the First Presidency and the Twelve Apostles

"Methuselah saw the future, prophesied by the power of the Holy Ghost, and dwelt in righteousness on earth for more years than any of the descendants of Adam of whom we have record." (Bruce R. McConkie, *Mortal Messiah*, 1:53.)

Moses 8:12

"Noah was four hundred and fifty years old, and begat Japheth"

Selected Statements of the First Presidency and the Twelve Apostles

"No mention is made of the marriage of Noah. He was 450 years old when Japheth was born. Whether there were any other children during those centuries is not mentioned, although it seems most improbable that there were not." (Mark E. Petersen, *Noah and the Flood*, p. 23.)

Moses 8:13

"Noah and his sons hearkened unto the Lord, and gave heed, and they were called the sons of God"

Selected Statements of the First Presidency and the Twelve Apostles

"Ham, who often is spoken of as an errant one, was fully faithful, and as other references show, he walked with God, as did Noah and the other sons. When Noah and these three sons, and the wives of all four, entered the ark, nothing is said about any children going in with them. Evidently none of their posterity was worthy of being saved from the flood." (Mark E. Petersen, *Noah and the Flood*, p. 23.)

"Because the daughters of Noah married the sons of men contrary to the teachings of the Lord, his anger was kindled, and this offense was one cause that brought to pass the universal flood. You will see that the condition appears reversed in the Book of Moses. It was the daughters of the sons of God who were marrying the sons of men, which was displeasing unto the Lord. The fact was, as we see it revealed, that the daughters who had been born, evidently under the covenant, and were the daughters of the sons of God, that is to say of those who held the priesthood, were transgressing the commandment of the Lord and were marrying out of the Church. Thus they were cutting themselves off from the blessings of the priesthood contrary to the teachings of Noah and the will of God. . . .

"Today there are foolish daughters of those who hold this same priesthood who are violating this commandment and marrying the sons of men; there are also some of the sons of those who hold the priesthood who are marrying the daughters of men. All of this is contrary to the will of God just as much as it was in the days of Noah." (Joseph Fielding Smith, *Answers to Gospel Questions*, 1:136–37.)

Selected Scripture References

"Neither shalt thou make marriages with them." (Deuteronomy 7:3.)

"Ye have transgressed, and have taken strange wives." (Ezra 10:10.)

"Be ye not unequally yoked together with unbelievers." (2 Corinthians 6:14.)

"A believer should not be united to an unbeliever." (D&C 74:5.)

Moses 8:16

"Noah prophesied, and taught the things of God, even as it was in the beginning"

Selected Statements of the First Presidency and the Twelve Apostles

"The principles of the gospel were taught from the beginning among the children of Adam. Some believed and accepted them; many others rejected them, bringing down upon their heads the wrath of God, for his anger was kindled against them because of their rebellion. In course of time, when the inhabitants of the earth were sufficiently corrupt, he caused the floods to come upon them, sweeping them off the earth. Noah, who was a preacher of righteousness, continued to preach these saving principles. The gospel was also taught to Abraham, and has always been among men when they were prepared to receive it." (Joseph Fielding Smith, *Doctrines of Salvation*, 1:160.)

"In his preaching, Noah 'taught the things of God, even as it was in the beginning.' (Moses 8:16) Evidently he knew the church history of his day. He was the tenth generation from Adam, but the generations overlapped, since everyone apparently lived hundreds of years. No doubt Methuselah, the oldest man, who lived nearly a thousand years, especially kept the memory of the human race and church well in mind." (Mark E. Petersen, *Noah and the Flood*, pp. 23–24.)

Moses 8:17

"His days shall be an hundred and twenty years"

Other Commentary

"Some people have concluded from God's statement that man's 'days shall be an hundred and twenty years' (verse 17) that Noah preached the gospel a hundred twenty years. That conclusion seems not to be justified, for that statement seems to indicate that the span of man's life from the time of the Flood would be cut down to a hundred and twenty years. The scriptures claim that prior to the Flood mortals lived many hundreds of years but following the Flood such characters as Father Abraham, Sarah, Isaac, Jacob, Joseph, Moses, and others, lived slightly over a hundred years. In fact, Moses died exactly at the time that he was 120 years of age." (Milton R. Hunter, *Pearl of Great Price Commentary*, p. 194.)

Moses 8:18

"And in those days there were giants on the earth"

See Statements and Scripture References under Moses 7:15.

Moses 8:19

"The Lord ordained Noah after his own order"

Selected Statements of the First Presidency and the Twelve Apostles

"Perhaps we might be permitted the reflection that it may have been possible that these men received some lesser office in the Priesthood before the authority of the evangelist was conferred upon them by father Adam. Such a thought is suggested by the statement that Cainan was called upon by the Lord in the wilderness in his fortieth year, but was ordained an evangelist by Adam when he was eighty-seven." (Joseph Fielding Smith, *Way to Perfection*, p. 73.)

"The Prophet Joseph taught us that father Adam was the first man on the earth to whom God gave the keys of the everlasting priesthood. He held the keys of the presidency, and was the first man who did hold them. Noah stood next to him, he being the father of all living in his day, as Adam was in his day. These two men were the first who received the priesthood in the eternal worlds, before the worlds were formed. They were the first who received the everlasting priesthood or presidency on the earth." (Wilford Woodruff, *Discourses of Wilford Woodruff*, p. 66.)

"Thus we behold the keys of this Priesthood consisted in obtaining the voice of Jehovah that He talked with him [Noah] in a familiar and friendly manner, that He continued to him the keys, the covenants, the power and the glory, with which He blessed Adam at the beginning." (Joseph Smith, *Teachings of the Prophet Joseph Smith*, p. 171.)

"The Priesthood was first given to Adam; he obtained the First Presidency, and held the keys of it from generation to generation. He obtained it in the Creation, before the world was formed, as in Genesis 1:26, 27, 28. He had dominion given him over every living creature. He is Michael the Archangel, spoken of in the Scriptures. Then to Noah, who is Gabriel; he stands next in authority to Adam in the Priesthood; he was called of God to this office, and was the father of all living in this day, and to him was given the dominion. These men held keys first on earth, and then in heaven." (Joseph Smith, *Teachings of the Prophet Joseph Smith*, p. 157.)

Selected Scripture References

See Moses 6:67.

Moses 8:19

The Lord commanded Noah "that he should go forth and declare his Gospel"

Selected Statements of the First Presidency and the Twelve Apostles

"In the days of Noah the people of that generation had the privilege of knowing whether Noah spoke from the Lord and whether the message that he claimed to have from the Lord was genuine or not. They could have had a revelation for themselves, because he preached the gospel as you and I now preach it in the world, and they could have known that their salvation depended upon their receiving and obeying this message which Noah delivered unto them. In the days of Jesus it was the same. But no person can know that Jesus is the son of God, except by revelation." (Lorenzo Snow, *Teachings of Lorenzo Snow*, p. 51.)

"Noah, a righteous man, ordained to the Priesthood, and knowing the gospel, taught the plan of salvation and the doctrine of the gospel to his day and generation. Some listened and obeyed, more heard the message with unwilling hearts. Self-conquest precedes full acceptance of the gospel. Nevertheless, even those who refused full obedience, took of the gospel such truths as they desired, and without authority built their religions in imitation of the full truth." (John A. Widtsoe, *Evidences and Reconciliations*, 1:83.)

"There was great contrast between the labors of Enoch and Noah and the results they obtained. Enoch was given tremendous power to do miracles. He could even move mountains. A land arose out of the sea in his day. He rebuked giants, fought off enemies, and converted an entire city to such a point of perfection that it was taken into heaven. Not so with Noah; his mission was different. He would continue with the divine warnings, but he had been chosen especially to survive the flood and begin the human race anew. In his day no longer was it necessary for great miracles to be performed to persuade the people. Matters had gone beyond that point. No record is made of any miracles performed by Noah or his sons. They merely preached to maintain the Lord's warning and to give to any who would receive it the opportunity to repent. But primarily they were assigned to build the ark and make ready for the cleansing of the earth. Then they must repopulate the world after the flood receded." (Mark E. Petersen, *Noah and the Flood*, p. 24.)

Selected Scripture References

God "spared not the old world, but saved Noah the eighth person, a preacher of righteousness." (2 Peter 2:5.)

Moses 8:21

"Behold, we are the sons of God; have we not taken unto ourselves the daughters of men?"

Selected Statements of the First Presidency and the Twelve Apostles

"Young men, take unto yourselves wives of the daughters of Zion, and come up and receive your endowments and sealings, that you may

raise up a holy seed unto the God of Abraham, even a holy and royal
Priesthood who shall be born legal heirs thereunto, having a right to
the keys thereof, and to administer in all the ordinances pertaining to
the House of the Lord. Cease your folly and become men of God; act
wisely and righteously before Him, and His choice blessings will attend
you." (The First Presidency: Brigham Young, Heber C. Kimball, and
Jedediah M. Grant, in James R. Clark, comp., *Messages of the First Presidency*, 2:186–87.)

"One of the great evils that existed among the people was that the
sons of God married the daughters of men; or, in other words, many
who were connected with the Church mixed themselves up with those
who were not; and thus their hearts were drawn away from God, and
in the sight of God they were no better than those who rejected His
servants." (John Taylor, in *Journal of Discourses*, 26:90. See also Bruce
R. McConkie, *Millennial Messiah*, p. 360; Brigham Young, *Discourses
of Brigham Young*, p. 304; Mark E. Petersen, *Noah and the Flood*, p.
25.)

"Whenever men are placed in communication with God and are in
possession of the Gospel of the Son of God, it brings life and immortality to light, and places them in relationship with God that other men
know nothing about.

"They were spoken of in former times as the 'sons of God.' " (John
Taylor, in *Journal of Discourses*, 21:159.)

Moses 8:22

"Every man was lifted up in the imagination of the thoughts of his heart, being only evil continually"

Selected Statements of the First Presidency and the Twelve Apostles

"The people became excessively wicked and corrupt, so much so,
that, as the Scriptures informs us 'Their thoughts were only evil, and
that continually;' and in consequence of this the Lord decreed that he
would destroy the people from the face of the earth. But before he did it
he gave revelation unto Noah, telling him that the destruction of all
flesh upon the earth had been decreed by the Almighty in consequences
of the wickedness of the people; and Noah had special revelation given
to him adapted to the circumstances which surrounded him, and the
age in which he lived. He was not told to build a city, to preach the
Gospel and gather the people as Enoch had done; but he was told that
the wickedness of all flesh had come up before the Almighty and that he

had determined to destroy them with a flood." (John Taylor, in *Journal of Discourses*, 14:358. See also 21:157; 26:89.)

"As far as we degenerate from God, we descend to the devil and lose knowledge, and without knowledge we cannot be saved, and while our hearts are filled with evil, and we are studying evil, there is no room in our hearts for good, or studying good." (Joseph Smith, *Teachings of the Prophet Joseph Smith*, p. 217.)

Selected Scripture References

"Every idle word that men shall speak, they shall give account thereof in the day of judgment." (Matthew 12:36.)

"Our words will condemn us, yea, all our works will condemn us; . . . and our thoughts will also condemn us." (Alma 12:14.)

Moses 8:24

"Believe and repent of your sins and be baptized . . . ; if ye do not this, the floods will come"

Selected Statements of the First Presidency and the Twelve Apostles

"Noah, going forth as a legal administrator and holding the same priesthood possessed by Enoch and his forebears, taught faith in the Lord Jesus Christ, repentance, baptism and the receipt of the Holy Ghost, telling his wicked and adulterous generation that unless they accepted the gospel, the floods would come in upon them and misery would be their doom." (Bruce R. McConkie, *Mortal Messiah*, 1:53.)

Moses 8:25

"And it repented Noah . . . that the Lord had made man on the earth"

Other Commentary

In the King James Version, Genesis 6:6 states, "And it repented the Lord that he had made man on the earth, and it grieved him at his heart." The Joseph Smith Translation corrects this troublesome passage of scripture. It was Noah, not the Lord, who was sorry that God had made man on the earth. (See Moses 8:25.)

Moses 8:26

"Noah . . . hath called upon me; for they have sought his life"

Selected Statements of the First Presidency and the Twelve

"It is not that every one who is reviled and who is persecuted possesses the truth. This does not always follow. But there never was a prophet of whom we have any account, raised up in the midst of the children of men to proclaim unto them divine truths, who did not receive in his life and experience these very things of which Jesus has spoken. They were hated, they were separated from the company of their fellows, they were reproached, their names were cast out as evil, they were reviled, their lives were sought." (George Q. Cannon, in *Journal of Discourses*, 20:333–34.)

"From Noah down one prophet after another was rejected by the generations unto whom they were sent and unto whom they bore messages from the Almighty. Even Moses, though successful in leading out the children of Israel, with difficulty escaped being stoned to death by his own adherents. And so with every prophet until the days of the Savior himself." (George Q. Cannon, in *Journal of Discourses*, 22:177.)

Moses 8:27

"Noah was a just man, and perfect in his generation"

Selected Statements of the First Presidency and the Twelve Apostles

"The people before the flood, and also the Sodomites and Canaanites, had carried these corruptions and degeneracies so far that God, in mercy, destroyed them and thus put an end to the procreation of races so degenerate and abominable; while Noah, Abraham, Melchizedek, and others who were taught in the true laws of procreation 'were perfect in their generation,' and trained their children in the same laws." (Parley P. Pratt, *Key to the Science of Theology*, p. 106.)

"Noah, who built the ark, was one of God's greatest servants, chosen before he was born as were others of the prophets. He was no eccentric, as many have supposed. Neither was he a mythical figure created only in legend. Noah was real. . . .

"Let no one downgrade the life and mission of this great prophet. Noah was so near perfect in his day that he literally walked and talked with God. . . .

"Few men in any age were as great as Noah. In many respects he was like Adam, the first man. Both had served as ministering angels in the presence of God even after their mortal experience." (Mark E. Petersen, *Noah and the Flood*, pp. 1–2.)

Moses 8:28

"The earth was corrupt before God, and it was filled with violence"

Selected Statements of the First Presidency and the Twelve Apostles

"But the people still rebelled. . . .

"So great was the apostasy that 'the earth was corrupt before God and it was filled with violence, and God looked upon the earth and behold it was corrupted for all flesh had corrupted its way upon the earth.'

"So came the flood, and Noah and his family—eight souls—were saved, together with the living creatures they had taken with them into the ark.

"But the Lord was not willing to give up. He was ready to start a new dispensation on the earth with Noah and his family.

"To make certain that they understood the gospel, and KNEW God, the Lord appeared, and walked and talked with Noah, and gave him commandments. Again the Lord was granting unto man a new revelation of himself as a means of convincing them of the truth of the Gospel." (Mark E. Petersen, *One Lord . . . One Faith!* pp. 186-87.)

Moses 8:30

"God said unto Noah: The end of all flesh is come before me"

Selected Statements of the First Presidency and the Twelve Apostles

"Those eight, including Noah, were the sole surviving remnant of the entire family of man. The antediluvian world numbered millions doubtless; millions were swept away from the face of the earth, and consigned to a place of torment, or to a prison. In this prison they were immured, doubtless in utter darkness." (George Q. Cannon, in *Journal of Discourses*, 26:81.)

" 'The end of all flesh is come before me, for the earth is filled with violence, and behold I will destroy all flesh from off the earth.' It should be remembered that the Lord said he would do it!

"So the Lord commanded Noah to build an ark into which he was to take his family and the animals of the earth to preserve seed after the flood, and all flesh that was not in the ark perished according to the Lord's decree. Of course this story is not believed by the wise and great among the children of men, any more than was Noah's story in his day." (Joseph Fielding Smith, *Doctrines of Salvation*, 3:38-39.)

"God destroyed the wicked of that generation with a flood. Why did he destroy them? He destroyed them for their benefit, if you can comprehend it." (John Taylor, in *Journal of Discourses*, 24:291.)

Selected Scripture References

"He that will not obey shall be cut off in mine own due time, after I have commanded and the commandment is broken." (D&C 56:3.)

Abraham 1

Abraham 1:1
"In the land of the Chaldeans, at the residence of my fathers"

Selected Statements of the First Presidency and the Twelve Apostles

"Ur was a city of about a half million population in the time of Abraham, according to archaeologists. It was given over to wickedness and idolatry. Yet it had beautiful buildings, good schools, and extensive business dealings by sea as well as on land. The remains of some of the docks are still discernible in the harbor.

"The site has been excavated for years by archaeologists. It is located 140 miles south of Babylon, about ten miles from the present bed of the Euphrates. In all likelihood the city was built originally on the banks of that river. . . .

"It is believed that Ur was founded some time in the fourth millennium B.C. Excavators say that their evidence indicates that it was wiped out by the flood of Noah's day, but that following the deluge, the city was rebuilt.

"Ur became the capital of the entire Mesopotamian valley under the reign of the Sumerian kings (2700 B.C.). Cemetery excavations have produced 'almost incredible treasures in gold, silver, bronze and semi-precious stones,' indicating not only wealth but also a high degree of civilization." (Mark E. Petersen, *Abraham, Friend of God*, p. 37.)

"The oldest cities known were located in the Mesopotamia and are mentioned in Genesis as Babel, Erech, Accad, Calneh, Nineveh, Hur, or Ur, the home of Abraham's father. It was at, or near, Babel that the confusion of the language of the people took place and from that place the Lord scattered them to all parts of the earth. One of the earliest countries beyond these borders where settlers immigrated was Egypt and this land was first settled by the daughter of Ham, so the time of its settlement goes back close to the days when Noah came forth from the ark." (Joseph Fielding Smith, *Man: His Origin and Destiny*, p. 456.)

Abraham 1:1

"I, Abraham, saw that it was needful for me to obtain another place of residence"

See Selected Statements, Scripture References, and Other Commentary under Abraham 1:5; 1:5; 1:5, 7.

Abraham 1:2

"Desiring also to be . . . a prince of peace, . . . I became a rightful heir, a High Priest, holding the right belonging to the fathers"

Selected Statements of the First Presidency and the Twelve Apostles

"The King of Shiloam (Salem) had power and authority over that of Abraham, holding the key and the power of endless life.

"What was the power of Melchizedek? . . . Those holding the fulness of the Melchizedek Priesthood are kings and priests of the Most High God, holding the keys of power and blessings. In fact, that Priesthood is a perfect law of theocracy, and stands as God to give laws to the people administering endless lives to the sons and daughters of Adam.

"Abraham says to Melchizedek, I believe all that thou hast taught me concerning the priesthood and the coming of the Son of Man; so Melchizedek ordained Abraham and sent him away. Abraham rejoiced, saying, Now I have a priesthood." (Joseph Smith, *Teachings of the Prophet Joseph Smith*, pp. 322–23. See also John Taylor, in *Journal of Discourses*, 22:304.)

"Who are the fathers? They were the righteous men who were the patriarchs to the nations in those first years. . . .

"This is something that we are heir to, we were born heir to it, and all we need to do is qualify for it to obtain this blessing, without which we never could go to the temple. And never going to the temple, we could never be sealed. And therefore, we could have no families; we could not go on with our work." (Spencer W. Kimball, in *Ensign*, Nov. 1975, p. 80. See also John Taylor, in *Journal of Discourses*, 19:80; 21:245.)

"Again there was an apostasy. During this time there was one man in the city of Ur, among the few that remained faithful to the Lord, who sought after righteousness.... The Lord answered Abraham's prayer, and he received the priesthood under the hands of Melchizedek, king of Salem." (Joseph Fielding Smith, *Doctrines of Salvation*, 3:82.)

Selected Scripture References

"Abraham received the priesthood from Melchizedek." (D&C 84:14.)

Other Commentary

Two men in the standard works are called "prince of peace": Melchizedek (see Alma 13:18) and the Savior (see Isaiah 9:6). Abraham 1:2 states that Abraham desired to be a "prince of peace" but does not say whether he ever attained such a title.

Abraham 1:3

The Priesthood came down "even from the beginning, or before the foundation of the earth"

Selected Statements of the First Presidency and the Twelve Apostles

"The Melchizedek Priesthood holds the right from the eternal God, and not by descent from father and mother; and that priesthood is as eternal as God Himself, having neither beginning of days nor end of life." (Joseph Smith, *Teachings of the Prophet Joseph Smith*, p. 323.)

"There are two Priesthoods spoken of in the Scriptures, viz., the Melchizedek and the Aaronic or Levitical. Although there are two Priesthoods, yet the Melchizedek Priesthood comprehends the Aaronic or Levitical Priesthood, and is the grand head, and holds the highest authority which pertains to the Priesthood, and the keys of the Kingdom of God in all ages of the world to the latest posterity on the earth; and is the channel through which all knowledge, doctrine, the plan of salvation and every important matter is revealed from heaven.

"Its institution was prior to 'the foundation of this earth, or the morning stars sang together, or the Sons of God shouted for joy.' " (Joseph Smith, *Teachings of the Prophet Joseph Smith*, pp. 166–67.)

Selected Scripture References

"This is the manner after which they were ordained—being called and prepared from the foundation of the world." (Alma 13:3.)

"This order was instituted in the days of Adam, and came down by lineage." (D&C 107:41.)

"All things were confirmed unto Adam, by an holy ordinance." (Moses 5:59.)

Abraham 1:3

"The first man, who is Adam, or first father"

See Selected Statements and Scripture References under Moses 1:34.

Abraham 1:4

"According to the appointment of God unto the fathers concerning the seed"

Selected Statements of the First Presidency and the Twelve Apostles

"The Patriarchal Order of Priesthood was revealed from heaven, and we are informed that 'the order of this priesthood was confirmed to be handed down from father to son, and rightly belongs to the literal descendants of the chosen seed, to whom the promises were made. This order was instituted in the days of Adam and came down by lineage.' " (Joseph Fielding Smith, *Progress of Man*, p. 100.)

"The first authority of Priesthood in the earth was Patriarchal. Adam was a patriarch, so were those who succeeded him. Being patriarchs, of course they were, as stated by Alma, high priests after the Holy Order. This Patriarchal (or Evangelical) order of Priesthood continued through the generations from Adam to Noah, and from Noah to Moses." (Joseph Fielding Smith, *Way to Perfection*, p. 72.)

"The father of Abraham from what we learn in the book of Abraham, turned to the worship of idols; therefore he either lost his priesthood or it passed him by; nevertheless the descent came through him to Abraham." (Joseph Fielding Smith, in *Improvement Era*, Nov. 1956, p. 789.)

Abraham 1:5

"My fathers, having turned from their righteousness, . . . utterly refused to hearken to my voice"

Selected Statements of the First Presidency and the Twelve Apostles

"We all know something of the courage it takes for one to stand in opposition to united custom, and general belief. None of us likes to be ridiculed. Few are able to withstand popular opinion even when they know it is wrong, and it is difficult to comprehend the magnificent courage displayed by Abraham in his profound obedience to Jehovah, in the midst of his surroundings. His moral courage, his implicit faith in God, his boldness in raising his voice in opposition to the prevailing wickedness, is almost beyond comparison. Without doubt this all had its part in the Lord granting the reward and blessings to Abraham and his posterity to the latest generations. Few greater blessings have been given to mortal man." (Joseph Fielding Smith, *Way to Perfection*, p. 86.)

Other Commentary

"Thus we find that Abraham, having sought for the privilege of becoming a preacher of righteousness, in answer to his desire the priesthood was given to him with the command to magnify it. It is not probable that such a man would fail in the hour of action. The friend of God and Father of the Faithful was one 'who knew no such word as fail,' in carrying out heaven's commands. That he did proclaim the law of the Lord wherever he went, is evidenced by his statement that in his youthful home in Ur, his kinsfolk utterly refused to hearken to his voice. So earnest did he become in his advocacy of the truth, that his death was decided upon, even by his own father, and he did not flinch from the issue, but the angel of God rescued him from the sacrificial altar; his work was not yet done." (George Reynolds, *Book of Abraham*, p. 77.)

Abraham 1:5

"My fathers, having turned from their righteousness, and from the holy commandments"

Selected Statements of the First Presidency and the Twelve Apostles

"Look at the days of Abraham, whose faith was so great that he was called the father of the faithful. He was an heir to the royal priesthood, another noble spirit, the friend of God. He came upon this earth, not in a way of light, but through idolatrous parents. His father was an idolator. I do not know who his grandfather was; but his father had false gods that he worshipped and sacrificed to. God inspired Abraham, and his eyes were opened so that he saw and understood something of the dealings of the Lord with the children of men. He understood that there was a God in heaven, a living and true God, and that no man should worship any other God but Him. These were the feelings of Abraham, and he taught his father's house, and all around him, as far as he had the privilege. The consequence was, his father and the idolatrous priests of that day sought to take his life. In the book of Abraham, translated in our day and generation, we are informed that Abraham was bound, and those priests sought to take his life, but the Lord delivered him from them. One reason why they did so was, that he had gone into those places which his father considered sacred, and among the wooden gods which were there, and, being filled with anger that his father should bow down and worship gods of wood and stone, he broke them. When his father saw that his son Abraham had broken his gods he was very angry with him. But Abraham, trying to reason with his father, said that probably the gods had got to fighting among themselves and had killed one another. He tried to bring him to reason, but his father did not believe they had life enough to kill one another. If he had possessed the spirit which his son had, he would have said there is no power with these gods; but he did not, and Abraham had to flee from his father's house, confiding in the Lord, who gave many promises to him and concerning his posterity." (Wilford Woodruff, in *Journal of Discourses*, 11:244.)

"Refusing to worship the true and living God, which they were taught from the beginning, and to walk in the light of divine revelation, they chose for their worship the forces of nature and set up idols representing such forces because they had to have visible aids to guide them in their religious rites and ceremonies. It is doubtful if these ancient people actually worshipped the images which they made with their own hands. These images merely represented the gods who were invisible; and they believed that the real god whom the image represented accepted this image worship. This was the condition in the days of Abraham. Governments had lost touch with the heavens." (Joseph Fielding Smith, *Progress of Man*, p. 103.)

Selected Scripture References

"Choose you this day whom ye will serve; whether the gods which your fathers served that were on the other side of the flood, or the gods of the Amorites." (Joshua 24:15.)

"They hearkened not, nor inclined their ear to turn from their wickedness." (Jeremiah 44:5.)

"Wo unto those that worship idols, for the devil of all devils delighteth in them." (2 Nephi 9:37.)

"They who will not hear the voice of the Lord, neither the voice of his servants, . . . shall be cut off from among the people." (D&C 1:14.)

Other Commentary

"That Abraham's fathers were idolaters, though the book of Genesis carries no such inferences, as also that Abraham was commanded by

Jehovah to leave his father's house because of this idolatry, is proven, we consider, by the following extracts. We will first turn to the Book of Judith, in the Apocrypha (chap. v, verses 6 to 9). It is there represented that when the invading hosts of the king of Nineveh were approaching the land of Israel, the commanding general made some inquiries with regard to the history of its people. Then Achior, the captain of all the sons of Ammon, in answer to his inquiries, replied: 'This people are descended of the Chaldeans, and they sojourned heretofore in Mesopotamia, because they would not follow the gods of their fathers which were in the land of Chaldea. For they left the way of their ancestors, and worshiped the God of heaven, the God whom they knew, so they cast them out from the face of their gods, and they flew into Mesopotamia and sojourned there for many days.'

"From the above it is very evident that the facts relating to the 'call of Abraham' were not only well known to the Hebrews, but to the people of the surrounding nations also. As Achior was one in high authority among the sons of Ammon, his words under the peculiar circumstances in which they were uttered, would carry great weight, and if unauthorized would meet with severe criticism and probable contradiction." (George Reynolds, *Book of Abraham*, p. 72.)

Abraham 1:5, 7

"My fathers, having turned from their righteousness, . . . endeavored to take away my life"

Selected Statements of the First Presidency and the Twelve Apostles

"Did Terah believe so much in the sun god that he would seek to placate that deity by sacrificing Abraham to him? The heathen priest already had sacrificed three young women on this same altar because they would not yield their virtue and refused to 'bow down to worship gods of wood or of stone. . . . ' (Abraham 1:11).

"It seemed to be Terah's intention to provide the same treatment for his son. It does not appear that there was any desire on his part to murder Abraham in a fit of anger because of a family quarrel. It seems more likely that it was a sacrifice of atonement that Terah sought, probably out of his fatherly love for his son. He may have thought that this extreme method should be used to save Abraham's soul. That at least is the charitable point of view, and most likely the correct one." (Mark E. Petersen, *Abraham, Friend of God*, pp. 47–48.)

"Abraham, the son of Terah, lived in the city of the Chaldees. The family of Abraham had turned from righteousness and had become idolators. Abraham therefore, himself a follower of God's truth, preached righteousness to them but without avail. For his insistence upon the worship of the only true and Living God, he was persecuted and his life sought. So intense was the hatred of the idolators that it was only by the intervention of the Lord that he was saved from being offered up as a sacrifice to the idols of the people." (John A. Widtsoe, *Evidences and Reconciliations* 3:25.)

Other Commentary

"We cannot prove, directly from the writings of any authors at our disposal, that an attempt was made to take Abraham's life for righteousness' sake; but we can show from the 'Antiquities' of Josephus that he was maltreated for that cause. This historian, after referring to the doctrines taught by Abraham, regarding God, writes, 'for which doctrines, when the Chaldeans and other people of Mesopotamia raised a tumult against him, he thought fit to leave that country; and at the command and by the assistance of God, he came and lived in the land of Canaan.' " (George Reynolds, *Book of Abraham*, p. 73.)

Abraham 1:7
"The priest of Elkenah was also the priest of Pharaoh"

Selected Statements of the First Presidency and the Twelve Apostles

"Abraham here not only spoke of the local gods of Ur, but also of the Egyptian gods. He mentions that the priest of Elkenah was also the priest of Pharaoh. The altar was obviously specially built for human sacrifice.

"How did this Egyptian infusion reach into Mesopotamia? What was the priest of Pharaoh doing in Ur?

"At this time Egyptian influence was felt throughout the Fertile Crescent. Much of the advanced learning of the people of the Nile was exported abroad, including some of their religious customs. . . .

" . . . the Egyptians had developed an alphabet, the earliest known to historians. This was borrowed by other nations, together with writing materials. . . .

"The Egyptians developed the use of papyrus. . . . This stimulated writing and greatly facilitated record keeping in neighboring countries. It was far more convenient than the use of clay tablets.

"In the same manner the religions of the Egyptians were also exported to nearby peoples. Hence there were priests of Pharaoh in Ur." (Mark E. Petersen, *Abraham, Friend of God*, pp. 42–43.)

Abraham 1:8

"It was the custom of the priest of Pharaoh, the king of Egypt, to offer up upon the altar . . . men, women, and children"

Selected Statements of the First Presidency and the Twelve Apostles

"The civilizations of Egypt, Chaldea, Assyria and the petty nations of Canaan, had been established. In the midst of this scattering the true worship of the Father was nearly lost. Sacrifice instituted in the days of Adam and continued in the practice and teaching of Noah, in the similitude of the great sacrifice of the Son of Man, had become perverted. Instead of offering clean animals, such as the lamb and bullock, the apostate nations had dwindled in unbelief to the extent that human sacrifice was offered to their idol gods." (Joseph Fielding Smith, *Way to Perfection*, p. 85.)

Selected Scripture References

"They have built also the high places of Baal, to burn their sons with fire for burnt offerings unto Baal." (Jeremiah 19:5.)

"And did take many prisoners both women and children, and did offer them up as sacrifices unto their idol gods." (Mormon 4:14.)

Other Commentary

"Human sacrifices were offered to the strange gods of the heathen in Abraham's day; more particularly in Egypt, as it is represented that it was the priest of Pharaoh who officiated on the occasions mentioned by the patriarch.

"To substantiate this point we shall make but one quotation, as its author mentions so many other historians, ancient and modern, as his authorities, that in quoting it we call upon them to become our witnesses also. It is taken from Dissertation II, Whiston's Josephus, and is as follows: 'It is evident from Sanchoniatho, Manetho, Pausanias, Diodorus, Siculus, Philo, Plutarch and Porphyry, that such [human] sacrifices were frequent both in Phoenicia and Egypt, and that long before the days of Abraham, as Sir John Marsham and Bishop Cumberland have fully proved: nay, that in other places (though not in Egypt) this cruel practice continued long after Abraham.'

"We may here draw attention to the statement that this cruel practice did not continue in Egypt after Abraham's day, owing, we doubt not, as will hereafter be shown, to the great influence that that patriarch wielded in later life with Pharaoh and his subjects, in favor of a more perfect way of serving heaven." (George Reynolds, *Book of Abraham*, p. 71-72.)

Abraham 1:10
"Which stood by the hill called Potiphar's Hill"

See Selected Statements under Abraham 1:20.

Abraham 1:11
"They [the three virgins] would not bow down to worship gods of wood or of stone, therefore they were killed upon this altar"

Selected Statements of the First Presidency and the Twelve Apostles

"In lands of idolatry and wickedness life must have been filled with constant anxiety and fear. The history of these nations is filled with carnage and bloodshed, intrigue and wickedness. The common people sank into abject misery and bondage. No person knew when he might be accused of some infraction of the law, or when the eye of the priest would be upon him, with the approval of the law, to make of him a sacrifice unto the gods. It was under conditions of this kind, and while Shem, son of Noah, was still living, that Abraham found it necessary to move from the land of his nativity and 'obtain another place of residence,' among the smaller nations and tribes of Canaan." (Joseph Fielding Smith, *Progress of Man*, pp. 101–2.)

Selected Scripture References

Shadrach, Meshach, and Abed-nego were cast into the fiery furnace for refusing to worship a golden image. (See Daniel 3:16–20.)

Other Commentary

"Among the ancient nations of the East, with the exception of the Jews, prostitution appears to have been connected with religious worship, and to have been not merely tolerated but encouraged. . . . In Egypt, Phoenicia, Assyria, Chaldea, Canaan and Persia, the worship of Isis, Moloch, Baal, Astarte, Mylitta and other deities consisted of the most extravagant sensual orgies and the temples were merely centers of vice. In Babylon some degree of prostitution appeared to have been even compulsory and imposed upon all women in honor of the goddess Mylitta. In India the ancient connection between religion and prostitution still survives." (*Encyclopedia Britannica*, 1952 ed., 18:596, as quoted in W. Cleon Skousen, *The First 2000 Years*, p. 362.)

Abraham 1:12–13
"That you may have a knowledge of this altar. . . . It was

made after the form of a bedstead"

Selected Statements of the First Presidency and the Twelve Apostles

"If we believe in present revelation, as published in the 'Times and Seasons' last spring, Abraham, the prophet of the Lord, was laid upon the iron bedstead for slaughter; and the book of Jasher, which has not been disproved as a bad author, says he was cast into the fire of the Chaldees." (Joseph Smith, *Teachings of the Prophet Joseph Smith*, p. 260.)

Abraham 1:15
"The angel of his presence stood by me, and immediately unloosed my bands"

Selected Statements of the First Presidency and the Twelve Apostles

"Divine guards had sped through space to save the life of Abraham on Potiphar's Hill in the land of Ur, to save Daniel and his companions in the lions' den, to save Nephi from the bitterness and bloodthirsty anger of his brothers, to save Isaac from the knife of sacrifice." (Spencer W. Kimball, in *Improvement Era*, June 1962, p. 437.)

Selected Scripture References

"Alma cried, saying . . . O Lord, give us strength according to our faith which is in Christ, even unto deliverance. And they broke the cords with which they were bound." (Alma 14:26.)

Abraham 1:16
"Abraham, Abraham, behold, my name is Jehovah"

Selected Statements of the First Presidency and the Twelve Apostles

"*Jehovah* is the Anglicized rendering of the Hebrew, *Yahveh* or *Jahveh*, signifying the *Self-existent One*, or *The Eternal*. This name is generally rendered in our English version of the Old Testament as LORD, printed in capitals. The Hebrew, *Ehyeh*, signifying *I Am*, is related in meaning and through derivation with the term *Yahveh* or *Jehovah*. . . .

"Jesus, when once assailed with question and criticism from certain Jews who regarded their Abrahamic lineage as an assurance of divine preferment, met their abusive words with the declaration. 'Verily, verily, I say unto you, Before Abraham was, I am.' The true significance of this saying would be more plainly expressed were the sentence punctuated and pointed as follows: 'Verily, verily, I say unto you, Before

Abraham, was I AM;' which means the same as had He said—Before Abraham, was I, Jehovah." (James E. Talmage, *Jesus the Christ*, pp. 36–37.)

"To believe in Abraham is to believe in Christ. No one can claim kinship to that ancient patriarch without believing what he believed and accepting the testimony he bore. Jesus once said to the unbelieving Jews: 'Had ye believed Moses, ye would have believed me: for he wrote of me. But if ye believe not his writings, how shall ye believe my words?' (John 5:46–47.) And so it is with Abraham. Had the Jews believed in their great patriarch—who of old worshiped Jehovah and looked forward to his mortal birth and atoning sacrifice—they would have accepted that same Jehovah when he ministered among them." (Bruce R. McConkie, *Promised Messiah*, p. 109.)

Selected Scripture References

"Thou, whose name alone is Jehovah, art the most high over all the earth." (Psalm 83:18.)

"Jehovah . . . Mighty God of Jacob." (D&C 109:68.)

"I appeared unto Abraham. . . . I am the Lord God Almighty; the Lord Jehovah. And was not my name known unto them?" (JST Exodus 6:3.)

Abraham 1:17

"I have come down to visit them, and to destroy him who hath lifted up his hand against thee, Abraham"

See Selected Statements and Scripture References under Abraham 1:20; 1:29.

Abraham 1:18

"I will take thee, to put upon thee my name, even the Priesthood of thy father"

Selected Statements of the First Presidency and the Twelve Apostles

"We have no account of the Lord's having organized a kingdom upon the earth in that day; but he gave the priesthood to Abraham, who taught his children the principles of righteousness. Isaac taught Jacob; and Jacob's sons, the twelve Patriarchs, were taught by the priesthood, and God gave unto them many great and glorious blessings." (Wilford Woodruff, in *Journal of Discourses*, 11:244.)

Selected Scripture References

"Why the first is called the Melchizedek Priesthood is because Melchizedek was such a great high priest. Before his day it was called the Holy Priesthood, after the Order of the Son of God." (D&C 107:2-3.)

"The Lord ordained Noah after his own order." (Moses 8:19.)

Abraham 1:19
"As it was with Noah so shall it be with thee"

Other Commentary

"It is not difficult for those who believe in the Bible as it is written, to understand that immediately after the flood there was but one form of faith upon the earth, and that the true one. Noah was a preacher of righteousness before and after the deluge, and because of their obedience to God's laws, he and his family were saved from the universal destruction that came upon the wicked. But their descendants, in an early day, began to depart from the purity of the truths that had saved 'the fathers,' and a knowledge of the forms of iniquity that existed amongst the antediluvians was in some manner conveyed to them, and incorporated in their debased new systems of worship. Noah, Melchizedek and others battled with but partial success against these growing infamies, and Abraham was especially called of the Lord to usher in a new dispensation." (George Reynolds, *Book of Abraham*, p. 84.)

In what way could Abraham be compared to Noah the great patriarch? Adam is the father of all and the great patriarch and prophet of the human family. Noah also is the father of all mankind since the Flood and is also a great prophet of God. When Abraham was compared to Noah by the Lord, it is easy to see that Abraham qualifies as a great prophet of God, as did Adam and Noah before him. But what of the patriarchal comparison? The scriptures teach that Abraham received a patriarchal honor in an unusual fashion. The Lord changed Abraham's name from Abram ("exalted father") to Abraham ("father of a multitude"). (Bible Dictionary, s.v. "Abraham.") The righteous spirits in the premortal life were to be born into mortality through Abraham's lineage. Abraham the patriarch was honored to become the father of the faithful; not only would he have a large posterity but he would have a righteous posterity who would "bear this ministry and Priesthood unto all nations." (Abraham 2:9.)

Abraham 1:19

"Through thy ministry my name shall be known in the earth forever"

Selected Statements of the First Presidency and the Twelve Apostles

"We often speculate about the extent of the Lord's subsequent promise of a vast posterity, but here is a promise that is seldom mentioned: 'Through thy ministry my name shall be known in the earth forever.' (Abraham 1:19.)

"This mighty prophet of God would not be left merely to propagate a great posterity. A ministry was given him! It must have included the preaching of the word. But to what congregations? The record is silent on this point. We do know that he taught the Egyptians astronomy. Could he have used that as a means of proclaiming the name of Christ in that spiritually benighted land?

"And surely if there were sufficient members of the Church in Palestine to justify having a 'great high priest,' there would have been congregations for Abraham to address. It is remembered that when Melchizedek preached repentance to his own people, he converted his entire city. (Alma 13:7–18.) Since he and Abraham were contemporaries and both were called of God, would they not have been associated together in the ministry?

"One means by which Abraham declares the name of Jehovah to all the world is through the generations of the Jews themselves." (Mark E. Petersen, *Abraham, Friend of God*, p. 53.)

See Selected Statements and Scripture References under Abraham 2:9–10; 2:10.

Abraham 1:20

"The Lord broke down the altar of Elkenah, and of the gods of the land"

Selected Statements of the First Presidency and the Twelve Apostles

"When the scripture says that the Lord broke down the altars of the gods of the land, it must have had broad repercussions because it brought great mourning in Chaldea 'and also in the court of Pharaoh.' Pharaoh and his court were in Egypt. Only a most unusual event could have caused such extensive and distant reactions.

"Abraham's brief account obviously does not tell the whole story. Abraham wrote that this attack took place on Potiphar's Hill in the land of Ur of Chaldea." (Mark E. Petersen, *Abraham, Friend of God*, pp. 48–49.)

Abraham 1:22

"And thus the blood of the Canaanites was preserved in the land"

See Selected Statements and Scripture References under Moses 7:8.

Selected Scripture References

"All worthy male members of the Church may be ordained to the priesthood without regard for race or color." (Official Declaration—2.)

Abraham 1:25

"The first government of Egypt . . . was after the manner of the government of Ham, which was patriarchal"

Selected Statements of the First Presidency and the Twelve Apostles

"Egypt was not the only nation, in these early times, which attempted to imitate the patriarchal order of government. We have seen in Abraham's record that this was the order of government in the reign of Adam, and down to the time of Noah.

" . . . Naturally that form of government would be perpetuated in large degree by all tribes as they began to spread over the face of the earth. As men multiplied they organized first in the family group, then into tribes and eventually into nations. The greater powers would naturally occupy the most favored spots. Stronger tribes would overcome the weaker and force them to join the national government, or else they would be subdued and treated as slaves, or placed under tribute. As the patriarchal order was handed down from father to son so also would the political authority be perpetuated with the same claims to authority. We know that in ancient times in Egypt, Assyria, Chaldea, Babylon, Persia, and among all the petty nations of the Mesopotamia and Palestine, the monarch was succeeded by his posterity in hereditary right." (Joseph Fielding Smith, *Progress of Man*, pp. 100–101.)

"For many years preceding the time of Abraham the descendants of Egyptus occupied and governed in Egypt. They extended their dominion into the land of Canaan and oppressed the people, but the time came when the people of Asia, who were of the Semitic race, rebelled and made war on the Egyptians and conquered the country, driving the original inhabitants farther south and up the Nile. These Semitic people known as Hyksos, or shepherds, for they had many flocks and herds, were in possession of the land of Egypt for many years before the time of Abraham. Their rule lasted for some five hundred years, and they were in possession of the land when Joseph was taken into Egypt. It was a Hyksos king who befriended Joseph and who was friendly with Abraham and Isaac. While these people occupied the land of Egypt, they were called Egyptians, although they were relatives of Abraham and Joseph, being descendants of Shem." (Joseph Fielding Smith, *Answers to Gospel Questions*, 1:169–70.)

Other Commentary

"It must be evident from the light thrown on the early history of the world, more especially of Egypt, by the Book of Abraham, that under the almost universally existing form of patriarchal government that 'the fathers' were not only High Priests unto God by right of their 'fatherhood,' but also the kings of the earth by that same right, and it was one of the easiest things in the world for the descendants of these men, who ruled by right divine, to not only reverence them as ministers of heaven's will in all things, temporal and spiritual, but also to deify and afterwards worship them." (George Reynolds, *Book of Abraham*, p. 86.)

Abraham 1:26–27

"Pharaoh being of that lineage by which he could not have the right of Priesthood"

Selected Scripture References

"All worthy male members of the Church may be ordained to the priesthood without regard for race or color." (Official Declaration—2.)

Abraham 1:28

"The records have come into my hands, which I hold unto this present time"

See Selected Statements, Scripture References, and Other Commentary under Moses 6:5; Abraham 1:31.

Abraham 1:29

"There came a fulfilment of those things which were said . . . , that there should be a famine in the land"

Selected Statements of the First Presidency and the Twelve Apostles

"As famine follows the sword, so the pangs of hunger gnawed in the bellies of the Lord's people during the third seal. From 2000 B.C. to

1000 B.C., as never in any other age of the earth's history, the black horse of hunger influenced the whole history of God's dealings with his people.

"In the beginning years of this seal, [Revelation 6:5-6] the famine in Ur of the Chaldees was so severe that Abraham's brother, Haran, starved to death, while the father of the faithful was commanded by God to take his family to Canaan. (Abraham 1:29-30; 2:15.) Of his struggle to gain sufficient food to keep alive, Abraham said: 'Now I, Abraham, built an altar in the land of Jershon, and made an offering unto the Lord, and prayed that the famine might be turned away from my father's house, that they might not perish.' Later he even had to leave Canaan in search of food. 'And I, Abraham, journeyed, going on still towards the south; and there was a continuation of a famine in the land; and I, Abraham, concluded to go down into Egypt, to sojourn there, for the famine became very grievous.' (Abraham 2:17, 21.)...

"Abraham's tenure in mortality was from 1996 to 1822 B.C.; the seven years of famine foretold in Pharaoh's dream commenced in 1709 B.C.; and the exodus from Egypt was in 1491 B.C. Truly the third seal was a millennium in which hunger among men affected the whole course of God's dealings with his people." (Bruce R. McConkie, *Doctrinal New Testament Commentary*, 3:479-80.)

Selected Scripture References

"Let there be a famine in the land, to stir them up in remembrance of the Lord their God." (Helaman 11:4.)

"How oft have I called upon you ... by the voice of famines and pestilences of every kind." (D&C 43:25.)

"And thus, ... with famine ... shall the inhabitants of the earth be made to feel the wrath, and indignation, and chastening hand of an Almighty God." (D&C 87:6.)

Abraham 1:31

"The records of the fathers ... the Lord my God preserved in mine own hands"

Selected Statements of the First Presidency and the Twelve Apostles

"The fact that Abraham had the records of the fathers is most interesting. ...

"It is notable that these records contained information about the stars and the planets. What an insight this gives concerning the 'fathers'! How had they learned astronomy? Did God teach them in the days of their righteousness as he later taught both Abraham and Moses? ...

" . . . Through his faithfulness, Abraham understood the value of those records, appreciated them, and sought to obtain the blessings that the gospel had offered to the fathers." (Mark E. Petersen, *Abraham, Friend of God*, p. 44.)

"Abraham must have been taught the true gospel in his youth, even though his father and other members of the family later apostatized. When his home became an open invitation for him to adopt idolatry, he did not yield. He remained true and faithful to the gospel teachings.

"It is not known how he obtained the record of his fathers, but that record certainly provided him with information concerning the priesthood and its many blessings, instilling in him a strong desire to be ordained to that priesthood." (Mark E. Petersen, *Abraham, Friend of God*, p. 41.)

Selected Scripture References

"It is wisdom in God that we should obtain these records . . . ; and also that we may preserve unto them the words which have been spoken by the mouth of all the holy prophets." (1 Nephi 3:19–20.)

"And a book of remembrance was kept, . . . for it was given unto as many as called upon God to write by the spirit of inspiration." (Moses 6:5.)

Other Commentary

The notes the Prophet Joseph Smith made about the original language of the book of Abraham, called the Egyptian Alphabet and Grammar, indicate that Methuselah and Abraham were well acquainted with the planetary system. The "Second Part, 1 Degree" reads: "Kolob in the first degree. It signifies the first great grand governing fixed star which is the fartherest that ever has been discovered by the fathers which was discovered by Methusela and also by Abraham."

Abraham 2

Abraham 2:1
"The Lord God caused the famine to wax sore"

See Selected Statements and Scriptural References under Abraham
1:29.

Abraham 2:2
"I, Abraham, took Sarai to wife"

Selected Statements of the First Presidency and the Twelve Apostles

"The Lord never sends apostles and prophets and righteous men to
minister to his people without placing women of like spiritual stature at
their sides. Adam stands as the great high priest, under Christ, to rule as
a natural patriarch over all men of all ages, but he cannot rule alone;
Eve, his wife, rules at his side, having like caliber and attainments to his
own. Abraham is tested as few men have been when the Lord commands him to offer Isaac upon the altar (Genesis 22:1–19); and Sarah
struggles with like problems when the Lord directs that she withhold
from the Egyptians her status as Abraham's wife. And so it goes, in all
dispensations and at all times when there are holy men there are also
holy women. Neither stands alone before the Lord. The exaltation of

the one is dependent upon that of the other." (Bruce R. McConkie, *Doctrinal New Testament Commentary*, 3:302.)

Abraham 2:3

"Abraham, get thee out of thy country, . . . unto a land that I will show thee"

Selected Statements of the First Presidency and the Twelve Apostles

"I fancy I see some of his neighbors coming to him, and saying: 'Abraham, where are you going?' 'Oh,' says he, 'I do not know.' 'You don't know.' 'No.' 'Well, who told you to go?' 'The Lord.' 'And you do not know where you are going?' 'Oh, no,' says he, 'I am going to a land that he will show me, and that he has promised to give me and my seed after me for an inheritance; and I believe in God, and therefore I am starting.' There was something very peculiar about it, almost as bad as us when we started to come off from Nauvoo . . . hardly knowing whither we went, just as Abraham did, and I do not think we were any bigger fools than he, for he went just about as we did, not knowing whither he went." (John Taylor, in *Journal of Discourses*, 14:359.)

Abraham 2:4

"Therefore I left the land of Ur, of the Chaldees, to go into the land of Canaan"

Selected Statements of the First Presidency and the Twelve Apostles

"Abraham was a chosen spirit, destined to be a great leader of the work of the Lord. He was commanded to move into another land to be shown him, where he might be free to worship the Lord of earth and the heavens. . . .

"In obedience to God's command, Abraham, with believing members of his family, moved into the promised land known to us as Palestine." (John A. Widtsoe, *Evidences and Reconciliations*, 3:25.)

"Except for Sarah, Lot, and Terah, who 'followed along' somewhat repentant, Abraham was alone. . . .

"On the way to Canaan they rested in northern Mesopotamia in a place that they named Haran, after the dead brother of Abraham. There the famine abated. With the return of prosperity, Terah went back to his idolatry. Not wishing to continue with Abraham to the promised land, he remained in Haran and subsequently died at the age of 205 years. . . .

"The region of Haran has other interests also. Bible dictionaries say that Nahor, who did not accompany Abraham on his journey north, afterward went to Haran to live, no doubt to be with his father and any other relatives who may have gathered there." (Mark E. Petersen, *Abraham, Friend of God*, p. 50.)

Abraham 2:6

"A strange land which I will give unto thy seed after thee for an everlasting possession"

Selected Statements of the First Presidency and the Twelve Apostles

"At the time of the calling of Abraham, the Lord entered into covenant with him and his posterity, in which He promised that Palestine should be theirs for an everlasting heritage. This promise was repeated to Isaac, and confirmed upon the head of Jacob.

"Prior to his death our father Jacob called his twelve sons to him, blessed them, and defined the future of their posterity, adding little to that which had before been promised, until he laid his hands upon the head of Joseph and not only conferred upon him the blessing and heritage of his fathers, but also declared that his heritage prevailed above that of his progenitors, unto the utmost bounds of the Everlasting Hills, to a land choice above all other lands, a land rich in the blessings of the earth, of the heavens above, and the sea beneath.

"Upon Ephraim, the younger of the two sons born to Joseph during his sojourn in Egypt, he sealed the heirship to the blessings and promises conferred upon his father." (The First Presidency: Heber J. Grant, Anthony W. Ivins, and Charles W. Nibley, in James R. Clark comp., *Messages of the First Presidency*, 5:279.)

"Abraham's inheritance in Canaan, for himself and his seed after him, was to be an eternal inheritance, one that would endure in time and in eternity. This promise is the hope of Israel, the hope that the meek shall inherit the earth, first during the millennial era and finally in that same immortal state when the earth becomes a celestial sphere. (*Mormon Doctrine*, 2nd ed., pp. 366–368.) The principle is the same as when the Lord spoke to his Latter-day Saints of their 'land of promise' [D&C 38:19–20]." (Bruce R. McConkie, *Doctrinal New Testament Commentary*, 2:71.)

"In Haran Abraham and his household remained for some time, and then took up their travels still towards the south and west to go into the land of Canaan. When Abraham entered Canaan the Lord spoke to him again, saying, 'Unto thy seed will I give this land: and there builded he an altar unto the Lord, who appeared unto him.' Moreover the Lord said, 'Lift up now thine eyes, and look from the place where thou art northward, and southward, and eastward and westward: For all the land which thou seest, to thee will I give it, and to thy seed forever.' This land which Abraham saw was not merely the little parcel known as Palestine, but it extended to the northward, and to the southward and from the ocean to Mesopotamia." (Joseph Fielding Smith, *Way to Perfection*, pp. 91–92.)

Abraham 2:6–11
The Abrahamic covenant

Selected Statements of the First Presidency and the Twelve Apostles

"Abraham first received the gospel by baptism (which is the covenant of salvation); then he had conferred upon him the higher priesthood, and he entered into celestial marriage (which is the covenant of exaltation), gaining assurance thereby that he would have eternal increase; finally he received a promise that all of these blessings would be offered to all of his mortal posterity. (Abraham 2:6–11; D&C 132:29–50.) Included in the divine promises to Abraham was the assurance that Christ would come through his lineage, and the assurance that Abraham's posterity would receive certain choice, promised lands as an eternal inheritance. (Abraham 2; Genesis 17; 22:15–18; Galatians 3.)

"All of these promises lumped together are called the Abrahamic covenant. This covenant was renewed with Isaac (Genesis 24:60; 26:1–4, 24) and again with Jacob. (Genesis 28; 35:9–13; 48:3–4.) Those portions of it which pertain to personal exaltation and eternal increase are renewed with each member of the House of Israel who enters the order of celestial marriage; through that order the participating parties become inheritors of all the blessings of Abraham, Isaac, and Jacob. (D&C 132; Romans 9:4; Galatians 3; 4.) (Bruce R. McConkie, *Mormon Doctrine*, p. 13.)

Other Commentary

"The most important item to be considered in this chapter is the covenant which was entered into between the Lord and the ancient Patriarch, Abraham. The Bible declares that God reconfirmed this holy covenant with Isaac, Jacob, and Joseph; therefore, the most far-reaching event in the Abrahamic Dispensation of the gospel was the covenant. Following are the main points of the covenant: (1) Abraham was to be a minister of the Gospel of Jesus Christ to a strange nation (Abraham 2:6); (2) he was to be the father of a great nation (Abraham 2:9); (3) his name would be great among all nations (*ibid.*); (4) Abraham and his posterity would be given a land which would be unto them an everlasting inheritance as long as they served God (Abraham 2:6, 19); (5) Abraham's posterity would be as numerous as the stars of the heavens and the sands of the sea (Abraham 3:14); (6) many of his descendants would bear the name of God, even the Holy Priesthood (Abraham 2:9); in fact, Abraham's posterity would be a nation of Priesthood holders (Abraham 2:11); (7) in Abraham and that Priesthood all families of the earth would be blessed (*ibid*.; Genesis 12:3); (8) those throughout the world from Abraham's time forward who received the Gospel of Jesus Christ would be accounted as the seed of Abraham (Abraham 2:10); (9) Christ would come through Abraham's seed (Abraham 2:11); (10) God promised to bless them that blessed Abraham and curse them that cursed Abraham (Abraham 2:11); (11) circumcision was to be the sign of the covenant (Genesis 17:10–14); (12) the covenant was to be an everlasting one, or a gospel covenant (Genesis 17:7); (13) in return for all of the foregoing blessings, Father Abraham and his posterity were to serve the Lord their God and keep all of His commandments.

"It should be observed at this point that on April 3, 1836, a heavenly messenger bestowed upon modern Israel through Joseph Smith and Oliver Cowdery the same blessings, covenants, and promises which had been made approximately 4,000 years ago to Father Abraham. The revelation states that: 'Elias appeared and committed the dispensation of the gospel of Abraham, saying, that in us and our seed, all generations after us should be blessed.' " (Milton R. Hunter, *Pearl of Great Price Commentary*, pp. 201–2.)

Abraham 2:8

"My name is Jehovah"

See Selected Statements and Scripture References under Abraham 1:16.

Abraham 2:8

"I know the end from the beginning"

See Selected Statements and Scripture References under Moses 1:6.

Abraham 2:9–10

"Thy seed . . . shall bear this ministry and Priesthood unto all nations; and I will bless them through thy name"

Selected Statements of the First Presidency and the Twelve Apostles

"The descent of this authority, or divine power, from Adam to Moses is here given in the Lord's own words to Joseph Smith. Moses received it from Jethro, a priest of the house of Midian. The Midianites were descendants of Abraham, through the children of Keturah, wife of Abraham, therefore the Midianites, who were neighbors to the Israelites in Palestine, were related to the Israelites, and were Hebrews. As descendants of Abraham they were entitled through their faithfulness to his blessings (see Abraham 2:9–11), and in the days of Moses and preceding them, in Midian the Priesthood was found." (Joseph Fielding Smith, *Church History and Modern Revelation*, 1:228.)

"The promise that in him all nations should be blessed, brought Abraham's work beyond that of flesh and blood relationships. It made of him a universal figure in the Lord's plan of salvation for all who were sent upon the earth. It would seem that the acceptance of the knowledge of the gospel, and the possession of the priesthood which Abraham bore would make all mankind heirs to the blessings promised Abraham." (John A. Widtsoe, *Evidences and Reconciliations*, 3:27.)

"This covenant with Abraham was also a call to leadership. Therefore, it has been interpreted to mean that Abraham and his descendants were chosen to conserve in purity and to advance on earth the eternal plan for human salvation." (John A. Widtsoe, *Gospel Interpretations*, p. 95.)

Selected Scripture References

"The scripture, foreseeing that God would justify the heathen through faith, preached before the gospel unto Abraham, saying, In thee shall all nations be blessed." (Galatians 3:8. See also v. 14.)

"The knowledge of a Savior has come unto the world, through the testimony of the Jews." (D&C 3:16.)

Abraham 2:10
"As many as receive this Gospel shall be called after thy name"

Selected Statements of the First Presidency and the Twelve Apostles

"Every person who embraces the gospel becomes of the house of Israel. In other words, they become members of the chosen lineage, or Abraham's children through Isaac and Jacob unto whom the promises were made. The great majority of those who become members of the Church are literal descendants of Abraham through Ephraim, son of Joseph. Those who are not literal descendants of Abraham and Israel must become such, and when they are baptized and confirmed they are grafted into the tree and are entitled to all the rights and privileges as heirs." (Joseph Fielding Smith, *Doctrines of Salvation*, 3:246.)

"As the Holy Ghost falls upon one of the literal seed of Abraham, it is calm and serene; and his whole soul and body are only exercised by the pure spirit of intelligence; while the effect of the Holy Ghost upon a Gentile, is to purge out the old blood, and make him actually of the seed of Abraham. That man that has none of the blood of Abraham (naturally) must have a new creation by the Holy Ghost. In such a case, there may be more of a powerful effect upon the body, and visible to the eye, than upon an Israelite, while the Israelite at first might be far before the Gentile in pure intelligence." (Joseph Smith, *Teachings of the Prophet Joseph Smith*, pp. 149–50. See also Bruce R. McConkie, *Mortal Messiah*, 1:56; 3:162.)

"There can be no misunderstanding of this statement. All who accept the gospel become by adoption members of the family of Abraham.

"Moreover, there is in the opinion of many, in this process of adoption, a subtle change in the body as well as in the spirit which makes a person a true heir of the promises to Abraham. . . .

"The oft-asked question, 'Who are the children of Abraham?' is well answered in light of the revealed gospel.

"All who accept God's plan for his children on earth and who live it are the children of Abraham. Those who reject the gospel, whether children in the flesh, or others, forfeit the promises made to Abraham and are not children of Abraham." (John A. Widtsoe, *Evidences and Reconciliations*, 3:28. See also Brigham Young, in *Journal of Discourses*, 7:290–91.)

" 'What was the purpose of Abraham's call? Why was he taken out of his own country and from his father's house and promised that he should become a great nation? It was because Mesopotamia was steeped in idolatry, and the time had arrived for the founding of a pure lineage through which the Lord Jesus Christ, the Savior, would come into the world. Abraham was required to separate himself from his idolatrous surroundings, that he might establish such a lineage. The strict laws given to Israel, Abraham's descendants, had as their object the preservation in purity of the lineage of our Lord.' " (Orson F. Whitney, in *Elder's Journal*, 17 June 1924, as quoted in Mark E. Petersen, *Abraham, Friend of God*, p. 58. See also John Taylor, in *Journal of Discourses*, 24:125; Joseph Fielding Smith, *Doctrines of Salvation*, 3:246, 249–50.)

Selected Scripture References

"Jesus Christ, the son of David, the son of Abraham." (Matthew 1:1.)

"If ye be Christ's, then are ye Abraham's seed, and heirs according to the promise." (Galatians 3:29.)

"As many of the Gentiles as will repent are the covenant people." (2 Nephi 30:2.)

Those who are "faithful unto the obtaining these two priesthoods . . . and the magnifying their callings" become "the seed of Abraham . . . and the elect of God." (D&C 84:33–34.)

Abraham 2:11

"In thee . . . and in thy seed . . . shall all the families of the earth be blessed, even with the blessings of the Gospel, which are the blessings of salvation, even of eternal life"

Selected Statements of the First Presidency and the Twelve Apostles

"It will be noticed that, according to Paul, (see Galatians iii:8) the Gospel was preached to Abraham. We would like to be informed in what name the Gospel was then preached, whether it was in the name of Christ or some other name. If in any other name, was it the Gospel? And if it was the Gospel, and that preached in the name of Christ, had it any ordinances? If not, was it the Gospel? And if it had ordinances what were they? Our friends may say, perhaps, that there were never any ordinances except those of offering sacrifices before the coming of Christ, and that it could not be possible for the Gospel to have been administered while the law of sacrifices of blood was in force. But we will recollect that Abraham offered sacrifice, and notwithstanding this, had the Gospel preached to him. That the offering of sacrifice was only to point the mind forward to Christ we infer from these remarkable words of Jesus to the Jews: [John 8:56]." (Joseph Smith, *History of the Church*, 2:17.)

"His seed are the ministers of Christ; they hold the holy priesthood; they have received the divine commission to preach the gospel in all the world and to every creature. And what are the blessings they offer mankind? They are salvation and eternal life.

"And what is salvation? Joseph Smith's definition is: 'Salvation consists in the glory, authority, majesty, power and dominion which Jehovah possesses and in nothing else; and no being can possess it but himself or one like him.' (*Lectures on Faith*, lecture 7, para. 9.) And what is eternal life? It is the name of the kind of life God lives. It consists of two things: life in the family unit, and the receipt of the fulness of the Father, meaning the fulness of the power, glory, and dominion of

God himself." (Bruce R. McConkie, *Millennial Messiah*, pp. 263–64. See also Bruce R. McConkie, in *Improvement Era*, June 1959, p. 474.)

Selected Scripture References

"Behold, you have my gospel before you, and my rock, and my salvation." (D&C 18:17.)

"This is my work and my glory—to bring to pass the immortality and eternal life of man." (Moses 1:39.)

Abraham 2:13

"Thou didst send thine angel to deliver me"

See Selected Statements and Scripture References under Abraham 1:15.

Abraham 2:13

"I will do well to hearken unto thy voice, therefore let thy servant rise up and depart in peace"

Selected Statements of the First Presidency and the Twelve Apostles

"Abraham was guided in all his family affairs by the Lord; was conversed with by angels, and by the Lord; was told where to go, and when to stop; and prospered exceedingly in all that he put his hand unto; it was because he and his family obeyed the counsel of the Lord." (Joseph Smith, *Teachings of the Prophet Joseph Smith*, pp. 251–52.)

Selected Scripture References

"In thy seed shall all the nations of the earth be blessed; because thou hast obeyed my voice." (Genesis 22:18.)

"Abraham obeyed my voice, and kept my charge, my commandments, my statutes, and my laws." (Genesis 26:5.)

Abraham 2:14

"I, Abraham, was sixty and two years old when I departed out of Haran"

Selected Statements of the First Presidency and the Twelve Apostles

"From the Book of Abraham we learn that Abraham was sixty-two and not seventy-five years of age when he left Haran (Genesis 12:4; Abraham 2:14), showing at least that much of an error in the Old Testament account." (Bruce R. McConkie, *Doctrinal New Testament Commentary*, 2:71.)

Abraham 2:15

"I took . . . all our substance that we had gathered, and the souls that we had won in Haran"

Selected Statements of the First Presidency and the Twelve Apostles

"Nothing is said about his possessions as he moved to Haran. He evidently went with little of this world's goods. But in Haran he prospered. He says that in leaving Haran, he took his wife and nephew 'and all our substance that we had gathered, and the souls that we had won in Haran.' (Abraham 2:15.) The scriptures say that he obtained many servants. Actually at one time he had in his retinue three hundred armed and trained fighting men. (Genesis 14:14.) Another paragraph says: 'There were many flocks in Haran.' (Abraham 2:5.) . . .

"There were several reasons why Abraham became rich. One must have been that he was a highly intelligent man, well educated in Ur, and trained no doubt in business as well as ranching. His business skill could have accounted for much of his successes, as it does with others. But there was a more important reason: He served the Lord!" (Mark E. Petersen, *Abraham, Friend of God*, p. 72.)

"When Abraham and his family left Ur to dwell in Canaan, he says they took with them 'the souls that we had won in Haran.' (Abraham 2:15.) Then, as now, the servants of the Lord were seeking to save their fellowmen." (Bruce R. McConkie, *Millennial Messiah*, p. 235.)

Abraham 2:17

"Prayed that the famine might be turned away"

See Selected Statements and Scripture References under Abraham 1:29.

Abraham 2:17

"I, Abraham, built an altar in the land of Jershon, and made an offering unto the Lord"

Selected Statements of the First Presidency and the Twelve Apostles

"The testimony in the Bible is direct and explicit that Abraham fulfilled the law requiring the offering of sacrifices, and furthermore was

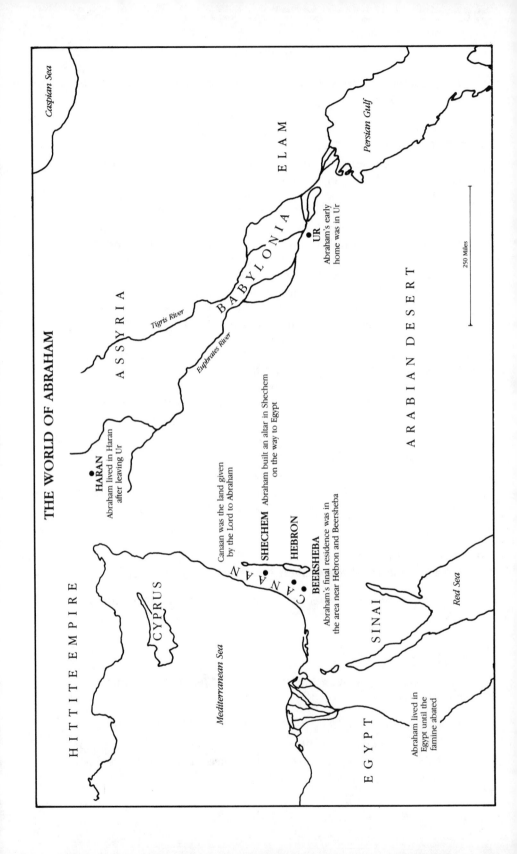

THE WORLD OF ABRAHAM

Caspian Sea

ELAM

Persian Gulf

HITTITE EMPIRE

ASSYRIA

BABYLONIA

Tigris River

Euphrates River

UR
Abraham's early
home was in Ur

ARABIAN DESERT

HARAN
Abraham lived in Haran
after leaving Ur

CYPRUS

Mediterranean Sea

CANAAN

Canaan was the land given
by the Lord to Abraham

SHECHEM   Abraham built an altar in Shechem
on the way to Egypt

HEBRON

BEERSHEBA
Abraham's final residence was in
the area near Hebron and Beersheba

SINAI

Red Sea

EGYPT

Abraham lived in
Egypt until the
famine abated

250 Miles

in possession of the principles of the Gospel and understood the saving value of the atonement.

"In the historical narrative of the Book of Genesis, we have numerous testimonies that Abraham offered up sacrifices, in connection with his worship of the Almighty." (John Taylor, *Mediation and Atonement*, p. 99.)

Abraham 2:19
"Unto thy seed will I give this land"

See Selected Statements, Scripture References, and Other Commentary under Abraham 1:2; 2:6.

Abraham 2:22–24
"The Lord said . . . : Let her [Sarai] say unto the Egyptians, she is thy sister, and thy soul shall live"

Selected Statements of the First Presidency and the Twelve Apostles

"There was good reason for this. It was customary for the kings and rulers to take to themselves any of the beautiful women their eyes fell upon. They had harems, of course, and did not mind adding to them. . . .

"To protect himself, Abraham had told Pharaoh that Sarah was his sister, which of course she was. Had he divulged that she was his wife, he might have been slain. But as his sister, Pharaoh was willing to buy her at a good price. . . .

"The scripture does not mention the response of Abraham. Naturally he must have refused the offer because he was a man of God." (Mark E. Petersen, *Abraham, Friend of God*, pp. 68–69.)

Selected Scripture References

"Say, I [Abraham] pray thee, thou art my sister: that it may be well with me for thy sake." (Genesis 12:13.)

"And Abraham said of Sarah his wife, She is my sister: and Abimelech King of Gerar sent, and took Sarah." (Genesis 20:2.)

"The men of the place asked him [Isaac] of his wife [Rebekah]; and he said, She is my sister." (Genesis 26:7.)

Other Commentary

"Josephus writes (Antiquities, book 1, chap viii) that when Pharaoh discovered that the woman, Sarah, whom he desired to take into his household, was the wife of Abraham, he made, as an excuse for his action, that believing her to be the patriarch's sister he wished to marry her, from his desire to be related to so distinguished a personage as Abraham. This could not be irony; Pharaoh was not in a condition to be ironical with his guest. It must have been an excuse that bore upon its face the probability of truth, and one that would be accepted as genuine by the powerful visitor from Canaan. Had it been otherwise, it would have been adding insult to injury, and instead of Abraham remaining in Egypt to become a teacher to its people, we should probably learn that in anger he returned to his own land." (George Reynolds, *Book of Abraham*, pp. 101–102.)

Some biblical commentators have questioned Abraham's integrity because of the Bible account of Abraham's asking Sarai to introduce herself as his sister to protect his life. The book of Abraham tells us that it was at the Lord's command that Abraham so introduced his beautiful wife to the Egyptians. The Lord used that method to introduce Abraham into the high courts of Egypt while protecting Sarai's virtue.

Abraham 3

Abraham 3:1
"I, Abraham, had the Urim and Thummim"

Selected Statements of the First Presidency and the Twelve Apostles

"Exactly how this precious instrument, the Urim and Thummim, operates, we can only surmise, but it seems to be infinitely superior to any mechanism ever dreamed of yet by researchers. It would seem to be a receiving set or instrument.... The abode of God is a master Urim and Thummim, and the synchronization of transmitting and receiving apparatus of this kind could have no limitation....

"Is it hard to project ourselves from the elemental world of puny man to the world of Omnipotent God, who with great purpose has developed precision instruments operated through his omnipotent knowledge? Is it difficult to believe that the Urim and Thummim, carried down through the ages by the prophets, even in the hands of our own modern-day prophet, could be that precision instrument which would transmit messages from God himself to his supreme creation—man? Can God have limitations? Can atmosphere or distance or space hold back the pictures? Would it be so difficult for Moses or Enoch or Abraham or Joseph to see a colorful, accurate, moving picture of all things past and present, and even future?" (Spencer W. Kimball, in *Improvement Era*, June 1962, p. 436. See also John Taylor, in *Journal of Discourses*, 25:215; Mark E. Petersen, *Abraham, Friend of God*, p. 128.)

"And the Lord communicated with him and gave him a Urim and Thummim by which he was enabled to interpret, to read and comprehend the mind and will and the laws and purposes of God. And, furthermore, I would state that he went still further. He asked God for certain blessings and privileges and powers which belonged to him and which he considered were within his reach, and which were his privilege to obtain. And the Lord revealed himself to him and communicated unto him certain eternal principles—that no man can comprehend unless God does reveal them—and many other things—the motion of the planets, and the planetary system of the earth on which we live, and the sun and the moon and the stars and the various bodies that compose our solar system; and then, of other suns, and other heavenly bodies and the laws governing them. Abraham wrote those things, and was well versed in those great principles." (John Taylor, in *Journal of Discourses*, 21:245.)

"The history concerning the *Urim and Thummim*, or *Interpreters* as they are called in the Book of Mormon, is not very clear. Abraham had the Urim and Thummim by which he received revelations of the heavenly bodies, as he has recorded in the Book of Abraham. What became of these after his death we do not know." (Joseph Fielding Smith, *Doctrines of Salvation*, 3:222.)

Selected Scripture References

"Whosoever is commanded to look in them, the same is called seer." (Mosiah 8:13.)

"There were two stones in silver bows—and these stones, fastened to a breastplate, constituted what is called the Urim and Thummim." (Joseph Smith—History 1:35.)

Abraham 3:2

"And I saw the stars, that they were very great"

Selected Statements of the First Presidency and the Twelve Apostles

"But, as far as our records reveal, Abraham stands preeminent as the greatest astronomer of all the ages. He saw, recorded, and taught the truths relative to the creation of the earth; of the movements and relationships of the sun, moon, and stars; and of the positions and revolutions of the various spheres in the sidereal heavens. (Abraham 3; 4; 5; *History of the Church*, vol. 2, p. 286.) When the Lord comes again, he will reveal all things (D&C 101:32–34); then the perfect knowledge of astronomy will be had again, and the faithful will know all things about all the creations of him who is omnipotent." (Bruce R. McConkie, *Mormon Doctrine*, p. 57.)

"Abraham knew far more in his day regarding the planets and the great fixed stars out in space than the greatest astronomer knows today. How did he get his knowledge? Not through the telescope; not through the spectroscope; but through the opening of his vision by the Spirit of God. He was taught by the Lord himself who revealed unto him all these things and explained the great heavenly bodies and their workings, also the earth, in a manner that never has been approached and cannot be approached by the scientific man with all his instruments to aid him and inspired by worldly learning." (Joseph Fielding Smith, *Doctrines of Salvation*, 1:147–48.)

"Many would wonder at the great Abraham, living nearly forty centuries ago, who was such a world authority, not only on the earth, its movements, and its conditions, but on the universe itself, extending to the very center of it.

"His supernatural knowledge was probably supplemented by research and observation in the clear, starry nights in the plains of Mesopotamia, but he must have received the major part through the Urim and Thummim which could have been far more revealing than the most powerful telescope in the most modern observatory. In his 175 brilliant years of life he accumulated knowledge in many fields, but especially in astronomy, in which field he seems to have excelled, and was perhaps equal or superior to even the highly trained Egyptian astronomers." (Spencer W. Kimball, in Conference Report, Apr. 1962, p. 60.)

Other Commentary

"Abraham tells us that there were three ways by which he received his knowledge of astronomy.

"1st. Through the records handed down to him from the antediluvian patriarchs.

"2nd. By the use of the Urim and Thummim, which he received from the Lord in Ur of Chaldea.

"3rd. By direct communication with the Almighty, who, face to face, and with His own voice, explained to him the laws that govern His countless creations." (George Reynolds, *Book of Abraham*, p. 104.)

Abraham 3:3, 16

"The name of the great one is Kolob, because it is near unto me"

Selected Statements of the First Presidency and the Twelve Apostles

"The Lord made known to him the following facts: That Kolob is the first creation, and is nearest to the celestial, or the residence of God. It is the first in government, the last pertaining to the measurement of time. This measurement is according to celestial time. One day in Kolob is equal to a thousand years according to the measurement of this earth, which by the Egyptians was called Jah-oh-eh. Oliblish, so called by the Egyptians, stands next to Kolob in the grand governing creation near the celestial, or place where God resides. This great star is also a governing star and is equal to Kolob in its revolutions and in its measuring of time. Other grand governing stars were also revealed to Abraham." (Joseph Fielding Smith, *Man: His Origin and Destiny*, p. 461.)

Other Commentary

"The Lord pointed out to Abraham that Kolob was immense in size. The fact that it took one thousand years of our time for it to make one complete turn on its axis—in other words, for one day's time to elapse— also is indicative of its enormity. Modern astronomers have discovered many stars which are gigantic in size. These they call 'super-giant stars.' One of the largest of them is named *Betelgeuse*. It has a diameter of approximately four hundred sixty millions of miles. Another super-giant star, being also enormous in size, is named *Antares*. This immense body of matter is located in the *Scorpia* constellation. It has a diameter of approximately three hundred millions of miles. Another giant star, being a little larger than Antares, is named *Myra*, and another is called *Arcturus*. The latter one has a diameter of thirty-six millions of miles. Any of these massive bodies of matter could easily be accepted as being comparable in size to the great star Kolob which God showed to Father Abraham." (Milton R. Hunter, *Pearl of Great Price Commentary*, p. 93.)

Read W. W. Phelps's lyrics to the hymn "If You Could Hie to Kolob." (*Hymns*, 1985, no. 284.)

Abraham 3:4

"Kolob was after the manner of the Lord according to its times

and seasons . . . , being one thousand years"

Selected Statements of the First Presidency and the Twelve Apostles

"According to this new revelation, there is a certain great world, called Kolob, placed near one of the celestial kingdoms, whose diurnal rotation takes place once in a thousand of our years; and that celestial time was measured by those celestial beings, by the rotations of Kolob, hence one day with the Lord was a thousand of our years." (Orson Pratt, in *Journal of Discourses*, 16:317.)

> *For thus saith the Lord, in the spirit of truth,*
> *I am merciful, gracious, and good unto those*
> *That fear me, and live for the life that's to come;*
> *My delight is to honor the saints with repose;*
>
> *That serve me in righteousness true to the end;*
> *Eternal's their glory, and great their reward;*
> *I'll surely reveal all my myst'ries to them, —*
> *The great hidden myst'ries in my kingdom stor'd—*
>
> *From the council in Kolob, to time on the earth.*
> *And for ages to come unto them I will show*
> *My pleasure & will, what my kingdom will do:*
> *Eternity's wonders they truly shall know.*

(Joseph Smith, poetic explanation of the vision [D&C 76], stanzas 5-7, in *Times and Seasons,* 4 [1 Feb. 1843]: 82.)

Selected Scripture References

"One day is with the Lord as a thousand years, and a thousand years as one day." (2 Peter 3:8.)

"I, Abraham, saw that it was after the Lord's time, which was after the time of Kolob." (Abraham 5:13.)

Other Commentary

"According to this, 1000 years of our time is equivalent to one day with the Lord. If you were to live to be 100 years old on earth, that would be 1/10 of one day with the Lord. Now suppose we divide the Lord's day into 24 equal parts, as our day is, just for comparative purposes: 100 years of our life would be equal to 1/10 of 24, or 2.4 hours. So according to this, if you live to be 100 on this earth, that would be equivalent to 2.4 hours in the Lord's time calendar. . . .

"Imagine yourself for a moment back in the spirit world before you came to earth. You were living in the presence of God in the celestial world. You knew from firsthand experience the fullness of the glory of God. You knew you could not participate in his glory, or become as he is, because you were only a spirit; you didn't have a physical body. Now the opportunity comes for you to go to earth where you can receive such a body and become as he is. . . .

"Wouldn't you promise to endure almost anything for two hours to get the blessings that the Lord has promised of eternal life and to become as he is?" (Eldred G. Smith, in *Improvement Era*, June 1966, p. 513.)

Abraham 3:6, 10

"It is given unto thee to know the times of reckoning, and the set time . . . of the earth," the sun, the moon, and "all the stars that are set to give light"

Selected Statements of the First Presidency and the Twelve Apostles

"The Lord creates worlds in a systematic manner. He places them throughout the Universe by perfect and infinite calculations. It is not a matter of chance but of divine order. Earths are created primarily as habitations for living creatures." (Joseph Fielding Smith, *Man: His Origin and Destiny*, p. 28.)

Selected Scripture References

"He appointed the moon for seasons: the sun knoweth his going down." (Psalm 104:19.)

"He hath given a law unto all things, by which they move in their times and their seasons." (D&C 88:42.)

Other Commentary

"In other words these great, governing planets control all others in their revolutions, or are the centres around which the others revolve. As the moon revolves around the earth, and the earth with the other primary and secondary planets belonging to this solar system revolve around the sun, so has the sun a centre around which it, with all its earths and moons, revolves, while this grand centre has a governing planet also, a sun or world around which it, with its attendant systems of suns and worlds, revolves, and so on until we come to Kolob, the 'nearest to the celestial or the residence of God,' which is the grand centre which governs all the suns and systems of suns 'which belong to the same order' as our earth and those that move with it." (George Reynolds, *Book of Abraham*, pp. 105–6.)

Abraham 3:9

"Kolob is set nigh unto the throne of God"

Selected Statements of the First Presidency and the Twelve Apostles

"There is throughout the Christian world the prevailing thought that heaven where the righteous will go is some place far off on some glorious sphere which is the home of the Eternal Father. He revealed to Abraham that his throne is near to Kolob, the great governing star of our universe. The heaven to which the righteous will go who dwell upon this earth, will be right here upon this earth." (Joseph Fielding Smith, *Man: His Origin and Destiny*, p. 537.)

"The planet Kolob became of great interest to Abraham. The Lord explained that it 'is set nigh unto the throne of God' and that it governs 'all those planets which belong to the same order as that upon which thou standest.' (Abraham 3:9.)

"It is interesting to note that the throne of God is on a separate planet in the sky, with Kolob being nearby." (Mark E. Petersen, *Abraham, Friend of God*, p. 128.)

Selected Scripture References

"After it [the earth] hath filled the measure of its creation, it shall be crowned with glory, even with the presence of God the Father." (D&C 88:19.)

"The angels do not reside on a planet like this earth; but they reside in the presence of God, on a globe like a sea of glass and fire." (D&C 130:6-7.)

"Kolob [signifies] the first creation, nearest to the celestial, or the residence of God." (Figure 1 of Facsimile 2 in the Pearl of Great Price.)

Abraham 3:11

"Thus I, Abraham, talked with the Lord, face to face, as one man talketh with another"

Selected Statements of the First Presidency and the Twelve Apostles

"Abraham was protected so that he could withstand the brilliance of the Lord and so that he could see and comprehend. The visions that Abraham saw at this time before his sojourn in Egypt were beyond all description. Perhaps no soul even with the strongest telescopes has ever seen the thousandth part of what Abraham saw as to this universe with all its limitless parts and functions. He also saw the creation of this earth." (Spencer W. Kimball, *Faith Precedes the Miracle*, p. 89.)

"In the knowledge of astronomical and other philosophical truths, which our modern great men are searching after and pride themselves in, they are but babes, compared with the ancient fathers. Do the wise men of modern ages understand the laws which govern the worlds that are, that were, and that are to come? They cannot fathom this matter. They have grown weaker when they ought to have grown stronger and wiser." (Brigham Young, *Discourses of Brigham Young*, pp. 162–63.)

"Suffice it to say, that the Lord himself instructed Abraham in things pertaining to this and other worlds, and that he in his day possessed more light and intelligence on the principles alluded to than all the combined wisdom of the world of to-day." (John Taylor, in *Journal of Discourses,* 21:245.)

See Selected Statements, Scripture References, and Other Commentary under Moses 7:4.

Abraham 3:12
"I saw those things which his hands had made, . . . and I could not see the end thereof"

Selected Statements of the First Presidency and the Twelve Apostles

"Here was a wonderful lesson to be learned by Abraham. In this vision the wonders of the universe were made plain to him. It was not merely a lesson in astronomy given under the tuition of the Master Astronomer, who built these vast worlds and knew them all by name. There were other and deeper meanings in this lesson. Abraham learned that the works of the Almighty are endless. He discovered that they are created as habitations for man. These glorified worlds are abodes of righteous celestial beings—the children of our eternal Father. Moreover, he learned that there is an eternal purpose in all the works of God, that many worlds have gone through their probation and on to eternal glory." (Joseph Fielding Smith, *Way to Perfection*, p. 94.)

"Could you gaze into heaven five minutes, you would know more than you would by reading all that ever was written on the subject." (Joseph Smith, *History of the Church*, 6:50.)

Selected Scripture References

"Worlds without number have I created." (Moses 1:33.)
"Were it possible that man could number the particles of the earth, . . . it would not be a beginning to the number of thy creations." (Moses 7:30.)

Abraham 3:14

"It was in the night time when the Lord spake these words unto me"

Selected Statements of the First Presidency and the Twelve Apostles

"It was in the night time when the Lord spoke these words to Abraham and revealed to him, in vision and by the Urim and Thummim, the greatest of the stars. As he gazed upon them—for his eyes were opened—they greatly multiplied before him so that he could not see the end thereof, for the stars were without number." (Joseph Fielding Smith, *Way to Perfection*, p. 94.)

Selected Scripture References

"And a vision appeared to Paul in the night." (Acts 16:9.)

"The voice of the Lord spake unto my father by night." (1 Nephi 16:9.)

"He hath heard my cry by day, and he hath given me knowledge by visions in the nighttime." (2 Nephi 4:23.)

Abraham 3:14

"I will multiply thee, and thy seed after thee, like unto these"

Selected Statements of the First Presidency and the Twelve Apostles

"Nor is this covenant confined to mortal life. It extends beyond the grave and into the celestial kingdom. The children of Abraham, if they will keep the covenant as they receive it in the house of the Lord, shall, as Abraham their father, continue on through all eternity to increase, and there shall be no end to their posterity. In this way the blessings of Abraham, Isaac and Jacob, are extended to them, and they become partakers to the fullest extent. For there is to be a continuation of the 'seeds forever' among those who receive exaltation in the kingdom of God. This is the promise, and there shall come through Abraham kings and priests and rulers, not only on this earth but in the heavens, and so shall it be worlds without end." (Joseph Fielding Smith, *Way to Perfection*, p. 96.)

"What, then, is the Abrahamic covenant? It is that Abraham and his seed (including those adopted into his family) shall have all of the blessings of the gospel, of the priesthood, and of eternal life. The gate to eternal life is celestial marriage, which holy order of matrimony enables the family unit to continue in eternity, so that the participating parties may have posterity as numerous as the sands upon the seashore or the

stars in heaven. The Abrahamic covenant enables men to create for themselves eternal family units that are patterned after the family of God our
Heavenly Father. A lesser part of the covenant is that the seed of Abraham
have the Millennial destiny of inheriting as an everlasting possession
the very land of Canaan whereon the feet of the righteous have trod in
days gone by." (Bruce R. McConkie, *New Witness for the Articles of
Faith*, p. 505.)

See Selected Statements and Scripture References under Abraham
2:9–10; 2:11.

Selected Scripture References

"Look now toward heaven, and tell the stars, if thou be able to
number them: . . . So shall thy seed be." (Genesis 15:5.)

"I will make thy [Isaac's] seed to multiply as the stars of heaven."
(Genesis 26:4.)

"Abraham received promises concerning his seed . . . ; both in the
world and out of the world should they continue as innumerable as the
stars." (D&C 132:30.)

Abraham 3:15

"Abraham, I show these things unto thee before ye go into
Egypt, that ye may declare all these words"

Selected Statements of the First Presidency and the Twelve Apostles

"Who taught the Egyptians? Abraham taught them the science of
astronomy, so we are informed, by late Egyptologists, and revealed unto
them the principle concerning the motions of the heavenly bodies."
(John Taylor, in *Journal of Discourses*, 25:215.)

"The learning of the Egyptians, and their knowledge of astronomy
was no doubt taught them by Abraham and Joseph, as their records
testify, who received it from the Lord." (Joseph Smith, *Teachings of the
Prophet Joseph Smith*, p. 251.)

Other Commentary

"The book of Abraham states that God commanded the patriarch to
show unto the Egyptians the things that He had revealed unto him.
Josephus, in narrating this portion of Abraham's history—being only
partially acquainted with the facts of the case from the authorities at his
disposal—tells us that Abraham went down into Egypt to avoid the
famine in Canaan, and to 'become an auditor of their priests, and to
know what they said concerning the gods; designing either to follow

them if they had better notions than he, or to convert them into a better way if his own notions proved the truest.' After his arrival in Egypt, and the circumstances arising out of the attempt of Pharoah to add Sarah to the number of his wives, the outcome of which placed the monarch under obligations to the patriarch, Joseph states that 'Pharoah gave Abraham leave to enter into conversation with the most learned among the Egyptians, from which conversation his virtue and his reputation became more conspicuous than they had been before.' . . . In another place the Jewish historian states, 'He (Abraham) was a person of great sagacity, both for understanding all things, and persuading his hearers, and not mistaken in his opinions; for which reason he began to have higher notions of virtue than others had, and he determined to renew and to change the opinion all men happened then to have concerning God.' " (George Reynolds, *Book of Abraham*, pp. 79–80.)

"That God did use Abraham, as stated in his book to convey astronomical knowledge to the Egyptians, is, we think, fully demonstrated by the following: Josephus (book 1, chapter viii) states that Abraham 'communicated to them (the Egyptians) arithmetic, and delivered to them the science of astronomy, for before Abraham came into Egypt they were unacquainted with those parts of learning, for that science came by the Chaldeans into Egypt, and from them to the Greeks also.' " (George Reynolds, *Book of Abraham*, p. 113.)

Selected Scripture References

See Facsimile 3 in the Pearl of Great Price.

Abraham 3:18

"Yet these two spirits, not withstanding one is more intelligent than the other, have no beginning"

Selected Statements of the First Presidency and the Twelve Apostles

"I want to reason a little on this subject. I learned it by translating the papyrus which is now in my house. I learned a testimony concerning Abraham, and he reasoned concerning the God of Heaven. 'In order to do that,' said he, 'suppose we have two facts: that supposes another fact may exist—two men on the earth, one wiser than the other, would logically show that another who is wiser than the wisest may exist. Intelligences exist one above another, so that there is no end to them.'

"If Abraham reasoned thus—If Jesus Christ was the Son of God, and John discovered that God the Father of Jesus Christ had a Father, you may suppose that He had a Father also. Where was there ever a son without a father? And where was there ever a father without first being a son? Whenever did a tree or anything spring into existence without a progenitor? And everything comes in this way. Paul says that which is earthly is in the likeness of that which is heavenly. Hence if Jesus had a Father, can we not believe that He had a Father also? I despise the idea of being scared to death at such a doctrine, for the Bible is full of it.

"I want you to pay particular attention to what I am saying. Jesus said that the Father wrought precisely in the same way as His Father had done before Him. As the Father had done before. He laid down his life, and took it up the same as His Father had done before." (Joseph Smith, *History of the Church*, 6:476-77.)

"Mankind are organized of element designed to endure to all eternity; it never had a beginning and never can have an end. There never was a time when this matter, of which you and I are composed, was not in existence, and there never can be a time when it will pass out of existence; it cannot be annihilated.

"It is brought together, organized, and capacitated to receive knowledge and intelligence, to be enthroned in glory, to be made angels, Gods—beings who will hold control over the elements, and have power by their word to command the creation and redemption of worlds, or to extinguish suns by their breath, and disorganize worlds, hurling them back into their chaotic state. This is what you and I are created for." (Brigham Young, in *Journal of Discourses*, 3:356.)

"I am dwelling on the immortality of the spirit of man. Is it logical to say that the intelligence of spirits is immortal, and yet that it had a beginning? The intelligence of spirits had no beginning, neither will it have an end. That is good logic. That which has a beginning may have an end. There never was a time when there were not spirits; for they are co-equal [co-eternal] with our Father in heaven. . . .

"I want to reason more of the spirit of man; . . . I take my ring from my finger and liken it unto the mind of man—the immortal part, because it has no beginning. Suppose you cut it in two; then it has a beginning and an end; but join it again, and it continues one eternal round. So with the spirit of man. As the Lord liveth, if it had a beginning, it will have an end. . . .

"Intelligence is eternal and exists upon a self-existent principle. It is a spirit from age to age, and there is no creation about it." (Joseph Smith, *Teachings of the Prophet Joseph Smith*, pp. 353-54.)

"God gave his children their free agency even in the spirit world, by which the individual spirits had the privilege, just as men have here, of choosing the good and rejecting the evil, or partaking of the evil to suffer the consequences of their sins. Because of this, some even there were more faithful than others in keeping the commandments of the Lord. Some were of greater intelligence than others, as we find it here, and were honored accordingly. . . .

"The spirits of men were not equal. They may have had an equal start, and we know they were all innocent in the beginning; but the right of free agency which was given to them enabled some to outstrip others, and thus, through the eons of immortal existence, to become more intelligent, more faithful, for they were free to act for themselves, to think for themselves, to receive the truth or rebel against it." (Joseph Fielding Smith, *Doctrines of Salvation*, 1:58-59.)

"Occasionally men arise who tower above the multitude in the extent of their knowledge, such as the Prophet Joseph and others whose names I need not mention; for, as the Lord revealed to Abraham, there are differences in spirits. He spoke of the Kokaubeam or the stars and of the difference manifest in them, that one star was greater and brighter than another until Kolob was reached, which is near the throne of the Eternal; and He said it was so with the spirits of men." (George Q. Cannon, *Gospel Truth*, 1:208.)

"The spirits of men were created with different dispositions and likes and talents. Some evidently were mechanically inclined, from them have come our inventors. Some loved music and hence they have become great musicians. We evidently brought to this world some if not all of the inclinations and talents that we had there. The fact that one person finds one bent, like mathematics easy and another finds it difficult, may, in my judgment, be traced to the spirit existence. So with other talents and skills. It was these characteristics that enabled our Eternal Father to choose certain individuals for certain work on the earth, such as Adam, Abraham, Moses and Joseph Smith. The Lord chose Cyrus and named him one hundred years before he was born to perform the work assigned to him on the earth. It is my judgment that thousands of others were chosen for their special fields because they showed talents and dispositions in that spirit world." (Joseph Fielding Smith, *Answers to Gospel Questions*, 5:138-39.)

Selected Scripture References

"He hath chosen us in him before the foundation of the world." (Ephesians 1:4.)

"They were ordained—being called and prepared from the foundation of the world according to the foreknowledge of God." (Alma 13:3.)

"Intelligence, or the light of truth, was not created or made, neither indeed can be." (D&C 93:29.)

"All spirit is matter, but it is more fine or pure." (D&C 131:7.)

"Choice spirits . . . were reserved to come forth in the fulness of times." (D&C 138:53.)

Abraham 3:19

"I am the Lord thy God, I am more intelligent than they all"

Selected Statements of the First Presidency and the Twelve Apostles

"Who controls the heavens and the earth? The Gods in the eternal worlds. Who has implanted certain principles in matter and in all creation? God has done it. All things are subject to these laws; and if men can place themselves under His guidance and find the way to approach the great Eloheim, they will know more in a very short time than all this world together know in all their lives and more than all the combined intelligence of the world, for God is the foundation of all wisdom, and the source of all intelligence and knowledge." (John Taylor, in *Journal of Discourses*, 25:215.)

"I witness that Jesus Christ is the only name under heaven whereby one can be saved! (See D&C 18:23.)

"I testify that He is utterly incomparable in what He *is*, what He *knows*, what He has *accomplished* and what He has *experienced*. . . .

"In *intelligence* and *performance*, He far surpasses the individual and the composite *capacities* and *achievements* of all who have lived, live now, and will yet live! (See Abraham 3:19.)" (Neal A. Maxwell, in *Ensign*, Nov. 1981, p. 8. See also Joseph Fielding Smith, *Way to Perfection*, p. 95.)

Selected Scripture References

"He comprehendeth all things, and all things are before him." (D&C 88:41.)

"The glory of God is intelligence." (D&C 93:36.)

Abraham 3:20

"The Lord thy God sent his angel to deliver thee from the hands of the priest of Elkenah"

See Selected Statements and Scripture References under Abraham 1:15.

Abraham 3:21

"I came down in the beginning in the midst of all the intelligences thou hast seen"

Selected Statements of the First Presidency and the Twelve Apostles

"The Lord made it known to Moses (see Book of Moses ch. 3) and also to Abraham (Abraham ch. 3) and it is expressed in several revelations, that man was in the beginning with God. In that day, however, man was a spirit unembodied. The beginning was when the councils met and the decision was made to create this earth that the spirits who were intended for this earth, should come here and partake of the mortal conditions and receive bodies of flesh and bones." (Joseph Fielding Smith, *Church History and Modern Revelation*, 2:162.)

Selected Scripture References

"O Father, glorify thou me with thine own self with the glory which I had with thee before the world was." (John 17:5.)

"Behold, my Beloved Son, which was my Beloved and Chosen from the beginning." (Moses 4:2.)

Abraham 3:22

"Intelligences that were organized before the world was"

Selected Statements of the First Presidency and the Twelve Apostles

"Some of our writers have endeavored to explain what an intelligence is, but to do so is futile, for we have never been given any insight into this matter beyond what the Lord has fragmentarily revealed. We know, however, that there is something called intelligence which always existed. It is the real eternal part of man, which was not created or made. This intelligence combined with the spirit constitutes a spiritual identity or individual.

"The spirit of man, then, is a combination of the intelligence and the spirit which is an entity begotten of God." (Joseph Fielding Smith, *Progress of Man*, p. 11.)

"The word *intelligence* as used by Latter-day Saints has two chief meanings, both found in the dictionary but of secondary use. First, a man who gathers knowledge and uses it in harmony with the plan of salvation is intelligent. He has intelligence. . . . Second, the word when preceded by the article an, or used in the plural as *intelligences*, means a person, or persons, usually in the spiritual estate. Just as we speak of a person or persons, we speak of an intelligence, or *intelligences*.

"This second use of the word has come into being among Latter-day Saints because of a statement made by the Lord to the Patriarch Abraham: [Abraham 3:21-23].

"This remarkable statement uses the words *intelligences, souls, spirits*, and *Abraham* (a man not yet on earth) interchangeably. Thus has come the frequent use in the Church of the term *an intelligence*, meaning usually a personage in the spirit world, who may come on earth.

"Implied in the use of this term is the doctrine of pre-existence." (John A. Widtsoe, *Evidences and Reconciliations*, 3:74. See also 3:77; Joseph Fielding Smith, *Church History and Modern Revelation*, 2:162.)

"I would just remark, that the spirits of men are eternal, that they are governed by the same Priesthood that Abraham, Melchizedek, and the Apostles were: that they are organized according to that Priesthood which is everlasting, 'without beginning of days or end of years.' " (Joseph Smith, *Teachings of the Prophet Joseph Smith*, p. 208. See also Bruce R. McConkie, *Millennial Messiah*, p. 12.)

Selected Scripture References

"Intelligence, or the light of truth, was not created or made, neither indeed can be." (D&C 93:29.)

Other Commentary

"Let it be observed that I say nothing as to the mode of the existence of these intelligences, beyond the fact of their eternity. But of their form, or the manner of their subsistence nothing, so far as I know, has been revealed, and hence we are without means of knowing anything about the modes of their existence beyond the fact of it, and the essential qualities they possess, which already have been pointed out." (B. H. Roberts, *Seventy's Course in Theology, Second Year*, p. 9. See also p. 11.)

Abraham 3:22-23

"There were many of the noble and great ones; . . . and [God] said: These I will make my rulers"

Selected Statements of the First Presidency and the Twelve Apostles

"Every man who has a calling to minister to the inhabitants of the world was ordained to that very purpose in the Grand Council of heaven before this world was. I suppose that I was ordained to this very office in that Grand Council." (Joseph Smith, *Teachings of the Prophet Joseph Smith*, p. 365.)

"In every dispensation the Lord has had those who were foreordained to do a certain work. We all dwelt in the presence of God before we came here, and such men as Abraham, Isaac, Jacob, the ancient Prophets, Jesus and the Apostles received their appointments before the world was made. They were ordained before the foundation of the world to come and tabernacle here in the flesh and to work for the cause of God, and this because of their faith and faithfulness." (Wilford Woodruff, in *Journal of Discourses*, 18:114.)

"Men have been raised up in almost all ages of the world to perform certain works, or accomplish certain missions; they have been inspired for that work and the mission from their infancy, and it may be even before they were born into the world. No doubt all the prominent men who have figured in any dispensation of the Gospel since the days of our father, Adam, until the present, were inspired of the Almighty from their childhood, and were chosen and selected even from or before their birth." (Joseph F. Smith, in *Journal of Discourses*, 25:52. See also Bruce R. McConkie, in *Ensign*, May 1974, p. 73; Joseph Fielding Smith, *Way to Perfection*, pp. 50–51.)

"Upon this principle was manifested the election, before the foundation of the world, of certain individuals to certain offices, as written in the scriptures.

"In other words, certain individuals, more intelligent than the others, were chosen by the Head, to teach, instruct, edify, improve, govern, and minister truth and salvation to others; and to hold the delegated powers or keys of government in the several spheres of progressive being.

"These were not only chosen, but set apart, by a holy ordinance in the eternal worlds, as ambassadors, foreign ministers, priests, kings, apostles, etc., to fill the various stations in the vast empire of the Sovereign of all." (Parley P. Pratt, *Key to the Science of Theology*, pp. 70–71. See also Bruce R. McConkie, *New Witness for the Articles of Faith*, p. 34.)

"God has raised up at different ages certain men to do a certain work, as he raised up father Abraham. He was a noble spirit, we are told, before he left the realms of glory to come and tabernacle in the flesh. He had the spirit of the Gods with him when he was born; and he was faithful to God, and he had confidence in him; and whatever God required at his hands, he performed." (Wilford Woodruff, *Discourses of Wilford Woodruff*, p. 233.)

"Many were chosen, as was Abraham, before they were born. . . .

"But now there is a warning: Despite that calling which is spoken of in the scriptures as 'foreordination,' we have another inspired declaration: 'Behold, there are many called, but few are chosen. . . . ' (D&C 121:34.)

"This suggests that even though we have our free agency here, there are many who were foreordained before the world was, to a greater state than they have prepared themselves for here. Even though they might have been among the noble and great, from among whom the Father declared he would make his chosen leaders, they may fail of that calling here in mortality. Then the Lord poses this question: ' . . . and why are they not chosen?' (D&C 121:34.)

"Two answers were given: First, 'Because their hearts are set so much upon the things of this world. . . . ' And second, they ' . . . aspire to the honors of men.' (D&C 121:35.)" (Harold B. Lee, *Stand Ye in Holy Places*, p. 9. See also Bruce R. McConkie, *Mortal Messiah*, 1:26.)

Selected Scripture References

"Before I formed thee in the belly I knew thee; . . . and I ordained thee a prophet unto the nations." (Jeremiah 1:5.)

"They were ordained—being called and prepared from the foundation of the world according to the foreknowledge of God." (Alma 13:3.)

"They were also among the noble and great ones who were chosen in the beginning." (D&C 138:55.)

Abraham 3:24

"And there stood one among them that was like unto God"

Selected Statements of the First Presidency and the Twelve Apostles

" 'Like unto God!' Like the Exalted Elohim who, in the ultimate sense, is the Creator, Upholder, and Preserver of the universe! Like unto God—how and in what way? Like him in length of days or the possession of progeny or the exalted nature of his tangible body? No, for the Son of the Father had yet to pass through a mortal probation, to overcome the world, to attain a resurrection, and to come back to his Father with his own glorious and tangible body. But like him in intelligence, in knowledge and understanding, in the possession of truth, in conformity to divine law, and therefore in power. Like him in plan and purpose, in desires for righteousness, in a willingness to serve his brethren, in all things that lead to that fulness of the glory of the Father which none can receive until they live in the eternal family." (Bruce R. McConkie, *Promised Messiah*, p. 53.)

Abraham 3:25

"We will prove them herewith, to see if they will do all things whatsoever the Lord their God shall command them"

Selected Statements of the First Presidency and the Twelve Apostles

"We have heretofore shown that the entire human race existed as spirit-beings in the primeval world, and that for the purpose of making possible to them the experiences of mortality this earth was created. They were endowed with the powers of agency or choice while yet but spirits; and the divine plan provided that they be free-born in the flesh, heirs to the inalienable birthright of liberty to choose and to act for themselves in mortality. It is undeniably essential to the eternal progression of God's children that they be subjected to the influences of both good and evil, that they be tried and tested and proved withal, 'to see if they will do all things whatsoever the Lord their God shall command them.' Free agency is an indispensable element of such a test." (James E. Talmage, *Jesus the Christ*, p. 17. See also Joseph Fielding Smith, *Doctrines of Salvation*, 2:6.)

"Justice, love, mercy, and truth will finally prevail in a universe presided over by a Lord who is a determined as well as loving Tutor. This mortal school is one of which the Father and the Son have solemnly declared, 'And we will prove them herewith, to see if they will do all things whatsoever the Lord their God shall command them.' (Abraham 3:25)

"The Lord knows how true individual development requires a setting of agency and opportunity. There is no other way." (Neal A. Maxwell, in *Ensign*, May 1983, p. 11. See also Spencer W. Kimball, *Miracle of Forgiveness*, pp. 4–5; Spencer W. Kimball, *Teachings of Spencer W. Kimball*, pp. 30–31.)

Selected Scripture References

"That I may prove them, whether they will walk in my law, or no." (Exodus 16:4.)

"The Lord giveth no commandments unto the children of men, save he shall prepare a way for them that they may accomplish the thing which he commandeth them." (1 Nephi 3:7.)

Abraham 3:26

"They who keep their first estate shall be added upon"

Selected Statements of the First Presidency and the Twelve Apostles

"We lived in the presence of God in the spirit before we came here. We desired to be like him, we saw him, we were in his presence. There is not a soul who has not seen both the Father and the Son, and in the spirit world we were in their presence; but it became necessary for us to gain experiences which could not be obtained in that world of spirits, and so we were accorded the privilege of coming down here upon this earth." (Joseph Fielding Smith, *Doctrines of Salvation*, 1:56.)

"God has taken these intelligences and given to them spirit bodies and given them instructions and training. Then he proceeded to create a world for them and sent them as spirits to obtain a mortal body, for which he made preparation. And when they were upon the earth, he gave them instructions on how to go about developing and conducting their lives to make them perfect, so they could return to their Father in heaven after their transitions. Then came the periods of time when souls were to be placed upon the earth and born to parents who were permitted to furnish the bodies. But no parent has ever yet on this earth been the parent of a spirit, because we are so far yet from perfection. Remember what I said a while ago, that 'As man is, God once was; and as God is, man may become.' They came with the definite understanding that they could return to become like God and go forward in their great development and progress." (Spencer W. Kimball, in *Ensign*, May 1977, p. 50.)

Selected Scripture References

"Before they were born, they, with many others, received their first lessons in the world of spirits and were prepared to come forth." (D&C 138:56.)

Abraham 3:26

"They who keep their second estate shall have glory added upon their heads for ever and ever"

Selected Statements of the First Presidency and the Twelve Apostles

"God himself, finding he was in the midst of spirits and glory, because he was more intelligent, saw proper to institute laws whereby the rest could have a privilege to advance like himself. The relationship we have with God places us in a situation to advance in knowledge. He has power to institute laws to instruct the weaker intelligences, that they may be exalted with Himself, so that they might have one glory upon another, and all that knowledge, power, glory, and intelligence, which is requisite in order to save them in the world of spirits." (Joseph Smith, *History of the Church*, 6:312. See also Joseph Fielding Smith, *Answers to Gospel Questions,* 4:151–52; Joseph Fielding Smith, *Doctrines of Salvation,* 1:56–57.)

"It is true that pre-existence is taught; but the pre-existence in which we believe is confined to our first estate. We are taught that our present life is our second estate, and this is a probation given unto us in which to gain experience and to be tried and purified to prepare us for our next estate." (George Q. Cannon, *Gospel Truth,* 1:28.)

"We are not now ready for all things the Lord has prepared in the City of God for them that love Him. (See 1 Corinthians 2:9.) Our present eyes are unready for things which they have not yet seen, and our ears are not prepared for the transcending sounds and music of that city.

"The trek will be proving and trying. Faith, patience, and obedience are essential (see Mosiah 23:21; Abraham 3:25), but he who completes the journey successfully will be unmeasurably added upon (see Abraham 3:26.) And he who does not will have subtracted from the sum of his possibilities.

"When we arrive home, we shall be weary and bruised. But at last our aching homesicknesses will cease. Meanwhile, our mortal home-comings are but faint foreshadowings of that Homecoming!" (Neal A. Maxwell, in Conference Report, Apr. 1986, p. 46.)

Selected Scripture References

"Eye hath not seen, nor ear heard, neither have entered into the heart of man, the things which God hath prepared for them that love him." (1 Corinthians 2:9.)

"This life is the time for men to prepare to meet God." (Alma 34:32.)

"If ye are faithful ye shall be . . . crowned with honor, and glory, and immortality, and eternal life." (D&C 75:5.)

"I . . . delight to honor those who serve me in righteousness and in truth unto the end. Great shall be their reward and eternal shall be their glory." (D&C 76:5–6.)

Abraham 3:27

"And the Lord said: Whom shall I send?"

See Selected Statements and Scripture References under Moses 4:1; 4:2; 4:3; 4:4.

Abraham 3:28

"And the second was angry, and kept not his first estate"

Selected Statements of the First Presidency and the Twelve

"This is our second estate. We kept our first estate. In the time of trial in the eternal worlds, when the spirits had to choose between Satan and Jesus, we and all the children of men who are on the face of the earth adhered to our Father. There was one-third of the hosts of heaven who joined Satan in his rebellion. The plan which he proposed for the salvation of the children of men was so specious and attractive that one-third of the children of God thought Satan was right and the Father wrong. These did not keep their first estate, and therefore they were denied the privilege of coming on earth and receiving a tabernacle. They are consigned to darkness—to hell—and are in torment. They are angels to the devil." (George Q. Cannon, *Gospel Truth*, 1:20.)

"Note the Lord's promise that 'they who keep their first estate shall be added upon.' This first estate is the life we lived in the spirit world before we were born. Abraham was chosen before he was born, and we will learn that others were also.

"Consider again the Lord's words: 'and they who keep not their first estate shall not have glory in the same kingdom with those who keep their first estate.' When the Lord chose the offer of his Son, Jesus, 'the second was angry, and kept not his first estate; and, at that day, many followed after him.'

"Thus, it was Satan, and a third of the hosts of heaven who kept not their first estate. They were, therefore, cast down to the earth and deprived of the privilege of taking upon themselves bodies, remaining bodies of spirit only, so they 'shall not have glory in the same kingdom with those who keep their first estate.' " (LeGrand Richards, *Marvelous Work and a Wonder*, p. 240.)

Selected Scripture References

"The angels which kept not their first estate, . . . he hath reserved in everlasting chains under darkness unto the judgment of the great day." (Jude 1:6.)

"The devil was before Adam, for he rebelled against me . . . ; and also a third part of the hosts of heaven turned he away from me." (D&C 29:36.)

Abraham 4

Abraham 4:1
"At the beginning"

See Selected Statements, Scripture References, and Other Commentary under Moses 2:1.

Abraham 4:1
"And they, that is the Gods, organized and formed the heavens and the earth"

Selected Statements of the First Presidency and the Twelve Apostles

"The account of creation as given in the Book of Abraham is distinctive in that it says that great work was done by 'the Gods' in contrast to the belief that one God—one Almighty Being—made all things by himself, and out of nothing. There was a plurality of Gods engaged in creation. This fact is well corroborated in the Bible, including some passages in Genesis. . . .

"Who were these Gods?

"We believe in a Godhead of Father, Son, and Holy Ghost. Who else would have participated in the creation?" (Mark E. Petersen, *Abraham, Friend of God*, pp. 144–45.)

285

"It is true that Adam helped to form this earth. He labored with our Savior Jesus Christ. I have a strong view or conviction that there were others also who assisted them. Perhaps Noah and Enoch; and *why not Joseph Smith*, and those who were appointed to be rulers before the earth was formed? We know that Jesus our Savior was a Spirit when this great work was done. He did all of these mighty works before he tabernacled in the flesh." (Joseph Fielding Smith, *Doctrines of Salvation*, 1:74–75.)

"Gods, even the sons of God, will be ordained to organize matter. How much matter do you suppose there is between here and some of the fixed stars which we can see? Enough to frame many, very many millions of such earths as this, yet it is now so diffused, clear and pure, that we look through it and behold the stars. Yet the matter is there. Can you form any conception of this? Can you form any idea of the minuteness of matter?" (Brigham Young, in *Journal of Discourses*, 15:137.)

"A General Assembly, Quorum or Grand Council of the Gods, with their President at their head, constitute the designing and creating power." (Parley P. Pratt, *Key to the Science of Theology*, p. 51.)

"In the beginning, the head of the Gods called a council of the Gods; and they came together and concocted a plan to create the world and people it." (Joseph Smith, *Teachings of the Prophet Joseph Smith*, p. 349.)

Abraham 4:2
"The earth, after it was formed, was empty and desolate"

See Selected Statements and Scripture References under Moses 2:2.

Abraham 4:2
"And darkness reigned upon the face of the deep"

See Selected Statements and Scripture References under Moses 2:2.

Abraham 4:2
"The Spirit of the Gods was brooding upon the face of the waters"

Selected Statements of the First Presidency and the Twelve Apostles

"Note that not only were the Gods in conversation while employed in this creative undertaking, but 'the Spirit of the Gods was brooding upon the face of the waters.'

"Then how was creation brought about? How were these materials organized into an earth? By the power of the Spirit of the Gods working under the direction of the Gods!

"Mankind at times has seen but slight expressions of the powers of so-called nature. Earthquakes have shaken large areas, even changed their shape. Floods have come, lightning has struck with death and destruction, and tidal waves have devastated the land. Would not such powers of nature have been employed in forming and organizing the earth?" (Mark E. Petersen, *Abraham, Friend of God*, p. 145.)

Abraham 4:3

"And they (the Gods) said: Let there be light"

See Selected Statements and Scripture References under Moses 2:3; 2:5.

Abraham 4:5

"The Gods called the light Day"

Selected Statements of the First Presidency and the Twelve Apostles

"But first, what is a day? It is a specified time period; it is an age, an eon, a division of eternity; it is the time between two identifiable events. And each day, of whatever length, has the duration needed for its purposes." (Bruce R. McConkie, in *Ensign*, June 1982, p. 11.)

Abraham 4:5

"And this was the first, or the beginning, of that which they called day and night"

See Selected Statements under Moses 2:5.

Abraham 4:6

"The Gods also said: Let there be an expanse in the midst of the waters"

See Selected Statements under Moses 2:6.

Abraham 4:9

"The Gods ordered, saying: Let the waters under the heaven be gathered together unto one place"

See Selected Statements under Moses 2:9.

Abraham 4:11

"The Gods said: . . . the herb yielding seed; the fruit tree yielding fruit, after his kind"

See Selected Statements under Moses 2:11.

Abraham 4:14

"The Gods organized the lights in the expanse of the heaven"

See Selected Statements and Scripture References under Moses 2:14.

Abraham 4:20

"The Gods said: Let us prepare the waters to bring forth abundantly the moving creatures . . . ; and the fowl, that they may fly above the earth"

See Selected Statements under Moses 2:20–23.

Abraham 4:24

"The God's prepared the earth to bring forth the living creature after his kind"

See Selected Statements under Moses 2:24–25.

Abraham 4:26

"Let us go down and form man in our image"

See Selected Statements and Scripture References under Moses 2:26.

Abraham 4:28

"We will cause them to have dominion over . . . every living thing that moveth upon the earth"

See Selected Statements and Scripture References under Moses 2:26.

Abraham 4:28

"We will cause them to be fruitful and multiply, and replenish the earth"

See Selected Statements and Scripture References under Moses 2:28.

Abraham 4:29

"The fruit of the tree yielding seed to them we will give it; it shall be for their meat"

See Selected Statements under Moses 2:29.

Abraham 5

Abraham 5:1

"Thus we will finish the heavens and the earth, and all the hosts of them"

Selected Statements of the First Presidency and the Twelve Apostles

"In the preceding six days was completed the formation or creation of the earth, after the spiritual order that man was formed or born in the heavens. All men, male and female, that ever have lived, or that ever will live on this earth, had a pre-existence before the formation of the earth commenced; and during our pre-existence in the heavens, the earth was undergoing this formation." (Orson Pratt, in *Journal of Discourses*, 16:318.)

Abraham 5:3

"The Gods concluded upon the seventh time, because that on the seventh time they would rest"

See Selected Statements and Scripture References under Moses 3:2–3.

Abraham 5:4

"The Gods came down and formed these the generations

of the heavens and of the earth"

See Selected Statements and Scripture References under Moses 3:4–5; 3:5.

Abraham 5:7

"The Gods formed man from the dust of the ground"

See Selected Statements and Scripture References under Moses 3:7, 22.

Abraham 5:7

"The Gods . . . took his spirit (that is, the man's spirit), and put it into him; and breathed into his nostrils the breath of life, and man became a living soul"

See Selected Statements and Scripture References under Moses 3:7.

Abraham 5:7–9, 17, 20

Life was placed on the earth during the seventh time

Selected Statements of the First Presidency and the Twelve Apostles

"There was no flesh upon the earth until the morning of the seventh day. On that morning God made the first fleshly tabernacle and took man's spirit and put within it, and man became a living soul—the first flesh upon the earth—the first man also. Though it was the seventh day, no flesh but this one tabernacle was yet formed. No fish, fowl and beast was as yet permitted to have a body of flesh. . . . On the seventh day he began the temporal portion. There was not yet a man to till the ground, 'and the gods formed man from the dust of the ground, and took his spirit—that is, the man's spirit—and put it into him and breathed into his nostrils the breath of life, and man became a living soul.' This we read in the second chapter of Genesis, and you will find it recorded on the 6th and 35th pages of the new edition of the 'Pearl of Great Price.'

" . . . We have been in the habit of thinking that the various kinds of animals that have lived, according to geologists, were the first flesh on the earth, and we go away back millions of ages to see that these lower formations of life existed before man. But the Lord gives us different information from this. He shows us that among all the animated creatures of flesh, man was the first that was ever placed upon the earth

in this temporal condition, contradicting the theories of geologists—
that is, so far as placing man on the earth in this present probation is
concerned. . . . Man was the first being that came upon the earth and
inhabited a body of flesh and bones. Afterwards, on the seventh day,
out of the ground the Lord God created the beasts of the field. Go back
to the first chapter of Genesis, and you will find that the beasts, etc.,
were formed on the sixth day or period, and that on the seventh there
was no flesh on the earth, and having created man as the first flesh
upon the earth, God then created, out of the ground, the beasts of the
field." (Orson Pratt, *Masterful Discourses of Orson Pratt*, pp. 70–72.)

Abraham 5:8

"The Gods planted a garden, eastward in Eden, and there they put the man"

Selected Statements of the First Presidency and the Twelve Apostles

"The Lord rested from his labors the seventh day. What particular
period of time within that day Adam fell I do not know; but one thing is
certain, that in the morning of the seventh day the Garden of Eden was
planted and he was placed therein, and during that morning a great
many things transpired pertaining to this temporal creation." (Orson
Pratt, in *Journal of Discourses*, 16:317–18.)

See Selected Statements under Moses 3:8.

Abraham 5:10

"There was a river running out of Eden . . . and became into four heads"

See Other Commentary under Moses 3:10–14.

Abraham 5:13

"Of the tree of knowledge of good and evil, thou shalt not eat of it"

See Selected Statements under Moses 3:17.

Abraham 5:13

"In the time that thou eatest thereof, thou shalt surely die"

See Selected Statements and Scripture References under Moses 3:17.

Abraham 5:13

"Now I, Abraham, saw that it was after the Lord's time, which was after the time of Kolob; for as yet the Gods had not appointed unto Adam his reckoning"

"When this earth was created, it was not according to our present time, but it was created *according to Kolob's time*, for the Lord has said it was created on celestial time which is Kolob's time. Then he revealed to Abraham that *Adam was subject to Kolob's time before his transgression*." (Joseph Fielding Smith, *Doctrines of Salvation*, 1:79. See also Joseph Fielding Smith, *Answers to Gospel Questions*, 2:60.)

"The adaptation of a thousand years to one day of celestial time is inapplicable to the years of all other planetary bodies of our system. Among the great variety of celestial kingdoms or glorified worlds, there may be many methods of measuring celestial time. There can be no doubt that each planet has its set time of creation, its set time of temporal continuance, and its set time or period of rest." (Orson Pratt, *Masterful Discourses of Orson Pratt*, p. 81.)

"This earthly ball, this little opake substance thrown off into space, is only a speck in the great universe; and when it is celestialized it will go back into the presence of God, where it was first framed." (Brigham Young, in *Journal of Discourses*, 9:317.)

"When the earth was framed and brought into existence and man was placed upon it, it was near the throne of our Father in heaven. . . . but when man fell, the earth fell into space, and took up its abode in this planetary system, and the sun became our light. When the Lord said—'Let there be light,' there was light, for the earth was brought near the sun that it might reflect upon it so as to give us light by day, and the moon to give us light by night. This is the glory the earth came from, and when it is glorified it will return again unto the presence of the Father, and it will dwell there, and these intelligent beings that I am looking at, if they live worthy of it, will dwell upon this earth." (Brigham Young, in *Journal of Discourses*, 17:143.)

"This earth will be rolled back into the presence of God, and crowned with celestial glory." (Joseph Smith, *Teachings of the Prophet Joseph Smith*, p. 181.)

Abraham 5:14

"It is not good that the man should be alone"

See Selected Statements, Scripture References, and Other Commentary under Moses 3:18; 3:22; 3:24.

Abraham 5:16

"Of the rib which the Gods had taken from man, formed they a woman"

See Selected Statements under Moses 3:22.

Abraham 5:18

"Therefore shall a man leave his father and his mother, and shall cleave unto his wife, and they shall be one flesh"

See Selected Statements and Scripture References under Moses 3:24.

Joseph Smith—Matthew

Joseph Smith—Matthew 1:1
"I am he of whom it is written by the prophets"

Selected Statements of the First Presidency and the Twelve Apostles

"The predictions of the early prophets concerning Christ's birth, life, and ministry were fulfilled, and those who sincerely believed were prepared to accept and follow him. This being true, we can reliably expect that the happenings prophesied of concerning his second coming will also be fulfilled." (Delbert L. Stapley, in *Ensign*, Nov. 1975, p. 47.)

Joseph Smith—Matthew 1:3
"There shall not be left here, upon this temple, one stone upon another that shall not be thrown down"

Selected Statements of the First Presidency and the Twelve Apostles

"How aptly Jesus chooses his illustrations. To those who saw the stones, to say that not one should be left upon another, symbolized the destruction of a once stable and securely built nation. Some single stones were about 67 ½ feet long, 7 ½ feet high, and 9 feet broad; the pillars supporting the porches, all one stone, were some 37 ½ feet tall. It is said that when the Romans destroyed and ploughed Jerusalem, six days battering of the walls failed to dislodge these mighty stones. The temple was, of course, finally leveled to the ground, and as the stones were rooted out and scattered elsewhere so was a once secure and great nation." (Bruce R. McConkie, *Doctrinal New Testament Commentary*, 1:637.)

"On three occasions of which we know, the Lord's own earthly house, as a priceless gem in a heaven-set crown, has graced the ground that is now claimed by the Jews and trodden down of the Gentiles. Solomon built a majestic mansion for the Lord in the day of Israel's glory. Zerubbabel built it anew when the remnant returned from bondage in Babylon. And Herod—a wretched, evil man whose every act bore Satan's stamp—built it for the final time in the day our Lord made flesh his tabernacle. This is the temple—one of the architectural wonders of the world, whose marble blocks were covered with gold, and whose influence upon the people cannot be measured—this is the temple that was torn apart, stone by stone, by Titus and his minions.

"Thus Herod's temple became a refuse heap, and with its destruction ancient Judaism died also." (Bruce R. McConkie, *Millennial Messiah*, p. 277.)

"The prophetic announcement of the desolation and destruction of the temple was thus more than the death knell of a building, even of a sacred building that was the 'Father's house.' It was in fact a prediction of gloom and doom upon a nation. It was the announcement of the final end of a dispensation, the end of a kingdom, the end of the Lord's people as a distinct nation." (Bruce R. McConkie, *Doctrinal New Testament Commentary*, 1:637.)

Selected Scriptural References

"O Jerusalem, Jerusalem, thou that killest the prophets. . . . Behold, your house is left unto you desolate." (Matthew 23:37–38.)

Joseph Smith—Matthew 1:4
"Jesus left them, and went upon the mount of Olives"

Selected Statements of the First Presidency and the Twelve Apostles

"In the course of His last walk from Jerusalem back to the beloved home at Bethany, Jesus rested at a convenient spot on the Mount of Olives, from which the great city and the magnificent temple were to be seen in fullest splendor, illumined by the declining sun in the late afternoon of that eventful April day. As He sat in thoughtful revery He was approached by Peter and James, John and Andrew, of the Twelve, and to them certainly, though probably to all the apostles, He gave instruction, embodying further prophecy concerning the future of Jerusalem, Israel, and the world at large." (James E. Talmage, *Jesus the Christ*, p. 569.)

Joseph Smith—Matthew 1:4

"Tell us when shall these things be which thou hast said concerning the destruction of the temple, and the Jews; and what is the sign of thy coming, and of the end of the world, or the destruction of the wicked, which is the end of the world?"

Selected Statements of the First Presidency and the Twelve Apostles

"Apparently the disciples thought these two events would be closely related in time. In reply Jesus will speak of *events* and not of *time*, and the key to understanding the whole discourse is to know which statements of our Lord pertain to the day of the ancient apostles and which to those ages following their ministries." (Bruce R. McConkie, *Doctrinal New Testament Commentary*, 1:640.)

"The compound character of the question indicates an understanding of the fact that the destruction of which the Lord had spoken was to be apart from and precedent to the signs that were to immediately herald His glorious advent and the yet later ushering in of the consummation commonly spoken of then and now as 'the end of the world.' An assumption that the events would follow in close succession is implied by the form in which the question was put." (James E. Talmage, *Jesus the Christ*, p. 569.)

"Now men cannot have any possible grounds to say that this is figurative . . . for He is now explaining what He had previously spoken in parables; and according to this language the end of the world is the destruction of the wicked, the harvest and the end of the world have an allusion directly to the human family in the last days, instead of the earth, as many have imagined; and that which shall precede the coming of the Son of Man, and the restitution of all things spoken of by the mouth of all the holy prophets since the world began; and the angels are to have something to do in this great work, for they are the reapers. As, therefore, the tares are gathered and burned in the fire, so shall it be in the end of the world; that is, as the servants of God go forth warning the nations, both priests and people, and as they harden their hearts and reject the light of truth, these first being delivered over to the buffetings of Satan, and the law and the testimony being closed up, as it was in the case of the Jews, they are left in darkness, and delivered over unto the day of burning; thus being bound up by their creeds, and their bands being made strong by their priests, are prepared for the fulfillment of the saying of the Savior—'The Son of Man shall send forth His angels, and gather out of His Kingdom all things that offend, and them which do iniquity, and shall cast them into a furnace of fire, there shall be wailing and gnashing of teeth.' We understand that the work of gathering together of the wheat into barns, or garners, is to take place while the tares are being bound over, and preparing for the day of burning; that after the day of burnings, the righteous shall shine forth like the sun, in the Kingdom of their Father. Who hath ears to hear, let him hear." (Joseph Smith, *Teachings of the Prophet Joseph Smith*, pp. 100-101. See also Bruce R. McConkie, *New Witness for the Articles of Faith*, p. 646.)

Other Commentary

The two questions that the disciples asked Jesus—What of the destruction of the temple and the Jews? and What of the second coming or the end of the world or the destruction of the wicked?—are given in both Matthew 24 and Joseph Smith—Matthew 1:3. The biblical account is somewhat unclear about when Jesus was answering which question. This passage has caused some confusion among Christians, allowing some to believe that the Second Coming was to be very soon after the destruction of Jerusalem (A.D. 70). The Joseph Smith—Matthew account, however, is clear. The apostles' first question is answered in verses 5 through 20, and their second question is answered in verses 21 through 55.

Joseph Smith—Matthew 1:5-6
"Take heed that no man deceive you"

Selected Statements of the First Presidency and the Twelve Apostles

"The inquiry referred specifically to time—when were these things to be? The reply dealt not with dates, but with events; and the spirit of the subsequent discourse was that of warning against misapprehension, and admonition to ceaseless vigilance. 'Take heed that no man deceive you' was the first and all-important caution; for within the lives of most of those apostles, many blaspheming imposters would arise, each claiming to be the Messiah. The return of Christ to earth as Lord and Judge was more remote than any of the Twelve realized." (James E. Talmage, *Jesus the Christ*, p. 570.)

Joseph Smith—Matthew 1:7
"Then shall they deliver you up to be afflicted, and shall kill you"

Selected Statements of the First Presidency and the Twelve Apostles

"In the providence of the Almighty persecution serves a most useful purpose. Every faithful Saint must perceive and acknowledge this. Each one feels its effect upon himself; he sees its effect upon his friends and neighbors. Persecution develops character. Under its influence we all know ourselves better than we did before we felt its pressure; and we discover traits in our brethren and sisters of the existence of which, perhaps, we were in entire ignorance. . . . It has also caused many who were careless and indifferent to arouse themselves from their lethargy and to renew their diligence in the work of God. It has also brought to light the hypocrisy of many, and caused them to throw off the mask of friendship and fellowship which they wore, and to exhibit themselves in their true lineaments." (John Taylor and George Q. Cannon, of the First Presidency of the Church, in James R. Clark, comp., *Messages of the First Presidency*, 3:48.)

"They, the apostles, were told to expect persecution, not only at the hands of irresponsible individuals, but at the instance of the officials such as they who were at that moment intent on taking the life of the Lord Himself, and who would scourge them in the synagogs, deliver them up to hostile tribunals, cite them before rulers and kings, and even put some of them to death—all because of their testimony of the Christ." (James E. Talmage, *Jesus the Christ*, p. 570.)

"The testing processes of mortality are for all men, saints and sinners alike. Sometimes the tests and trials of those who have received the gospel far exceed any imposed upon worldly people. Abraham was called upon to sacrifice his only son. Lehi and his family left their lands and wealth to live in a wilderness. Saints in all ages have been commanded to lay all they have upon the altar, sometimes even their very lives. . . .

" . . . Sometimes the Lord's people are hounded and persecuted. Sometimes He deliberately lets His faithful saints linger and suffer, in both body and spirit, to prove them in all things, and to see if they will abide in His covenant, even unto death, that they may be found worthy of eternal life. If such be the lot of any of us, so be it.

"But come what may, anything that befalls us here in mortality is but for a small moment, and if we are true and faithful God will eventually exalt us on high. All our losses and sufferings will be made up to us in the resurrection." (Bruce R. McConkie, in Conference Report, Oct. 1976, pp. 158–60.)

Joseph Smith—Matthew 1:9
"Many false prophets shall arise, and shall deceive many"

Selected Statements of the First Presidency and the Twelve Apostles

"What are false prophets? They are teachers and preachers who profess to speak for the Lord when, in fact, they have received no such appointment. They are ministers of religion who have not been called of God as was Aaron. They may suppose—often sincerely and with pious devoutness—that it is their right to tell others what they must do to be saved when, in fact, they have received no such commission from on high.

"They are teachers of religion who do not receive revelation and have not gained from the Holy Ghost the true testimony of Jesus. They are ministers of religion who do not hold either the Aaronic or Melchizedek priesthoods, and try as they may it is beyond their power to bind on earth and have their acts sealed eternally in the heavens.

"False prophets are false teachers; they teach false doctrine; they neither know nor teach the doctrines of salvation. Rather, they have followed cunningly devised fables that they suppose make up the gospel of Christ, and they preach them as such." (Bruce R. McConkie, *Millennial Messiah,* pp. 70–71.)

Joseph Smith—Matthew 1:10
"The love of many shall wax cold"

Selected Statements of the First Presidency and the Twelve Apostles

"Their [the apostles'] labors would be complicated and opposed by the revolutionary propaganda of many false prophets, and differences of creed would disrupt families, and engender such bitterness that brothers would betray one another, and children would rise against their parents, accusing them of heresies and delivering them up to death. Even among those who had professed discipleship to Christ many would be offended and hatred would abound; love for the gospel would wax cold, and iniquity would be rampant among men." (James E. Talmage, *Jesus the Christ,* p. 571.)

Joseph Smith—Matthew 1:12

"The abomination of desolation, spoken of by Daniel the prophet"

Selected Statements of the First Presidency and the Twelve Apostles

"Whatever may be said of the sufferings and sorrows and death of the Lord's saints in the age of martyrdom, it was but a type of a shadow of the vengeance and slaughter destined to be poured out upon the Jews of that generation. The synagogues in which apostles were scourged would soon be drenched in the blood of those who wielded the lash. The currents of hatred that swept many of Jesus' disciples to untimely deaths would soon become a great tidal wave of anger and animosity against the Jewish people that would destroy their city, overrun their nation, and scatter their people. Those who with Roman hands crucified their King at Jerusalem would soon themselves be hanging by the thousands upon Roman crosses in that same benighted area." (Bruce R. McConkie, *Mortal Messiah*, 3:429. See also 3:433; Bruce R. McConkie, *Doctrinal New Testament Commentary*, 1:644.)

Other Commentary

"And thus was the holy house burned down. . . .

"Now although anyone would justly lament the destruction of such a work as this was, since it was the most admirable of all the works that we have seen or heard of, both for its curious structure and its magnitude, and also for the vast wealth bestowed upon it, as well as for the glorious reputation it had for its holiness; yet might such a one comfort himself with this thought, that it was fate that decreed it so to be, which is inevitable, both as to living creatures and as to works and places also. . . .

"While the holy house was on fire, everything was plundered that came to hand, and ten thousand of those that were caught were slain; nor was there a commiseration of any age, or any reverence of gravity, but children, and old men, and profane persons, and priests were all slain in the same manner. . . . The people also that were left above were beaten back upon the enemy and under a great consternation, and made sad moans at the calamity they were under; the multitude also that was in the city joined in this outcry with those that were upon the hill. And besides, many of those that were worn away by the famine, and their mouths almost closed, when they saw the fire of the holy house, they exerted their utmost strength, and brake out into groans and outcries again: Perea did also return the echo, as well as the mountains round about [the city], and augmented the force of the entire noise. Yet was the misery itself more terrible than this disorder; for one would have thought that the hill itself, on which the temple stood, as seething hot, as full of fire on every part of it, that the blood was larger in quantity than the fire, and those that were slain more in number than those that slew them; for the ground did no where appear visible, for the dead bodies that lay on it; but the soldiers went over heaps of those bodies, as they ran upon such as fled from them." (Flavius Josephus, *Wars of the Jews*, bk. 6, chap. 4, pars. 7–8; bk. 6, chap. 5, par. 1.)

Joseph Smith—Matthew 1:12
"Then you shall stand in the holy place"

Selected Statements of the First Presidency and the Twelve Apostles

"Guided by inspiration, the primitive saints withdrew from Jerusalem and Judea before the desolating scourges fell upon the city and the people. The saints left the unholy city and went to a place of safety, a holy place, a place made holy by their presence, for it is not places but people that are holy." (Bruce R. McConkie, *Millennial Messiah*, p. 472.)

"As one studies the Lord's commandments and attending promises upon compliance therewith, one gets some definite ideas as to how we might 'stand in holy places,' as the Lord commands—if we will be preserved with such protection as accords with his holy purposes, in order that we might be numbered among the 'pure in heart' who constitute Zion. . . .

"As one studies the commandments of God, it seems to be made crystal clear that the all-important thing is not where we live but whether or not our hearts are pure." (Harold B. Lee, in Conference Report, Oct. 1968, p. 62. See also Harold B. Lee, in Conference Report, Apr. 1943, p. 129.)

Joseph Smith—Matthew 1:13
"Let them who are in Judea flee into the mountains"

Selected Statements of the First Presidency and the Twelve Apostles

"In all this, speedy flight is enjoined. 'Flee to the mountains. Let him who is on the housetop take the outside staircase, or go over the roofs of the houses. Let him who is in the field go in his work clothes. Abandon your property. Those who are in country areas must not return into the city. The time for escape will be short. Look not back to Sodom and the wealth and luxury you are leaving. Stay not in the burning house, in the hope of salvaging your treasures, lest the flame destroy you. Pray that your flight will not be impeded by the cold of winter or the shut gates and travel restrictions of the Sabbath. Flee, flee to the mountains.' (And when the day came, the true saints, guided as true saints always are by the spirit of revelation, fled to Pella in Perea and were spared.)" (Bruce R. McConkie, *Mortal Messiah*, 3:430.)

"For the saints in that dread and evil day, Jesus counseled: 'Then let them who are in Judea flee into the mountains.' They are to leave the city and the land and go to a place of safety. 'Let him who is on the housetop flee, and not return to take anything out of his house; Neither let him who is in the field return back to take his clothes.' Their flight must be in haste. Roman steel will take the life of any who linger. Houses and crops and property are of no moment. If their lives are to be spared, they must forsake the things of this world and assemble with the fleeing saints in holy places, there to prepare themselves for a better world where the riches of eternity are found." (Bruce R. McConkie, *Millennial Messiah*, p. 472.)

Joseph Smith—Matthew 1:18

"Tribulation . . . such as was not before sent upon Israel, of God"

Selected Statements of the First Presidency and the Twelve Apostles

"You all know the sequel, how the Jews carried through their awful plot and crucified the Son of God, and how thereafter they continued to fight against his gospel. You remember, too, the price they paid, how in 70 A.D. the city fell into the hands of the Romans as the climax of a siege in which the historian Josephus tells us there were a million one hundred thousand people killed and ' . . . tens of thousands were taken captive, to be afterwards sold into slavery, or to be slain by wild beasts, or in gladiatorial combat for the amusement of Roman spectators.'

"All of this destruction and the dispersion of the Jews would have been avoided had the people accepted the gospel of Jesus Christ and had their hearts changed by it." (Marion G. Romney, in Conference Report, Oct. 1948, pp. 76–77.)

"And what a desolation it was! As the Roman legions swept through the Holy Land only a few years later and wiped out Jerusalem, it was such a catastrophe that it fully reflected the Savior's prediction when he said, 'Then shall be great tribulation, such as was not since the beginning of the world to this time, no, nor ever shall be.' (Matthew 24:21.)

"As Josephus describes it in his writings, it is dreadful to contemplate, even after almost two thousand years." (Mark E. Petersen, in *Ensign*, Nov. 1979, p. 12.)

"God does it; the merciful Lord is also a God of justice. The penalty for sin must be paid. Similarly, it was the loving Christ who himself sent death and destruction to the Nephite cities to cleanse them before he came to minister personally to the ancient inhabitants of America. (3 Nephi 9.)" (Bruce R. McConkie, *Doctrinal New Testament Commentary*, 1:645.)

"Let this fact be engraved in the eternal records with a pen of steel: the Jews were cursed, and smitten, and cursed anew, because they rejected the gospel, cast out their Messiah, and crucified their King. Let the spiritually illiterate suppose what they may, it was the Jewish denial and rejection of the Holy One of Israel, whom their fathers worshipped in the beauty of holiness, that has made them a hiss and byword in all nations and that has taken millions of their fair sons and daughters to untimely graves." (Bruce R. McConkie, *Millennial Messiah*, pp. 224–25.)

Joseph Smith—Matthew 1:20

"Except those days should be shortened, there should none of their flesh be saved"

Selected Statements of the First Presidency and the Twelve Apostles

"I have before me a quotation of Will Durrant in his book, *The Story of Civilization,* in which he states that 'no people in history fought so tenaciously for liberty as the Jews, nor any other people against such odds.' He says further, 'No other people has ever known so long an exile, or so hard a fate.'

"Then referring to the siege of Jerusalem under Titus, lasting for 134 days, during which 1,100,000 Jews perished and 97,000 were taken captive; he states that the Romans destroyed 987 towns in Palestine and slew 580,000 men, and a still larger number, we are told, perished through starvation, disease, and fire.

" . . . And even their banishment and scattering didn't end their persecution. . . .

" . . . Yes, the prophecies regarding the dispersion and the suffering of Judah have been fulfilled. But the gathering and re-establishment of the Jews is also clearly predicted." (Ezra Taft Benson, in Conference Report, Apr. 1950, pp. 74–75.)

Other Commentary

"Over a million Jews had been killed in the revolt, and it is estimated that as many as 900,000 were taken captive. Thousands were carried off to Egypt to work in the quarries and mines as lifelong slaves. Boys and women were sold to slave traders, and thousands of others died of starvation in the prison camps. A remnant of this conquered people was scattered to the ends of the earth.

"It appears that only a small segment of the Jews escaped the terrible destruction. These were members of the Church of Jesus Christ, who followed the counsel of the Savior and fled as the siege was to begin." (H. Donl Peterson, in *Ensign,* May 1972, pp. 42.)

Joseph Smith—Matthew 1:20
"For the elect's sake, according to the covenant, those days shall be shortened"

Selected Statements of the First Presidency and the Twelve Apostles

"The whole history of the world—the rise and fall of nations; the discovery of islands and continents; the peopling of all lands and the fates which have befallen all people—for four millenniums the whole earth has been governed and controlled for the benefit of the children of Israel. And now the day of their glory and triumph is at the door.

"The concept of a chosen and favored people, a concept scarcely known in the world and but little understood even by the saints of God, is one of the most marvelous systems ever devised for administering salvation to all men in all nations in all ages. Israel, the Lord's chosen people, were a congregation set apart in preexistence. In large measure, the spirit children of the Father who acquired a talent for spirituality, who chose to heed the divine word then given, and who sought, above their fellows, to do good and work righteousness—all these were foreordained to be born in the house of Israel. They were chosen before they were born. This is the doctrine of election." (Bruce R. McConkie, *Millennial Messiah*, p. 182.)

"The tribulations of the time then foreshadowed would prove to be unprecedented in horror and would never be paralleled in all their awful details in Israel's history; but in mercy God has decreed that the dreadful period should be shortened for the sake of the elect believers, otherwise no flesh of Israel would be saved alive. Multitudes were to fall bythe sword; other hosts were to be led away captive, and so be scattered amongst all nations." (James E. Talmage, *Jesus the Christ*, p. 572.)

Joseph Smith—Matthew 1:21

"If any man shall say unto you, Lo, here is Christ, or there, believe him not"

Selected Statements of the First Presidency and the Twelve Apostles

"After the destruction of Jerusalem and the scattering of the Jews, and after the establishment of the primitive Church, an era of false religions is to commence, an era of division, disunity, discord and disagreement, an era of change and apostasy, so that among those who profess to follow Christ, some will advocate one doctrine of salvation and some another. Perfect Christianity will be lost; and Jesus' warning is to beware of all false and conflicting claims made in his name.

"A perfect illustration of this religious turmoil is found in the religious revival which swept the frontier areas of America in the Prophet's day." (Bruce R. McConkie, *Doctrinal New Testament Commentary*, 1:647.)

Joseph Smith—Matthew 1:22

"For in those [last] days there shall also arise false Christs, and false prophets . . . insomuch, that, if possible, they shall deceive the very elect"

Selected Statements of the First Presidency and the Twelve Apostles

"False Christs preceded the destruction of Jerusalem and the temple, both of which occurred in A.D. 70, and they shall be manifest again before the Second Coming. They are, in fact, now here, and their presence is one of the least understood of all the signs of the times. . . .

"True, there may be those deranged persons who suppose they are God, or Christ, or the Holy Ghost, or almost anything. None but the lunatic fringe among men, however, will give them a second serious thought. The promise of false Christs who will deceive, if it were possible, even the very elect, who will lead astray those who have made eternal covenant with the Lord, is a far more subtle and insidious evil.

"A false Christ is not a person. It is a false system of worship, a false church, a false cult that says: 'Lo, here is salvation; here is the doctrine of Christ. Come and believe thus and so, and ye shall be saved.' It is any concept or philosophy that says that redemption, salvation, sanctification, justification, and all of the promised rewards can be gained in any way except that set forth by the apostles and prophets." (Bruce R. McConkie, *Millennial Messiah*, pp. 47–48.)

"One of the surest and most certain signs of the times is the near-omnipresence of false prophets. 'There shall also arise . . . false prophets,' saith the holy word. (JS–M 1:22.) It is now almost as though every fool or near-fool, and every person filled with self-conceit and a desire to be in the spotlight of adulation, fancies himself a prophet of religion or politics, or what have you. Streets and stadiums and temples are overrun, as the ancient prophets foretold, with the false ministers and teachers and politicians of the latter days. And all this shall continue until the greedy, the power hungry, and the self-called preachers go the way of all the earth when He comes to rule whose right it is both to instruct and to govern." (Bruce R. McConkie, *New Witness for the Articles of Faith*, p. 626.)

Joseph Smith—Matthew 1:23
"Behold, I speak these things unto you for the elect's sake"

Selected Statements of the First Presidency and the Twelve Apostles

"Our attention now turns to what the inspired word has to say about the false teachers, false ministers, and false prophets who shall spew forth their damning doctrines in the days of desolation and sorrow that precede the Second Coming of the true Teacher, the chief Minister, and the presiding Prophet. Their presence is one of the signs of the times, and they shall prophesy and teach so near the truth 'that, if possible, they shall deceive the very elect.' (JS–M 1:22.)

"Lest we be deceived, we must know the differences between true and false prophets. 'Beware of false prophets,' Jesus said (Matthew 7:15), and we cannot recognize a false prophet unless we know what a true one is." (Bruce R. McConkie, *Millennial Messiah*, p. 68. See also Bruce R. McConkie, *Doctrinal New Testament Commentary*, 1:654.)

"The Prophet Joseph Smith, in his inspired version of that same scripture, added these significant words: *'who are the elect, according to the covenant.'* This is what has been said, in effect, in this conference: Unless every member of this Church gains for himself an unshakable testimony of the divinity of this Church, he will be among those who will be deceived in this day when the 'elect according to the covenant' are going to be tried and tested. Only those will survive who have gained for themselves that testimony." (Harold B. Lee, in Conference Report, Oct. 1950, p. 129.)

Joseph Smith—Matthew 1:25

"If they shall say unto you: Behold, he is in the desert; . . . Behold, he is in the secret chambers; believe it not"

Selected Statements of the First Presidency and the Twelve Apostles

"If these false religious systems with their false teachers invite you to the desert to find Christ in a life of asceticism, go not forth, he is not there; if they call you to the secret chambers of monastic seclusion to find him, believe them not, he is not there." (Bruce R. McConkie, *Doctrinal New Testament Commentary, 1:648.*)

"Deceiving prophets, emissaries of the devil, would be active, some alluring people into the deserts, and impelling them to hermit lives of pernicious asceticism, others insisting that Christ could be found in the secret chambers of monastic seclusion; and some of them showing forth through the power of Satan, such signs and wonders as 'to seduce, if it were possible, even the elect'; but of all such scheming of the prince of evil, the Lord admonished His own: 'Believe it not'; and added, 'take ye heed; behold I have foretold you all things.' " (James E. Talmage, *Jesus the Christ*, pp. 572-73. See also p. 589.)

Joseph Smith—Matthew 1:26

"As the light of the morning cometh out of the east, . . . so shall also the coming of the Son of Man be"

Selected Statements of the First Presidency and the Twelve Apostles

"For when, in this age of apostasy and discord, the true religion of Christ comes again, it will be as the light of the morning, dawning gradually and increasing in brilliance until the millennial day when it shall cover the whole earth. Then shall the Son of Man come to reign personally upon the earth." (Bruce R. McConkie, *Doctrinal New Testament Commentary*, 1:648.)

Joseph Smith—Matthew 1:27

"Wheresoever the carcass is, there will the eagles be gathered together"

Selected Statements of the First Presidency and the Twelve Apostles

"By inserting this epigrammatic parable in his discourse on the Second Coming of the Son of Man, Jesus endorses the teachings and hopes of nearly all the prophets of ancient Israel. These inspired teachers had seen with seeric vision that the Lord's elect, the chosen of Israel, would first be scattered among all nations, and, then, before the ushering in of the millennial era, be gathered again to the lands of their inheritance. (Isaiah 2:1-5; 5:26-30; 11:10-16; 29; Jeremiah 3:12-18; 16:11-21; 23:1-8; 31:6-14; Ezekiel 11: 16-20; 20:33-42; 37.)

"In the parable, as here given, the carcass is the body of the Church to which the eagles, who are Israel, shall fly to find nourishment. 'The gathering of Israel is first *spiritual* and second *temporal*. It is spiritual in that the lost sheep of Israel are first "restored to the true Church and fold of God," meaning that they come to a true knowledge of the God of Israel, accept the gospel which he has restored in latter days, and join the Church of Jesus Christ of Latter-day Saints. It is temporal in that these converts are then "gathered home to the lands of their inheritance, and . . . established in all their lands of promise" (2 Nephi 9:2; 25:15-18; Jeremiah 16:14-21), meaning that the house of Joseph will be established in America, the house of Judah in Palestine, and that the Lost Tribes will come to Ephraim in America to receive their blessings in due course. (D&C 133.)' (*Mormon Doctrine*, p. 280.)" (Bruce R. McConkie, *Doctrinal New Testament Commentary*, 1: 648-49. See also Bruce R. McConkie, *Millennial Messiah*, p. 351-52.)

"The gathering of Israel in the last days was pictured as the flocking of eagles to the place where the body of the Church would be established." (James E. Talmage, *Jesus the Christ*, p. 573.)

"This world today is full of wickedness. That wickedness is increasing. True there are many righteous people scattered throughout the earth, and it is our duty to search them out and give unto them the gospel of Jesus Christ and bring them out of Babylon." (Joseph Fielding Smith, *Doctrines of Salvation*, 3:30. See also George Q. Cannon, in *Millennial Star*, 25 [14 Mar. 1863]: 169.)

"The spirit of gathering has been with the Church from the days of that restoration. Those who are of the blood of Israel, have a righteous desire after they are baptized, to gather together with the body of the Saints at the designated place. This, we have come to recognize, is but the breath of God upon those who are converted turning them to the promises made to their fathers.

"But the designation of gathering places is qualified in another revelation by the Lord to which I would desire to call your attention. After designating certain places in that day where the Saints were to gather, the Lord said this:

" 'Until the day cometh when there is found no room for them; and then I have other places which I will appoint unto them.' (D&C 101:21.)

"Thus, clearly, the Lord has placed the responsibility for directing the work of gathering in the hands of the leaders of the Church to whom he will reveal his will where and when such gatherings would take place in the future. It would be well—before the frightening events concerning the fulfillment of all God's promises and predictions are upon us, that the Saints in every land prepare themselves and look forward to the instruction that shall come to them from the First Presidency of this Church as to where they shall be gathered and not be disturbed in their feelings until such instruction is given to them as it is revealed by the Lord to the proper authority." (Harold B. Lee, in Conference Report, Apr. 1948, p. 55.)

Joseph Smith—Matthew 1:29

"Nation shall rise against nation, and kingdom against kingdom"

Selected Statements of the First Presidency and the Twelve Apostles

"Have we not had numerous rumors of wars? Have we not had wars, such wars as the world never saw before? Is there not today commotion among the nations, and are not their rulers troubled? Have not kingdoms been overturned and great changes been made among nations? . . . We know this to be the case, both from observation and from the predictions of the prophets. Elijah, one hundred years ago, told Joseph Smith that the great and dreadful day of the Lord was near, 'even at the doors.' " (Joseph Fielding Smith, *Way to Perfection*, pp. 282–83. See also Joseph Smith, *History of the Church*, 1:315.)

"The Lord says he has decreed wars. Why? Because of the hatred in the hearts of men, because of the wickedness in the hearts of men, because they will not repent." (Joseph Fielding Smith, *Doctrines of Salvation*, 3:42.)

"Be it remembered that tribulations lie ahead. There will be wars in one nation and kingdom after another until war is poured out upon all nations and two hundred million men of war mass their armaments at Armageddon.

"Peace has been taken from the earth, the angels of destruction have begun their work, and their swords shall not be sheathed until the Prince of Peace comes to destroy the wicked and usher in the great Millennium.

"It is one of the sad heresies of our time that peace will be gained by weary diplomats as they prepare treaties of compromise, or that the Millennium will be ushered in because men will learn to live in peace and to keep the commandments, or that the predicted plagues and promised desolations of latter days can in some way be avoided.

"We must do all we can to proclaim peace, to avoid war, to heal disease, to prepare for natural disasters—but with it all, that which is to be shall be." (Bruce R. McConkie, in *Ensign*, May 1979, p. 93.)

Other Commentary

"As one of the signs that would precede his coming, Jesus said that there would be wars and rumors of wars, and an awful hate would exist among people. . . .

" . . . We can now drop concentrated fire on a nation and literally roast its population. War doesn't solve a single human problem, and yet the one place where our generation excels most is in its ability to make war. Modern war is undoubtedly the most highly developed of all of our sciences. Even a horrible kind of destructive cold war now seems to have become a fixed part of our unfortunate way of life. But sinful, unstable man now holds in his hands the ability to destroy everything upon the earth in just a few hours. Our failure has been that while we have perfected weapons, we have failed to perfect the men who may be asked to use them. But still there is no letup in our evil. Like the ancients, we can discern the face of the sky, but we fail in reading the signs of the times. This has always been one of the world's most serious problems." (Sterling W. Sill, in Conference Report, Apr. 1966, pp. 20–21.)

Joseph Smith—Matthew 1:29
"There shall be famines, and pestilences, and earthquakes, in divers places"

Selected Statements of the First Presidency and the Twelve Apostles

" 'Ah' but says sapient man—editors, clergymen and others—'we have had hundreds of earthquakes and wars and famines and pestilences; we have had thunderings, lightnings, tempests, and the sea heaving itself beyond its bounds; but the end has not come yet; and we think those who view such events as the messages of wrath from Heaven, the victims of a vulgar superstition.' Yes, and in their very anxiety to escape deception and superstition, they will become the victims of both; the voices of the elements—nature's voice speaking in God-like power— will be suffered to pass by as unheeded, so far as repentance is concerned, as is the voice of feeble, though inspired man, until the consumption decreed shall be fulfilled, and the vengeance of a rejected and offended God shall be fully executed." (George Q. Cannon, in *Millennial Star*, 25 [24 Oct. 1863]: 682.)

"There are among us many loose writings predicting the calamities which are about to overtake us. Some of these have been publicized as though they were necessary to wake up the world to the horrors about to overtake us. Many of these are from sources upon which there cannot be unquestioned reliance.

"Are you priesthood bearers aware of the fact that we need no such publications to be forewarned, if we were only conversant with what the scriptures have already spoken to us in plainness?

"Let me give you the sure word of prophecy on which you should rely for your guide instead of these strange sources which may have great political implications.

"Read the 24th chapter of Matthew—particularly that inspired version as contained in the Pearl of Great Price. [Joseph Smith—Matthew.]

"Then read the 45th section of the Doctrine and Covenants where the Lord, not man, has documented the signs of the times.

"Now turn to section 101 and section 133 of the Doctrine and Covenants and hear the step-by-step recounting of events leading up to the coming of the Savior.

"Finally, turn to the promises the Lord makes to those who keep the commandments when these judgments descend upon the wicked, as set forth in the Doctrine and Covenants, section 38.

"Brethren, these are some of the writings with which you should concern yourselves, rather than commentaries that may come from those whose information may not be the most reliable and whose motives may be subject to question. And may I say, parenthetically, most of such writers are not handicapped by having any authentic information on their writings." (Harold B. Lee, in Conference Report, Oct. 1972, p. 128. See also Joseph Fielding Smith, *Doctrines of Salvation*, 3:27; Melvin J. Ballard, in Conference Report, Oct. 1923, p. 31; Brigham Young, in *Journal of Discourses*, 8:123.)

"I will prophesy that the signs of the coming of the Son of Man are already commenced. One pestilence will desolate after another. We shall soon have war and bloodshed. The moon will be turned into blood. I testify of these things, and that the coming of the Son of Man is nigh, even at your doors. If our souls and our bodies are not looking forth for the coming of the Son of Man; and after we are dead, if we are not looking forth, we shall be among those who are calling for the rocks to fall upon them." (Joseph Smith, *History of the Church*, 3:390.)

Joseph Smith—Matthew 1:30

"Because iniquity shall abound, the love of men shall wax cold"

Selected Statements of the First Presidency and the Twelve Apostles

"I saw men hunting the lives of their own sons, and brother murdering brother, women killing their own daughters, and daughters seeking the lives of their mothers. I saw armies arrayed against armies. I saw blood, desolation, fires. The Son of Man has said that the mother shall be against the daughter, and the daughter against the mother. These things are at our doors. They will follow the Saints of God from city to city. Satan will rage, and the spirit of the devil is now enraged. I know now how soon these things will take place." (Joseph Smith, *History of the Church*, 3:391.)

" 'Love' here means Christian unity, harmony. Where in the Christian world does that love, that oneness, prevail? There is an abundance of co-operation based on self-interest, or family connections: but where is there genuine Christian love, true, unselfish, constant? Its absence in the majority of men is one of the signs of the end." (Hyrum M. Smith and Janne M. Sjodahl, *Doctrine and Covenants Commentary*, p. 262.)

Joseph Smith—Matthew 1:30

"He that shall not be overcome, the same shall be saved"

Selected Statements of the First Presidency and the Twelve Apostles

"Can you tell me where the people are who will be shielded and protected from these great calamities and judgments which are even now at our doors? I'll tell you. The priesthood of God who honor their priesthood, and who are worthy of their blessings are the only ones who shall have this safety and protection. They are the only mortal beings. No other people have a right to be shielded from these judgments. They are at our very doors; not even this people will escape them entirely. They will come down like the judgments of Sodom and Gomorrah. And none but the priesthood will be safe from their fury." (Wilford Woodruff, in *Young Woman's Journal*, Aug. 1894, p. 512. See also Joseph Fielding Smith, in Conference Report, Oct. 1940, p. 117.)

"Do not think for a moment that the days of trial are over. They are not. If we keep the commandments of the Lord, we shall prosper, we shall be blessed; the plagues, the calamities that have been promised will be poured out upon the peoples of the earth, and we shall escape them, yea, they shall pass us by.

"But remember the Lord says if we fail to keep his word, if we walk in the ways of the world, they will not pass us by, but we shall be visited with floods and with fire, with sword and with plague and destruction. We may escape these things through faithfulness. Israel of old might have escaped through faithfulness." (Joseph Fielding Smith, *Doctrines of Salvation*, 3:34.)

Joseph Smith—Matthew 1:31
"Again, this Gospel of the Kingdom shall be preached in all the world"

Selected Statements of the First Presidency and the Twelve Apostles

"When the prophetic word says the gospel shall be preached in every nation, it means every nation. It includes Russia and China and India. When it speaks of every kindred and people, it embraces the people of Islam and the believers in Buddha. When it mentions every tongue, it includes all the confusing dialects of all the sects and parties of men. The gospel is to go to them all. And the Lord will not come until it does." (Bruce R. McConkie, *Millennial Messiah*, p. 136.)

"Today The Church of Jesus Christ of Latter-day Saints is extending the heralded message of the restoration of the gospel to every nation which permits us entrance through its borders. This is a fulfillment of the vision and revelation received by Daniel, the prophet, 'Who foresaw and foretold the establishment of the kingdom of God in the latter days, never again to be destroyed nor given to other people.' (Joseph F. Smith—Vision of the Redemption of the Dead 1:44.)" (Ezra Taft Benson, in *Ensign*, May 1978, p. 32. See also Bruce R. McConkie, *New Witness for the Articles of Faith*, p. 630.)

"Our missionaries are going forth to different nations, and in Germany, Palestine, New Holland, Australia, the East Indies, and other places, the Standard of Truth has been erected; no unhallowed hand can stop the work from progressing; persecutions may rage, mobs may combine, armies may assemble, calumny may defame, but the truth of God will go forth boldly, nobly, and independent till it has penetrated every continent, visited every clime, swept every country, and sounded in every ear, till the purposes of God shall be accomplished, and the Great Jehovah shall say the work is done." (Joseph Smith, *History of the Church*, 4:540.)

Joseph Smith—Matthew 1:32

"Again shall the abomination of desolation, spoken of by Daniel the prophet, be fulfilled"

Selected Statements of the First Presidency and the Twelve Apostles

"All the desolation and waste which attended the former destruction of Jerusalem is but prelude to the coming siege. Titus and his legions slaughtered 1,100,000 Jews, destroyed the temple, and ploughed the city. In the coming reenactment of this 'abomination of desolation,' the whole world will be at war, Jerusalem will be the center of the conflict, every modern weapon will be used, and in the midst of the siege the Son of Man shall come, setting his foot upon the mount of Olives and fighting the battle of his saints." (Bruce R. McConkie, *Doctrinal New Testament Commentary*, 1:659.)

Selected Scripture References

"My servants, go ye forth . . . , reproving the world in righteousness of all their unrighteous and ungodly deeds, setting forth clearly and understandingly the desolation of abomination in the last days." (D&C 84:117.)

"I will gather all nations against Jerusalem to battle; and the city shall be taken, and the houses rifled, and the women ravished." (Zechariah 14:2.)

Joseph Smith—Matthew 1:33

"The sun shall be darkened, and the moon shall not give her light"

Selected Statements of the First Presidency and the Twelve Apostles

"There may be more than one occasion when the light of the sun and the moon shall be withheld from men, and when it will seem as though the very stars in the firmament are being hurled from their places. What is here recited could mean that the light of the sun is blotted out by smoke and weather conditions, which would also make the moon appear 'as blood.' This falling of the stars 'unto the earth' could be meteoric showers, as distinguished from the stars, on another occasion, appearing to fall because the earth itself reels to and fro." (Bruce R. McConkie, *Millennial Messiah*, p. 380.)

"The words of the prophets are rapidly being fulfilled, but it is done on such natural principles that most of us fail to see it. . . . Wonders in heaven and in the earth should be seen, and there should be fire, blood and pillars of smoke. Eventually the sun is to be turned into darkness and the moon as blood, and then shall come the great and dreadful day of the Lord. Some of these signs have been given; some are yet to come. The sun has not yet been darkened. We are informed that this will be one of the last acts just preceding the coming of the Lord." (Joseph Fielding Smith, *Way to Perfection*, p. 280.)

Joseph Smith—Matthew 1:34

"This generation, in which these things shall be shown forth, shall not pass away until all I have told you shall be fulfilled"

Selected Statements of the First Presidency and the Twelve Apostles

"Consult any reliable unabridged dictionary of the English language for evidence of the fact that the term 'generation' as connoting a period of time, has many meanings, among which are 'race, kind, class.' The term is not confined to a body of people living at one time. Fausett's *Bible Cyclopedia, Critical and Expository*, after citing many meanings attached to the word, says: 'In Matthew 24:34 "this generation shall not pass (viz. the Jewish race, of which the generation in Christ's days was a sample in character: compare Christ's address to the 'generation,' 23:35, 36, in proof that 'generation' means at times the whole Jewish race) till all these things be fulfilled"—a prophecy that the Jews shall be a distinct people still when He shall come again.' " (James E. Talmage, *Jesus the Christ*, p. 590.)

"There have been various interpretations of the meaning of a generation. It is held by some that a generation is one hundred years; by others that it is one hundred and twenty years; by others that a generation as expressed in this and other scriptures has reference to a period of time which is indefinite. The Savior said: 'An evil and adulterous generation seeketh after a sign.' This did not have reference to a period of years, but to a period of wickedness. A generation may mean the time of this present dispensation." (Joseph Fielding Smith, *Church History and Modern Revelation*, 2:102. See also James E. Talmage, *Jesus the Christ*, pp. 574-75.)

Selected Scripture References

"This generation of Jews shall not pass away until every desolation which I have told you concerning them shall come to pass." (D&C 45:21.)

Joseph Smith—Matthew 1:35
"My words shall not pass away, but all shall be fulfilled"

Selected Statements of the First Presidency and the Twelve Apostles

"I am just simple-minded enough, my brethren and sisters, to stand upon the rock of assurance that not one jot or tittle of the word of the Lord shall fail. Do not allow yourselves to think that the coming of the Christ means merely the spread of different or more advanced ideas among men, or simply the progress and advancement of society as an institution. These shall be but incidents of the great consummation, the consummation of this particular stage or epoch of the Lord's work. The Lord Jesus Christ shall come in the clouds of heaven, accompanied by the heavenly hosts, and His advent shall be marked by a great extension of the resurrection of the just, which has been in progress since that resurrection Sunday on which He came forth from the tomb and took up the wounded, pierced body which He had laid down; and those who are not able to bear the glory of His coming because of their wickedness, their foulness, and wilful state of sin, shall, by natural means, perish." (James E. Talmage, in Conference Report, Apr. 1916, pp. 130–31.)

"I do not know how long it will be before this mission shall be accomplished and these words of our Lord and Savior Jesus Christ shall be fulfilled, but that he will work *speedily*, that he will accomplish his purposes within the time that he has set, I fully believe, and his promises shall not fail." (Joseph Fielding Smith, *Doctrines of Salvation*, 3:7.)

"This may be understood as applying to the generation in which the portentous happenings before described would be realized. So far as the predictions related to the overthrow of Jerusalem, they were literally fulfilled within the natural lifetime of several of the apostles and of multitudes of their contemporaries; such of the Lord's prophecies as pertain to the heralding of His second coming are to be brought to pass within the duration of the generation of some who witness the inauguration of their fulfilment." (James E. Talmage, *Jesus the Christ*, pp. 574–75.)

Selected Scripture References

"Think not that I am come to destroy the law, or the prophets . . . one jot or one tittle shall in no wise pass from the law, till all be fulfilled." (Matthew 5:17–18.)

"I do not destroy that which hath been spoken concerning things which are to come." (3 Nephi 15:7.)

"And all things that he [Isaiah] spake have been and shall be, even according to the words which he spake." (3 Nephi 23:3.)

Joseph Smith—Matthew 1:36

"The powers of the heavens shall be shaken"

Selected Statements of the First Presidency and the Twelve Apostles

"From the *Inspired Version* we learn that the signs promised in Matthew 24:29 are to occur after the abomination of desolation sweeps Jerusalem for the second time. They will thus come almost at the very hour of the Second Coming. From other scriptural accounts of these same signs we learn that 'the earth shall tremble and reel to and fro as a drunken man' (D&C 88:87), and 'shall remove out of her place' (Isaiah 13:10–13); that 'the islands shall become one land' (D&C 133:23); and that 'the stars shall be hurled from their places.' (D&C 133:49.) Thus it would seem, when the Lord makes his appearance and the earth is restored to its paradisiacal state, that there will be great physical changes. When the continents become one land and the earth reels to and fro, with all that then occurs, it will surely appear unto men as though the very stars of heaven were being hurled from their places, and so they will be as far as their relationship to the earth is concerned. That there may be other heavenly bodies, having the appearance of stars, that shall fall on the earth may also well be. Truly the scriptures testify of many signs and wonders in the heavens above. (D&C 29:14; Joel 2:31; Revelations 6:12–17.)" (Bruce R. McConkie, *Doctrinal New Testament Commentary*, 1:678.)

"One wonders if we are not now seeing some of the wonders of heaven—Not all, for undoubtedly some of them will be among the heavenly bodies, such as the moon and the sun, the meteors and comets, but in speaking of the heavens, reference is made to that part which surrounds the earth and which belongs to it. It is in the atmosphere where many of the signs are to be given. Do we not see airships of various kinds traveling through the heavens daily? Have we not had signs in the earth and through the earth with the radio, railroad trains, automobiles, submarines, and satellites, and in many other ways? There are yet to be great signs; the heavens are to be shaken, the sign of the Son of Man is to be given; and then shall the tribes of the earth mourn. . . .

"If the great and dreadful day of the Lord was near at hand when Elijah came, we are just one century nearer it today." (Joseph Fielding Smith, *Way to Perfection*, pp. 280–81, 284.)

Joseph Smith—Matthew 1:36
"Then shall appear the sign of the Son of Man in heaven"

Selected Statements of the First Presidency and the Twelve Apostles

"The sign of the coming of the Son of Man—what is it? We do not know. Our revelation says simply: 'And immediately there shall appear a great sign in heaven, and all people shall see it together.' (D&C 88:93.)" (Bruce R. McConkie, *Millennial Messiah*, p. 418.)

"We are informed that there will be a great sign in the heavens. It is not to be limited so that some few only of the human family can see it; but it is said, 'All people shall see it together!' At least, it is to be like our sun seen over one entire side of the globe, and then passing immediately round to the other, or else it will encircle the whole earth at the same time. But the bridegroom does not come then. These are only the preceding events to let the Latter-day Saints and the pure in heart know that these are the times that they may trim up their lamps and prepare for the triumphant appearing of their Lord." (Orson Pratt, in *Journal of Discourses*, 8:50. See also Joseph Smith, *History of the Church*, 5:291.)

"There will be wars and rumors of wars, signs in the heavens above and on the earth beneath, the sun turned into darkness and the moon to blood, earthquakes in divers places, the seas heaving beyond their bounds; then will appear one grand sign of the Son of Man in heaven. But what will the world do? They will say it is a planet, a comet, etc. But the Son of Man will come as the sign of the coming of the Son of Man, which will be as the light of the morning cometh out of the east." (Joseph Smith, *Teachings of the Prophet Joseph Smith*, pp. 286–87.)

Joseph Smith—Matthew 1:37
"And whoso treasureth up my word, shall not be deceived"

Selected Statements of the First Presidency and the Twelve Apostles

"Not *read*, not *study*, not *search*, but *treasure up* the Lord's word. *Possess* it, *own* it, *make it yours* by both believing it and living it. For instance: the voice of the Lord *says* that if men have faith, repent, and are baptized, they shall receive the Holy Ghost. It is not sufficient merely to *know* what the scripture *says*. One must *treasure it up*, meaning take it into his possession so affirmatively that it becomes a part of his very being; as a consequence, in the illustration given, one actually receives the companionship of the Spirit. Obviously such persons will not be deceived where the signs of the times and the Second Coming of the Messiah are concerned." (Bruce R. McConkie, *Doctrinal New Testament Commentary*, 1:662.)

Selected Scripture References

"Beware lest ye are deceived; ... seek ye earnestly the best gifts, always remembering for what they are given." (D&C 46:8.)

Other Commentary

The word of God comes to mankind primarily through the living prophets, the scriptures, and the promptings of the Holy Ghost.

Joseph Smith—Matthew 1:37
"He shall send his angels before him"

Selected Statements of the First Presidency and the Twelve Apostles

"These choice young people [referring to the youth of the Church] are not an aristocracy of the rich, but of those who are rich in the Spirit of God. It is not an aristocracy of the politically or socially powerful, but of those who have great moral influence. It is and would be of those who are the elect of God. It is an aristocracy of the young Saints of God, even as those who are on the stand this afternoon and who will be on the stand singing for us this evening.

"Jesus spoke of them when he said: 'He shall send his angels with a great sound of a trumpet, and they shall gather together his elect from the four winds.' (Matthew 24:31.)" (James E. Faust, in *Ensign*, Nov. 1974, p. 60.)

Joseph Smith—Matthew 1:37
"They shall gather together the remainder of his elect from the four winds"

Selected Statements of the First Presidency and the Twelve Apostles

"It is ... the concurrent testimony of all the Prophets, that this gathering together of all the Saints, must take place before the Lord comes to 'take vengeance upon the ungodly,' and 'to be glorified and admired by all those who obey the Gospel.' " (Joseph Smith, *History of the Church*, 4:272.)

"There must come a time, for the Lord has spoken it, when by some miraculous manner, he will gather from the four ends of the earth his people in a gathering which does not have to do with that which has already taken place.

"This seems to be a time to come—near the great day of resurrection (D&C 45:46 and Moses 7:62–63), and just preceding the time when the 'arm of the Lord shall fall upon the nations.' In that day the City of Enoch—the other City of Zion—will return and men shall again exercise perfect faith and have the guidance of divine power." (Joseph Fielding Smith, *Signs of the Times*, p. 169.)

"Those of Israel who live on earth and are worthy, and who are not gathered before the Lord comes, shall be gathered thereafter. . . . How shall this work be performed, and who shall do the actual gathering in of the lost sheep? . . . The message itself shall come from on high, and the Lord, as his custom is, will work through his servants on earth. They will do the work as they are now doing it. The elders of Israel will gather Israel after the Lord comes, on the same basis as at present." (Bruce R. McConkie, *Millennial Messiah*, p. 314.)

Joseph Smith—Matthew 1:38
"Now learn a parable of the fig-tree"

Selected Statements of the First Presidency and the Twelve Apostles

"In giving the Parable of the Fig Tree, Jesus both reveals and keeps hidden the time of his coming. The parable is perfect for his purposes. It announces that he will most assuredly return in the 'season' when the promised signs are shown. But it refrains from specifying the day or the hour when the figs will be harvested, thus leaving men in a state of expectant hope, ever keeping themselves ready for the coming harvest." (Bruce R. McConkie, *Doctrinal New Testament Commentary*, 1:664.)

"The hearts of men in the nations are failing them. Earthquakes are extremely frequent and 'in divers places.' In these and numerous other ways we see the fig tree putting forth its leaves, and we have had the warning. Yet many, if not most, of the inhabitants of the world fail to see anything significant in all of this, and they say that things are going on as they have been doing from the beginning." (Joseph Fielding Smith, *Doctrines of Salvation*, 3:22. See also Melvin J. Ballard, in Conference Report, Oct. 1923, p. 32.)

"Directing their attention to the fig tree and other trees which flourished on the sunny slopes of Olivet, the Master said: 'Behold the fig tree, and all the trees; when they now shoot forth, ye see and know of your own selves that summer is now nigh at hand. So likewise ye, when ye see these things come to pass, know ye that the kingdom of God is nigh at hand.' Of the fig tree in particular the Lord remarked: 'When his branch is yet tender, and putteth forth leaves, ye know that summer is nigh.' This sign of events near at hand was equally applicable to the premonitory conditions which were to herald the fall of Jerusalem and the termination of the Jewish autonomy, and to the developments by which the Lord's second advent shall be immediately preceded." (James E. Talmage, *Jesus the Christ*, p. 574.)

Other Commentary

"Before the second coming of Jesus Christ, certain promised signs and wonders are to take place, making it possible for his Saints to know the approximate time of his coming. . . .

"President Kimball gave this counsel, 'The leaves are commencing to show on the fig tree.' That is prophetic." (Bernard P. Brockbank, in *Ensign*, May 1976, p. 74.)

Joseph Smith—Matthew 1:40
"But of that day, and hour, no one knoweth"

Selected Statements of the First Presidency and the Twelve Apostles

"Each passing year brings us nearer the date of the Lord's coming in power and glory. True, the hour and the day when this great event is to take place, no man knoweth; but all the promised signs indicate that it is not far distant. Meanwhile the duty of the Saints is to watch and work and pray, being valiant for truth, and abounding in good works. Despite the uneasiness and discontent in many parts of the earth, the suspicions and jealousies among the nations, the mounting wave of lawlessness and crime, and the seeming spread of the elements of destruction even in our own beloved country—despite these symptoms denoting the apparent growth of the power of evil, those who continue to stand in holy places can discern through it all the handworking of the Almighty in consummation of His purposes and in furtherance of His will. That which, viewed with the natural eye, is portentous and dreadful, causes no apprehension to those who have faith that whatever happens, the Lord God omnipotent reigneth." (First Presidency: Heber J. Grant, Anthony W. Ivins, and Charles W. Nibley, in James R. Clark, *Messages of the First Presidency*, 5:256.)

"Of the day and the hour of the coming of Christ no man knoweth. It is not yet, neither is it far off; there are prophecies yet to be fulfilled before that event takes place; therefore, let no man deceive the Saints with vain philosophy and false prophecy; for false prophets will arise, and deceive the wicked, and, if possible, the good; but while the wicked fear and tremble at surrounding judgments, the Saints will watch and pray; and, waiting the final event in patience, will look calmly on the passing scenery of a corrupted world, and view transpiring events as confirmation of their faith in the holy gospel which they profess, and rejoice more and more, as multiplied signs shall confirm the approach of the millennial day." (First Presidency: Brigham Young, Heber C. Kimball, and Willard Richards, in James R. Clark, comp., *Messages of the First Presidency*, 2:64. See also Bruce R. McConkie, *Doctrinal New Testament Commentary*, 1:665–67; Bruce R. McConkie, in *Ensign*, May 1979, p. 93.)

Joseph Smith—Matthew 1:41
"As it was in the days of Noah, so it shall be also at the coming of the Son of Man"

Selected Statements of the First Presidency and the Twelve Apostles

"This similitude lets us know that the normal activities of life will continue unabated until the day of cleansing comes, and also that these ordinary activities will be as evil and wicked as they were in that day when men were drowned by the flood lest their evil deeds further offend their Maker.

"Wickedness and evil commenced in the days of Adam; it spread and increased until, by the time of the flood, it covered the earth and contaminated every living soul save Noah and his family. . . . As it was then, so it is today." (Bruce R. McConkie, *Millennial Messiah*, p. 357.)

"That His advent in power and glory is to be sudden and unexpected to the unobserving and sinful world, but in immediate sequence to the signs which the vigilant and devout may read and understand, was made plain by comparison with the prevailing social conditions of Noah's time, when in spite of prophecy and warning the people had continued in their feasting and merry-making, in marrying and giving in marriage, until the very day of Noah's entrance into the ark." (James E. Talmage, *Jesus the Christ*, p. 575.)

"At the coming of Christ—which scoffers would postpone, or deny— there shall come another cleansing of the earth; but the second time by fire. Is not the condition among the people today similar to that in the days of Noah? Did the people believe and repent then? Can you make men, save with few exceptions, believe today that there is any danger?" (Joseph Fielding Smith, *Way to Perfection*, p. 285. See also Joseph Fielding Smith, *Doctrines of Salvation*, 3:20.)

Selected Scripture References

"And they were married, and given in marriage, and were blessed according to the multitude of the promises which the Lord had made unto them." (4 Nephi 1:11.)

Joseph Smith—Matthew 1:44
"Two shall be in the field, the one shall be taken, and the other left"

Selected Statements of the First Presidency and the Twelve Apostles

"In saying that two persons shall be together and one shall be taken and the other left, Jesus is inviting solemn attention to the same awesome truth. When the Lord returns some will be taken and others left, some will abide the day and others will not.

"The key to this seeming mystery is the revealed truth relative to the creation, fall, the coming renewal, and the eventual celestializing of the earth. . . .

"According to the divine program, as long as the earth remains in its telestial or fallen state, men who are living a telestial law—the law of wickedness and carnality—can dwell on its surface. When the earth becomes a terrestrial or millennial globe, then none can remain on its surface unless they conform to at least a terrestrial law. . . .

"Thus those who shall abide the day, who shall remain on the earth when it is transfigured (D&C 63:20-21), are those who are honest and upright and who are living at least that law which would take them to a terrestrial kingdom of glory in the resurrection. Anyone living by telestial standards can no longer remain on earth and so cannot abide the day." (Bruce R. McConkie, *Doctrinal New Testament Commentary*, 1:668-69.)

"These words can be used in a dual way. They can be applied to the destruction of the wicked in the day of burning, when only the righteous abide the day, or they can be applied to the gathering of the remainder of the elect by the angels, when they are caught up to meet their Lord, with those who are unworthy of such a quickening being left on earth." (Bruce R. McConkie, *Millennial Messiah*, p. 687.)

Selected Scripture References

"There shall be two men in one bed; the one shall be taken, and the other shall be left." (Luke 17:34.)

Joseph Smith—Matthew 1:48

"Be ye also ready, for in such an hour as ye think not, the Son of Man cometh"

Selected Statements of the First Presidency and the Twelve Apostles

"Many of us are prone to think that the day of His coming, the day of the setting up of the Kingdom of Heaven in its power and glory is yet far distant. . . . How would you feel if authoritative proclamation were made here today that on the literal morrow, when the sun shall rise again in the east, the Lord would appear in His glory to take vengeance upon the wicked, and to establish His Kingdom upon the earth? Who amongst you would rejoice? The pure in heart would, the righteous in soul would, but many of us would wish to have the event put off. . . . We are very loath to accept and believe that which we do not want to believe, and the world today does not wish to believe that the coming of the Christ is near at hand, and consequently all kinds of subterfuges are invented for explaining away the plain words of scripture. We rejoice in simplicity. The Gospel of Jesus Christ is wonderfully simple. . . . It is the proud and they who do wickedly who close their eyes and their ears and their hearts to the signs of the times, to the word of the Gospel and to the testimony of the Christ. It has long been a favorite excuse of men who were not ready for the advent of the Lord, to say, 'The Lord delayeth His coming.' Don't attach too much importance to the fact that He has thus far delayed His coming, for He has repeatedly told us that the day of His coming is very, very near, even at our doors." (James E. Talmage, in Conference Report, Apr. 1916, pp. 129–30. See also Bruce R. McConkie, *Doctrinal New Testament Commentary*, 1:674–75; Bruce R. McConkie, in *Ensign*, May 1979, p. 92.)

"Brothers and sisters, this is the day the Lord is speaking of. You see the signs are here. Be ye therefore ready. The Brethren have told you in this conference how to prepare to be ready. We have never had a conference where there has been so much direct instruction, so much admonition; when the problems have been defined and also the solution to the problem has been suggested.

"Let us not turn a deaf ear now, but listen to these as the words that have come from the Lord, inspired of him, and we will be safe on Zion's hill, until all that the Lord has for his children shall have been accomplished." (Harold B. Lee, in Conference Report, Oct. 1973, p. 170.)

Joseph Smith—Matthew 1:49
"Who, then, is a faithful and wise servant?"

Selected Statements of the First Presidency and the Twelve Apostles

"Jesus speaks here of his ministers, his servants, the holders of his holy priesthood. They are the ones whom he has made rulers in the household of God to teach and perfect his saints. Theirs is the responsibility to be so engaged when the Master returns. If they are so serving when the Lord comes, he will give them exaltation. But if the rulers in the Lord's house think the Second Coming is far distant, if they forget their charge, contend with their fellow ministers, and begin to live after the manner of the world, then the vengeance of their rejected Lord shall, in justice, fall upon them when he comes again." (Bruce R. McConkie, *Doctrinal New Testament Commentary*, 1:675.)

"The Lord's ministers are appointed to feed the flock of God. 'Blessed is that servant whom his lord, when he cometh, shall find so doing; and verily I say unto you, he shall make him ruler over all his goods.' In the true sense this could only apply to the elders in latter-day Israel who, in fact, are the only legal administrators on earth, whose authority is traced to the Lord, and whose power and authority come in full measure from him." (Bruce R. McConkie, *Millennial Messiah*, p. 688.)

Joseph Smith—Matthew 1:51
"If that evil servant shall say in his heart: My lord delayeth his coming"

Selected Statements of the First Presidency and the Twelve Apostles

"Do not think the Lord delays his coming, for he will come at the appointed time, not the time which I have heard some preach when the earth becomes righteous enough to receive him. I have heard some men in positions and places of trust in the Church preach this, men who are supposed to be acquainted with the word of the Lord, but they failed to comprehend the scriptures. Christ will come in the day of wickedness, when the earth is ripe in iniquity and prepared for the cleansing, and as the cleanser and purifier he will come, and all the wicked will be as stubble and will be consumed." (Joseph Fielding Smith, *Doctrines of Salvation*, 3:3.)

Selected Scripture References

"Woe unto them . . . that say: Let him make speed, and hasten his work, that we may see it: and let the counsel of the Holy One of Israel draw nigh and come, that we may know it!" (Isaiah 5:18–19; 2 Nephi 15:18–19.)

The wicked in the western hemisphere at the time of Christ's birth were saying, "Behold the time is past." (3 Nephi 1:6.)

Joseph Smith—Matthew 1:55
"The end of the earth is not yet, but by and by"

Selected Statements of the First Presidency and the Twelve Apostles

"Jesus, on Olivet, after speaking of unfaithful servants who ate and drank with the drunken, who forsook the labors of their ministry, and who, accordingly, were cut asunder and appointed their portion with the hypocrites, where there was weeping and gnashing of teeth—Jesus said: 'And thus cometh the end of the wicked, according to the prophecy of Moses, saying: They shall be cut off from among the people.' To this Jesus added, 'But the end of the earth is not yet, but by and by,' meaning that the destruction of the wicked is the end of the world but not the end of the earth." (Bruce R. McConkie, *Millennial Messiah*, p. 556.)

Joseph Smith—History

Joseph Smith—History 1:1

"Many reports . . . have been put in circulation by evil-disposed and designing persons"

Selected Statements of the First Presidency and the Twelve Apostles

"We have been asked a good many times, 'Why do you not publish the truth in regard to these lies which are circulated about you?' We might do this if we owned all the papers published in Christendom. Who will publish a letter from me or my brethren? Who will publish the truth from us? If it gets into one paper, it is slipped under the counter or somewhere else; but it never gets into a second. They will send forth lies concerning us very readily. The old adage is that a lie will creep through the keyhole and go a thousand miles while truth is getting out of doors; and our experience has proved this. We have not the influence and power necessary to refute the falsehoods circulated about us. We depend on God, who sits in the heavens." (Brigham Young, *Discourses of Brigham Young*, p. 540.)

"Whenever the servants of the Lord in our day teach and testify that Joseph Smith is a prophet of God, Satan's ministers immediately spew forth a stream of venomous evil and falsehood, belittling, defaming, and opposing that prophet whom the Lord appointed to bring to pass his strange act in the last days. It is their wont to wrest the scriptures, falsify history, and give a false color to the spoken word." (Bruce R. McConkie, *New Witness for the Articles of Faith*, p. 8.)

Joseph Smith—History 1:1
"I have been induced to write this history, to disabuse the public mind"

Selected Statements of the First Presidency and the Twelve Apostles

"In consequence of certain false and slanderous reports which have been circulated, justice would require me to say something upon the private life of one whose character has been so shamefully traduced. By some he is said to have been a lazy, idle, vicious, profligate fellow. These I am prepared to contradict, and that too by the testimony of many persons with whom I have been intimately acquainted, and know to be individuals of the strictest veracity, and unquestionable integrity. All these strictly and virtually agree in saying, that he was an honest, upright, virtuous, and faithfully industrious young man. And those who say to the contrary can be influenced by no other motive than to destroy the reputation of one who never injured any man in either property or person." (Oliver Cowdery, in *Messenger and Advocate*, 2 [Oct. 1835]: 200.)

Joseph Smith—History 1:3
"I was born [23 December 1805] in the town of Sharon, Windsor County, State of Vermont"

Selected Statements of the First Presidency and the Twelve Apostles

"This modern man, with a most ordinary name, our revered and honored Prophet Joseph Smith, began his mortal life on December 23, 1805, in Sharon, Windsor County, Vermont. He was born with all of the scriptural talents and capacities he had acquired through long ages of obedience and progression among his fellow prophets. Men are not born equal in talents and capacities; mortality commences where preexistence ends, and the talents earned in the life that went before are available for use in this mortal life." (Bruce R. McConkie, *New Witness for the Articles of Faith*, p. 4.)

Other Commentary

"After selling the farm at Tunbridge, we moved only a short distance to the town of Royalton. Here we resided a few months, then moved again to Sharon, Windsor county, Vermont. In the latter place my husband rented a farm of my father, which he cultivated in the summer, teaching school in the winter. In this way my husband continued laboring for a few years, during which time our circumstances gradually improved until we found ourselves quite comfortable again." (Lucy Mack Smith, *History of Joseph Smith*, p. 46.)

Joseph Smith—History 1:3
"My father, Joseph Smith, Sen., left the State of Vermont, and moved to Palmyra"

Selected Statements of the First Presidency and the Twelve Apostles

"Continued sickness pursued the family for a year; this, together with three successive years of crop failure, placed the family in rather straitened circumstances. So discouraged did they become that the decision was reached to move to the milder climate and more fertile region of western New York, where there would be a better opportunity to retrieve their fortunes.

"As soon as arrangements could be made and obligations settled, Joseph Smith and family moved to Palmyra, New York, a distance of about three hundred miles from their home in New Hampshire. . . . It should be remembered that western New York, at that time, was sparsely settled." (Joseph Fielding Smith, *Essentials in Church History*, p. 38.)

"As I stood at the Smith home, I thought of the early struggles of the family, and wondered what means the Lord might have used to get them to move from Vermont or New Hampshire, if they had not been forced from these states by poverty. Their poverty was not the result of indolence, as the wicked have proclaimed, but the poverty and reverses of Providence, sent to give experience and to lead the family to a better land where the Lord could perform his work through the youthful Seer, yet to be raised up." (Joseph Fielding Smith, *Doctrines of Salvation*, 3:241.)

Other Commentary

"It was in these places, Palmyra and Manchester, and in the midst of these family struggles for existence and these sorrows, that the boyhood of Joseph Smith, the Prophet, was spent. Western and much even of central New York was a wilderness in those years. Rochester, some twenty miles to the northwest of Palmyra, in 1815, consisted of but two or three log houses. The region was known as 'the western wilderness,' and two years before the arrival of the Smiths the Indians had 'desolated the whole Niagara frontier.' " (B. H. Roberts, *Comprehensive History of the Church*, 1:36.)

Joseph Smith—History 1:5
"There was in the place where we lived an unusual excitement on the subject of religion"

Selected Statements of the First Presidency and the Twelve Apostles

"Western New York in the early nineteenth century was essentially frontier territory, a place of opportunity to those for whom the tremendous task of clearing and breaking the virgin land held little fear. Among these were Joseph and Lucy Mack Smith and their eight children, who in 1816 came to the vicinity of Palmyra, not far from Rochester.

"They were a typical New England family of English and Scottish extraction who prized the independence their fathers on both lines had fought for in the American Revolution of 1776. And they were religious folk who read the Bible and had family prayer, although like many of their kind they belonged to no church.

"This condition among the people of the frontier areas of America became a matter of serious concern to religious leaders, and a crusade was begun to convert the unconverted. It was carried over a vast area from the New England states to Kentucky. In 1820 it reached western New York. The ministers of the various denominations united in their efforts, and many conversions were made among the scattered settlers. One week a Rochester paper noted: 'More than 200 souls have become hopeful subjects of divine grace in Palmyra, Macedon, Manchester, Lyons and Ontario since the late revival commenced.' The week following it was able to report 'that in Palmyra and Macedon . . . more than four hundred souls have already confessed that the Lord is good.' " (Gordon B. Hinckley, *Truth Restored*, pp. 1–2.)

"In the accounts of the Prophet and his mother, Lucy Mack Smith, there is also considerable historical background which has been confirmed by secondary sources as being accurate. As an example, the Prophet refers in the published account of the First Vision to the religious fervor in the area where the Smith family was living at the time. Among others, Brigham Young later affirmed: 'I very well recollect the reformation which took place in the country among the various denominations of Christians—the Baptists, Methodists, Presbyterians, and others—when Joseph was a boy.' (*Journal of Discourses*, 12:67.)" (James E. Faust, in *Ensign*, May 1984, p. 68.)

Joseph Smith—History 1:5

"Some crying, 'Lo, here!' and others, 'Lo, there!' "

Selected Statements of the First Presidency and the Twelve Apostles

"To prepare for the day of burning which was to be, a spirit of religious concern and unrest swept the frontier areas where the Lord's future prophet dwelt in peaceful obscurity. The ministers of a decadent Christendom plied their trade with fanatical valor. Their cries went forth, ' "Lo, here is Christ" and, "lo, there." ' [Joseph Smith—History 1:50.]

"Each professor of religion used all his powers of reason and sophistry to gain converts to his particular system of salvation." (Bruce R. McConkie, in *Ensign*, Nov. 1975, p. 16.)

Joseph Smith—History 1:6

"All their good feelings . . . were entirely lost in a strife of words and a contest about opinions"

Selected Statements of the First Presidency and the Twelve Apostles

"For a length of time the reformation seemed to move in a harmonious manner, but, as the excitement ceased, or those who had expressed anxieties, had professed a belief in the pardoning influence and condescension of the Savior, a general struggle was made by the leading characters of the different sects, for proselytes. Then strife seemed to take the place of that apparent union and harmony which had previously characterized the moves and exhortations of the old professors, and a cry—I am right—you are wrong—was introduced in their stead." (Oliver Cowdery, in *Messenger and Advocate*, 1 [Dec. 1834]: 42.)

Other Commentary

"There was a great revival in religion, which extended to all the denominations of Christians in the surrounding country in which we resided. Many of the world's people, becoming concerned about the salvation of their souls, came forward and presented themselves as seekers after religion. Most of them were desirous of uniting with some church, but were not decided as to the particular faith which they would adopt. When the numerous meetings were about breaking up, and the candidates and the various leading church members began to consult upon the subject of adopting the candidates into some church or churches, as the case might be, a dispute arose, and there was a great contention among them.

"While these things were going forward, Joseph's mind became considerably troubled with regard to religion." (Lucy Mack Smith, *History of Joseph Smith*, pp. 68–69.)

"Revival encampments as well as other revival services were often held as 'union services.' That is, the different sects would unite for the conversion of those who had made no profession of christianity, and for the reclamation of backsliders; for with the passing away of the excitement under which they professed religion, the converts all too frequently experienced a reversion to the worldly life, and there were many backsliders. It frequently happened, however, that the good feelings engendered during the union revival services were dissipated by jealousies and wranglings when the converts came to elect the religious body in which they desired to hold their fellowship; for notwithstanding it was nominally held that membership in any one of the Christian sects styled 'orthodox,' was all-sufficient for proper church connection, it was in those times—and especially in the states and parts of states herein designated, one of the inconsistencies of Protestant christendom that there was a sharp rivalry, and bitterness between the sects save only when hostilities were suspended on such occasions as those mentioned above. There were cries of 'lo, here! here is Christ'; to which the response—'nay, but lo, here! here is Christ!' Fierce debates followed, and great divisions in judgment obtained as to what even constituted the essentials of christianity. Grave doubts perplexed the minds of many people, and hindered the progress of religion." (B. H. Roberts, *Comprehensive History of the Church*, 1: 50–51.)

Joseph Smith—History 1:7
"My father's family was proselyted to the Presbyterian faith"

Other Commentary

"The question 'which of the sects shall we join,' had been a problem in the Smith household even before their removal from Vermont. Lucy Smith was baptized in that state by a minister who was willing to leave to her the question of choosing the sect she would join, and to a time subsequent to her baptism. During the family's residence in Tunbridge, Lucy's desire to be identified with some one or other of the churches became acute; but, owing to the disagreeable feelings which such a step seemed likely to engender among their friends, and especially with the eldest brother of Joseph Smith, Sen.—Jesse Smith,—she abandoned, for the time being, her desire. In 1820, however, when the religious revival that swept through the Western Reserve and New York state reached Palmyra, she determined upon membership in the Presbyterian church, and in this was followed by her sons Hyrum and Samuel Harrison, and by her daughter Sophronia. Joseph Smith, the future Prophet of the New Dispensation, inclined to the Methodist persuasion, but did not join their church. The father held aloof from formal connection with any of the sects, but was none the less a staunch, Christian man." (B. H. Roberts, *Comprehensive History of the Church*, 1:34-35.)

Joseph Smith—History 1:10

"Who of all these parties are right; or, are they all wrong together?"

Selected Statements of the First Presidency and the Twelve Apostles

"After strong solicitations to unite with one of those different societies, and seeing the apparent proselyting disposition manifested with equal warmth from each, his mind was led to more seriously contemplate the importance of a move of this kind. To profess godliness without its benign influence upon the heart, was a thing so foreign from his feelings, that his spirit was not at rest day nor night. To unite with a society professing to be built upon the only sure foundation, and that profession be a vain one, was calculated, in its very nature, the more it was contemplated, the more to arouse the mind to the serious consequences of moving hastily, in a course fraught with eternal realities. To say he was right, and still be wrong, could not profit; and amid so many, some must be built upon the sand." (Oliver Cowdery, in *Messenger and Advocate*, 1 [Dec. 1834]: 43.)

Joseph Smith—History 1:11

"I was one day reading the Epistle of James, first chapter and fifth verse"

Selected Statements of the First Presidency and the Twelve Apostles

"This single verse of scripture has had a greater impact and a more far reaching effect upon mankind than any other single sentence ever recorded by any prophet in any age. It might well be said that the crowning act of the ministry of James was not his martyrdom for the testimony of Jesus, but his recitation, as guided by the Holy Ghost, of these simple words which led to the opening of the heavens in modern times.

"And it might well be added that every investigator of revealed truth stands, at some time in the course of his search, in the place where Joseph Smith stood. He must turn to the Almighty and gain wisdom from God by revelation if he is to gain a place on that strait and narrow path which leads to eternal life." (Bruce R. McConkie, *Doctrinal New Testament Commentary*, 3: 246-47.)

Other Commentary

"The Reverend Mr. Lane of the Methodist church preached a sermon on the subject, 'What church shall I join?' He quoted the golden text of James—

" 'If any of you lack wisdom, let him ask of God that giveth to all men liberally and up-braideth not, and it shall be given him.'

"The text made a deep impression on the mind of the Prophet. He read it on returning home, and pondered it deeply. Here was a message from the word of God. A message to all men; but to him especially, since he had been made to feel that of all men he lacked wisdom, in respect of a matter to him vital." (B. H. Roberts, *Comprehensive History of the Church*, 1:52–53.)

Joseph Smith—History 1:12

"Never did any passage of scripture come with more power to the heart of man than this did at this time to mine"

Selected Statements of the First Presidency and the Twelve Apostles

"Joseph Smith was the noble and great one who had been prepared from all eternity to receive the heaven-sent word, 'Never did any passage of scripture come with more power to the heart of man,' he said, 'than this did at this time to mine.' (Joseph Smith—History 1:12.) The Spirit of God rested mightily upon him. Not even Enoch and Abraham and Moses and the ancient prophets had been overpowered by such yearnings for truth and salvation as then filled Joseph's soul. As guided from on high, he retired to the place before appointed by the Lord of heaven and there began to offer up to God the desires of his heart." (Bruce R. McConkie, *New Witness for the Articles of Faith*, p. 5.)

"Revelation comes to men in an unlimited number of ways. Three separate mediums are mentioned in the first recorded account of revelation—the spoken word, the visitation of angels, and the power of the Holy Ghost. . . .

"Another medium is an impelling impulse of the nature received by the Prophet when he read James 1:5." (Marion G. Romney, in *Improvement Era*, June 1964, p. 506.)

Joseph Smith—History 1:13

"I came to the conclusion that I must either remain in darkness and confusion, or else I must do as James directs"

Selected Statements of the First Presidency and the Twelve Apostles

"This budding prophet had no preconceived false notions and beliefs. He was not steeped in the traditions and legends and superstitions and fables of the centuries. He had nothing to unlearn. He prayed for knowledge and direction. The powers of darkness preceded the light. When he knelt in solitude in the silent forest, his earnest prayer brought on a battle royal which threatened his destruction. For centuries, Lucifer with unlimited dominion had fettered men's minds. He could ill-afford to lose his satanic hold. This threatened his unlimited dominion. . . .

" . . . For this young boy, clean, free from all antagonistic and distorted ideas and with a sincere desire to find the truth, knelt in a secluded spot in a New York forest and poured out his soul to God, and with a faith the size of mountains he asked serious questions that none of the sects upon the earth had been able to fully answer.

"A new truth, a concept not understood by the myriads of people on the earth, burst forth, and in that moment there was only one man on the face of the whole earth who knew with an absolute assurance that God was a personal being, that the Father and Son were separate individuals with bodies of flesh and bones [and that he] had been created in their image. As the Son was in the image of his Father, the Father God was the same kind of image as the Son." (Spencer W. Kimball, *Teachings of Spencer W. Kimball*, pp. 428–29.)

Joseph Smith—History 1:14

"In accordance with this, my determination to ask of God, I retired to the woods to make the attempt"

Selected Statements of the First Presidency and the Twelve Apostles

"He must ask of God, as all men must, and ask he did. He walked a short distance from his country home to a secluded place in a grove of trees. There, alone, he knelt and prayed, pouring out his soul to his Maker, offering up the desires of his heart to God.

"This was the hour of destiny and hope. Amid the gloom of apostate darkness a light would shine forth. Creation's decree, the great proclamation—'Let there be light'—was to be issued anew. The light of the gospel, the light of the Everlasting Word, would soon shed its rays o'er all the earth." (Bruce R. McConkie, in *Ensign*, Nov. 1975, p. 18.)

Joseph Smith—History 1:14

"Early in the spring of eighteen hundred and twenty"

Selected Statements of the First Presidency and the Twelve Apostles

"The occurrence of which we desire more particularly to speak, and which ranks in importance alongside the greatest verities of revealed religion, is one that took place in a grove of trees near Palmyra, New York, on a beautiful, clear day early in the spring of 1820. Was it on the sixth of April? Perhaps—such at least is the tradition. But be that as it may, what transpired at that time was destined to affect the salvation of the billions of our Father's children." (Bruce R. McConkie, in *Ensign*, Nov. 1975, p. 15.)

Joseph Smith—History 1:14-19
The First Vision

Selected Statements of the First Presidency and the Twelve Apostles

"There has been no event more glorious, more controversial, nor more important in the story of Joseph Smith than this vision. It is possibly the most singular event to occur on the earth since the Resurrection. Those who do not believe it happened find it difficult to explain away. Too much has happened since its occurrence to summarily deny that it ever took place." (James E. Faust, in *Ensign*, May 1984, p. 67.)

"What was learned from the First Vision?

"1. The existence of God our Father as a personal being, and proof that man was made in the image of God.

"2. That Jesus is a personage, separate and distinct from the Father.

"3. That Jesus Christ is declared by the Father to be his Son.

"4. That Jesus was the conveyer of revelation as taught in the Bible.

"5. The promise of James to ask of God for wisdom was fulfilled.

"6. The reality of an actual being from an unseen world who tried to destroy Joseph Smith.

"7. That there was a falling away from the Church established by Jesus Christ—Joseph was told not to join any of the sects, for they taught the doctrines of men.

"8. Joseph Smith became a witness for God and his Son, Jesus Christ." (James E. Faust, in *Ensign*, May 1984, p. 68.)

Joseph Smith—History 1:15-16
"I was seized upon by some power which entirely overcame me"

Selected Statements of the First Presidency and the Twelve Apostles

"He therefore, retired to a secret place in a grove, but a short distance from his father's house, and knelt down, and began to call upon the Lord. At first, he was severely tempted by the powers of darkness, which endeavored to overcome him; but he continued to seek for deliverance, until darkness gave way from his mind, and he was enabled to pray in fervency of the spirit, and in faith." (Orson Pratt, as quoted in Milton V. Backman, Jr., *Joseph Smith's First Vision*, pp. 171-72.)

"Such are the ways of Satan that when the God of heaven seeks to send the greatest light of the ages into the world, the forces of evil oppose it with the deepest darkness and iniquity of their benighted realm. Lucifer, our common enemy, fought the promised restoration as he now fights the accomplished restoration." (Bruce R. McConkie, in *Ensign*, Nov. 1975, p. 18.)

See Selected Statements under Moses 1:20.

Joseph Smith—History 1:16
"I saw a pillar of light exactly over my head"

Selected Statements of the First Presidency and the Twelve Apostles

"Just as prayer is the means by which men address the Lord, so revelation is the means by which God communicates to men. In doing so, He uses various means. The spoken word, for example, was the method He used to answer Adam's prayer . . .

"In addition to the spoken word, the Lord at times appears personally. . . .

"Sometimes the Lord sends personal representatives to communicate with men. He sent Moroni, for example, to visit and instruct the Prophet Joseph Smith several times. [See Joseph Smith—History 1:28-59.] . . .

"On other occasions the Lord has communicated with men by means of dreams and visions. . . .

"Most often, however, revelation comes to us by means of the still, small voice." (Marion G. Romney, in Conference Report, Apr. 1978, pp. 75-76.)

"A pillar of fire appeared above my head; which presently rested down upon me, and filled me with unspeakable joy. A personage appeared in the midst of this pillar of flame, which was spread all around and yet nothing consumed. Another personage soon appeared like unto the first: he said unto me thy sins are forgiven thee." (Joseph Smith, "1835 Recital of the First Vision," as recorded by Warren Cowdery, in Milton V. Backman, Jr., *Joseph Smith's First Vision*, p. 159.)

Joseph Smith—History 1:17
"When the light rested upon me I saw two Personages"

Selected Statements of the First Presidency and the Twelve Apostles

"The God of all these worlds and the Son of God, the Redeemer, our Savior, in person attended this boy. He saw the living God. He saw the living Christ. Few of all the man-creation had ever glimpsed such a vision—Peter, James, and John, yes, and Moses, Abraham, and Adam, but few others. Joseph now belonged to an elite group—the tried and trusted, and true. He was in a select society of persons whom Abraham describes as 'noble and great ones' that were 'good' and that were to become the Lord's rulers. (Abraham 3:22-23.)" (Spencer W. Kimball, *Teachings of Spencer W. Kimball*, p. 430.)

"It was necessary in the very outset of this work that there should be a revelation of this character. Up to that time men for generations had been ignorant of the character of God. It was believed, as many now believe, that He was a Being diffused through space—a spiritual Being, without an entity or without a tabernacle. But the first revelation that was given in our day, in answer to the prayer of the boy, Joseph Smith, Jun., and seemingly the most necessary one that could be given to lay the foundation of faith in the human mind, was the appearance of God the Father and His Son Jesus Christ. . . .

"There were two Personages appeared unto Joseph Smith, Jun.,— God the Father and His Son Jesus Christ. Whatever errors had existed, whatever doubts had prevailed up to that time concerning the being of God were swept away, never to return." (George Q. Cannon, *Gospel Truth*, 1:130.)

"There is no account in history or revelation extant, where ever before both the Father and the Son appeared in the presence of mortal man in glory. Most wonderful was the honor bestowed upon this unsophisticated boy. Great was his faith—so great that he was able, like the brother of Jared, to penetrate the veil and behold the glory of these holy Beings, whose glory rested upon him. Without this power overshadowing him, he could not have endured their presence, for their brightness was far greater than the brightness of the noonday sun. . . . Joseph Smith, through the power of the Lord, was able to behold the presence of the Great Creator and his Glorified Son, for they deigned to honor him, with their presence and converse with him." (Joseph Fielding Smith, *Essentials in Church History*, pp. 46-47. See also Bruce R. McConkie, *New Witness for the Articles of Faith*, pp. 72-73; Joseph Fielding Smith, *Doctrines of Salvation*, 1:2.)

Joseph Smith—History 1:17
"Whose brightness and glory defy all description"

Selected Statements of the First Presidency and the Twelve Apostles

"We may after baptism and confirmation become companions of the Holy Ghost who will teach us the ways of the Lord, quicken our minds and help us to understand the truth. The people of the world do not receive the gift of the Holy Ghost.

"Joseph Smith did not have the gift of the Holy Ghost at the time of the First Vision, but he was overshadowed by the Holy Ghost; otherwise, he could not have beheld the Father and the Son." (Joseph Fielding Smith, *Doctrines of Salvation*, 1:42–43.)

See Selected Statements and Scripture References under Moses 1:11.

Joseph Smith—History 1:17
"This is My Beloved Son. Hear Him!"

Selected Statements of the First Presidency and the Twelve Apostles

"I would like to call your attention to one little thing in the first vision of the Prophet Joseph Smith. It is very significant, and Joseph Smith did not know it. If he had been perpetrating a fraud, he would not have thought of it. You will recall in your reading that the Father and the Son appeared, and the Father introduced the Son and told the Prophet to hear the Son.

"Now suppose the Prophet had come back from the woods and had said the Father and the Son appeared to him, and the Father said, 'Joseph, what do you want?' and when he asked the question and told him what he wanted, the Father had answered him; then we would know that the story of the Prophet could not be true.

"All revelation comes through Jesus Christ." (Joseph Fielding Smith, *Answers to Gospel Questions*, 1:16.)

" '*This is My Beloved Son. Hear Him!*' Have more blessed words ever saluted human ears? Is it not again as it was at Bethabara when John baptized the Lamb of God who takes away the sin of the world? Is it not once more as it was when the Son of God was transfigured before the chief of his ancient apostles? The voice of God is heard again! The Father bears witness of the Son and introduces him to the world!" (Bruce R. McConkie, *New Witness for the Articles of Faith*, p. 6.)

Joseph Smith—History 1:18

"I asked the Personages who stood above me in the light, which of all the sects was right"

Selected Statements of the First Presidency and the Twelve Apostles

"Joseph Smith sought seclusion, by himself, alone, as a teenage individual to attempt to pray. He asked the Lord two questions: first, which of all the churches is true, and next, which he should join. These two questions are appropriate for every teenager to ask, those of you who are in the Church and those of you who are seeking after truth. Now, if you have the inclination or the desire to find out for yourselves, you are entering in by the way." (Boyd K. Packer, in *Improvement Era*, Dec. 1962, p. 926.)

Other Commentary

"It gives evidence of the intellectual tenacity of Joseph Smith that in the midst of all these bewildering occurrences he held clearly in his mind the purpose for which he had come to this secluded spot, the object he had in view in seeking the Lord. As soon, therefore, as he could get sufficient self-possession to speak, he asked the Personages in whose resplendent presence he stood, which of the sects was right, and which he should join." (B. H. Roberts, *Comprehensive History of the Church*, 1:54.)

"His seeking knowledge from God upon this very question—'which of all the sects is right?' is a confession of his own inability to determine the matter. No human wisdom was sufficient to answer that question. No man in all the world was so preeminent as to be justified in proclaiming out of his own wisdom the divine acceptance of one church in preference to another, or God's rejection of them all. Divine wisdom alone was sufficient to pass judgment upon such a question as that. And there is peculiar force in the circumstance that the announcement which Joseph Smith makes with reference to this subject is not formulated by him nor by any other man, but is given to him of God. God has been the judge of the status of modern christendom, Joseph Smith but his messenger, to herald that judgment to the world." (B. H. Roberts, *Comprehensive History of the Church*, 1:62.)

Joseph Smith—History 1:19

"I was answered that I must join none of them, for they were all wrong"

Selected Statements of the First Presidency and the Twelve Apostles

"We are there when the heavens open. There is a pillar of light. Two Personages, 'whose brightness and glory defy all description,' stand above the seeking seer-to-be. The Father testifies of his Beloved Son and commands, '*Hear Him!*' Joseph asks which of all the sects is right and which he should join. The word that comes back from the Son of God causes the very pillars of Christendom to totter and sway. Joseph is to 'join none of them,' for they are 'all wrong.' Some words are spoken about creeds that are an abomination in the Lord's sight and about professors of religion who are corrupt and whose hearts are far removed from divine standards. (JS–H 1: 16–19.) Thus is ushered in the dispensation of the fulness of times; it comes in a day when all churches are false; it is a day in which Satan has power over his own dominions." (Bruce R. McConkie, *Millennial Messiah*, p. 57. See also Bruce R. McConkie, *New Witness for the Articles of Faith*, p. 141; B. H. Roberts, *Comprehensive History of the Church*, 1:60–61.)

Joseph Smith—History 1:19

"Those professors were all corrupt; . . . they teach for doctrines the commandments of men, having a form of godliness, but they deny the power thereof"

Selected Statements of the First Presidency and the Twelve Apostles

"In the early centuries of the Christian era, the apostasy came not through persecution, but by relinquishment of faith caused by the superimposing of a man-made structure upon and over the divine program. Many men with no pretense nor claim to revelation, speaking without divine authority or revelation, depending only upon their own brilliant minds, but representing as they claim the congregations of the Christians and in long conference and erudite councils, sought the creation process to make a God which all could accept. . . .

" . . . They replaced the simple ways and program of the Christ with spectacular rituals, colorful display, impressive pageantry, and limitless pomposity, and called it Christianity. They had replaced the glorious, divine plan of exaltation of Christ with an elaborate, colorful, man-made system. They seemed to have little idea of totally dethroning the Christ, nor terminating the life of God, as in our own day, but they put together an incomprehensible God idea." (Spencer W. Kimball, *Teachings of Spencer W. Kimball*, p. 425.)

"No man, in and of himself, without the aid of the Spirit of God and the direction of revelation, can found a religion, or promulgate a body of doctrine, in all particulars in harmony with revealed truth. If he has not the inspiration of the Lord and the direction of messengers from his presence, he will not comprehend the truth, and therefore such truth as he teaches will be hopelessly mixed with error. This is proved to be the case with many professed founders of religious creeds. Their teachings cannot be made to square themselves with the revelations of Jesus Christ and his prophets." (Joseph Fielding Smith, *Doctrines of Salvation*, 1:189.)

"Apostasy and false churches go hand in hand; they aid and abet each other. When men forsake the gospel they find a form of godliness in churches of their own creation, and these churches teach doctrines that sustain men in their apostasy. . . .

" . . . [The Book of Mormon] shall come forth and go to the world in a day when there are churches for homosexuals, churches that accept adulterers, churches containing murderers, and even churches for those who worship Satan. It shall come in a day when there shall be churches for sinners who imagine their sins are remitted, without any act on their part, simply because Christ died for sinners." (Bruce R. McConkie, *Millennial Messiah*, pp. 60–61.)

"The world crisis we now face is upon us precisely because men have been and now are seeking the abundant life, for men, and peace among nations—the fruits of looking to God—by preaching the doctrine of the fatherhood of God and the brotherhood of man without actually believing them. Of such, the Lord says, ' . . . they draw near to me with their lips, but their hearts are far from me, . . . ' (Joseph Smith 2:19.) . . .

"The need for us to look to God, however, in order to live is inherent in the very nature of man and his environment. It is not founded on arbitrary command but on universal law." (Marion G. Romney, in Conference Report, Oct. 1962, p. 94.)

Other Commentary

" 'Those professors are all corrupt' . . . should not be taken as referring to the whole body of Christians; but rather as referring to the teachers of their creeds—the 'professors;' that term not being used in the sense of 'confessors' of the creeds, who merely accept doctrine from the teachings of the 'professors'—the following and not the leaders.

"This distinction is justified from the immediate context of the passage: 'they (the 'professors') draw near to me with their lips, but their hearts are far from me; *they* (the 'professors') *teach for doctrine the commandments of men.*' This context clearly proves that the charge of 'corruption' is limited at least to the 'teachers,' not to the whole body of Christians. Moreover, I am convinced myself that the declaration is still further limited to the 'professors' who founded, and by that act taught to the world the creeds that are an 'abomination' in the sight of

God—a fact not at all difficult of belief, or of proof, upon an analysis of the creeds themselves. And those who originally could form such conceptions of God and man, and the purpose of human existence, as the creeds teach, were certainly men of warped understanding, men of perverted, or 'corrupted' minds." (B. H. Roberts, *Comprehensive History of the Church*, 1:61.)

Joseph Smith—History 1:20
"Many other things did he say unto me, which I cannot write at this time"

Selected Statements of the First Presidency and the Twelve Apostles

"The message that Joseph received from the Father and the Son was that the full truth was not upon the earth and that he should not affiliate with the religions of the day, as well as other things of transcending importance which were not written.

"Joseph stated in that account: 'Many other things did he say unto me, which I cannot write at this time.' (JS–H 1:20.) Obviously, Joseph was overwhelmed by the occasion and the instructions he received." (James E. Faust, in *Ensign*, May 1984, p. 67.)

"But on another occasion the Prophet was permitted to write one of these other things. He was told, in effect, that if he remained faithful and true, he would be the instrument in the hands of the Lord to restore the everlasting gospel. In process of time he became that instrument; he received revelation upon revelation; heavenly ministers visited him; keys and powers, rights and prerogatives were restored, until the gospel in its fulness had been given again, which means that everything had been restored that was needed to enable men to gain a fulness of exaltation hereafter. The Church of Jesus Christ of Latter-day Saints was set up, and the power of God was again manifest to men on the earth." (Bruce R. McConkie, in *Improvement Era*, Dec. 1962, p. 908.)

Joseph Smith—History 1:21
"There were no such things as visions or revelations in these days"

Selected Statements of the First Presidency and the Twelve Apostles

"When we stop to reflect, it is not strange that this message of light and truth should be rejected by the world, for the Lord had said long years before, 'Men love darkness rather than light, because their deeds are evil.' As for the priests, was not their craft in danger? The message left with the youthful seer by the God of heaven was most drastic. It had been declared in language that could be clearly understood, that the creeds of men were not in accord with his Gospel. This was not a message to please the religious teachers of the day. Moreover, the vision had shattered the traditions of the times. The doctrines taught in the churches were emphatically contradicted and disproved. The world was teaching and believing that the canon of scripture was full; that there was not to be and could not be, more revelation; that the visitation of angels had ceased with the early Christian fathers, and such things as these had passed away forever. Again, the doctrine was taught that the Father, Son and Holy Ghost were incomprehensible, without body, parts and passions. A revelation of the Father and the Son as separate persons, each with a body tangible and in the form of the body of man, was destructive of this doctrine, as revelation was of the doctrine of the closed heavens. The world had held that perfection in religion and the organization of the Church of Christ was not to be expected, but that men were led by their own human reason to interpret the word of the Lord as set forth in the scriptures." (Joseph Fielding Smith, *Essentials in Church History*, pp. 48–49.)

Joseph Smith—History 1:21

"He treated my communication not only lightly, but with great contempt, saying it was all of the devil"

Selected Statements of the First Presidency and the Twelve Apostles

"As might be expected, so unusual a story caused considerable excitement. In good faith he spoke of it to one of the preachers who had been engaged in the revival. The boy was taken aback when the man treated the story with contempt, telling him that such things were of the devil, that all visions and revelations had ceased with the apostles, 'and that there would never be any more of them.' Nor was this the end of the matter for the young boy. He soon found himself singled out for ridicule; and men, who ordinarily would have paid little attention to such a young lad, took pains to revile him. It was a source of great sorrow to him." (Gordon B. Hinckley, *Truth Restored*, p. 5.)

"God the Father and his Son Jesus Christ revealed themselves to Joseph Smith in a marvelous vision. After that glorious event, Joseph Smith told a minister about it. Joseph was surprised to hear the minister say that there were no such things as visions or revelations in these days, that all such things had ceased. [See Joseph Smith—History 1:21.]

"This remark symbolizes practically all of the objections that have ever been made against the Church by nonmembers and dissident members alike. Namely, they do not believe that God reveals his will today to the Church through prophets of God. All objections, whether they be on abortion, plural marriage, seventh-day worship, etc., basically hinge on whether Joseph Smith and his successors were and are prophets of God receiving divine revelation." (Ezra Taft Benson, in Conference Report, Apr. 1975, p. 95.)

Joseph Smith—History 1:22

"I soon found, however, that my telling the story had excited a great deal of prejudice against me among professors of religion"

Selected Statements of the First Presidency and the Twelve Apostles

"Joseph soon declared this marvelous experience to others outside his family. As a result, much ridicule, contempt, and even hatred were visited upon him. His mother, Lucy Mack Smith, relates that after the First Vision, 'from this time until the twenty-first of September, 1823, Joseph continued, as usual, to labor with his father, and nothing during this interval occurred of very great importance—though he suffered every kind of opposition and persecution from the different orders of religionists.' (*History of Joseph Smith by His Mother*, p. 74.)" (James E. Faust, in *Ensign*, May 1984, p. 67.)

"No wonder Joseph Smith rejoiced, he now possessed greater knowledge than all the professors and diviners in all the world! Naturally he desired that others should share his joy and partake of his wonderful information. He would proclaim it to them with gladness, surely they would be pleased to receive it and would rejoice with him! But great disappointment awaited him, for with one accord his message was rejected. Only the members of his household would believe. He was treated with scorn by great men of learning, although he was but a boy. He was mocked and shamed. Instead of the spirit of love and gratefulness following him for revealing this glorious message of truth, it was the spirit of contempt and hatred with which he had to contend. In sorrow he learned to hold his peace and wait—wait for further light and inspiration which he had been promised. Though all the world would mock and former friends deride, he knew he had beheld the vision. There was one Friend to whom he now could go and pour out his soul in humble hope of encouragement and succor. What did it matter though the whole world should laugh, if the Son of God would hearken to his humble pleadings?" (Joseph Fielding Smith, *Essentials in Church History*, pp. 47-48.)

"Why should so many religionists unite against an unknown youth of no renown or standing in the community? Would the whole sectarian world shiver and shake and call for a sword if some other unknown fourteen-year-old youth in an obscure frontier village should claim that he was visited by angels and that he saw the Lord? The problem when Joseph Smith announced such a claim was that it was true and that Lucifer knew of its verity." (Bruce R. McConkie, *New Witness for the Articles of Faith*, pp. 8-9.)

Other Commentary

"His experience indicated how far removed men were from a sincere belief in those scriptures so frequently found upon their lips. Here a text of scripture had been used as the foundation of a public discourse upon a most important subject. A subsequent reading of it had deepened the impression made upon the mind of a sincere believer in the scriptures, until it became to him a veritable message from the word of God— the voice of God to his soul. He acted upon the message thus received. That act of faith brought forth its results, which were now ridiculed and denounced by the teachers of the word of God." (B. H. Roberts, *Comprehensive History of the Church*, 1:56.)

Joseph Smith—History 1:25

"I could not deny it, neither dared I do it; at least I knew that by so doing I would offend God, and come under condemnation"

Selected Statements of the First Presidency and the Twelve Apostles

"Members of the Church are sometimes guilty of the same sins that afflict fallen man generally. When they are, their condemnation is greater than it otherwise would be, because of their greater light and knowledge. In addition, many acts become sinful for the saints that would not be so considered had they not taken upon themselves the obligations of the gospel." (Bruce R. McConkie, *New Witness for the Articles of Faith*, p. 225.)

Joseph Smith—History 1:26

"I had found the testimony of James to be true—that a man

who lacked wisdom might ask of God, and obtain, and not be upbraided"

Selected Statements of the First Presidency and the Twelve Apostles

"Another day dawned, another soul with passionate yearning prayed for divine guidance. A spot of hidden solitude was found, knees were bended, hearts were humbled, pleadings were voiced, and a light brighter than the noonday sun illuminated the world—the curtain never to be closed again, the gate never again to be slammed, this light never again to be extinguished. A young lad of incomparable faith broke the spell, shattered the 'heavens of iron' and reestablished communication. Heaven kissed the earth, light dissipated the darkness, and God again spake to man revealing 'his secret unto his servants the prophets.' (Amos 3:7.) A new prophet was in the land, and through him God set up his kingdom—a kingdom never to be destroyed nor left to another people—a kingdom that will stand forever." (Spencer W. Kimball, *Teachings of Spencer W. Kimball*, pp. 424-25.)

"On the great problem that had perplexed him, Joseph Smith's mind was now settled. He joined none of the churches that had sought his interest. And more important, he had learned that the promise of James was true: One who lacked wisdom might ask of God, and obtain, and not be upbraided." (Gordon B. Hinckley, *Truth Restored*, p. 6.)

Joseph Smith—History 1:27
"I continued to pursue my common vocations in life"

Selected Statements of the First Presidency and the Twelve Apostles

"Life for Joseph Smith was never the same once he had told the story of his vision. For one thing, that remarkable experience had left an indelible impression upon him. The knowledge he had thus received placed him in a unique position. Nevertheless, his manner of living was not greatly different from that of the ordinary farm boy of his day, except that he was often made an object of ridicule. But he continued to work on his father's farm, to work for others in the area, and to associate with companions of his own age. Those acquainted with him describe him as a strong, active boy of cheerful disposition, who enjoyed wrestling and other sports." (Gordon B. Hinckley, *Truth Restored*, p. 7.)

Joseph Smith—History 1:29

"On the evening of the above-mentioned twenty-first of September"

Other Commentary

"There was an interval of more than three years between the first vision of Joseph Smith and a second manifestation in the same kind. Three years! That is a long interval in such matters. Had Joseph Smith been a mere enthusiast, self-deceived, and his vision subjectively induced, would he have waited so long before another manifestation was secured? The length of time between his visions strongly argues for the reality of the first one. Had it not been real he would not have waited three years for the fulfillment of the promise made by the Divine Personages of his first vision, viz., that 'the fulness of the gospel would at some future time be made known to him.' " (B. H. Roberts, *Comprehensive History of the Church*, 1:69.)

Joseph Smith—History 1:29

"I had full confidence in obtaining a divine manifestation"

Selected Statements of the First Presidency and the Twelve Apostles

"On the evening of the 21st of September, 1823, previous to retiring to rest, our brother's mind was unusually wrought up on the subject which had so long agitated his mind—his heart was drawn out in fervent prayer, and his whole soul was so lost to every thing of a temporal nature, that earth, to him, had lost its claims, and all he desired was to be prepared in heart to commune with some kind messenger who could communicate to him the desired information of his acceptance with God.

"At length the family retired, and he, as usual, bent his way, though in silence, where others might have rested their weary frames 'locked fast in sleep's embrace,' but repose had fled, and accustomed slumber had spread her refreshing hand over others beside him—he continued still to pray—his heart, though once hard and obdurate, was softened, and that mind which had often flitted, like the 'wild bird of passage,' had settled upon a determined basis not to be decoyed or driven from its purpose." (Oliver Cowdery, in *Messenger and Advocate*, 1 [Feb. 1835]: 78–79.)

Other Commentary

"The family were still living in the log house they had first erected on their farm. . . . This log house had a low garret divided into two apartments, and it was doubtless to one of these apartments that the Prophet retired. He betook himself to prayer and supplication to God for forgiveness of all his sins and follies; and also pleaded for a manifestation that would make known to him his standing before the Lord. There was a heart-yearning to know if the youthful follies had alienated him from God. He felt confident that he would receive a manifestation, but would it be one of reproof and rejection, or one of pardon and further instruction? He was not long left in doubt." (B. H. Roberts, *Comprehensive History of the Church*, 1:71.)

Joseph Smith—History 1:30
"A personage appeared at my bedside"

"In this situation hours passed unnumbered—how many or how few I know not, neither is he able to inform me; but supposes it must have been eleven or twelve, and perhaps later, as the noise and bustle of the family, in retiring, had long since ceased.—While continuing in prayer for a manifestation in some way that his sins were forgiven; endeavoring to exercise faith in the scriptures, on a sudden a light like that of day, only of a purer and far more glorious appearance and brightness, burst into the room.—Indeed, to use his own description, the first sight was as though the house was filled with consuming and unquenchable fire. This sudden appearance of a light so bright, as might naturally be expected, occasioned a shock or sensation, visible to the extremities of the body. It was, however, followed with a calmness and serenity of mind, and an overwhelming rapture of joy that surpassed understanding, and in a moment a personage stood before him." (Oliver Cowdery, in *Messenger and Advocate*, 1 [Feb. 1835]: 79. See also Joseph Fielding Smith, *Answers to Gospel Questions*, 1:37.)

"A remarkable fact is to be noticed with regard to this vision. In ancient times the Lord warned some of his servants in dreams. . . . But the one of which I have been speaking is what would have been called an open vision. And though it was in the night, yet it was not a dream. There is no room for conjecture in this matter, and to talk of deception would be to sport with the common sense of every man who knows when he is awake, when he sees and when he does not see.

"He could not have been deceived in the fact that a being of some kind appeared to him; and that it was an heavenly one." (Oliver Cowdery, in *Messenger and Advocate*, 1 [July 1835]: 156.)

"It is no easy task to describe the appearance of a messenger from the skies—indeed, I doubt there being an individual clothed with perishable clay, who is capable to do this work. . . .

" . . . The stature of this personage was a little above the common size of men in this age; his garment was perfectly white, and had the appearance of being without seam." (Oliver Cowdery, in *Messenger and Advocate*, 1 [Feb. 1835]: 79.)

Joseph Smith—History 1:32
"His whole person was glorious beyond description"

Selected Statements of the First Presidency and the Twelve Apostles

"Notwithstanding the room was previously filled with light above the brightness of the sun, as I have before described, yet there seemed to be an additional glory surrounding or accompanying this personage, which shone with an increased degree of brilliance, of which he was in the midst; and though his countenance was as lightning, yet it was of a pleasing, innocent and glorious appearance, so much so, that every fear was banished from the heart, and nothing but calmness pervaded the soul." (Oliver Cowdery, in *Messenger and Advocate*, 1 [Feb. 1835]: 79.)

Joseph Smith—History 1:33
"He called me by name, and said unto me that he was a messenger sent from the presence of God to me"

Selected Statements of the First Presidency and the Twelve Apostles

"Though fear was banished from his heart, yet his surprise was no less when he heard him declare himself to be a messenger sent by commandment of the Lord, to deliver a special message, and to witness to him that his sins were forgiven, and that his prayers were heard; and that the scriptures might be fulfilled, which say—'God has chosen the foolish things of the world to confound the things which are mighty; and base things of the world, and things which are despised, has God chosen; yea, and things which are not, to bring to nought things which are, that no flesh should glory in his presence.' " (Oliver Cowdery, in *Messenger and Advocate*, 1 [Feb. 1835]: 79.)

Joseph Smith—History 1:33
"My name should be had for good and evil among all nations"

Selected Statements of the First Presidency and the Twelve Apostles

"He has therefore chosen you as an instrument in his hand to bring to light that which shall perform his act, his strange act, and bring to pass a marvelous work and a wonder. Wherever the sound shall go it shall cause the ears of men to tingle, and wherever it shall be proclaimed, the pure in heart shall rejoice, while those who draw near to God with their mouths, and honor him with their lips, while their hearts are far from him, will seek its overthrow, and the destruction of those by whose hands it is carried. Therefore, marvel not if your name is made a derision, and had as a by-word among such, if you are the instrument in bringing it, by the gift of God, to the knowledge of the people." (Oliver Cowdery, in *Messenger and Advocate*, 1 [Feb. 1835]: 79–80.)

Joseph Smith—History 1:35
"The Urim and Thummim"

Selected Statements of the First Presidency and the Twelve Apostles

"Why didn't he translate it himself? Moroni could read those writings. He wrote some of them. He was familiar with the language. How easy it would have been for him to say to Joseph Smith, 'Here is the record. I sealed it up. I did the writing of two of these books. My father did the writing of others. I understand the language perfectly, and I am going to write this in your language and give it to you.'

"It seems to me that is what a fraud would have said. If Joseph Smith had been an imposter he would have said: 'The angel revealed this record to me, but I couldn't read it so the angel, who understood the language, interpreted it and I wrote it at his dictation.'

"But if he had said that it would have been fatal. Instead of doing that he said, 'The angel placed in my hands the Urim and Thummim and said: "These interpreters will enable you to translate this record. Now you go and do it." ' That, in substance, is what he said. He has been ridiculed for it, and the great people of the earth, the scientists, say it is an impossibility, but that it is the consistent thing." (Joseph Fielding Smith, *Doctrines of Salvation*, 1:197–98.)

See Selected Statements and Scripture References under Moses 6:36; Abraham 3:1.

Joseph Smith—History 1:39
"He shall plant in the hearts of the children the promises made to the fathers, and the hearts of the children shall turn to their fathers"

Selected Statements of the First Presidency and the Twelve Apostles

"Now, the word *turn* here should be translated *bind*, or seal. But what is the object of this important mission? or how is it to be fulfilled?

The keys are to be delivered, the spirit of Elijah is to come, the Gospel to be established, the Saints of God gathered, Zion built up, and the Saints to come up as saviors on Mount Zion." (Joseph Smith, *Teachings of the Prophet Joseph Smith*, p. 330.)

"This work of salvation for the dead came to the Prophet like every other doctrine—piecemeal. It was not revealed all at once. When the Angel Moroni came to the Prophet Joseph Smith, one of the things he told him was that the hearts of the children should turn to their fathers and the hearts of the fathers to the children, so that when the Lord should come the earth should not be smitten with a curse. That is significant. That was the first inkling the Prophet had concerning salvation for the dead, and he did not know just what it meant. He had a very vague idea of the meaning of the words that Elijah would come to 'plant in the hearts of the children the promises made to the fathers,' and I suppose he pondered over it a good deal." (Joseph Fielding Smith, *Doctrines of Salvation*, 2:168.)

"Now comes the point, what is this office and work of Elijah? It is one of the greatest and most important subjects that God has revealed. He should send Elijah to seal the children to the fathers, and the fathers to the children.

"Now was this merely confined to the living, to settle difficulties with families on earth? By no means. It was a far greater work. Elijah! what would you do if you were here? Would you confine your work to the living alone? No; I would refer you to the Scriptures, where the subject is manifest: that is, without us, they could not be made perfect, nor we without them; the fathers without the children, nor the children without the fathers.

"I wish you to understand this subject, for it is important; and if you will receive it, this is the spirit of Elijah, that we redeem our dead, and connect ourselves with our fathers which are in heaven, and seal up our dead to come forth in the first resurrection; and here we want the power of Elijah to seal those who dwell on earth to those who dwell in heaven. This is the power of Elijah and the keys of the kingdom of Jehovah." (Joseph Smith, *History of the Church*, 6:251–52.)

"When I went before the Lord to know who I should be adopted to (we were then being adopted to prophets and apostles), the Spirit of God said to me, 'Have you not a father, who begot you?' 'Yes, I have.' 'Then why not honor him? Why not be adopted to him?' 'Yes,' says I, 'that is right.' I was adopted to my father, and should have had my father sealed to his father, and so on back; and the duty that I want every man who presides over a Temple to see performed from this day henceforth and forever, unless the Lord Almighty commands otherwise, is, let every man be adopted to his father. When a man receives the endowment, adopt him to his father; not to Wilford Woodruff, nor to any other man outside the lineage of his fathers. That is the will of God to this people. I want all men who preside over these temples in these mountains of Israel to bear this in mind. What business have I to take away the rights of the lineage of any man? What right has any man to do this? No; I say let every man be adopted to his father; and then you will do exactly what God said when he declared He would send Elijah the prophet in the last days. Elijah the prophet appeared unto Joseph Smith and told him the day had come when this principle must be carried out. Joseph Smith did not live long enough to enter any further upon these things. His soul was wound up with this work before he was martyred for the word of God and testimony of Jesus Christ. He told us that there must be a welding link of all dispensations and of the work of God from one generation to another. This was upon his mind more than most any other subject that was given to him. In my prayers the Lord revealed to me, that it was my duty to say to all Israel to carry this principle out, and in fulfillment of that revelation I lay it before this people." (Wilford Woodruff, in James R. Clark, comp., *Messages of the First Presidency*, 3:256.)

Other Commentary

"This turning of hearts to family relationships means establishing and sealing patriarchal lineage within the sacred confines of the temple and carrying that family inheritance into our daily lives. That is why, even if we do build temples, if we do not keep the covenants made in them, we will be rejected as a people." (Theodore M. Burton, in Conference Report, Oct. 1967, p. 81.)

Joseph Smith—History 1:40
"He quoted the eleventh chapter of Isaiah"

Selected Statements of the First Presidency and the Twelve Apostles

"The Angel Moroni told the Prophet Joseph that, quoting the words of Isaiah, the Lord should gather scattered Israel and bring in the dispersed of Judah and set up an ensign for the nations. Well, hasn't he done it? Let us consider what has happened here in these valleys of the mountains as a part of the fulfillment of the promises the Lord has made through his prophets of old: how he should cause the waters to flow down from the high places where it has been reservoired in these mountains, how the rivers should flow in the deserts (and if you go up through Idaho and see those great canals out of that Snake River, you will see that those canals are larger than the average rivers you see in the world), and how the waters should spring up in the dry places. When I was in Arizona recently, I saw pipes at least twenty inches in diameter running day and night, all the time, full of water, and as I saw them, I said to myself, this is what the prophets saw when the Lord declared through their mouths that he would turn the wilderness and make it to blossom as the rose. And we are living here in that day." (LeGrand Richards, in Conference Report, Apr. 1951, p. 41.)

"The Lord by direct revelation has also taken occasion in our day to interpret, approve, clarify, and enlarge upon the writings of Isaiah.

"When Moroni came to Joseph Smith on September 21, 1823, that holy messenger 'quoted the eleventh chapter of Isaiah, saying that it was about to be fulfilled.' [Joseph Smith—History 1:40.] . . .

"It truly takes revelation to understand revelation, and what is more natural than to find the Lord Jehovah, who revealed his truths anciently, revealing the same eternal verities today and so tying his ancient and modern words together, that we may be blessed by our knowledge of what he has said in all ages." (Bruce R. McConkie, in *Ensign*, Oct. 1973, p. 81.)

Joseph Smith—History 1:42
"The vision was opened to my mind that I could see the place where the plates were deposited"

Selected Statements of the First Presidency and the Twelve Apostles

"While describing the place where the record was deposited, he gave a minute relation of it, and the vision of his mind being opened at the same time, he was permitted to view it critically; and previously being acquainted with the place, he was able to follow the direction of the vision, afterward, according to the voice of the angel, and obtain the book." (Oliver Cowdery, in *Messenger and Advocate*, 1 [Feb. 1835]: 80.)

Other Commentary

The following are some of the things Moroni taught Joseph Smith. They are taken from the writings of Oliver Cowdery.

1. Considerable information on the Restoration (see Isaiah 29); "his strange act" (Isaiah 28:21); "their hearts are far from him" (Isaiah 29:39). (See *Messenger and Advocate*, 1 [Feb. 1835]: 79.)

2. The fulness of the Gentiles was described as "one fold and one shepherd" (John 10:16. (See *Messenger and Advocate,* 1 [Feb. 1835]: 79.)

3. The Nephites and Lamanites are "literal descendants of Abraham." (*Messenger and Advocate,* 1 [Feb. 1835]: 80.)

4. The words of the book must be delivered to the learned "before it is translated." (*Messenger and Advocate*, 1 [Feb. 1835]: 80.)

5. The sealed portion "contains the same revelation which was given to John upon the isle of Patmos," and when we are worthy it will be unfolded to us. (*Messenger and Advocate*, 1 [Feb. 1835]: 80.)

6. Isaiah's prophecies about Israel were reiterated. (See Isaiah 2; *Messenger and Advocate*, 1 [Apr. 1835]: 110.)

7. A new covenant will be made with Israel. (See Isaiah 2; *Messenger and Advocate*, 1 [Apr. 1835]: 110.)

8. Many fishers and hunters will be sent in the last days. (See Jeremiah 16:16).

9. Moroni spoke on the "gospel and the gathering." (*Messenger and Advocate*, 1 [Apr. 1835]: 112.)

10. Joseph saw as well as heard. "While those glorious things were being rehearsed, the vision was also opened, so that our brother was permitted to see and understand much more full and perfect than I am able to communicate in writing. I know much may be conveyed to the understanding in writing, and many marvellous truths set forth with the pen, but after all it is but a shadow, compared to an open vision of seeing, hearing and realizing eternal things." (*Messenger and Advocate*, 1 [Apr. 1835]: 112.)

"During our evening conversations, Joseph would occasionally give us some of the most amusing recitals that could be imagined. He would describe the ancient inhabitants of this continent, their dress, mode of traveling, and the animals upon which they rode; their cities, their buildings, with every particular; their mode of warfare; and also their religious worship. This he would do with as much ease, seemingly, as if he had spent his whole life among them." (Lucy Mack Smith, *History of Joseph Smith*, p. 83.)

Joseph Smith—History 1:45

"He [Moroni] informed me of great judgments which were coming upon the earth"

See Selected Statements, Scripture References, and Other Commentary under Joseph Smith—Matthew 1:29; 1:30; 1:31; 1:32; 1:33; 1:34.

Joseph Smith—History 1:46

"I must have no other object in view in getting the plates but to glorify God"

Selected Statements of the First Presidency and the Twelve Apostles

"Now, nearly every temptation that comes to you and me comes in one of those forms. Classify them, and you will find that under one of those three nearly every given temptation that makes you and me spotted, ever so little maybe, comes to us as (1) *a temptation of the appetite*; (2) *a yielding to the pride and fashion and vanity of those alienated from* the things of God; or (3) *a gratifying* of the passion, or a desire for the riches of the world, or power among men." (David O. McKay, in Conference Report, Oct. 1911, p. 59.)

"But it is necessary to give you more fully the express instructions of the angel, with regard to the object of this work in which our brother had now engaged—He was to remember that it was the work of the Lord, to fulfil certain promises previously made to a branch of the house of Israel, of the tribe of Joseph, and when it should be brought forth must be done expressly with an eye, as I said before, single to the glory of God, and the welfare and restoration of the house of Israel.

"You will understand, then, that no motive of pecuniary, or earthly nature, was to be suffered to take the lead of the heart of the man thus favored. The allurements of vice, the contaminating influence of wealth, without the direct guidance of the Holy Spirit, must have no place in the heart nor be suffered to take from it that warm desire for the glory and kingdom of the Lord, or, instead of obtaining, disappointment and reproof would most assuredly follow." (Oliver Cowdery, in *Messenger and Advocate*, 1 [July 1835]: 156-57.)

Joseph Smith—History 1:48

"I found my strength so exhausted as to render me entirely unable"

Other Commentary

"The next day, my husband, Alvin, and Joseph, were reaping together in the field, and as they were reaping, Joseph stopped quite suddenly, and seemed to be in a very deep study. Alvin, observing it, hurried him, saying, 'We must not slacken our hands or we will not be able to complete our task.' Upon this Joseph went to work again, and after laboring a short time, he stopped just as he had done before. This being quite unusual and strange, it attracted the attention of his father, upon which he discovered that Joseph was very pale. My husband, supposing that he was sick, told him to go to the house, and have his mother doctor him. He accordingly ceased his work, and started, but on coming to a beautiful green, under an apple tree, he stopped and lay down, for he was so weak he could proceed no further. He was here but a short time, when the messenger whom he saw the previous night, visited him again, and the first thing he said was, 'Why did you not tell your father that which I commanded you to tell him?' Joseph replied, 'I was afraid my father would not believe me.' The angel rejoined, 'He will believe every word you say to him.' " (Lucy Mack Smith, *History of Joseph Smith*, p. 79.)

Joseph Smith—History 1:50

"I returned to my father in the field, and rehearsed the whole matter to him"

Other Commentary

"Joseph then promised the angel that he would do as he had been commanded. Upon this, the messenger departed, and Joseph returned to the field, where he had left my husband and Alvin; but when he got there, his father had just gone to the house, as he was somewhat unwell. Joseph then desired Alvin to go straightway and see his father, and inform him that he had something of great importance to communicate to him, and that he wanted him to come out into the field where they were at work. Alvin did as he was requested, and when my husband got there Joseph related to him all that had passed between him and the angel the previous night and that morning. Having heard this account, his father charged him not to fail in attending strictly to the instruction which he had received from this heavenly messenger.

"Soon after Joseph had this conversation with his father, he repaired to the place where the plates were deposited." (Lucy Mack Smith, *History of Joseph Smith*, pp. 79-80.)

Joseph Smith—History 1:50

"I left the field, and went to the place where the messenger had told me"

Selected Statements of the First Presidency and the Twelve Apostles

"As Joseph Smith journeyed to the Hill Cumorah on that memorable first visit, he was beset by many conflicting emotions. His father's family were poor and in financial distress. Creditors had been bearing down heavily upon them. The adversary of all righteousness took advantage of these conditions to sorely tempt the youth with all his power. The plates of the book were made of gold and were of great intrinsic value. Could they not be used to relieve the financial embarrassment of the family? Or was there not something else deposited with the plates that might be used for such purpose? Such were the thoughts Satan put into his heart as he approached the hill, and the admonition of the angel was temporarily forgotten." (Joseph Fielding Smith, *Essentials in Church History*, pp. 56–57.)

"It is sufficient to say that such were his reflections during his walk of from two to three miles: the distance from his father's house to the place pointed out. And to use his own words it seemed as though two invisible powers were influencing, or striving to influence his mind— one with the reflection that if he obtained the object of his pursuit, it would be through the mercy and condescension of the Lord, and that every act or performance in relation to it, must be in strict accordance with the instruction of that personage who communicated the intelligence to him first; and the other with the tho'ts and reflections like those previously mentioned—contrasting his former and present circumstances in life with those to come. That precious instruction recorded on the sacred page—pray always—which was expressly impressed upon him, was at length entirely forgotten, and as I previously remarked, a fixed determination to obtain and aggrandize himself, occupied his mind when he arrived at the place where the record was found." (Oliver Cowdery, in *Messenger and Advocate*, 1 [July 1835]: 157–58.)

Joseph Smith—History 1:51
The Hill Cumorah

Selected Statements of the First Presidency and the Twelve Apostles

"I must now give you some description of the place where, and the manner in which these records were deposited. . . .

" . . . about four miles from Palmyra, you pass a large hill on the east side of the road. Why I say large, is, because it is as large perhaps, as any in that country. . . . The north end rises quite sudden until it assumes a level with the more southerly extremity, and I think I may say an elevation higher than at the south a short distance, say half or three fourths of a mile. As you pass toward Canandaigua it lessens gradually until the surface assumes its common level, or is broken by other smaller hills or ridges, water courses and ravines. I think I am justified in saying that this is the highest hill for some distance round, and I am certain that its appearance, as it rises so suddenly from a plain on the north, must attract the notice of the traveller as he passes by.

"At about one mile west rises another ridge of less height, running parallel with the former, leaving a beautiful vale between. The soil is of the first quality for the country, and under a state of cultivation." (Oliver Cowdery, in *Messenger and Advocate*, 1 [July 1835]: 158.)

"The hill of which I have been speaking, at the time mentioned, presented a varied appearance: the north end rose suddenly from the plain, forming a promontory without timber, but covered with grass. As you passed to the south you soon came to scattering timber, the surface having been cleared by art or by wind; and a short distance farther left, you are surrounded with the common forest of the country. It is necessary to observe, that even the part cleared was only occupied for pasturage, its steep ascent and narrow summit not admitting the plow of the husbandman, with any degree of ease or profit. It was at the second mentioned place where the record was found to be deposited, on the west side of the hill, not far from the top down its side; and when myself visited the place in the year 1830, there were several trees standing: enough to cause a shade in summer, but not so much as to prevent the surface being covered with grass—which was also the case when the record was first found." (Oliver Cowdery, in *Messenger and Advocate*, 2 [Oct. 1835]: 195-96.)

Joseph Smith—History 1:52
"And there indeed did I behold the plates"

Selected Statements of the First Presidency and the Twelve Apostles

"Eagerly he removed the earth so that he might get a lever under the edge. Lifting the rock, he looked into a box formed by a stone in the bottom with other stones cemented together to form the sides. There, indeed, was the treasure!—a breastplate, two stones set in silver bows, and a book of gold leaves bound together with three rings." (Gordon B. Hinckley, *Truth Restored*, p. 11.)

"First, a hole of sufficient depth, (how deep I know not,) was dug. At the bottom of this was laid a stone of suitable size, the upper surface being smooth. At each edge was placed a large quantity of cement, and into this cement, at the four edges of this stone, were placed, erect, four others, their bottom edges resting in the cement at the outer edges of the first stone. The four last named, when placed erect, formed a box, the corners, or where the edges of the four came in contact, were also cemented so firmly that the moisture from without was prevented from entering. It is to be observed, also, that the inner surface of the four erect, or side stones was smooth. This box was sufficiently large to admit a breast-plate, such as was used by the ancients to defend the chest, &c. from the arrows and weapons of their enemy. From the bottom of the box, or from the breast-plate, arose three small pillars composed of the same description of cement used on the edges; and upon these three pillars was placed the record of the children of Joseph. . . . When it was first visited by our brother, in 1823, a part of the crowning stone was visible above the surface while the edges were concealed by the soil and grass, from which circumstance you will see, that however deep this box might have been placed by Moroni at first, the time had been sufficient to wear the earth so that it was easily discovered, when once directed, and yet not enough to make a *perceivable* difference to the passer by. . . . A few years sooner might have found even the top stone concealed, and discouraged our brother from attempting to make a further trial to obtain this rich treasure, for fear of discovery; and a few later might have left the small box uncovered, and exposed its valuable contents to the rude calculations and vain speculations of those who neither understand common language nor fear God." (Oliver Cowdery, in *Messenger and Advocate*, 2 [Oct. 1835]: 196–97.)

Joseph Smith—History 1:53
"I made an attempt to take them out, but was forbidden by the messenger"

Selected Statements of the First Presidency and the Twelve Apostles

"You will have wondered, perhaps, that the mind of our brother should be so occupied with the thoughts of the goods of this world, at the time of arriving at Cumorah, on the morning of the 22nd of September, 1823, after having been rapt in the visions of heaven during the night, and also seeing and hearing in open day; but the mind of man is easily turned, if it is not held by the power of God through the prayer of faith, and you will remember that I have said that two invisible powers were operating upon his mind during his walk from his residence to Cumorah, and that the one urging the certainty of wealth and ease in this life, had so powerfully wrought upon him, that the great object so carefully and impressively named by the angel, had entirely gone from his recollection that only a fixed determination to obtain now urged him forward. . . .

"After arriving at the repository, a little exertion in removing the soil from the edges of the top of the box, and a light pry, brought to his natural vision its contents. No sooner did he behold this sacred treasure than his hopes were renewed, and he supposed his success certain; and without first attempting to take it from its long place of deposit, he thought, perhaps, there might be something more equally as valuable, and to take only the plates, might give others an opportunity of obtaining the remainder, which could he secure, would still add to his store of wealth. These, in short, were his reflections, without once thinking of the solemn instruction of the heavenly messenger, that all must be done with an express view of glorifying God.

"On attempting to take possession of the record a shock was produced upon his system, by an invisible power, which deprived him, in a measure, of his natural strength. He desisted for an instant, and then made another attempt, but was more sensibly shocked than before. What was the occasion of this he knew not—there was the pure unsullied record, as had been described—he had heard of the power of enchantment, and a thousand like stories, which held the hidden treasures of the earth, and supposed that physical exertion and personal strength was only necessary to enable him to obtain the object of his wish. He therefore made the third attempt with an increased exertion, when his strength failed him more than at either of the former times, and without premeditating he exclaimed, 'Why can I not obtain this book?' 'Because you have not kept the commandments of the Lord,' answered a voice, within a seeming short distance. He looked, and to his astonishment, there stood the angel who had previously given him the directions concerning this matter. In an instant, all the former instructions, the great intelligence concerning Israel and the last days, were brought to his mind." (Oliver Cowdery, in *Messenger and Advocate*, 2 [Oct. 1835]: 197–98. See also Joseph Fielding Smith, *Essentials in Church History*, p. 57; Gordon B. Hinckley, *Truth Restored*, p. 12.)

Other Commentary

"Joseph prayed at that moment, and as he prayed the darkness in his mind began to dispel. His soul was filled with light as it had been the evening before, and he was filled with the Holy Spirit. Once again the Lord manifested 'his condescension and mercy; the heavens were opened and the glory of the Lord shone round about and rested upon him. While he thus stood gazing and admiring, the angel said 'Look!'

"The scene quickly changed from light to darkness. Joseph 'beheld the prince of darkness, surrounded by his innumerable train of associates.' As this scene unfolded before Joseph, Moroni explained:

" 'All this is shown, the good and the evil, the holy and impure, the glory of God and the power of darkness, that you may know hereafter the two powers and never be influenced or overcome by that wicked one. Behold, whatever entices and leads to good and to do good, is of God, and whatever does not is of that wicked one: It is he that fills the hearts of men with evil, to walk in darkness and blaspheme God; and you may learn from hence forth, that his ways are to destruction, but the way of holiness is peace and rest.' [See *Messenger and Advocate* 2:198.]" (H. Donl Peterson, *Moroni: Ancient Prophet, Modern Messenger,* pp. 93–94.)

Joseph Smith—History 1:54
"Each time I found the same messenger there, and received instruction and intelligence"

Selected Statements of the First Presidency and the Twelve Apostles

"Joseph Smith, the humble farmer boy, was trained and instructed as, perhaps, no other prophet was ever taught and trained, by divine instructors sent from the throne and presence of our Eternal Father." (Joseph Fielding Smith, *Doctrines of Salvation*, 1:201.)

Other Commentary

"The Prophet has not given a more extended description of these annual interviews than is here set down; but undoubtedly the knowledge obtained in them was subsequently inter-woven in the doctrine and organization of the church." (B. H. Roberts, *Comprehensive History of the Church*, 1:81.)

Joseph Smith—History 1:55
"We were under the necessity of laboring with our hands, hiring out by day's work"

Other Commentary

"The male members of the Smith family were still under the necessity of occasionally obtaining work outside of cultivating their own farm, in order to sustain themselves and meet the payments on their land. Hence they were sometimes at home and sometimes abroad. About a year after the death of Alvin, in October, 1825, to be exact, Joseph engaged to work for an elderly gentleman, Josiah Stoal, of Bainbridge, Chenango county, in the south part of New York state." (B. H. Roberts, *Comprehensive History of the Church*, 1:81.)

Joseph Smith—History 1:56

"Hence arose the very prevalent story of my having been a money-digger"

Selected Statements of the First Presidency and the Twelve Apostles

"During the interval of four years, from 1823 to 1827, Joseph Smith was under the necessity of aiding his father's family in paying their debts and procuring a living. At times he found employment at home and at times abroad, as opportunity afforded. The death of his oldest brother Alvin, in 1823, made it all the more needful that he exert himself for the benefit of the family. In October, 1825, he entered the employ of an aged gentleman named Josiah Stowel. Mr. Stowel had heard of some old Spanish silver mines in Harmony, Pennsylvania, and employed his hired help in searching for hidden treasure. Joseph, after about one month of fruitless search, persuaded this kindly gentleman to forsake the foolish venture. From this employment came the cry that Joseph Smith, the 'Mormon' Prophet, was a 'money-digger.' " (Joseph Fielding Smith, *Essentials in Church History*, p. 59.)

"Soon after this visit to Cumorah, a gentleman from the south part of the State, (Chenango County), employed our brother as a common laborer, and accordingly he visited that section of the country: and had he not been accused of digging down all, or nearly so, the mountains of Susquehannah, or causing others to do it by some art of necromancy, I should leave this, for the present, unnoticed. . . . In the town of Harmony, Susquehannah County, Pa. is said to be a cave or subterraneous recess . . . where a company of Spaniards, a long time since, when the country was uninhabited by white settlers, excavated from the bowels of the earth ore, and coined a large quantity of money; after which they secured the cavity and evacuated, leaving a part still in the cave, purposing to return at some distant period. A long time elapsed and this account came from one of the individuals who was first engaged in this mining business. The country was pointed out and the spot minutely described. This, I believe, is the substance, so far as my memory serves, though I shall not pledge my veracity for the correctness of the account as I have given.—Enough however, was credited of the Spaniard's story, to excite the belief of many that there was a fine sum of the precious metal lying coined in this subterraneous vault, among whom was our employer; and accordingly our brother was required to spend a few months with some others in excavating the earth, in pursuit of this treasure." (Oliver Cowdery, in *Messenger and Advocate*, 2 [Oct. 1835]: 200–201.)

Other Commentary

"A man by the name of Josiah Stoal came from Chenango county, New York, with the view of getting Joseph to assist him in digging for a silver mine. He came for Joseph on account of having heard that he possessed certain means by which he could discern things invisible to the natural eye.

"Joseph endeavored to divert him from his vain pursuit, but he was inflexible in his purpose and offered high wages to those who would dig for him in search of said mine, and still insisted upon having Joseph to work for him. Accordingly, Joseph and several others returned with him and commenced digging. After laboring for the old gentleman about a month, without success, Joseph prevailed upon him to cease his operations, and it was from this circumstance of having worked by the month, at digging for a silver mine, that the very prevalent story arose of Joseph's having been a money digger." (Lucy Mack Smith, *History of Joseph Smith*, pp. 91–92. See also B. H. Roberts, *Comprehensive History of the Church*, 1:82.)

Joseph Smith—History 1:57

"It was there I first saw my wife . . . Emma Hale"

Other Commentary

"While Joseph was in the employ of Mr. Stoal, he boarded a short time with one Isaac Hale, and it was during this interval that Joseph became acquainted with his daughter, Miss Emma Hale, to whom he immediately commenced paying his addresses. . . .

" . . . Joseph called my husband and myself aside and said, 'I have been very lonely ever since Alvin died and I have concluded to get married, and if you have no objections to my uniting myself in marriage with Miss Emma Hale, she would be my choice in preference to any other woman I have ever seen.' We were pleased with his choice and not only consented to his marrying her, but requested him to bring her home with him and live with us. Accordingly, he set out with his father for Pennsylvania." (Lucy Mack Smith, *History of Joseph Smith*, 1:92–93.)

Joseph Smith—History 1:58

"My wife's father's family were very much opposed to our being married"

Other Commentary

"The report that Joseph Smith had received a revelation had followed him into Pennsylvania, and as he steadfastly adhered to the reality of that revelation, prejudice and persecution followed him more or less into every neighborhood. Owing to these circumstances the Hale family was considerably prejudiced against him and opposed his marriage with Emma. He was, therefore, under the necessity of taking her elsewhere for the ceremony, and was married at the home of Squire Tarbil, in South Bainbridge, Chenango county, New York. It is usually charged by anti-'Mormon' writers that Joseph Smith 'stole his wife,' but since she was born on July 10, 1804, and therefore at the time of her marriage was in her twenty-third year, and under the law mistress of her own actions, it is a little difficult to see where the charge of 'stealing' or 'abduction' can be made to hold good." (B. H. Roberts, *Comprehensive History of the Church*, 1:82–83.)

Joseph Smith—History 1:59

"At length the time arrived for obtaining the plates" (22 September 1827)

Selected Statements of the First Presidency and the Twelve Apostles

"After having received many visits from the *angels* of God unfolding the majesty and glory of the events that should transpire in the last days, on the morning of the 22nd of September, A.D. 1827, the angel of the Lord delivered the records into my hands." (Joseph Smith, *History of the Church*, 4:537.)

Other Commentary

"We always had a peculiar anxiety about him whenever he was absent, for it seemed as though something was always taking place to jeopardize his life. But to return. He did not get home till the night was far spent. On coming in he threw himself into a chair, apparently much exhausted. . . .

"Presently he smiled and said in a calm tone, 'I have taken the severest chastisement that I have ever had in my life.'

"My husband, supposing that it was from some of the neighbors, was quite angry and observed, 'I would like to know what business anybody has to find fault with you!'

" 'Stop, father, stop,' said Joseph, 'it was the angel of the Lord. As I passed by the hill of Cumorah, where the plates are, the angel met me and said that I had not been engaged enough in the work of the Lord; that the time had come for the record to be brought forth; and that I must be up and doing and set myself about the things which God had commanded me to do. But, father, give yourself no uneasiness concerning the reprimand which I have received, for I now know the course that I am to pursue, so all will be well.'

"It was also made known to him at this interview that he should make another effort to obtain the plates, on the twenty-second of the following September, but this he did not mention to us at that time." (Lucy Mack Smith, *History of Joseph Smith*, pp. 100–101.)

Joseph Smith—History 1:59

"I should be responsible for them [the gold plates] . . . until he, the messenger, should call for them"

Selected Statements of the First Presidency and the Twelve Apostles

"The question has been asked many times of our elders: Where are the plates? Does the Church have in its possession the plates from which the Book of Mormon was translated by Joseph Smith?

"When the answer is given that the plates were received again by the Angel Moroni, who through the centuries since they were hid up unto the Lord has been their special guardian, the reply is generally made: What a wonderful aid it would be to your people in convincing the world of the truth of your story if you could show the plates to prove that Joseph Smith really had them.

"Perhaps it is natural for a man who hears for the first time the story of Joseph Smith and the coming forth of the Book of Mormon to propound such a question and to think that the plates, if they had been placed in some museum where the public could examine them, would have added much to prove the authenticity of the Prophet's story. With deeper reflection we discover that this would not have been the case, for it is not the way the Lord proves his truth, now or at any other time." (Joseph Fielding Smith, *Doctrines of Salvation*, 3:227.)

Joseph Smith—History 1:59–60

"If I would use all my endeavors to preserve them, . . . they should be protected"

Selected Statements of the First Presidency and the Twelve Apostles

"Joseph soon learned why Moroni had charged him so strictly to guard the record taken from the hill. No sooner was it rumored that he had the plates than efforts were made to seize them from him. To preserve them, he first carefully hid them in a hollow birch log. Then he locked them in a chest in his father's home. Later they were buried beneath the hearthstone of the family living room. A cooper's shop across the street was their next hiding place. All of these and other stratagems were employed to keep the plates safe from neighborhood mobs who raided and ransacked the Smith home and surrounding premises, and even employed a diviner in their zeal to locate the record." (Gordon B. Hinckley, *Truth Restored*, p. 13.)

Other Commentary

"When Joseph first got the plates, the angel of the Lord stood by and said:

" 'Now you have got the Record into your own hands, and you are but a man, therefore you will have to be watchful and faithful to your trust, or you will be overpowered by wicked men; for they will lay every plan and scheme that is possible to get it away from you, and if you do not take heed continually, they will succeed. While it was in my hands, I could keep it, and no man had power to take it away! but now I give it up to you. Beware, and look well to your ways, and you shall have power to retain it, until the time for it to be translated.' " (Lucy Mack Smith, *History of Joseph Smith*, p. 110.)

"Joseph kept the Urim and Thummim constantly about his person, by the use of which he could in a moment tell whether the plates were in any danger. . . .

"The plates were secreted about three miles from home, in the following manner: Finding an old birch log much decayed, excepting the bark, which was in a measure sound, he took his pocket knife and cut the bark with some care, then turned it back and made a hole of sufficient size to receive the plates, and, laying them in the cavity thus formed, he replaced the bark; after which he laid across the log, in several places, some old stuff that happened to lay near, in order to conceal as much as possible the place in which they were deposited.

"Joseph, on coming to them, took them from their secret place, and, wrapping them in his linen frock, placed them under his arm and started for home.

"After proceeding a short distance, he thought it would be more safe to leave the road and go through the woods. Traveling some distance after he left the road, he came to a large windfall, and as he was jumping over a log, a man sprang up from behind it and gave him a heavy blow with a gun. Joseph turned around and knocked him down, then ran at the top of his speed. About half a mile farther he was attacked again in the same manner as before; he knocked this man down in the like manner as the former and ran on again; and before he reached home he was assaulted the third time. In striking the last one, he dislocated his thumb, which, however, he did not notice until he came within sight of the house, when he threw himself down in the corner of the fence in order to recover his breath. As soon as he was able, he arose and came to the house. He was still altogether speechless from fright and the fatigue of running." (Lucy Mack Smith, *History of Joseph Smith*, pp. 107–8. See also B. H. Roberts, *Comprehensive History of the Church*, 1:91.)

Joseph Smith—History 1:61
"The persecution, however, became so intolerable that I was under the necessity of . . . going with my wife to . . . Pennsylvania"

Selected Statements of the First Presidency and the Twelve Apostles

"So intense and bitter became the opposition in Manchester that the Prophet sought a place of refuge in another locality. Having received an invitation from his wife's parents to come to their home in Harmony, Pennsylvania, he accepted the invitation and prepared to go. Being very poor he experienced some difficulty in procuring the necessary means to meet his obligations and make the journey. In this hour of distress, and in the midst of persecution, he found a friend in Martin Harris, of Palmyra, New York. Joseph, with his wife's brother, Alva Hale, had gone to Palmyra to transact some business, and while there he was approached by Martin Harris, who said to him: 'How do you do, Mr. Smith? Here are fifty dollars. I give this to you to do the Lord's work with; no, I give it to the Lord for His own work.' Joseph offered to take the money and give his note which Alva Hale also agreed to sign, but Martin Harris refused to take the note. This money enabled the prophet to make the journey to Harmony where he found a haven of rest." (Joseph Fielding Smith, *Essentials in Church History*, p. 61.)

Other Commentary

"Alva Hale, Joseph's brother-in-law, came to our house from Pennsylvania, for the purpose of moving Joseph to his father-in-law's, as word had been sent to them that Joseph desired to move there as soon as he could settle up his business. During the short interval of Alva's stay with us, he and Joseph were one day in Palmyra, at a public-house, transacting some business. As they were thus engaged, Mr. Harris came in: he stepped immediately up to my son and taking him by the hand, said, 'How do you do, Mr. Smith.' After which he took a bag of silver from his pocket and said again, 'Here, Mr. Smith, is fifty dollars; I give this to you to do the Lord's work with; no, I give it to the Lord for his own work.'

" 'No,' said Joseph, 'We will give you a note, Mr. Hale, I presume, will sign it with me.'

" 'Yes,' said Alva, 'I will sign it.'

"Mr. Harris, however, insisted that he would give the money to the Lord, and called those present to witness the fact that he gave it freely and did not demand any compensation, that it was for the purpose of helping Mr. Smith to do the Lord's work. And as I have been informed, many were present on that occasion who witnessed the same circumstance.

"Joseph in a short time arranged his affairs and was ready for the journey." (Lucy Mack Smith, *History of Joseph Smith*, pp. 117–18.)

Joseph Smith—History 1:62

"I commenced copying the characters off the plates"

Selected Statements of the First Presidency and the Twelve Apostles

"Once comfortably settled, he commenced work on the record. It was a strange volume, approximately six inches in width by eight inches in length, and six inches thick. The golden pages, or plates, were not quite so thick as common tin, and were bound together by three rings on one side. Approximately one-third of the plates could be turned freely, similar to the pages of a loose-leaf book, but the remaining two-thirds were 'sealed' so that they could not be examined. Beautiful engravings, small and finely cut, were found on the plates.

"Joseph began his work by copying onto paper several pages of the strange characters. Some of these he translated by means of the Urim and Thummim, the 'interpreters' which he had received with the plates." (Gordon B. Hinckley, *Truth Restored*, pp. 14–15.)

Joseph Smith—History 1:63

"Mr. Martin Harris came to our place, got the characters which I had drawn off the plates, and started with them to the city of New York"

Selected Statements of the First Presidency and the Twelve Apostles

"Martin Harris took the transcript that had been made together with the partial translation, and departed for New York. Just what his object was, and what he had in mind, is not made clear. That he was led to do so by inspiration was later shown. . . .

"A number of years later, when he discovered the use to which his testimony had been given, Professor Anthon denied the statement of

Martin Harris, although he did confess that such a person called to see him with such characters, but he treated it as a hoax. There may be some slight errors in the account of Martin Harris, but in the main his story must be true for it is the fulfilment of an ancient prophecy of Isaiah almost word for word. It is not likely that Martin Harris was familiar with the prophecy of Isaiah at that time and without question Professor Anthon had no intention of fulfilling prophecy in making his answer, but nevertheless such proved to be the case." (Joseph Fielding Smith, *Essentials in Church History*, pp. 62, 64. See also Gordon B. Hinckley, *Truth Restored*, pp. 16–17.)

"The words of the book, Isaiah says, are to be delivered to the learned, not the book itself. I have had people rise up and say, 'Why did not Joseph Smith send the plates to the learned?' Because that would have been a violation of this prophecy. The words of the book, not the book itself were to be delivered to the learned, requesting him to read them—'Read this I pray thee.' But he says, 'I can not, for it is sealed.' Martin Harris told him a portion of these plates were sealed and were not to be translated during the present generation; but the portion that were unsealed were to be translated. He replied, 'I can not read a sealed book,' thus fulfilling the words of Isaiah.

" . . . Now in regard to Joseph Smith's qualifications or attainments in learning, they were very ordinary. He had received a little education in the common country schools in the vicinity in which he had lived. He could read a little, and could write, but it was in such an ordinary hand that he did not venture to act as his own scribe, but had to employ sometimes one and sometimes another to write as he translated. This unlearned man did not make the same reply that the learned man did. For when the book was delivered to this unlearned youth and he was requested to read it, he replied, 'I am not learned.' I suppose he felt his weakness when the Lord told him to read this book; for he thought it was a great work." (Orson Pratt, in *Journal of Discourses*, 5:186. See also B. H. Roberts, *Comprehensive History of the Church*, 1:99; Joseph Fielding Smith, *Doctrines of Salvation*, 3:201–2.)

Joseph Smith—History 1:67
"Two days after the arrival of Mr. Cowdery . . . I commenced to translate the Book of Mormon"

Selected Statements of the First Presidency and the Twelve Apostles

"For a time the Prophet was without assistance. For several months he was under the necessity of 'laboring with his hands' on his small farm in Harmony and otherwise seeking employment. The work of the Lord was lagging. He must be about his mission. He prayed to the Lord for help. On the 5th of April 1829, a young school teacher, Oliver Cowdery, came to Harmony to inquire of Joseph Smith regarding his work. Oliver Cowdery had been teaching school near the home of the Smiths in Manchester, and part of the time boarded with that family. From them he learned of the Prophet's vision, the coming of Moroni, and of the plates. He had a feeling that these stories were true and desired to investigate at close quarters. He was convinced of the truth of Joseph's story, and two days after his arrival in Harmony, commenced to write as the Prophet translated from the record. Later in the month of April the Lord gave to Oliver a revelation through Joseph Smith in which he was called to the work. In that revelation things were revealed that only Oliver Cowdery knew. From that time forth he continued to act as the amanuensis for Joseph Smith, until the Book of Mormon was finished." (Joseph Fielding Smith, *Essentials in Church History*, pp. 66–67.)

"We may conclude from the evidence that the actual time of translating the record, as we have it in the Book of Mormon, was between April 7, 1829, and the first week of June of that same year, or not to exceed two full months." (Joseph Fielding Smith, *Doctrines of Salvation*, 3:218.)

Other Commentary

"Soon after we returned from Harmony, a man by the name of Lyman Cowdery, came into the neighborhood, and applied to Hyrum (as he was one of the trustees), for the district school. A meeting of the trustees was called, and Mr. Cowdery was employed. But the following day, this Mr. Cowdery brought his brother Oliver to the trustees, and requested them to receive him instead of himself, as circumstances had transpired which rendered it necessary for him to disappoint them, or which would not allow of his attending to the school himself; and he would warrant the good conduct of the school under his brother's supervision. All parties being satisfied, Oliver, commenced his school, boarding for the time being at our house. He had been in the school but a short time, when he began to hear from all quarters concerning the plates, and as soon began to importune Mr. Smith upon the subject, but for a considerable length of time did not succeed in eliciting any information. At last, however, he gained my husband's confidence, so far as to obtain a sketch of the facts relative to the plates.

"Shortly after receiving this information, he told Mr. Smith that he was highly delighted with what he had heard, that he had been in a deep study upon the subject all day, and that it was impressed upon his mind, that he should yet have the privilege of writing for Joseph. Furthermore, that he had determined to pay him a visit at the close of the school, which he was then teaching." (Lucy Mack Smith, *History of Joseph Smith*, pp. 138–39. See also p. 141.)

Joseph Smith—History 1:68

"We . . . went into the woods to pray and inquire of the Lord respecting baptism for the remission of sins"

Selected Statements of the First Presidency and the Twelve Apostles

"Among the doctrines taught in the ancient record was that of baptism for the remission of sins. Joseph Smith had never been baptized, for he had not become a member of any church. As he and Oliver discussed the matter, he resolved to inquire of the Lord concerning the ordinance.

"They retired to the seclusion of the woods along the banks of the Susquehanna River. It was the 15th day of May 1829. While they were engaged in prayer a light appeared above them, and in it a heavenly messenger descended. He announced himself to them as John, known in scripture as John the Baptist." (Gordon B. Hinckley, *Truth Restored*, p. 20. See also Joseph Fielding Smith, *Essentials in Church History*, p. 67.)

"Every time keys were restored, two men received them. Why? Because it was necessary according to the divine law of witnesses for Joseph Smith to have a companion holding those keys; otherwise it would not have happened. So, as Oliver Cowdery states, when John the Baptist came, he and Joseph Smith received the Aaronic Priesthood under his hands; and when Peter, James, and John came, he was with Joseph Smith. . . .

"If Joseph Smith had said, 'I testify, and I testify alone,' his testimony would not be true. There had to be two, that the testimony might be valid." (Joseph Fielding Smith, *Doctrines of Salvation*, 1:211.)

"Another thing very significant in the coming of John is the fact that he, who was at the time a resurrected personage, conferred upon Joseph Smith and Oliver Cowdery the priesthood and then required of them that they baptize each other. In the natural order of things, men are baptized before the priesthood is conferred upon them. In this case the order was reversed.

"We may conclude quite safely that with the limited knowledge which they had at that time, these two inexperienced young men, had they been guilty of perpetrating a fraud, would not have thought of this. It is most likely that they would have made the claim that the angel first baptized them and then gave them priesthood. Had they made such a statement as this it would have been fatal to their story." (Joseph Fielding Smith, *Doctrines of Salvation*, 3:90.)

Joseph Smith—History 1:69

"Upon you my fellow servants, in the name of Messiah, I confer the Priesthood of Aaron"

Selected Statements of the First Presidency and the Twelve Apostles

"As it was anciently, so it is today. Priesthoods and keys and heavenly powers are just as important as they ever were. Where they are present, there is a hope of salvation; if they are absent, there is no true gospel, no power of God unto salvation, no redeeming power, no hope of eternal life.

"But thanks be to God, all that mortals possessed anciently in the way of priesthoods and keys has been restored. John the Baptist, ministering as a resurrected and glorified being, on the 15th day of May in 1829, conferred upon Joseph Smith and Oliver Cowdery the Aaronic Priesthood and all of the keys and powers that unto it do appertain. It 'holds the keys of the ministering of angels, and of the gospel of repentance, and of baptism by immersion for the remission of sins.' (D&C 13.) It is the power by which Aaron and his sons and the Levites in general administered the temporal and spiritual affairs of the Lord in ancient Israel. What those ancient worthies did in their day, legal administrators can do now, because the same ancient power is vested in modern hands. (JS–H 1:68–72.)" (Bruce R. McConkie, *New Witness for the Articles of Faith*, p. 321.)

Joseph Smith—History 1:69

"Until the sons of Levi do offer again an offering unto the Lord in righteousness"

Selected Statements of the First Presidency and the Twelve Apostles

"It is generally supposed that sacrifice was entirely done away when the Great Sacrifice [i.e.,] the sacrifice of the Lord Jesus was offered up, and that there will be no necessity for the ordinance of sacrifice in future; but those who assert this are certainly not acquainted with the duties, privileges and authority of the Priesthood, or with the Prophets.

"The offering of sacrifice has ever been connected and forms a part of the duties of the Priesthood. It began with the Priesthood, and will be continued until after the coming of Christ, from generation to generation. . . .

"These sacrifices, as well as every ordinance belonging to the Priesthood, will, when the Temple of the Lord shall be built, and the sons of Levi be purified, be fully restored and attended to in all their powers, ramifications, and blessings. This ever did and ever will exist when the powers of the Melchizedek Priesthood are sufficiently manifest; else how can the restitution of all things spoken of by the Holy Prophets be brought to pass. It is not to be understood that the law of Moses will be established again with all its rites and variety of ceremonies; this has never been spoken of by the prophets; but those things which existed prior to Moses' day, namely, sacrifice, will be continued.

"It may be asked by some, what necessity for sacrifice, since the Great Sacrifice was offered? In answer to which, if repentance, baptism, and faith existed prior to the days of Christ, what necessity for them since that time? The Priesthood has descended in a regular line from father to son, through their succeeding generations." (Joseph Smith, *Teachings of the Prophet Joseph Smith*, pp. 172-73. See also Joseph Fielding Smith, *Doctrines of Salvation*, 3:93-94.)

Joseph Smith—History 1:71
"After which I laid my hands upon his head and ordained him to the Aaronic Priesthood"

Selected Statements of the First Presidency and the Twelve Apostles

" 'After we [Joseph Smith and Oliver Cowdery] baptized each other the angel said, "Joseph, you lay your hands upon Oliver and *reconfirm* the ordination that I have given you, and Oliver, put your hands upon the head of Joseph Smith and reconfirm the ordination that I have given you" '—or the restoration of the priesthood, which is a better term. And they did that. Why? Because of this very thing I am telling you.

"It was out of order to ordain men and then baptize them. We never think today of doing that. We do not take a man and confer upon him the Aaronic Priesthood and then baptize him, or send him to be baptized. Why? Because we have a Church organization. So the angel did what was essential—the only thing that was, as far as he was then concerned—and then he commanded them to baptize each other, and then had them lay hands on each other and *reseal* those blessings in the proper order." (Joseph Fielding Smith, *Doctrines of Salvation*, 1:196-97.)

Joseph Smith—History 1:72

"His name was John, the same that is called John the Baptist in the New Testament"

Selected Statements of the First Presidency and the Twelve Apostles

"Few prophets rank with John the Baptist. Among other things, his ministry was foretold by Lehi (1 Nephi 10:7-10), Nephi (1 Nephi 11:27; 2 Nephi 31: 4-18), and Isaiah (Isaiah 40:3); Gabriel came down from the courts of glory to announce John's coming birth (Luke 1:5-44); he was the last legal administrator, holding keys and authority under the Mosaic dispensation (D&C 84:26-28); his mission was to prepare the way before, baptize, and acclaim the divine Sonship of Christ (John 1); and in modern times, on the 15th of May, 1829, he returned to earth as a resurrected being to confer the Aaronic Priesthood upon Joseph Smith and Oliver Cowdery. (Joseph Smith 2:66-75; D&C 13.)" (Bruce R. McConkie, *Mormon Doctrine*, p. 393.)

Joseph Smith—History 1:73

"Immediately on our coming up out of the water after we had been baptized, we experienced great and glorious blessings"

Selected Statements of the First Presidency and the Twelve Apostles

"Immediately after coming out of the water they experienced great and glorious blessings, and being filled with the Holy Spirit, began to prophesy of the coming forth of the Church and the establishment of the great work of the Lord in the latter days. Their minds were now enlightened and the scriptures were opened to their understandings. For the first time in many centuries there now stood on the earth men with power to officiate in baptism for the remission of sin." (Joseph Fielding Smith, *Essentials in Church History*, pp. 68-69. See also Bruce R. McConkie, *New Witness for the Articles of Faith*, p. 269.)

Other Commentary

"The next morning they commenced the work of translation, in which they were soon deeply engaged.

"One morning they sat down to their work, as usual, and the first thing which presented itself through the Urim and Thummim was a commandment for Joseph and Oliver to repair to the water and attend to the ordinance of baptism." (Lucy Mack Smith, *History of Joseph Smith*, p. 142.)

Joseph Smith—History 1:74
"Our minds being now enlightened, we began to have the scriptures laid open to our understandings"

Selected Statements of the First Presidency and the Twelve Apostles

"Truth seekers must heed the voices of the legal administrators sent to teach the truth in their day, and they must search the scriptures and ponder the inspired writings of the apostles and prophets of all ages. The light and truth they received from the spoken word and from the written record will depend on their own spiritual status. Each pronouncement in the holy scriptures, for instance, is so written as to reveal little or much, depending on the spiritual capacity of the student. To a carnal person, a passage of scripture may mean nothing; to an honest though uninformed truth seeker, it may shed forth only a few rays of heavenly light; but to one who has the mind of Christ, the same passage may blaze forth an effulgence of celestial light. That which is a mystery to one is plain and simple to another. The things of the Spirit can be understood only by the power of the Spirit." (Bruce R. McConkie, *New Witness for the Articles of Faith*, pp. 71–72.)

Joseph Smith—History 1:74
"We were forced to keep secret the circumstances of having received the Priesthood and our having been baptized"

Other Commentary

"For a season, doubtless in order to avoid persecution, which constantly increased in bitterness, Joseph and Oliver kept their baptism and ordination to the Aaronic Priesthood a secret; but as men's minds were wrought upon to inquire after the truth, they at last let it be known that they had received authority to baptize for the remission of sins, and a number of people received the ordinance at their hands." (B. H. Roberts, *Outlines of Ecclesiastical History*, p. 317.)

"The ordination of these brethren and their baptism, events so important in the history of the church, occurred on the 15th of May, 1829, while they were still residing at Harmony, in Pennsylvania, and engaged in the translation of the *Book of Mormon*. At first they felt it necessary to keep secret the fact of their ordination and baptism, as in Harmony and vicinity there were threats of mob violence which were only prevented from being executed by the influence of Isaac Hale, the Prophet's father-in-law; who, though not believing in the work of Joseph Smith, was nevertheless opposed to mobs and lawlessness, and gave the young Prophet the benefit of his influence, which for some time had amounted to protection." (B. H. Roberts, *Comprehensive History of the Church*, 1:180–81.)

Bibliography

Backman, Milton V., Jr. *Joseph Smith's First Vision: The First Vision in Its Historical Context.* Salt Lake City: Bookcraft, 1971.

Benson, Ezra Taft. *The Constitution, a Heavenly Banner.* Salt Lake City: Deseret Book Co., 1986.

_____. In Conference Report, Apr. 1950, pp. 74–75.

_____. In Conference Report, Apr. 1978, p. 48.

_____. In *Ensign,* May 1978, p. 32.

British Mission Manuscript History. LDS Church Historical Department, Salt Lake City, Utah.

Brockbank, Bernard P. In *Ensign,* May 1976, p. 74.

Brown, Hugh B. *What Is Man and What He May Become.* Brigham Young University Speeches of the Year. Provo, Utah, 25 Mar. 1958.

Budge, E. A. Wallis. *Osiris, Volume II.* New Hyde Park, New York: University Books, 1961.

_____. *The Gods of the Egyptians.* 2 vols. New York: Dover Publications, 1969.

BYU Studies: A Voice for the Community of LDS Scholars. Vols. 11, 18. Provo, Utah: Brigham Young University Press, 1971 and 1978.

Cannon, George Q. *Gospel Truth.* 2 vols. Salt Lake City: Deseret Book Co., 1957.

Champdor, Albert. *Das Agyptisch Totunbuch.* Zurich: n.p., 1979.

Charge to Religious Educators. 2d ed. Salt Lake City: The Church of Jesus Christ of Latter-day Saints, 1982.

Clark, James R., comp. *Messages of the First Presidency of The Church of Jesus Christ of Latter-day Saints.* 6 vols. Salt Lake City: Bookcraft, 1970.

Clark, R. T. Rundle. *Myth and Symbol in Ancient Egypt.* London: Thames and Hudson, Ltd., 1978.

Conference Reports. Salt Lake City: The Church of Jesus Christ of Latter-day Saints, 1910–86.

Cook, Melvin Alonzo, and Melvin Garfield Cook. *Science and Mormonism: Correlations, Conflicts, and Conciliations.* Salt Lake City: Deseret Book Co., 1967.

Cowdery, Oliver. In *Latter-day Saints' Messenger and Advocate.* Vols. 1–2. 1835.

de Horrack, Peter J. *Proceedings of the Society of Biblical Archaeology.* London: British Museum, 1884.

Doxey, Roy W. *The Pearl of Great Price (Lectures 1 through 8): Education Weeks Lectures 1970.* Provo, Utah: Brigham Young University Press.

Dunn, Paul H. In Conference Report, Oct. 1969, pp. 128–29.

Dyer, Alvin R. In Conference Report, Oct. 1969, p. 54.

Elders' Journal of The Church of Jesus Christ of Latter-day Saints. July 1838.

Ensign. 1972–86.

Evans, Richard L. In Conference Report, Oct. 1959, p. 127.

Eyring, Henry. *The Faith of a Scientist.* Salt Lake City: Bookcraft, 1967.

Faust, James E. In *Ensign,* Nov. 1974, p. 60.

Frost, Edward. Letter to Levi Richards, Oct. 1852

Gardiner, Alan. *Egyptian Grammar.* London: Oxford University Press, 1975.

Gates, Susa Young. In *Young Woman's Journal,* Aug. 1894.

Grant, Heber J. *Gospel Standards.* Comp. G. Homer Durham. Salt Lake City: Deseret Book Co., 1976.

Hanks, Marion D. In Conference Report, Apr. 1980, pp. 40–41.

―――――――――. In *Ensign,* Nov. 1984, p. 36.

Helck, H. E. In *Orientalia* 19 (1950).

Hinckley, Gordon B. *Truth Restored: A Short History of The Church of Jesus Christ of Latter-day Saints.* Salt Lake City: The Church of Jesus Christ of Latter-day Saints, 1979.

―――――――――. In Conference Report, Oct. 1986, p. 65.

―――――――――. In *Ensign,* Nov. 1986, p. 42.

Hunter, Howard W. In Conference Report, Apr. 1980, p. 34.

―――――――――. In Conference Report, Apr. 1986, p. 18.

Hunter, Milton R. *The Gospel through the Ages.* Salt Lake City: Stevens and Wallis, 1945.

―――――――――. *Pearl of Great Price Commentary.* Salt Lake City: Bookcraft, 1951.

_____. In Conference Report, Oct. 1968, p. 37.

Hymns of The Church of Jesus Christ of Latter-day Saints. Salt Lake City: The Church of Jesus Christ of Latter-day Saints, 1985.

Improvement Era. 1917–68.

Jessee, Dean C. In *BYU Studies,* Summer 1971, p. 439.

Josephus, Flavius. *Antiquities of the Jews.* Trans. William Whiston. Philadelphia: John C. Whiston Co., n.d.

Journal History of The Church of Jesus Christ of Latter-day Saints. LDS Church Historical Department, Salt Lake City, Utah.

Journal of Discourses. London: Latter-day Saints' Book Depot, 1854–86.

Kelsey, Eli B. In *Millennial Star,* 13 [1 Feb. 1851]: 34.

Kimball, Spencer W. *Faith Precedes the Miracle.* Salt Lake City: Deseret Book Co., 1972.

_____. *The Miracle of Forgiveness.* Salt Lake City: Bookcraft, 1969.

_____. *The Teachings of Spencer W. Kimball.* Ed. Edward L. Kimball. Salt Lake City: Bookcraft, 1982.

_____. In Conference Report, Oct. 1954, p. 52.

_____. In Conference Report, Apr. 1962, pp. 60–62.

_____. In Conference Report, Apr. 1964, pp. 94–96.

_____. In Conference Report, Oct. 1967, p. 30.

_____. In Conference Report, Apr. 1974, p. 66.

_____. In *Ensign,* Nov. 1975, p. 80.

_____. In *Ensign,* Mar. 1976, pp. 71–72.

_____. In *Ensign,* May 1977, p. 50.

_____. In *Ensign,* Nov. 1977, p. 78.

_____. In *Ensign,* May 1978, p. 77.

_____. In *Improvement Era,* June 1962, pp. 436–37.

Lee, Harold B. *Ye Are the Light of the World.* Salt Lake City: Deseret Book Co., 1974.

_____. In Conference Report, Apr. 1948, p. 55.

_____. In Conference Report, Oct. 1950, p. 129.

_____. In Conference Report, Oct. 1966, p. 116.

_____. In Conference Report, Oct. 1968, p. 62.

_____. In Conference Report, Oct. 1972, p. 128.

_____. In Conference Report, Oct. 1973, p. 170.

Letters of Count Carlo Vidua. Vol. 2. Ed. Giuseppe Pomba. Turin: Cesare Balbo, 1834. Translated at Brigham Young University from the Italian by Dr. Cinzia Noble and Murray A. Lowe.

Ludlow, Daniel H., comp. *Latter-day Prophets Speak: Selections from the Sermons and Writings of the Presidents of The Church of Jesus Christ of Latter-day Saints.* Salt Lake City: Bookcraft, 1951.

Matthews, Robert J. *"A Plainer Translation": Joseph Smith's Translation of the Bible, a History and Commentary.* Provo, Utah: Brigham Young University Press, 1975.

Maxwell, Neal A. In Conference Report, Apr. 1984, p. 30.

——————. In Conference Report, Apr. 1986, p. 46.

——————. In *Ensign,* Nov. 1981, pp. 8, 10.

——————. In *Ensign,* May 1983, p. 11.

McConkie, Bruce R. *Doctrinal New Testament Commentary.* 3 vols. Salt Lake City: Bookcraft, 1973.

——————. *The Millennial Messiah: The Second Coming of the Son of Man.* Salt Lake City: Deseret Book Co., 1982.

——————. *Mormon Doctrine.* 2d ed. Salt Lake City: Bookcraft, 1966.

——————. *The Mortal Messiah.* 4 vols. Salt Lake City: Deseret Book Co., 1980.

——————. *A New Witness for the Articles of Faith.* Salt Lake City: Deseret Book Co., 1985.

——————. *The Promised Messiah: The First Coming of Christ.* Salt Lake City: Deseret Book Co., 1978.

——————. In Conference Report, Oct. 1976, pp. 158–60.

——————. In Conference Report, Oct. 1977, p. 50.

——————. In *Ensign,* Apr. 1977, p. 4.

——————. In *Ensign,* May 1979, p. 93.

——————. In *Ensign,* June 1982, pp. 11–12.

——————. In *Improvement Era,* May 1953, p. 322.

McKay, David O. *Gospel Ideals.* Salt Lake City: The Improvement Era, 1953.

——————. In Conference Report, Apr. 1968, p. 92.

——————. In *Improvement Era,* Feb. 1964, p. 84.

——————. In *Improvement Era,* July 1968, p. 3.

Mercatante, Anthony S. *Who's Who in Egyptian Mythology.* New York: Clarkson N. Potter, 1978.

Messages for Exaltation: Eternal Insights from the Book of Mormon [Gospel Doctrine class manual]. Salt Lake City: Deseret Sunday School Union, 1967.

Millet, Robert L., and Kent P. Jackson, eds. *The Pearl of Great Price*. Studies in Scripture Series, vol. 2. Salt Lake City: Randall Book Co., 1985.

Morenz, S. *Religions en Egypte Hennenistique et Romaine*. Colloque de Strebourg. Paris: University Press, 1969.

Morris, George Q. In Conference Report, Apr. 1958, p. 38.

Oaks, Dallin H. In Conference Report, Oct. 1984, p. 16.

_____. In *Ensign*, Nov. 1986, p. 20.

Packer, Boyd K. In Conference Report, Oct. 1984, p. 85.

The Pearl of Great Price, Being a Choice Selection from the Revelations, Translations, and Narrations of Joseph Smith . . . to The Church of Jesus Christ of Latter-day Saints. Liverpool: F. D. Richards, 1851.

Pearl of Great Price. Salt Lake City: The Church of Jesus Christ of Latter-day Saints, 1981.

Penrose, Charles W. *"Mormon" Doctrine, Plain and Simple, or, Leaves from the Tree of Life*. Salt Lake City: Juvenile Instructor Office, 1888.

Perry, L. Tom. In Conference Report, Oct. 1984, p. 21.

Petersen, Mark E. *Abraham, Friend of God*. Salt Lake City: Deseret Book Co., 1979.

_____. *Moses: Man of Miracles*. Salt Lake City: Deseret Book Co., 1977.

_____. *Noah and the Flood*. Salt Lake City: Deseret Book, 1982.

_____. *One Lord . . . One Faith!* Salt Lake City: Deseret Book, 1963.

_____. In *Ensign*, Nov. 1979, p. 12.

_____. In *Ensign*, Nov. 1981, p. 66.

Peterson, H. Donl. *Moroni: Ancient Prophet, Modern Messenger*. Bountiful, Utah: Horizon Publishers, 1983.

_____. In *Ensign*, May 1972, p. 42.

Pratt, Orson. *Masterful Discourses and Writings of Orson Pratt*. Comp. N. B. Lundwall. Salt Lake City: Bookcraft, n.d.

_____. In *The Seer*, Apr. 1854, pp. 249–50.

_____. Letter to [John] Davis, 14 July 1850. LDS Church Historical Department, Salt Lake City, Utah.

_____, and Franklin D. Richards. Letter to [?] Phillips and [John] Davis, 3 Dec. 1850. LDS Church Historical Department, Salt Lake City, Utah.

Pratt, Parley P. *Key to the Science of Theology*. Classics in Mormon Literature Series. Salt Lake City: Deseret Book, 1978.

Reynolds, George F. *The Book of Abraham: Its Authenticity Established as a Divine and Ancient Record*. 3d ed. Salt Lake City: Deseret Sunday School Union, 1948.

Rhodes, Michael Dennis. In *BYU Studies,* Spring 1977, p. 270.

Richards, LeGrand. *A Marvelous Work and a Wonder.* Salt Lake City: Deseret Book Co., 1950.

Richards, Levi. Correspondence, 6 Feb. 1851, 12 Feb. 1851, 21 Feb. 1851. LDS Church Historical Department, Salt Lake City, Utah.

Roberts, B. H. *A Comprehensive History of The Church of Jesus Christ of Latter-day Saints, Century 1.* 6 vols. Salt Lake City: The Church of Jesus Christ of Latter-day Saints, 1930.

_____. *Outlines of Ecclesiastical History: A Text Book.* 6th ed. Salt Lake City: The Church of Jesus Christ of Latter-day Saints, 1950.

_____. *The Seventy's Course in Theology, Second Year: Outline History of the Dispensations of the Gospel.* Reprint. Dallas: S. K. Taylor Publishing Co, 1976.

Romney, Marion G. In Conference Report, Oct. 1948, pp. 76–77.

_____. In Conference Report, Apr. 1953, p. 124.

_____. In Conference Report, Apr. 1969, p. 107.

_____. In Conference Report, Apr. 1971, p. 24.

_____. In Conference Report, Oct. 1976, p. 168.

_____. In Conference Report, Apr. 1977, p. 76.

_____. In *Ensign,* May 1983, p. 17.

_____. In *Ensign,* Nov. 1981, p. 43.

_____. In *Improvement Era,* June 1953, p. 442.

_____. In *Improvement Era,* Nov. 1968, pp. 46, 48.

Sill, Sterling W. In Conference Report, Apr. 1966, pp. 19–21.

_____. In Conference Report, Apr. 1970, pp. 29–30.

Smith, Eldred G. In Conference Report, Apr. 1971, p. 146.

_____. In *Improvement Era,* June 1966, p. 513.

Smith, George Albert. In *Church News,* 17 June 1944, p. 4.

Smith, Joseph. *History of The Church of Jesus Christ of Latter-day Saints.* 2d ed. Salt Lake City: The Church of Jesus Christ of Latter-day Saints, 1951.

_____. *Lectures on Faith.* Comp. N. B. Lundwall. Salt Lake City: Bookcraft, n.d.

_____. *Teachings of the Prophet Joseph Smith.* Comp. Joseph Fielding Smith. Salt Lake City: The Deseret News Press, 1938.

Smith, Joseph F. *Gospel Doctrine.* Salt Lake City: Deseret Book Co., 1939.

_____. In Conference Report, Apr. 1900, p. 40.

_____. In *Improvement Era,* Nov. 1917, p. 7.

_____. In *Improvement Era,* Dec. 1917, p. 104.

_____. In *Juvenile Instructor,* vol. 37, no. 18 [15 Sept. 1902], p. 562.

_____. Letter to Franklin D. Richards, 30 Nov. 1852. LDS Church Historical Department, Salt Lake City, Utah.

Smith, Joseph Fielding. *Answers to Gospel Questions.* 5 vols. Salt Lake City: Deseret Book Co., 1960.

_____. *Church History and Modern Revelation.* 2 vols. Salt Lake City: The Council of the Twelve Apostles of The Church of Jesus Christ of Latter-day Saints, 1947.

_____. *Doctrines of Salvation.* Comp. Bruce R. McConkie. 3 vols. Salt Lake City: Bookcraft, 1954.

_____. *Essentials in Church History.* 13th ed. Salt Lake City: Deseret Book Co. for The Church of Jesus Christ of Latter-day Saints, 1950.

_____. *Man, His Origin and Destiny.* Salt Lake City: Deseret Book Co., 1954.

_____. *The Progress of Man.* Salt Lake City: Deseret Book Co., 1973.

_____. *Seek Ye Earnestly . . . .* Comp. Joseph Fielding Smith, Jr. Salt Lake City: Deseret Book Co., 1970.

_____. *The Signs of the Times: A Series of Discussions.* Independence, Mo.: Press of Zions Printing and Publishing Co., 1947.

_____. *The Way to Perfection: Short Discourses on Gospel Themes.* 8th ed. N.p.: Genealogical Society of Utah, 1949.

_____. In *Improvement Era,* Nov. 1956, p. 789.

_____. In *Improvement Era,* Apr. 1962, p. 231.

Smith, Hyrum M., and Janne M. Sjodahl. *The Doctrine and Covenants, Containing Revelations Given to Joseph Smith, Jr., the Prophet, with an Introduction and Historical and Exegetical Notes.* Rev. ed. Salt Lake City: Deseret Book Co., 1951.

Smith, Lucy Mack. *History of Joseph Smith by His Mother, Lucy Mack Smith.* Edited by Preston Nibley. Salt Lake City: Bookcraft, 1958.

Snow, Lorenzo. *The Teachings of Lorenzo Snow.* Comp. Clyde J. Williams. Salt Lake City: Bookcraft, 1984.

Spencer, A. J. *Death in Ancient Egypt.* Middlesex, England: Penguin Books, 1982.

Stapley, Delbert L. In Conference Report, Apr. 1967, p. 34.

_____. In *Ensign,* Nov. 1975, p. 47.

Talmage, James E. *Jesus the Christ.* 18th ed. Salt Lake City: The Church of Jesus Christ of Latter-day Saints, 1922.

_____. *The Articles of Faith.* 30th ed. Salt Lake City: The Church of Jesus Christ of Latter-day Saints, 1949.

—————. *The Earth and Man.* Address delivered in the Tabernacle, Salt Lake City, 9 Aug. 1931. Reprint. Brigham Young University Printing Service, 1976.

—————. In Conference Report, Apr. 1916, pp. 129–31.

Tanner, N. Eldon. In Conference Report, Oct. 1974, p. 121.

Taylor, John. *The Mediation and Atonement of Our Lord and Savior Jesus Christ.* Salt Lake City: Deseret News Co., 1882. Photolithographic reprint of original edition, Salt Lake City, 1979.

—————. *The Gospel Kingdom: Selections from the Writings and Discourses of John Taylor.* 4th ed. Comp. G. Homer Durham. Salt Lake City: Bookcraft, 1964.

—————. *The Government of God.* Liverpool: S. W. Richards, 1852.

Times and Seasons. 1843, 1845.

Walker, Ronald W. In *BYU Studies,* Spring 1978, pp. 469–72.

Whitney, Orson F. *Life of Heber C. Kimball.* 2d ed. Salt Lake City: Stevens and Wallis, 1945.

—————. In Conference Report, Apr. 1910, p. 60.

Widtsoe, John A. *Evidences and Reconciliations.* 5th ed. 3 vols. Salt Lake City: Bookcraft, 1943.

—————. *Gospel Interpretations: Aids to Faith in a Modern Day.* Salt Lake City: Bookcraft, 1947.

—————. *Man and the Dragon, and Other Essays.* Salt Lake City: Bookcraft, 1945.

Widtsoe, John A. *A Rational Theology: As Taught by The Church of Jesus Christ of Latter-day Saints.* 7th ed. Salt Lake City: Deseret Book Co., 1965.

—————, and Leah D. Widtsoe. *The Word of Wisdom: A Modern Interpretation.* Rev. ed. Salt Lake City: Deseret Book Co., 1950.

Wilford Woodruff Journal. LDS Church Historical Department, Salt Lake City, Utah.

Woodruff, Wilford. *Discourses of Wilford Woodruff.* Ed. G. Homer Durham. Salt Lake City: Bookcraft, 1946.

—————. In *Young Woman's Journal,* Aug. 1894, p. 512.

Young, Brigham. *Discourses of Brigham Young.* Comp. John A. Widtsoe. Salt Lake City: Deseret Book Co., 1925.

Young Woman's Journal. Aug. 1894.

Index

Aaronic Priesthood, 234. *See also*
Priesthood
Abel, 163–65; 167–68
Abraham: in land of Chaldeans, 232;
became High Priest, 233–34;
people refused to hearken to,
235–36; people turned from righteousness in days of, 236–38;
men sought to kill, 238–39; and
Jehovah, 242–43; priesthood
given to, 243–44; compared to
Noah, 244; ministry of, 245; took
Sarai to wife, 250; went to promised land, 251; promised Palestine, 252–53; and Abrahamic
Covenant; 253–54; and seed to
bless families of earth, 257; left
Haran, at age 62, 258–59; built
altar in Jershon, 259–60;
instructed to say Sarai is sister,
261–62; had Urim and Thummim, 263–64; saw stars, 264–65;
told of Kolob, 266; talked with
Lord face to face, 269–70; saw
things Almighty had made,
270–71; to have no end to posterity, 271–72; taught Egyptians,
272–73; reasoned that spirits
have no beginning, 273–76;

taught that man was in beginning
with God, 277; received calling
before coming to earth, 278–80
Abraham, Book of: and Abraham's
writings found in Egypt, 36–37;
and events leading to discovery of
Abraham papyri, 37–38; and
Antonio Lebolo, 38–39; and
Michael H. Chandler, 40–41; and
mummies in America, 41–42;
papyrus of, translated, 42–44;
publication of, 44–45; contributions of, 45–46
Accad, 233
Achior, 238
Acusilaus, 180
Adam: was first of all men, 104–5;
was given breath of life, 132; had
choice whether to eat of tree,
135; ate of forbidden fruit,
135–36; transgression was choice
of, 146–47; brought mortality to
posterity, 149; was driven out of
Garden of Eden, 152; ate bread
by sweat of brow, 152–53; was
shut out from presence of God,
154; was commanded to offer
sacrifice, 154–55; partook of
forbidden fruit to have seed, 159;

vocation, 348–49; personage appeared at bedside of, 349–52; received Urim and Thummim, 352; work for dead revealed to, 352–54; saw place where plates were deposited, 355–56; was informed of great judgments coming on earth, 356; to glorify God, 357; was exhausted after Moroni's visit, 357–58; returned to father in field, 358; left field to go to Hill Cumorah, 358–60; beheld plates, 361–63; instructed by messenger, 363; worked for Josiah Stoal, 363–64; met and married Emma Hale, 365–66; obtained plates, 366–67; to protect plates, 367–69; was persecuted, 369–70; copied characters from plates, 370; commenced to translate Book of Mormon, 371–73; prayed about baptism for remission of sins, 373–74; received priesthood, 374; ordained Oliver Cowdery, 375; received blessings after baptism, 376–77; kept baptism secret, 377–78

Smith, Joseph, quotations by: on state of early Church, 7; on difficulties faced while attempting to write history, 58; on Almighty's dwelling in eternal fire, 75–76; on God's having all knowledge, 83–84; on revelation, 87; on discerning spirits, 91; on Satan's desire to influence righteous men, 93; on power of priesthood to rebuke Satan, 94; on Satan's desire to dethrone Jehovah, 94; on Satan's desire to possess men's bodies, 94; on three separate members of Godhead, 96; on creation of earth, 103, 286; on eternal life, 108; on organization of earth, 111; on earth being without form, 115; on man as organized in heaven, 125; on Satan's rebellion in heaven, 141; on Adam's teaching posterity, 161; on sacrifice, 163–64; on obedience to God's commandments, 164; on Abel's sacrifice, 164–65; on those with bodies vs. those without, 166; on sons of perdition, 167; on Cain and Abel, 167–68; on secret combinations, 168; on free agency, 189; on translation, 202; on Second Coming of Christ, 215; on Zion, 217–18; on Millennium, 219; on Adam's and Noah's holding priesthood on earth and in heaven, 226; on people being wicked, 229; on Abraham's receiving priesthood, 233; on priesthood, 234; on Abraham's courage, 235–36; on Abraham's being cast into fire, 241-42; on becoming of house of Israel, 256; on Abraham's seed to bless families of earth, 257; on Abraham's being guided by Lord, 258; on Kolob, 267; on Abraham's learning from Lord, 270; on Abraham's teaching Egyptians, 272; on spirits having no beginning, 273–74; on men foreordained to certain work, 278–79; on keeping second estate, 282; on earth to be crowned with celestial glory, 293; on end of world, 297–98; on signs of Second Coming, 312, 319; on love to wax cold, 313; on gospel to be preached to every country, 314; on gathering of elect, 320; on First Vision, 338; on modern churches, 343; on hearts of children turning to fathers, 352–53; on work for dead, 353; on obtaining golden plates, 366; on sacrifice, 274–75; on John the Baptist, 376

Smith, Joseph F., quotations by: on extreme poverty of early Saints, 21; on accepting revelations contained in Doctrine and Covenants and Pearl of Great Price, 23; on Moses' seeing God face to face, 73; on man as child of God, 77; on how to be sons and daughters of God; 78; on having no other God save Eternal Father, 82–83;